D1231991

Ellen Immergut vividly demonstrates the tremendous impact political institutions can have on policy in this comparative analysis of the politics of national health insurance in Sweden, France, and Switzerland – three countries where the same legislative proposals have been considered but where the policy results vary widely.

In each country, politicians proposed programs of national health insurance and measures to regulate the economic activities of the medical profession. Although these proposals triggered similar political conflicts and reactions in all the countries, the Swiss, French, and Swedish health systems developed in divergent directions as a result of the specific legislative proposals enacted into law in each country: The Swedish system can be considered the most "socialized" in Western Europe, the Swiss the most "privatized," and the French a conflict-ridden compromise between the two.

Immergut argues that institutional rules and procedures, and not the demands and resources of social groups, set the terms for political conflicts. By providing distinct opportunities and impediments to both politicians and interest groups, political institutions establish distinct "rules of the game" that explain the ability of various groups to influence policy making. Political institutions thus play a primary role both in structuring political conflicts and in accounting for divergent policy outcomes.

HEALTH POLITICS

CAMBRIDGE STUDIES IN COMPARATIVE POLITICS

General editor

PETER LANGE Duke University

Associate editors

ELLEN COMISSO University of California, San Diego
PETER HALL Harvard University
JOEL MIGDAL University of Washington
HELEN MILNER Columbia University
SIDNEY TARROW Cornell University

This series publishes comparative research that seeks to explain important cross-national domestic political phenomena. Based on a broad conception of comparative politics, it hopes to promote critical dialogue among different approaches. While encouraging contributions from diverse theoretical perspectives, the series will particularly emphasize work on domestic institutions and work that examines the relative roles of historical structures and constraints, of individual or organizational choice, and of strategic interaction in explaining political actions and outcomes. This focus includes an interest in the mechanisms through which historical factors impinge on contemporary political choices and outcomes.

Works on all parts of the world are welcomed, and priority will be given to studies that cross traditional area boundaries and that treat the United States in comparative perspective. Many of the books in the series are expected to be comparative, drawing on material from more than one national case, but studies devoted to single countries will also be considered, especially those that pose their problem and analysis in such a way that they make a direct contribution to comparative analysis and theory.

OTHER BOOKS IN THE SERIES

David D. Laitin, *Language Repertoires and State Construction in Africa*
Allan Kornberg and Harold D. Clarke, *Citizens and Community:
Political Support in a Representative Democracy*

HEALTH POLITICS
INTERESTS AND INSTITUTIONS IN
WESTERN EUROPE

ELLEN M. IMMERGUT
Massachusetts Institute of Technology

CAMBRIDGE
UNIVERSITY PRESS

Published by the Press Syndicate of the University of Cambridge
The Pitt Building, Trumpington Street, Cambridge CB2 1RP
40 West 20th Street, New York, NY 10011, USA
10 Stamford Road, Oakleigh, Melbourne 3166, Australia

First published 1992

Printed in the United States of America

Library of Congress Cataloging-in-Publication Data
Immergut, Ellen M.
Health politics: interests and institutions in Western Europe/
Ellen M. Immergut.
p.   cm. – (Cambridge studies in comparative politics)
Includes bibliographical references and index.
ISBN 0-521-41335-4 (hardback)
1. Medicine, State – Switzerland.   2. Medicine, State – Sweden.
3. Medicine, State – France.   I. Title.   II. Series.
[DNLM: 1. Health Policy – France – legislation.   2. Health Policy –
Sweden – legislation.   3. Health Policy – Switzerland – legislation.
4. National Health Programs – France – legislation.   5. National
Health Programs – Sweden – legislation.   6. National Health Programs –
Switzerland – legislation.   7. Politics – France.   8. Politics –
Sweden.   9. Politics – Switzerland.   WA 540.1 I33h]
RA412.5.S9I45   1992
DNLM/DLC   92-8128
for Library of Congress   CIP

A catalog record for this book is available from the British Library

ISBN 0-521-41335-4 hardback

For Brita, Ed, Eva, and Karin

Contents

Preface

When I began the research for this book, I was concerned with the limits of politics: Why was national health insurance deemed politically impossible in the United States, when similar programs already existed in other nations? If the American medical profession appeared able to block such government efforts, what had happened elsewhere? Were European doctors more predisposed to government intervention, or were they simply less powerful politically? By reading statements from interest groups kept in government archives in several nations, I found that doctors' opinions in Western Europe did not seem so very different from those in the United States. I compared the politics of national health insurance in Switzerland, France, and Sweden – three countries where national health insurance had been proposed, but where, as a result of political struggles, the final policy results are three health systems that represent the two extremes and the center of the private–public mix in health. Medical associations in all three countries had opposed national health insurance on the grounds that doctors preferred to work as private practitioners and not as government employees. "Socialized medicine," it was thought, would undermine professional autonomy. How then could one explain the fact that Switzerland rejected national health insurance, France accepted it, and Sweden not only enacted national health insurance, but later converted its health system to a de facto national health service?

As the research continued, I was forced to widen my angle of vision from the medical profession to other actors, ones that are not always seen as central to health policy. Strange characters, like the Swiss chiropractors, French small businessmen, or Swedish local county council politicians, stole center stage from the commonly studied insurers, physicians, and hospital administrators, and turned the course of events in unexpected directions. It became increasingly clear that in each country, the trajectory of health care politics had followed paths not predicted by the leading explanations for health policy or the welfare state. At the same time, the study turned up some historical regularities. The history of each case pointed insistently to the role played by standard political institutions. The Swiss referendum, the French parliament, and the Swedish executive bureaucracy emerged as key elements in an explanation of national health insurance politics in those countries. Indeed, clues to the salient elements of each national pattern were embedded even in the constitutions of these nations.

The resulting book argues for the primacy of these institutions in explaining policy outcomes precisely because they facilitate or impede the entry of different groups into the policy-making process. Different procedures for making policy decisions frame policy debates: They change the array of actors that are brought into the decision-making process and they provide distinct sets of advantages and disadvantages to groups wishing to promote their interests. Not only do political institutions radically change the balance of pressure-group power, they also have an impact on the role played by professional politicians, by the policy makers within government bureaucracies, and by the general public. More fundamentally, the procedural rules by which policy decisions are made affect the ways in which issues are defined and the types of evidence that can be brought to bear in resolving policy disputes. Procedures for representing interests select out different sorts of information in different political systems, thereby structuring political conflicts.

More broadly, we can say that these rules construct interests because, being based on different conceptions of the proper mechanism for arriving at the public interest, they channel debates along different cleavages of interest in different political cultures. In Switzerland, the public interest on any specific policy issue is viewed as the sum of the demands of individual citizens as expressed in national referenda. In Sweden, on the other hand, proper representation for policy issues is a matter of consensual agreements between interest groups, whose large memberships and democratic procedures ensure their responsiveness to the public. In other nations, the rules of representation might emphasize discussion of policy goals in legislatures, or the importance of an impartial executive standing above the particularistic claims of interest groups (as in the French case), or perhaps the need to maintain equitable representation of different regional or ethnic groups. These visions of representation, as they might be called, stem from different traditions and from conflicts among different political and social movements. But whatever their origins, the formal procedural mechanisms that each national history has left in place continue to affect the treatment of policy issues in contemporary polities in ways that are often quite different from what one would imagine.

The centrality of these procedures for interest representation has several implications for public policy. First, public policies should not be viewed merely as the result of the demands of various groups competing for political influence without greater attention being paid to the procedural mechanisms that allow these demands to be voiced. Health policy, for example, is often discussed in terms of the organized medical profession; unemployment policy is viewed as the result of struggles between labor unions and business associations. Even alternative approaches that emphasize actors such as bureaucrats and policy elites focus on the demands of these actors rather than on the framework in which these demands are expressed. This book argues that the analysis of policy making should focus more explicitly on the procedures for making policies and less exclusively on the demands themselves, though demands never disappear altogether. These procedures do not simply represent the views of interest groups. They select the groups whose views will be represented and they shape demands by changing the strategic environment in which the demands of groups are formulated. Union representatives, for example, will take into account the institutional context within which they must organize when deciding how best to negotiate with employers. The procedures for representation that create such strategic environments are central to understanding both the origins and the maturation of public policies.

Second, the importance of the procedural framework has repercussions for those directly involved in the policy-making process. Through procedures such as hearings, written statements, and public debates, modern democracies strive to represent the views of interested parties as they create policies. Much of the strategy of policy makers and policy advocates has been designed to achieve compromises and bargains on the demands of competing groups. But if the procedures for achieving compromise change both the demands of these groups and the relative effectiveness of these groups in promoting their demands, a new strategy is called for. Policy strategists need to target these policy procedures so that they provide incentives for group leaders to agree to majority decisions. What is politically feasible may depend as much on the way in which interest groups are brought into the policy process as on their initial preferences about a particular policy. Furthermore, if these procedures have repercussions for the balance of power, then we should know the consequences of these different methods of interest representation.

Third, the significance of procedural frameworks points toward a different approach to comparative public policy. Different nations have designed their political institutions in different ways and rely on different procedures for representing interests. These procedural mechanisms are intertwined with institutionalized relationships among interest groups, parties, and governments that have developed over long periods of time. Both the procedures and these political relationships set the stage for specific policy conflicts. Consequently, we cannot apply models of policy making to a series of nations as though they shared a common point of departure. The rules of representation establish a logic for policy making that is different in different nations. Indeed, the very concept of political power depends on the ways in which procedural rules organize political contests. Because different sets of political institutions are susceptible to different sorts of political pressures, these institutions determine whether politics is best understood as "interest-group" politics, "professional" politics, "bureaucratic" politics, or "class" politics. Thus, we must look first at these different starting points in order to understand why a particular view of policy making may be more appropriate to some polities than to others.

At the same time, however, institutional procedures are continually renegotiated through political bargaining. This adds an unpredictable element to policy outcomes. Institutions are simply tools of political decision making whose significance changes as political actors put them to new uses. An understanding of political institutions can provide insights into why the history of health care politics in these nations unfolded as it did, but the history itself is far richer and less determined than the bare bones of the institutional analysis. Institutional analysis can provide some generalizations about the types of interest groups that will tend to exert political leverage under different institutional conditions. But it cannot produce a science of interest-group influence. There is no linear relationship between a specific set of political institutions and the interest groups that will succeed or the health system that results. For, whereas the structures for decision making provide incentives for actors to act as they do, and therefore help to account for the choices that they have made, the freedom to choose remains in the hands of these actors. Consequently, these histories are filled with unexpected events, sudden about faces, and new strategies. This book is a call to look at these histories, not just at the broad sweep of major events, but also at the seemingly minor struggles that make up daily political life. These are the battles that establish the constraints on politics, but they are also the junctures that extend the limits of the possible.

Acknowledgments

Like many books that have their origins in a doctoral dissertation, this one has generated a long list of persons and institutions to thank. The thesis research was funded by an International Doctoral Research Fellowship from the Social Science Research Council and the American Council of Learned Societies, an American Scandinavian Foundation Grant, and a Krupp Foundation Dissertation Fellowship from the Center for European Studies at Harvard. The Center for European Studies at Harvard, the Institute for Social Research at the University of Stockholm, and the Ecole Normale Supérieure de Jeunes Filles at Montrouge, France, provided institutional support for the thesis. For these arrangements, I am grateful to Abby Collins, Guido Goldman, Stanley Hoffmann, Walter Korpi, Shamus Malin, Mme Serre, Mme Thiebaut, and Mlle Follet. In particular, I wish to thank my thesis committee, Alessandro Pizzorno, Paul Starr, and, especially, Lee Rainwater.

Much of the reworking of the argument, rewriting, and new research was carried out at the Max-Planck-Institut für Gesellschaftsforschung in Cologne and the Instituto Juan March in Madrid. The directors of these institutes – Renate Mayntz, Fritz Scharpf, and Victor Pérez-Díaz – provided not only institutional support, but gave me the opportunity to present the argument of the book in seminars, and took the time to comment personally on the manuscript or parts of it. Fritz Scharpf has read every page of the manuscript – as well as many of those that were thrown into the recycling bin – and spent many hours discussing specific points and how to present them. Jens Alber, Douglas Ashford, Suzanne Berger, William Glaser, Peter Hall, Vicky Hattam, Arnold J. Heidenheimer, Christopher Howard, Peter Katzenstein, Peter Lange, Michael Lipsky, Richard Locke, Uday Mehta, Paul Osterman, Dietrich Rueschemeyer, Chuch Sabel, Richard Samuels, Harvey Sapolsky, Theda Skocpol, Deborah Stone, Rosemary Taylor, Margy Weir, Reinhard Zintl, and anonymous reviewers commented on the manuscript. To all these persons, I am grateful. I also wish to thank Emily Loose, my editor at Cambridge, and Ronald Cohen, whose manuscript editing skills greatly improved the text.

List of abbreviations and organizations

Allmänna Svenska Läkarföreningen. First Swedish Medical Association.

AMA. American Medical Association.

Arbeiterbund. Nineteenth century Swiss workers' alliance.

Ärztekammer. German Chamber of Physicians; legislative organ of the Swiss medical association.

Ärztekommission. Late nineteenth-century committee of representatives of Swiss cantonal medical societies.

ATP. Allmänna Tilläggspensioneringen (Swedish General Supplemental Pension Scheme).

CFTC. Confédération Française des Travailleurs Chrétiens (French Confederation of Christian Workers).

CGC. Confédération Générale des Cadres (French Union of White-Collar Employees and Managers).

CGPF. Confédération Générale de la Production Française (pre-Second World War French employers association).

CGPME. Confédération Générale des Petites et Moyennes Entreprises (French General Confederation of Small and Medium Enterprises).

CGT. Confédération Générale du Travail (General Confederation of Labor, French Communist trade union).

CGT-FO. Confédération Générale du Travail-Force Ouvrière (moderate scission from CGT).

CGTU. Confédération Générale du Travail Unitaire (Communist scission from CGT in 1920s).

CNAMTS. Caisse Nationale d'Assurance Maladie des Travailleurs Salariés (French National Health Insurance Fund for Salaried Employees).

CNPF. Conseil National du Patronat Français (National Council of French Employers).

Collegium Medicum. Swedish Royal Academy of Medicine.

Conseil Supérieur d'Assurances Sociales. Government Council on Social Insurance.

CREDOC. Centre de Recherches et de Documentation sur la Consommation (French Center for Research and Documentation of Comsumption).

CSMF. Confédération des Syndicats Médicaux Français (Confederation of French Medical Unions).

FMF. Fédération des Médecins de France (Federation of French Physicians).

FNOSS. Fédération Nationale des Organismes de la Sécurité Sociale (French National Federation of Social Security Organizations).

KSK. Konkordat der Schweizerischen Krankenkassen (Association of Swiss Sickness Funds).

Lex Forrer. First Swiss national health insurance law.

LO. Landsorganisationen i Sverige (literally, Country Organization in Sweden, Swedish Trade Union Confederation).

MRP. Mouvement Républicain Populaire (Popular Republican Movement, French Christian Democratic Party).

NHS. British National Health Service.

Ordre des Médécins. French order of physicians.

Rikssjukkassornas Centralorganisation. Swedish National Sickness Funds Central Organization.

SAF. Sveriges Arbetsgivarförening (Swedish Employers Association).

SAV. Schweizerischer Arbeitgeberverein (also called Zentralverband Schweizerischer Arbeitgeber Organisationen, Swiss Employers Association).

SÄV. Schweizerischer Ärzteverein (Swiss Medical Association, also called Verbindung der Schweizer Ärzte).

SBV. Schweizerischer Bauernverein (Swiss Farmers Association).

SFIO. Section Française de l'Internationale Ouvrière (French section of the Workers' International, French Socialist Party).

SGB. Schweizerischer Gewerkschaftsbund (Swiss Trade Union Confederation).

SGV. Schweizerischer Gewerbeerein (Swiss Artisans Association).

Skattebetalarnas Förening. Taxpayers Association.

SOU. Statens Offentliga Utredningar (Swedish Royal Committee Reports).

Svenska Sjukkasseförbundet. Swedish Sickness Fund Association.

Sveriges Allmänna Sjukkasseförbund. Swedish General Sickness Fund Association.

Sveriges Läkarförbund. Swedish Medical Association.

Sveriges Läkarsällskapet. Swedish Medical Society.

Svenska Provinsialläkarföreningen. Swedish Provincial Doctors Association.

TCO. Tjänstemännens Centralorganisation (Swedish White-Collar Employees and Managers Central Organization).

USMF. Union des Syndicats Médicaux Français (Union of French Medical Unions).

Glossary of foreign-language terms

Botschaft. Legislative proposal presented by the executive government in Switzerland and Germany.

Bundesrat. Swiss Federal Council.

Caisses d'assurance maladie. French sickness funds.

Code de Déontologie. French medical code of ethics.

Comité d'organisation. French compulsory works councils consisting of employer and employee representatives during the Vichy regime.

Cumul des mandats. Simultaneous holding of several political posts.

Dépassement. Exemption from fee schedule.

Entente directe. Direct payment.

Kungliga Kommittéväsendet. Swedish Royal Committee Proceedings.

La médecine libérale. French liberal medical model.

Nationalrat. National Council – First Chamber (lower house) of the Swiss Parliament.

Proporz. Swiss practice of electing Bundesrat according to a stable formula of two representatives each from the Radical Democratic, Christian Conservative, and Social Democratic Parties, and one from the Swiss People's Party.

Remiss. Swedish procedure of submitting legislative proposals to interest groups for comment. Used for both the procedure and the statements written by the groups.

Riksdag. Swedish parliament.

Sociétés de secours mutuelles (also called **mutuelles**). French mutual aid societies, carriers of public social insurance from 1930 to 1945. After 1945, provided supplementary insurance.

Ständerat. States' Council – Second Chamber (upper house) of the Swiss Parliament.

Tarif d'autorité. Official fee schedule. Applies in the absence of conventions.

Tarif de responsabilité. Reimbursement fee schedule. Limits sickness fund liability.

Ticket modérateur. Patient's insurance deductible.

Tiers garant. Third-party guarantor (reimbursement payment).

Tiers payant. Third-party payment.

Vernehmlassung. Swiss procedure of submitting legislative proposals to interest groups for comment. Refers to both the procedure and the statements written by the groups.

Wundearzt. Swiss and German nineteenth-century apprenticeship-trained doctor.

Tables

1

Institutions of representation and national health insurance politics

Of all social programs, national health insurance is perhaps the most controversial. It constitutes what Martha Derthick calls a "boundary issue" of the welfare state. Such "issues of principle," she says, have "stirred passions and mobilized interest groups on a massive scale."[1] These programs are not automatically accepted as part of the welfare state; they have entailed political contestation that has tested the boundaries of the political sphere. National health insurance symbolizes the great divide between liberalism and socialism, between the free market and the planned economy. Doctors, unions, employers, and other interest groups actively engage in national health insurance conflicts. Political parties look to national health insurance programs as a vivid expression of their distinctive ideological profiles and as an effective means of getting votes. To the politicians in the executive, the introduction of such programs demonstrates that their administration has actually accomplished something. To the bureaucrats, health insurance provides an ample domain to exercise their administrative power.

National health insurance, in sum, is a highly politicized issue. Yet, the results of these conflicts vary considerably. Whereas virtually every industrialized country in North America and Western Europe has introduced workmen's compensation, unemployment insurance, and at least a basic, universal pension plan, health insurance stands out as an exception. Some countries, such as the United States, provide public health insurance coverage for certain limited segments of the population. Others simply subsidize private health insurance, as is the case in Switzerland. At the opposite end of the spectrum, we find nations like Britain, Spain, Italy, and Sweden that guarantee medical care to all citizens through nationalized hospitals and publicly paid doctors. Most Western European nations, including France, the Federal Republic of Germany, Belgium, and the Netherlands, as well as Canada, have introduced some form of national health insurance legislation. Again, these programs vary a great deal in the benefits they offer, their cost to patients, and the restrictions they place on doctors.

Government programs that finance and provide medical care determine to what extent a health care system is predominantly public or private.

These programs have important consequences for the autonomy of the medical profession, the control and steering of health services, and the distribution and financing of health care. Nevertheless, different nations have chosen very different approaches to the provision of medical care. Even a cursory examination of the development of health care systems in Europe and the United States demonstrates that these systems did not evolve naturally. In each country, there were a variety of conflicting opinions about the proper role of government in health. How then can one explain these very different outcomes? Why do nations with very similar levels of economic development and medical technology produce such different health care systems?

The answer is important not only for our understanding of health policy, but also for what it says about the politics of the welfare state more generally. In trying to understand why national health insurance programs are politically feasible in some countries but not in others, we will gain insight into the constraints on other social programs as well. National health insurance is an example – albeit an especially controversial one – of the type of social program we associate with the concept of a welfare state. At issue is the question of when and why democratic processes result in an extension of social rights. Indeed, this is the core question of the debate on the welfare state. Whereas scholars writing in the aftermath of the Second World War (like T.H. Marshall, William Beveridge, and Richard Titmuss) viewed the welfare state as a natural step in the expansion of democracy, their assumptions came into question during the 1970s and 1980s. It is not clear that democracy inevitably results in the growth of social programs. Nor is it clear from a normative perspective that these social programs should indeed be the goal of liberal democracies.[2]

Rather than discussing the relationship between democracy and the welfare state in the abstract, this book addresses these larger questions by examining specific instances of reform. It compares the politics of national health insurance in Switzerland, France and Sweden – three countries where the same legislative proposals have been considered, but where the pattern of failed and successful attempts at lawmaking has resulted in health programs that represent a broad range of government intervention in health. Switzerland has the most private health system in Western Europe, Sweden the most public, and France a conflict-ridden compromise between the two. In each case, the source of differences in national health insurance programs is a specific law. Legislative battles have determined whether or not there will be a public program, who is to be covered, the form the insurance will take, and what is to be provided. These laws thus affect individual citizens directly. Moreover, they effect a reshaping of the market for medical care that touches the interests of doctors, hospitals, insurers, and employers. To be sure, market forces, changes in demography, etiology, and technology, as well as negotiations and collective agreements have had a tremendous impact on the health sector. Nevertheless, these forces operate within a framework created through laws. Laws set the boundaries between the public and private health care sectors. Laws determine the extent to which access to health care is a right of citizenship. They redistribute the costs of health care between individuals, employers, and the larger society. To the extent that democracy has shaped the health care system, its effects have been mediated through specific laws.

This is a book about the politics of making these laws. The limits and possibilities of the democratic process in enacting social reforms are analyzed by looking at concrete instances of legislative conflict. The book argues that in order to understand the politics of national health insurance, we must look beyond the clash of ideologies and the clash of interest groups to the political context in which these interests are defined. By tracing political conflicts over national health insurance in a number of Western European nations, the book shows how procedures for representing interests structure the policy choices made by these nations. These procedures draw in distinct groups of participants and exclude others. They encourage the formation of distinct types of lobby associations. And they influence the strategies the leaders of these organizations use to pursue their own interests and those of their members.

This is therefore a book about why some interest groups win and others lose. It is also a book about why we make the policy choices we do and about the ways in which some policy choices are moved on and off the political agenda. And it is a book about how we might change the ways in which we go about making policy choices. Further, by stressing the procedural framework for policy decisions, it confronts the problem that no single explanation has yet emerged for the development of national health insurance policies – or for the welfare state. Whereas some other views of social policy have gone directly to various causal factors, such as modernization or the strength of the labor movement, the book argues that these approaches will remain unsuccessful until they examine the political context that makes these variables relevant.

THE RULES OF THE GAME

This political context is an institutional context.[3] Different nations have developed different institutions, formal and informal, for making political decisions. The formal institutions of government as defined by constitutions are critical to these decisions. But equally important to public policy are the informal practices that have developed around these institutions as interest groups, political parties, individual politicians, and bureaucrats have struggled to bend these institutions to their wills. These "rules of the game" define a different political logic for each nation. This is a logic that public policy, no matter how technical the subject matter, cannot escape. As we look at individual political decisions, we see this national pattern constantly reemerging.[4]

Different procedures for representing interests form the core of these logics. These have developed from different philosophies about the representation of interests and from concrete political conflicts over the institutions of representation. The political struggles that forged modern parliaments left an enduring political legacy. Yet, as new actors used these institutions to promote their interests, they changed the ways in which these institutions worked. Consequently, different nations involve interest groups in different ways in the policy process. Particular procedures offer these groups distinct channels of access to political decision making.

For some countries, the effective point of decision is in the executive, for others it is the parliament or the courts, and in others, policy issues are put directly before the electorate through referenda. These policy procedures have an impact on the kinds of groups that are included in a given policy decision, and offer distinct advantages and disadvantages to the various groups that wish to influence these decisions. They offer the general public very different routes for voicing opinions on policy issues. And they change the ability of representatives of the governing party to carry out their legislative program.

Much of the literature on public policy has concerned itself with these policy procedures. Many of these authors share a concern that public policy entails administrative processes and restricted policy networks that undermine the democratic process. Theodore J. Lowi, for example, has criticized the tendency in the United States to parcel out public decisions to private groups, allowing administrative agencies to negotiate with pressure groups over decisions of state. E.E. Schattschneider has noted the problems posed for democracy by the weakened role of political parties and the rise of interest groups. Although their evaluation of the outcomes is somewhat different, Philippe Schmitter and Charles Maier have described the growth of centralized organizations for interest intermediation and the displacement of parliamentary decisions to these associations in Western Europe. The common theme is that administrative processes have replaced political decisions made by legislatures, with the consequence that interest groups rather than democratically elected representatives now make policy.[5]

The case of national health insurance, however, shows that legislative decisions remain important. Open political battles in formal institutional arenas have had a significant impact on the health programs that have been introduced in these European nations. Meaningful political changes have indeed been made during the course of political deliberations within standard political institutions. Thus, rather than considering policy procedures as essentially opposed to democratic formalisms, this particular case of policy making allows us to examine the ways in which formal democratic institutions constitute a framework within which policy making takes place. While we can acknowledge the general trend toward a growth in organized interest groups and the role they play in policy decisions, these groups have not replaced traditional forms of democratic representation. Rather, interest group activities are embedded within these political institutions, and the scope of interest-group influence depends upon the logic of these political institutions. Political decisions taken in representative institutions set boundaries and create opportunities for the more hidden policy processes that occur within administrative agencies and interest-group associations.

But the ways in which these political decisions are made is different in different polities. Constitutional rules, the organization of political parties, and patterns of electoral participation – the standard political variables – create decision-making structures, each of which has its own logic. These formal institutional features and the ways in which they are combined with electoral results produce different kinds of political dynamics. For example, different patterns of consensus and conflict ensue when an executive government can make unilateral decisions than when the upper chamber of a divided parliament can be counted on to veto executive proposals. Consequently, the ability of executive governments to impose programs of reform, as well as the ability of interest groups to resist these reforms or to demand concessions, depends upon this institutional and political framework.

Political institutions do not neutrally transmit demands or merely ratify agreements previously worked out through preparliamentary interest-group bargains. Specific institutional configurations establish strategic contexts for political contests that determine those interests that can be effectively expressed and which ones will prevail over others. In this way, political institutions help to shape the definition of interests and their expression in politics.

THE POLITICS OF HEALTH

This book traces the effects of political institutions on policy decisions by following specific decisions as they travel through these institutional configurations. It investigates a series of reforms in Switzerland, France, and Sweden that established (or failed to establish) their national health insurance programs, in the process redrawing the boundaries between the public and the private sectors. As late as the 1920s, these systems looked similar. In all three countries, the role of government in health insurance was limited to providing subsidies to voluntary mutual associations – the type of system that remains in Switzerland today. As the book will show, from similar starting points the health systems of Switzerland, France, and Sweden developed in divergent directions as a consequence of the individual legislative proposals that were enacted into law in each country. Consequently, today these three systems represent three ideal types of government financing and provision of health services, which is why I chose them for this study.

In Switzerland, the role of government is limited to providing financial subsidies to private insurance carried by government-approved mutual aid societies. France has introduced national health insurance, a compulsory program of public health insurance that pays for medical treatment provided by private doctors. Sweden has gone the furthest, first establishing national health insurance and then converting this program to a de facto national health service that provides medical treatment directly to citizens through publicly employed doctors working in public hospitals. Roughly speaking, one could characterize the Swedish health system as the most socialized, while the Swiss could be viewed as the most privatized. It is not surprising, however, that Sweden is the country that ends up with the most expanded public programs in health, or that Switzerland is the one with the least. For these overall outcomes fit our stereotypes of the politics of these nations. Sweden is often thought of as a leader in welfare state programs, whereas Switzerland is generally viewed as having a more conservative political culture. But if one looks at what actually happened, at the ways in which these programs were enacted or rejected, these results are indeed quite surprising.

The three countries initially considered very similar types of policy proposals; politicians in all three nations attempted to introduce national health insurance programs. Indeed, of the three, Switzerland moved earliest to enact national health insurance, and established a program in 1911 that was considered a policy breakthrough by the standards of the time. Further, similarly situated interest groups in these three countries tended to view their interests in similar ways. The medical profession, for example, opposed national health insurance in all three countries. Political parties, too, reacted to the idea of national health insurance in similar ways. Even in Switzerland, all of the political parties were willing to enact national health insurance as early as 1900. In no case did the politics of national health insurance boil down to partisan conflicts.

Interest-group power

If the differences do not stem from basic differences in the ideas of policy makers, party politics, or the interests of different groups, do they depend on differences in the power of these groups? The answer presented in this book is yes. But the conception of power is somewhat different than that used in other studies. Differences in the power of the interest groups in these nations cannot be explained solely by features particular to the resources of any particular lobbying association. As an interest group, the medical profession, for example, had access to similar cultural, organizational, and market resources. Swedish, French, and Swiss doctors all enjoyed a recognized monopoly on medical practice. They were endowed with considerable technical expertise and social status. They earned relatively high incomes. Similar types of professional associations represented doctors in political matters and during negotiations with health insurance authorities in all three nations. And if membership figures can be used as a measure of organizational strength, we find that organizational differences do not explain these different outcomes. Since the 1930s, over 90 percent of Swedish and Swiss doctors have joined the national medical associations, whereas at the height of its success, the French medical association enrolled only 60 percent of French doctors. But French doctors were not the least successful as a lobby group – Swedish doctors were the least successful in the political sphere.

As exclusive providers of medical care, doctors should have been able to boycott government programs in all three nations. Indeed, in terms of market scarcity, the Swedish medical profession was the most advantageously placed of the three, with 89 doctors for every 100,000 inhabitants in 1959, compared with 107 in France and 141 in Switzerland.[6] In other words, although physicians were in relatively shorter supply in Sweden than in either France or Switzerland, the Swedish physicians were less successful in blocking government initiatives in health than doctors elsewhere. Thus, the theory that physicians achieve political power because they exercise a monopoly over medical practice or maintain the numbers of licensed physicians at low levels does not fit these three cases.

It is not differences in numbers and organizational strength that explain differences in the ability of medical professions to veto health policies in different nations. Rather, it is the opportunities for using these resources, and therefore the *value* of these resources, that varies from nation to nation. Successful political influence depends not only on the resources of particular interest groups, but also on the properties of the targets at which political pressures are aimed. Institutional configurations are vulnerable to political influence to different extents and at different points. Political decision making in different polities emphasizes different political arenas and different decision-making rules. Depending upon which arena constituted the de facto point of decision, different groups were privileged by the political institutions in each country.

In Switzerland, the constitutional right of voters to challenge legislation through referenda pulled decision making into the electoral arena. In this arena, the instability of majority rule proved a deterrent to proposals for

policy change; referendum votes were more often negative than positive. Consequently, the referendum was viewed as a threat to legislation. This created a strategic opportunity for the interest groups, like Swiss doctors, who found that they could use the referendum threat to gain concessions from policy makers. Swiss doctors never resorted to medical strikes; they simply threatened to block legislation by calling for referenda.

In France, the problem-riddled parliaments of the Third and Fourth Republics offered unexpected opportunities for interest group influence. Unstable parliamentary coalitions impeded executive governments from enacting legislation. The parliament became a bottleneck in the French political process, and hence was the de facto point of decision. French doctors profited from their parliamentary contacts to demand legislative concessions, and as a group that generally wished to block legislation rather than see it enacted, these doctors were inadvertently advantaged by the difficulty of French parliamentarians in reaching any decision at all. Only when the executive resorted to constitutional change in order to circumvent the parliamentary veto point, could French health legislation be enacted.

In Sweden, a pattern of executive dominance, made possible by institutions established to conserve the power of the monarchy and the Conservative Party during the transition to democracy, precluded the kinds of interest-group veto opportunities found elsewhere. With decision making effectively contained in the executive arena, Swedish doctors were politically disadvantaged. In this arena, their views were outweighed by those of the main producer groups – employers and trade unions – and, in contrast to French and Swiss doctors, they did not have recourse to an alternative veto point to override the executive-level consensus.

Thus, this book argues that power is not an essential or invariant characteristic of particular interest groups. Rather, the political impact of a particular group is contingent on strategic opportunities stemming from the logic of political decision processes. In sum, we could say that we do not have veto *groups* within societies, but rather veto *points* within political systems.

Of course, doctors are not the only group that is important to health policy making. Unions, employers, farmers, small businessmen, and even chiropractors participated in these legislative conflicts. In fact, case studies will show that the role of the profession is less important than is generally assumed. Nevertheless, the same general argument – that political influence depends upon strategic opportunities offered by particular political systems – can be applied to the other social and political actors engaged in these conflicts over national health insurance. Different institutional configurations allowed both the proponents and opponents of national health insurance very different opportunities for promoting their interests. This changed the outcomes of these struggles and changed the strategies the leaders of these organizations used to pursue their interests.

The book describes in close detail the political events that are responsible for the important differences in Swedish, French, and Swiss health care policy. In each case, national health insurance legislation responded both to common problems and to unpredictable, conjunctural events. But in each country a continuity in policy making is apparent, one that is singular and unpredicted by leading views on the welfare state. The critical difference between the cases was not the plans for reform or the resources of particular interest groups, but the institutional contexts in which political decisions were made. Political institutions changed the balance of power in these nations because they provided the same groups with different opportunities to influence political decisions. This historical material provides the basis for the book's main claim. Institutions for political representation play a primary role in structuring political conflicts and hence in accounting for divergent policy outcomes.

A COMPARATIVE INSTITUTIONAL APPROACH

In order to highlight the distinctiveness of the institutional approach, the balance of this chapter will examine some traditional ways of looking at the politics of health policy. The first generation of theories about the politics of health and social policy was concerned with a single issue: convergence versus divergence among nations. Factors such as economic growth and advances in medical technology were thought to stimulate increases in the public provision of medical services and to create pressures for policy convergence among nations. Factors such as national culture and distinct political ideologies, on the other hand, were viewed as barriers to convergence that account for distinctive and divergent national patterns of health policy. In response, a variety of approaches stressed the importance of politics in accounting for the particular path of welfare state development. Many of these theories featured the power of interest groups, with an emphasis on the medical profession by one camp and big business and unions by another. Each of these explanations will be taken up in turn and found wanting. The social forces that create pressures for political action are not a sufficient explanation for the emergence of national health insurance. Comparisons with other countries show that the factors that may seem overpowering in one nation – such as the peculiarities of its liberal tradition, the attitude of the medical profession, or the strength of its labor movement – have resulted in quite different outcomes in other nations. The comparative perspective shows that some factors are neither as unique nor as critical as they may appear, whereas others stand out as truly significant. Further, the comparative perspective brings to the fore the institutional framework within which these political conflicts take place.

ECONOMIC FACTORS AND MEDICAL TECHNOLOGY

In health policy, as in many other areas of policy, economic growth and technological progress are often thought of as setting the parameters for policy making. Although there is little doubt that such factors are indeed important, debate has ensued about how much scope remains for democratic choice within these apparently objective constraints. The strongest statement of the view that constraints on reform are objective rather than political was made by a group of writers known as the "convergence theorists." In a series of seminal studies, Pryor, Wilensky, Lebeaux, and others shattered conventional notions about democracy by pointing out that the levels of social expenditure were similar in both democratic capitalist and communist nations.[7] Despite differences in the type of political regime, the views of elites and political parties, and commonly held ideas about popular ideology, nations with similar levels of economic development and similar demographic factors (especially the age of the population) developed similar social policies. By analogy, such unilineal models of development were also applied to health by such writers as Roemer and Abel-Smith. Advances in medical technology and economic growth, they claimed, result in an ever greater public role in the financing and organization of health care systems.[8]

This vision of modernization, however, cannot explain the variations in response to common health problems. Despite similar medical break-throughs and economic pressures, different nations have enacted very different health care programs. As many of the convergence theorists themselves have pointed out, once we narrow the range of comparisons to a more homogeneous group of nations from the standpoint of development, political differences emerge more clearly.[9] Public policy making cannot be explained simply as the rational response of any society to a technical problem. Political factors help to determine whether or not a problem is defined as a public problem that requires political action, they shape the way in which that problem is perceived, and they intervene in the resolution of that problem.[10]

LIBERAL IDEOLOGY

A second common approach stresses cultural and ideological limitations on policy making. Economic growth and technical progress occur, according to the advocates of this approach, but distinct national traditions, and especially the strength of liberal ideology, ensure that no two nations – or health care systems – become alike.[11] Ideological or cultural conceptions set limits to the types of policies that can be enacted to solve similar problems in different nations. The surprising thing about national health insurance, though, is that politicians from distinct political cultures considered very similar types of programs. Reformers perceived their problems in similar ways, and the same ideas for solutions arose in many countries simultaneously. Nearly every country in Western Europe considered compulsory national health insurance or even a national health service at some point. In addition, reformers followed developments in neighboring countries with great interest and actively borrowed ideas that had been tried out elsewhere. Indeed, as this book will show, the ideas proposed in Western Europe were not very different from those proposed in the United States.

The political history of national health insurance is not a matter of a particular set of ideas about health care that remain distinct for each nation over long periods of time. Furthermore, whether one considers political culture to be the beliefs of individual citizens or the more elaborated doctrines of formally organized political parties or political movements, these sets of ideas rarely include well worked out proposals extending to specific details of the health care system. Instead, concrete policy proposals tend to emerge from political negotiations during which political leaders consider the fit between their party doctrine and the proposal at hand, but at the same time are also swayed by practical considerations (often brought to their attention by members of the bureaucracy) and by the positions taken by competing party leaders. Thus, the connection between cultural or ideological traditions and specific health policies must take into account the political lineup at any particular moment.[12]

Not only was the linkage between political ideology and policy proposals rather loose, but the passage of a single piece of legislation was in itself sufficient to completely change the health policy profile of a nation. The divergence of Swedish, French, and Swiss health policy was caused by the enactment of new laws. By contrast, the United States failed to enact the national health insurance proposals of the Progressive Era (1909–1920) and the Truman era. Had it done so, the United States would not now be distinct from the European group of nations. In other words, we find not distinct political cultures that only consider certain types of proposals, but rather an international policy debate, where particular episodes of reform constituted watersheds in the development of a nation's health policies. It is to these seemingly small turning points that different nations owe their specific sets of programs – the passage of individual laws has had major repercussions for the future development of national health systems.

PROFESSIONAL AUTONOMY

A prevalent approach to the analysis of the politics of just such policy reforms is to study the demands and activities of interest groups. In the health policy area, these studies often focus on the role of the medical profession. It is obvious that the medical profession should be a dominant actor in national health insurance policy making. After all, these programs directly affect the working conditions and incomes of doctors. Doctors are also the sole experts qualified to judge the effects of these public programs on health. Finally, these programs depend on the cooperation of doctors, for health insurance is meaningless unless doctors agree to treat insurance patients.

The involvement of the medical profession is in fact what makes national health insurance so controversial. In this area of social policy, governments do not merely provide transfer payments; they pay for the services of a private profession that is highly organized and politically influential. From the perspective of governments, such an open-ended commitment is problematic. Whereas the costs of pensions, for example, can be predicted, the costs of national health insurance depend upon the costs of medical treatment. These costs are potentially limitless, for they increase as doctors experiment with new therapies, patients demand new treatments, and the charges for medical procedures go up. Indeed, opponents of national health insurance have often argued that this is a Pandora's box of never-ending costs.[13]

Consequently, once governments begin to pay for medical services, they generally attempt to control the price of these services and to make sure that physicians are available to participate in the public programs. But here, government regulation encroaches on professional privilege. Heated political battles have taken place over whether national health programs should merely support the market for private medical practitioners by providing public payment for private services, or whether governments should regulate, restrict, or even replace private practice by providing health services directly, through a kind of medical "civil service" of government-employed doctors.

If national health insurance programs almost inevitably lead to conflicts between doctors and governments, how can we account for the particular resolution of these conflicts in different nations? An obvious place to look is at the theories that seek to explain the "power" of doctors. Whereas some studies of health policy have analyzed medical influence using the standard variables of pluralist policy analysis[14] – examining the superior organizational and financial resources as well as the political contacts available to doctors – a group of more sociological theories has stressed inherent features of medical practice. Theories of professional power have been developed to explain the pivotal role of doctors, not just for health policy, but for modern societies more generally. The independence of the medical profession, or professional autonomy as it has been called, is viewed as the key to the privileged position of doctors according to this school, although each theory analyses the sources of autonomy differently.

The sociology of the profession

Early studies of the medical profession saw autonomy as crucial for the social functions performed by doctors. Curing the sick requires a relationship of trust between doctor and patient that must be protected by measures to ensure that doctors are qualified and ethical. To this end, doctors need to be not only specially trained, but free from outside pressures. Writers such as Talcott Parsons viewed the traits of professionalism – special training, codes of ethics, supervision only by professional colleagues – as arising out of social necessity.[15] Many professional associations, as well, have stressed the need for independent physicians to assure quality care. Financial independence, and in particular the right of doctors to receive payments directly from patients without intervening bodies such as government agencies or insurance companies, was incorporated into several medical codes of ethics on the grounds that economic independence was critical if medical judgments were to be made on purely medical grounds. Patients would trust doctors only, it was argued, if they felt sure that doctors were completely loyal to them, and not to an outside party that was paying the bill.[16]

Later views of professional power criticized this notion of social necessity. Not every socially necessary occupation was granted the same autonomy and privileges as the medical profession. Moreover, the medical profession had not always been equally well-respected or autonomous. These criticisms led to alternative views that focused on the historical processes that resulted in professional autonomy. According to Eliot Freidson, the critical aspect of autonomy is that only fellow members of the profession are recognized as capable of judging the technical aspects of medical work. Although technical autonomy may now appear as self-evident, Freidson argues that this was not always a natural state of affairs. Rather, the unique professional status of physicians was achieved through campaigns by the profession to prove to governments the efficacy of medicine as a scientific body of knowledge and to convince these governments to approve exclusive routes for medical training and licensing. Many occupations, in other words, require specialized training, but the medical profession is one of the few that successfully convinced governments to require legal licenses for practice and asserted its right to technical autonomy in all spheres of medical practice.[17]

An offshoot of this view focuses more squarely on medical licensing. Following the Weberian tradition, Berlant and Larson, for example, regard medical organizations as a kind of modern guild. The key to professional autonomy, in their view, is not technical expertise, which by itself is quite hard to define, but market monopoly. Once the medical profession managed to control entry into the profession through licensing – a feat these writers agree with Freidson was achieved through political skill and historical luck – the profession could use its monopoly position to increase doctors' incomes, require direct payment, and improve the social status of doctors. Likewise, several economists – including Adam Smith – have viewed medical licensing as a barrier to competition that generates an economic advantage to physicians. This liberal profession is based on not-so-liberal market arrangements.[18]

Paul Starr points out that the American medical profession is a case apart as the early democratic political culture in the United States eschewed the role of the state that made European educational and licensing controls possible. It took a series of broad social and cultural changes, as well as political campaigns to reform medical education and establish both general and specialty licensing, for the profession to achieve what Starr calls its "cultural authority." This concept encompasses the status of physicians, but stresses in particular the authority of the profession to define medical issues and even the language permitted to discuss health, an authority that underlies the political role of the American Medical Association (AMA).[19]

Political influence

Whatever the historical origins of professional autonomy – whether its roots lie in technical expertise, market monopoly, or broader cultural factors – the implications of these studies of the power of the medical profession is that professional autonomy, once established, places the medical profession in a unique position as a political lobby group. If national health insurance requires the cooperation of physicians as the only group qualified to carry out medical treatment, then doctors should be able to bargain quite successfully for their conditions of practice under these programs. "As producers of a crucial service in industrial countries, and a service for which governments can seldom provide short-run substitutes, physicians have the overwhelming political resources to influence decisions regarding payment methods quite apart from the form of bargaining their organizations employ. . . . Hence whatever the political and medical structure of the western industrial country, medical preferences determine the methods of payment used in public medical care programs."[20]

But the case of national health insurance poses a puzzle. As one might imagine, doctors in many countries viewed national health insurance with alarm. From 1930 to 1970, it was not so much the insurance itself but the increasing government regulation of the profession that was sure to follow that doctors opposed. Medical associations throughout Western Europe viewed national health insurance as a threat to their professional autonomy. These associations were concerned that government insurance would undermine the independence of physicians. Whereas the model of medicine favored by the profession was that of the independent practitioner responsible directly to the patient and to professional colleagues, the entry of government into this relationship would place doctors under the control of government agencies. Proponents of national health insurance sometimes argued that this concern for professional autonomy was merely a disguised concern for professional incomes.

Whatever the true motives of these professional associations, the case studies that follow show that the initial reaction of organized doctors to national health insurance was one of resistance. At the same time, these physicians should have had equivalent opportunities to veto national health insurance programs. Through different routes, doctors throughout Western Europe and North America had been able to achieve the basic components of professionalism: Medicine was recognized as a highly valued technical skill to be practiced exclusively by doctors, and all of these nations introduced educational and licensing requirements. Why, then, were doctors in some countries more successful at blocking national health insurance programs than doctors in others?

To explain the differing impact of national medical associations on policy decisions, we must move away from the concept of professional autonomy to an analysis of the political institutions to which these lobbying efforts are addressed. Rather than limiting ourselves to factors related to the internal structure of this pressure group, such as its social status, organizational form, or market position, we might turn, as Harry Eckstein suggests, to the "structure of the decision-making processes which pressure groups seek to influence." In the British case, Eckstein found that the British Medical Association (BMA) had greater success as a pressure group during administrative negotiations within the Ministry of Health than in the more open political debates in parliament. Further, he related the general trend for British policy decisions to be made in the executive to features of the political system, such as single-member districts that allow a party to take decisive majorities in elections and enforce party discipline. Similarly, Rudolf Klein has stressed the importance of "old-fashioned party politics" and the type of public that is included in any particular political decision – what we could call the arena of policy making – as critical for medical influence in Britain. For legislative decisions, such as the passage of Medicare in 1965, Theodore Marmor has pointed to the importance of political factors such as the electoral position of the Democratic Party and the disproportionate power of Southern Democrats within the American congressional structure. Deborah Stone demonstrates that corporatist institutions have been important *both* as a source of the quasi-governmental power of the German profession and for successful efforts to control the economic activities of the profession. Such comparative studies, sensitive to the

political and institutional variables stressed here, have laid the groundwork for this book.[21]

In sum, the concept of professional autonomy emerged as an explanation of professional privilege. At their core, these theories point to the
ability of the profession to move decisions out of the sphere of politics,
the state, or the market and into exclusive professional jurisdictions.
The theories have been highly successful in explaining why, in any one
country, the medical profession has been more successful than many
other occupational groups in achieving a publicly sanctioned status as
experts. And, because explaining occupational stratification rather than
policy outcomes per se was the intent of many of these theories of
professionalization, its theorists have indeed met their goal. But if we
wish to understand the political role of the profession, we must understand how the various sources of professional autonomy are brought to
bear in the formal process of politics and, conversely, what it is that
enables the public to use the political sphere to constrain professional
autonomy. Even with similar resources, medical professions in different
countries have achieved different degrees of political influence. To
explain the political impact of professional power, we need to disentangle
the various strands of professional autonomy – technical expertise, licensing, associational membership, economic independence. And we must
turn to the mechanisms that translate aspects of professional autonomy
into political influence and hence to the receptivity of different political
institutions to professional power.

CLASS THEORIES

Paralleling debates about professional autonomy, and completely unrelated, another perspective has stressed the role of class-based politics in
accounting for the presence or absence of welfare state policies. Some of
these theories have focused on capitalism as a system and have analyzed
the functions of social policy in eliminating political conflicts and solving
economic problems within capitalism. In contrast to some conservative
critics of the welfare state, who view welfare state programs as a drain on
market economies, Marxist functionalists claimed that the welfare state is
an adjunct to capitalist economies. More recent versions of class theories
have tended to focus either on the role of business interests in shaping
social programs, or on the ability of organized labor, in conjunction with
social democratic political parties, to make political demands for social
programs.[22]

There are good reasons to think that the politics of national health
insurance may indeed be linked to these larger questions of economic
regulation and class conflict. A new insight into national health insurance
legislation is added if we consider it as part of a set of Keynesian
programs. Public health insurance does stimulate demand for medical

services, and the cash benefits portions of these programs add disposable income to the economy. Major initiatives in health insurance have come at times when governments looked to other Keynesian programs as well, such as during the 1930s, 1940s and 1960s. Moreover, interest groups, parties, and government officials discussed these programs as part of debates about economic, fiscal, and anti-inflation policies. As the case studies will indicate, both the perceived need for program expansion and the fears of medical costs were discussed within the framework of ideological and practical debates about the issues of economic planning, demand stimulus, and incomes policies. There is also evidence that the views of employers counted heavily in national health insurance debates, supporting the views of a number of scholars that business interests have shaped the welfare state. On the other hand, unions and socialist parties have also played a leading role in championing national health insurance programs.

None of these class theories, however, provides a full explanation for national health insurance politics. Although broad economic changes may have made national health insurance programs more appealing in some periods than in others, the type of program chosen to fill an economic exigency cannot be anticipated from economic conditions alone. In these conflicts, there is no clear historical pattern either of employer or union dominance. Like other interest groups, these actors have suffered both political victories and political losses. French employers, for instance, challenged the first compulsory health insurance law of 1928 and forced members of parliament to redraft the legislation with lower payroll-tax rates. In 1946, however, the Liberation government introduced universal national health insurance despite the opposition of employers. Furthermore, the relative political impact of employers and workers is not clearly correlated to the size of the unionized labor force. Although Swiss workers were more highly unionized than the French, for example, for reasons related to the organization of Swiss political institutions, Swiss unions were nevertheless less effective than French unions in demanding health insurance reform. Moreover, many other interest groups have participated in these conflicts. Recent studies have pointed, for example, to the decisive role of the middle classes and farmers' parties. Neither does the history of national health insurance merely mirror the history of social democratic electoral victories. National health insurance programs were introduced by political parties across the political spectrum for a variety of political reasons. The "new history" of the welfare state indicates that the impulse for social reform cannot be reduced to a class model, or to any other monocausal view.[23]

More importantly, in its efforts to depict the transformative potential of the "democratic class struggle," the class perspective has neglected some fundamental problems of representation. There is a logical and empirical gap between the class structure and the emergence of organizations, such as labor unions and social democratic parties, that purport to represent class interests. Unionization is not merely a matter of getting the working class to "see" its objective interests. In countries such as Sweden, the idea of "one big union" is viewed as legitimate. But in others, class interests are subordinate to other bases of solidarity, such as political ideology (France), religion (the Netherlands), or language (Belgium). To those who believe that class interests override all others, these social, cultural, or political cleavages are viewed as obstructions. But why should one cleavage rather than another – such as gender, age, or risk group – naturally or inevitably be preeminent? Further, as the empirical facts show that class cleavages are not always paramount, an important task is to explain the emergence of interest organizations based on different cleavages in different polities.

The cases of national health insurance policy-making will show that political institutions in different nations responded differently to different types of pressure group activity. Swedish institutions responded well to class-based interest associations, amplifying the impact of organizational gains and encouraging the continued growth of centralized union, employer, and white-collar associations. Swiss political institutions, on the other hand, proved to be more sensitive to organizations based on narrowly defined conceptions of interest, such as professional and small business associations. Indeed, despite the lack of women's suffrage, Switzerland is the one country included in this study in which social movements based on *gender* as opposed to *class* were important in placing health insurance reform on the political agenda, although, in the end, these groups did not succeed in getting the legislation they proposed enacted into law. For the United States, Quadagno has pointed out that the most successful promoters of welfare state policies were based on *age* as a category.[24]

By responding differentially to alternatively organized social and political movements, political institutions help to select the very conceptual categories that form the basis of organizational life. The ways in which social groups have organized themselves – the membership densities and degree of centralization – are certainly important. But in order to understand where these organizations come from and why some are more effective than others in translating membership strength into political results, it is equally important to examine the political arenas – specifically the representatives within them and the logic according to which they work – that respond to these organized social actors.

INSTITUTIONS AND ANALYZING POLICY

Many of the approaches sketched out thus far criticize pluralist theories of public policy. By pointing to elements of civil society – such as the economy, the ideological or cultural realm, the division of labor into professional groupings, or the system of class relations – these theories emphasize systematic pressures that facilitate or impede social policy legislation. Such theories are inherently critical of the pluralist view that political decisions result from a balance of interest group pressures.[25] If social power can bias political outcomes, then quite evidently the process cannot be said to be balanced. This brief and schematic survey raises a troublesome issue, however. Although there is plenty of evidence for a social skew to political decision making, no study has been able to find an inherent logic to the development of the welfare state. The historical variation is simply much greater than is predicted by social views of politics. Social programs have been enacted for a wide variety of reasons, and through extremely different political processes. As this book will show, health-policy conflicts often involved issues and actors completely unrelated to these theories. For example, after the First World War the French enacted their first national health insurance law not as a result of interest group, professional, or class conflicts – although these factors did indeed play a role – but mainly because of issues of nationhood that became relevant after the return of Alsace and Lorraine to France. Such historical discrepancies are not minor details; they must be confronted if these theories of the welfare state are to meet their own goal of showing that "politics matter."

The growing body of historical evidence that does not fit the predictions of macro-social theories of the welfare state indicates a fundamental flaw in the sociological approach. Whatever the source of social pressure, social demands must be channeled through political institutions if they are to have an impact on political decisions. The attempt to analyze political struggles in terms of social pressures runs into trouble precisely because the political institutions that mediate between the social and the political worlds do not respond consistently to the same social pressures. Whereas one set of political institutions may react quite strongly to, for instance, class pressures – whether from employers or workers – another set of institutions may not. Social theories of political power help us to understand the potential power of social actors. But these theories will remain necessarily incomplete until they address the political institutions that allow these actors to realize this potential. Without attention to these political institutions, social variables are divorced from the political context that gives them meaning.

Whereas social theories of political pressure assume that the expression of demands is efficient – that is, that the final result is proportional to the strength of the initial demand – an alternative approach asserts that the mechanisms by which social pressures are transmitted to political decision-makers are critical. Institutional theories of politics have addressed both the organization of social and political actors as well as the larger political and institutional frameworks in which political conflicts take place. Broadly speaking, we can categorize the institutionalists into three basic theoretical types: historical institutionalist, rational choice, and organization theory.[26]

Historical institutionalists emphasize the legacy of distinct national experiences, unique patterns of institution building and organization of social interests, as well as, in many cases, the role of states in demarcating the boundaries of conflict and representation. New political conflicts are fought out by groups that have already been formed and within distinctive political systems that already have a history. These preexisting organizations structure the paths of political debates and policy outcomes. They determine – out of all of the myriad possible social cleavages – which ones will be important in the political sphere. Institutions for representing interests often constitute what Suzanne Berger has called "preformed lines of division" that set the terms for discussing new issues.[27]

The rational choice perspective has concentrated on the ways in which institutional rules – for example, the sequence of parliamentary votes, or the division of legislatures into committees – affect the strategic interactions of political participants. These rules – and not the initial preferences of the various players – determine where the equilibrium balance point between the different interests concerned will be found.[28]

The third approach to institutional analysis comes from organization theory, and in particular from the Carnegie school. This approach starts from a recognition of the limits on human cognition. It stresses the ways in which techniques for processing information compensate for these limitations, and analyzes their impact on organizational decisions. Standard operating procedures decide what kinds of information should be used to make decisions and how to make those decisions. This sort of "bounded rationality" restricts choice by ordering information, and hence enables individuals with contrary purposes to achieve coordinated action.[29]

These institutional theories differ in significant ways – particularly in their assumptions about human rationality and in their recognition of collective sources of differences in the power and resources of individuals. Yet, to some extent, the differences have been overdrawn and some important similarities overlooked. Despite different theoretical vocabularies and different methodological concerns, there is indeed a coherence to the institutionalist approach. Institutionalists all view individual interests or preferences as diverse, and potentially aligned along a number of different dimensions. In this, they are no different than liberal or pluralist theorists. Where they depart from these other views, however, is in their stress on the role of institutions in articulating these preferences. Political demands cannot be understood, according to the institutionalists, without attention to the institutional rules that allow these demands to become visible and politically significant. Further, these institutions do not merely aggregate these preferences in an additive way. By indicating rules for adjudicating among divergent interests, institutions order preferences, and hence privilege some dimensions of conflict and consensus at the expense of other potential dimensions.

Institutions thus create order not just by the ways of thinking or courses of action they allow, but also by those they exclude. In fact, many institutionalists go further. Not only may information be lost or distorted by these institutions, but it is in fact only when institutions establish rules for ordering and perceiving information that it is possible to have "information" at all. Consequently, decisions – whether made by members of interest groups, business organizations, or polities – are contingent upon institutional rules for making these decisions. Nevertheless, each of the institutionalist approaches keeps in mind the tension between choices constructed through institutions and the underlying diversity of preferences.

As we will see in the case studies, this tension is critical to understanding the institutional dynamics of political decision making. Institutions forge political consensus by setting forth procedures for arriving at decisions and rules for resolving conflicts. Yet they do not erase the underlying differences of opinion that make consensus difficult to achieve. Policy proposals are vetoed when institutions leave an opening that allows such differences to reemerge. Thus, the telling point of the institutionalist perspective is not whether a given organization counts as an "institution." The gist of institutionalism is the way in which institutional rules adjudicate among a variety of preferences, and hence give different weights to these preferences, no matter where the adjudication occurs.

INSTITUTIONS AS ACTORS AND STRUCTURES

Corporatist theories

One way to apply these institutional approaches to public policy is to focus on institutions as an independent variable. Whether institutions are envisioned as institutional actors or as institutional structures, a number of studies have looked for correlations between institutional inputs and policy outputs. The literature on corporatism, and particularly the works of Philippe Schmitter, has analyzed single interest groups as well as national patterns of interest groups as organizations whose features – for example, the degree of vertical and horizontal integration – account for interest group behavior and policy results. The array of organized groups accounts for the political pressures that will be felt by governments; the ways in which individual groups are structured helps to account for the ways in which members of those groups perceive their interests. A centralized, corporatist union movement, for example, is thought to be more capable of getting its members to agree to incomes policies than is a fragmented movement, split along different skill lines as well as vertically between the top union leadership and representatives such as shop stewards, who may be closer to the rank-and-file. The organization of the group thus shapes the ways in which members view their interests as well as their capacity to act on those interests.

Corporatist theories are quite important for policy making. Not only does the pattern of interest representation help to explain political pressures that result in specific policies, groups recognized (or even sponsored) by governments also provide a means for implementing policies. The West German national health insurance system, for instance, is organized and run through agreements negotiated by such corporatist interest groups representing the medical profession, unions, employers, and insurance agencies. Without these institutional actors, such agreements could not be made. These official representatives not only present the views of their memberships, they enforce compliance with negotiated agreements by their members.[30] Nevertheless, the extent to which interest organizations have achieved a corporatist form of organization, as we will see, does not explain the differences in Swiss, French, and Swedish health politics. Under some political circumstances, corporatist interest organizations may be extremely important, whereas under others they may be irrelevant.[31]

States as actors and structures

Other policy analysts focus on governments as actors and structures. These analysts focus variously on the role of bureaucrats, state administrative capacities, policy legacies, state structures, and the more classical issues of state, such as the national interest and political legitimacy. The work of Theda Skocpol, in particular, points out that these institutions of government are critical for the enactment of social programs. The institutionalist twist is that these analysts understand both the motivations and capacities for action of policy-makers in organizational terms. Three different levels of government appear as important: the nation-state as part of a system of nation-states, the bureaucratic and administrative level, and the political leadership.[32]

The nation-state. Several writers have pointed out that there is a link between social insurance and international security considerations – that is, between the welfare state and the nation-state. Many national health and other insurance programs have been enacted following wars. Other writers have pointed to the connection between exposure to the international economy and the introduction of social programs – the more "open" the economy, the greater the tendency to expand the welfare state. Nevertheless, although wars may have tended to produce postwar political climates favorable to social policies, it is unclear if this is a matter of a new ideological commitment to equality, growth of unionization during wars, fears of postwar social unrest, or an economic necessity to tradeoff surplus capital between warfare and welfare expenditures.

Not only are the causal linkages unclear, but the outcomes are irregular as well. For instance, how can we explain that neutral countries such as Sweden and Switzerland reacted to the end of the two world wars with similar social policy proposals, but the actual legislative results were polar opposites: Sweden enacted national health insurance and went on to change the system to a de facto national health service, whereas Switzerland's national health insurance law was rejected by a national referendum. Similarly, the open economies of Sweden, Austria, and Switzerland, as Katzenstein shows, have produced very different balances between corporatist organizations representing capital and labor, and very different social policies as well. The security interests of nation-states may help to place programs of social reform on the political agenda, but there is no direct correlation between such interests and subsequent policy outcomes.[33]

Bureaucracy and organizations. At the bureaucratic level, we may note that no program was ever introduced without the very active participation of high-level bureaucrats. Reforms tended to be prepared initially in the executive governments, with interest group consultation following, indicating that interest group opinions responded to government policies rather than initiating them. Further, reforms built upon preexisting programs and administrative structures, so that we could say that policy legacies and administrative capacities exerted an influence on the range of policies considered. Here the institutional actor is impersonal, and could be thought of as a structure. Empirically, however, there is no direct correlation between governmental structures and social policies. Among federal political systems, Canada has enacted Federal-Provincial hospital and medical insurance, West Germany has a national health insurance system, and Switzerland has rejected national health insurance. Italy and the United States are both known for patronage political parties, yet Italy introduced a national health service that eliminated a source of patronage, whereas the United States has not enacted national health insurance and certainly would not consider a national health service. The United States is said to have a weak administrative capacity for social programs, yet the Social Security Administration was set up virtually overnight.

Despite differences in civil service traditions and bureaucratic politics, members of different European bureaucracies prepared quite similar proposals for national health insurance, and the differences in what was ultimately enacted cannot be traced to differences in the implementing bureaucracies. Thus, although bureaucrats and bureaucratic structures are most certainly important for policy making in general, here we have a case where national health insurance laws seem to fall within the zone of indifference of many different civil servants. This allows us to concentrate on the impact of the legislative process itself.[34]

Political executives. At the level of political leaders, there is a tremendous amount of evidence for what we could call an "executive-centered" approach. Although the term "state" has been the subject of a continuing debate, in Europe, the narrow, constitutionally precise meaning of the term is the executive branch of government as opposed to the legislative. Depending on the particular constitution, the political executive may be a king, a president, a prime minister (whose political rights are then based on a parliamentary coalition or single-party rule), or, as in the Swiss case, a seven-member collegial executive composed of representatives of the leading parties. The executive-centered approach – which comes closest to a clear view of the state as an actor – makes sense of the wide variation in partisanship in enacting national health insurance. It may be the position of politicians as rulers and an interest in stabilizing their regime that is the common thread.

This view leads to a more careful consideration of the specifically *political* motivations of leaders as opposed to social pressures. Flora and Alber have pointed out that even with similar levels of working-class unrest, the reactions of nineteenth-century political elites differed according to their need for popular legitimacy – leaders of monarchical regimes expanded social programs at earlier dates as they sought an alternative to the political legitimacy afforded by parliamentary institutions. Bismarck, for example, may have been more concerned about the liberals in the parliament than the socialists in the streets when he proposed compulsory health insurance in 1881. Concerns of executive power can explain why Napoléon III, de Gaulle, and FDR each played a decisive role in promoting new social programs in quite different historical periods.[35] The "state" in this very specific sense plays an important role as an institutional actor in national health insurance politics; but so do sets of formally organized interest groups, political parties, bureaucrats, and units of local government.

POLITICAL INSTITUTIONS AS CONFIGURATIONS

This book pulls out a different strand of institutionalist thinking. Rather than emphasizing particular actors or parts of political systems, it focuses on the organization of political systems as wholes and the overall logic by which they work. It tries to make sense of the variation in national health insurance politics by focusing on the institutional frame within which political decisions are made. Given the wide variety of historical contingencies and causal factors that are implicated in national health insurance legislation, the explanatory strategy used here has been to show how the institutional framework for political decisions can explain why some factors are relevant in some polities or historical periods but not in others.

By mediating political conflicts in distinctive ways, political institutions bring together different constellations of organized actors and change the ways in which they interact. Social problems, organized interest groups, or governmental structures alone are not sufficient to explain the different legislative measures taken to combat similarly perceived problems. More broadly, we cannot analyze public policy results by correlating political inputs to policy outputs. For political institutions reconfigure these political pressures and redefine the policy alternatives. The design of national political institutions and the ways in which these institutions work in practice create different linkages between political inputs and policy outputs. Indeed, to borrow from the language of systems theory, we could say that the "input–output functions" themselves are different in different political systems. This book views political institutions as complex configurations and tries to pinpoint the mechanisms by which these institutions produce different logics of interest group power in different polities.

The formal institutions of representative government are at the heart of this analysis. The rules for electing representatives and investing a government empower representatives of a particular political view. The rules of governance provide opportunities and obstacles for translating these views into concrete policies. These procedural advantages and impediments are the product of years of struggle among various political movements over the institutional design of political systems.

Generally speaking, specific institutional provisions represent historic compromises between pressures for representation of new actors and the wishes of elites to maintain the status quo. Institutional veto points, such as the separation of powers, were explicitly incorporated into national constitutions in order to check centralized power and to impede popular movements from usurping the reins of government. But in order to understand how such institutional provisions continue to exert an influence, particularly when the cast of relevant actors has changed significantly from the monarchs, nobles, and priests that often designed these institutions, we must examine the incentives that these institutions provide to the actors involved in contemporary policy conflicts.

Institutional hurdles direct political decisions along particular paths through the different political arenas where representatives must concur for a final decision to be made. Formal institutional rules and the distribution of politicians with different partisan loyalties into these arenas result in different patterns of certainty and uncertainty in decision making. These institutions, together with the partisan distribution of votes, do not determine the final outcome, but they do determine the places in the process where passage is certain and those where bottlenecks are likely to arise. These patterns of predictability and indecision, established by specific institutional mechanisms, are the key to understanding the dynamics of the legislative aspects of policy making. They affect both the ability of executive governments to enact their legislative programs and the ability of interest groups to influence the legislative outcome.

Rules and procedures

The division of power among elected representatives established by constitutional rules is a key distinguishing feature of different political systems. The extent of executive power is of particular interest in this book. To what degree can the political executive act independently of representatives in other arenas, such as the legislature, the courts, or the electorate? Constitutional provisions define the autonomy of these representatives by setting forth rules for making individual political decisions and rules for the investiture in office of these representatives. Members of the separate branches of government may be restricted to specific policy domains; provisions for executive vetoes, legislative override, procedures for presenting executive proposals, and parliamentary motions all delineate the freedom of action of these various representatives. The rules for investiture prescribe a more long-lasting autonomy – for example, by specifying whether the political executive will be elected directly or appointed by a parliamentary coalition – and, in the latter case, dependent therefore on the members of the coalition and their majority status in the parliament.

These rules affect not only the initial investiture, but the continued rule of these representatives. Legislatures may have the right to impeach even a directly elected president or to call for a vote of confidence against a prime minister. Conversely, the executive may be allowed to dissolve a legislature and proceed with new elections. By specifying the network of rules that prescribe and limit the powers and jurisdictions of members of these different political arenas, we can describe the formal structure for making political decisions. By examining these rules, we know whether the political executive can make unilateral decisions, whether parliamentary approval is required, or whether voters may recall legislation directly, as in Switzerland. These rules comprise the institutional design of a political system.

The de jure rules of institutional design are the foundation stones of political decision structures. But to understand how these institutions work in practice, we must add the de facto rules that arise from electoral results and party systems. For political power depends on votes – but votes as they are distributed within particular political institutions. The effective power of a political executive and the dynamics of executive–legislative relations depend on the partisan composition of the various houses of parliament, on whether the executive enjoys a stable parliamentary majority, and on whether party discipline is in force.

The implications of different types of electoral results could be spelled out in much more detail, as they will be in the individual case studies, but here these comments are limited to the overall point that the need for assenting votes limits the scope for action of the political executive. Patterns of electoral participation change the functioning of a given institutional design in a particular country. To some extent, although the exact extent is still under debate, voter turnout, electoral patterns, and features of the party system may be explained by the formal rules of electoral laws.[36] However, although worthy of further investigation, the ultimate causes of these electoral patterns are less germane to the argument of this book than the observation that, together, de jure constitutional rules and de facto electoral results create a political framework for policy making.

This maze of institutional rules establishes the background conditions for the actions of politicians, bureaucrats, interest groups, and voters who wish to enact or to block policies. These rules do not predetermine any particular policy outcome or dictate a particular definition of interests. There is no direct correlation between a particular set of political institutions and a given health policy. Rather, institutions change the course of policy making by the ways in which these rules link particular decision makers or allow them greater or lesser independence of action. This changes the ability of any particular actor to force policy provisions through the legislative process. The ability of an executive leader to introduce legislation and to see it ultimately enacted, for instance, depends upon the potential for unilateral executive action – that is, on whether politicians at subsequent points of decision will ratify or oppose the executive proposal.

The probability of veto is not random, however. Political decisions can be viewed as a series of decisions made by representatives in a linked chain of political arenas. Depending upon how these political arenas are configured – that is, upon the rules for transferring decisions from one political arena to the next and on the rules for partisan representation within each – the probability of agreement with the executive will vary. In this way, the veto points depend both on constitutional rules and electoral results. These points are not physical entities but points of strategic uncertainty where decisions may be overturned; even a small shift in electoral results or constitutional provisions may change the location and strategic importance of such veto points.

The political system taken as a whole, with all of its institutional provisions and a particular distribution of partisan representatives – which I call an "institutional configuration" – comprises an environment of conduct. Without an understanding of this political environment, the activities of political actors do not make sense – this institutional environment is the frame of reference for their actions. The particular policy conflicts we are about to examine all take place within the framework of such institutional configurations, and the strategies and tactics of these various actors all refer to a particular political and institutional configuration. Like the view of the historical institutionalists, this view of political institutions recognizes the importance of the historical origins of these institutions and the ways in which preexisting institutions create power inequalities such that political conflicts do not start out on an even playing field. But in tracing out the logic of the institutions as they work in practice, it draws as well from the rational choice and organization theory perspectives.

Institutions and interests

In order to understand interest group influence, one must examine each link in the chain of political decision making, seeing which politicians occupy strategically important positions and analyzing why they might react favorably to interest group lobby efforts. Particularly for a group such as doctors, who represent only a tiny minority of voters, electoral significance, and even financial considerations, do not explain why doctors would have a great deal of political clout or why it should vary across nations. Further, as discussed previously, their role as health experts, or as holders of a market monopoly, does not account for different degrees of political influence. The same observation holds true for much larger groups. Labor unions have achieved very different degrees of political influence that do not vary merely according to the number of members they enroll or the number of voters they represent. If a given group is to insist that specific legislative provisions be added or dropped, it must be able to threaten the passage of the law. Particular institutional configurations with their veto opportunities determine whether interest groups can make such threats, and at what stage in the legislative proceedings interest groups can intervene.

Interest groups are often consulted directly during the formulation of policy proposals at the executive stage. But their relative importance depends on whether they are politically essential to the executive, or whether they can count on concentrations of politicians to overturn executive decisions at a later stage in the legislative process. Interest group influence thus depends on the institutional context of political decision making. If the political executive can enact legislation un-impeded by parliamentary or electoral vetoes, the average interest group has little chance of stopping the legislation. On the other hand, if the executive is dependent on, say, the approval of a parliamentary com-mittee, certain select interest groups – those that for one reason or another are relevant to the members of that committee – have an oppor-tunity for a veto.

Such interest group influence may be direct or indirect. In some cases, interest groups have direct access to decision makers at the veto point through personal contacts or other forms of lobby networks; even a small group may be a critical constituency for a given politician. In these cases, the interest groups can threaten the passage of a law by directly influenc-ing the politicians at the veto point. In other cases, influence is indirect. Interest groups may be able to take advantage of unintended features of the decision-making process – for example, a stalemated parliament or coordination problems stemming from a divided government. In these cases, interest groups enhance their bargaining power by relying on points of strategic uncertainty that they themselves cannot control.

Institutional configurations thus give different interests differential chances of attaining favorable policy outcomes.[37] Because interest groups can anticipate these results, however, the institutional effects are impor-tant not just for the final policy outcome, but for interest group behavior during the entire process. The willingness of interest groups to make concessions early on or to stand their ground depends upon their assess-ment of the veto opportunities. If there is no chance of veto, they may as well cooperate. On the other hand, if they can veto – or they think uncertainties in the process make a veto likely – they may as well insist that their demands be met, and they may in fact escalate their demands. This strategic aspect of demands is worth stressing. Interest groups do not hold one interest. They come to negotiations with long lists of potential demands, and, depending on their view of the opportunity structure, they will go down the list as far as possible. Interest groups adjust their strategies and reformulate their demands in light of the peculiarities of particular institutional configurations.

SWISS, FRENCH, AND SWEDISH HEALTH POLITICS

In order to show these political institutions at work, this book presents a description of selected instances of legislative conflict, each of which was critical to the development of national health insurance policy in a given nation. As will be seen, the political conflicts examined all involve a central conflict between executive governments and doctors. Although governments in these three nations attempted to expand their control over medical markets, doctors fought to maintain a free market. Each victory by the state brought about reduced market freedom for doctors; each success of the medical profession improved, or at least safeguarded, its market position. The extent to which either governments or doctors achieved their objectives depended on the political institutions in each country.

In Sweden, we observe a pattern of executive dominance. The political executive could be sure of parliamentary support for its proposals because the executive was based on stable parliamentary majorities and party discipline was in force. Under these circumstances, one could not expect the majority of members of parliament, who were bound by party loyalty, to deviate from the executive decision. Consequently, the executive could take action without fearing parliamentary vetoes. Because executive decisions could not be vetoed elsewhere, political negotiation was contained within the executive arena. This, of course, privileged groups with executive importance, such as employers or unions, while it disadvantaged those with better contacts or greater sympathy in the parliamentary or electoral arenas, such as doctors. Bargains reached in the executive preparliamentary process were final as they could not be overturned elsewhere. This gave interest groups, particularly small ones, an incentive to cooperate and try to obtain concessions at the executive stage. These institutional advantages enabled the Swedish government to introduce national health insurance and controls on doctors' fees and to convert the system to a national health service by introducing salaried employment for hospital doctors.

In France, although constitutionally also a parliamentary system, the executive lacked the support of stable parliamentary majorities. Not only did electoral results not establish a clear majority, but lack of party discipline allowed for continual renegotiation of the parliamentary coalition. Consequently, the executive could not count on proposals being ratified in the parliament, as in the Swedish case. Rather, significant policy changes and even vetoes could be expected from parliamentary representatives. Furthermore, the shifting alliances in the parliament made it difficult to reach any policy decision at all. This made the parliamentary arena a critical decision point in France. And it proved to be a tremendous advantage for interest groups that were essential to the members of parliament that could bring down the executive government by exiting from the governing coalition – particularly for those that aimed to block increased government intervention, such as doctors, small employers, and farmers. As might be expected, groups with such parliamentary recourse were not inclined to make concessions to the executive. It was only when the executive made itself independent from the parliament through the special provisions of the brief Liberation period and then more permanently after the constitutional changes of the Fifth Republic that major changes in health policy were introduced, despite the continued resistance of these interest groups. At these times, the executive could enact laws without parliamentary ratification, thereby bypassing the parliamentary veto point. The executive relied on these institutional provisions to introduce national health insurance, controls on doctors' fees, and salaried employment for some groups of hospital doctors. Thus, the pattern of health politics depended on the dynamic of political contestation between executive and parliament.

In Switzerland, the referendum provided a means for opponents of national health insurance to veto legislation even after it had been approved by all major interest groups and political parties. Even when decisions had been made in the executive and approved in the parliament, a referendum campaign could force issues into the electoral arena. Although we might expect that popular access of this sort would hasten the enactment of progressive programs, it proved to be quite easy to assemble counter-majorities among the electorate. Even though voters voted predictably for the same political parties (and even for the Social Democratic Party, which became the largest party in 1943), once these parties proposed policies, the underlying diversity of preferences in the electorate became apparent, and legislative proposals were more often rejected than accepted. As we will see, this uncertainty in the electoral arena afforded interest groups willing to call for referenda, such as doctors, an unusual route of political influence. For, simply by threatening to launch referenda, these groups were granted concessions throughout the policy process. The Swiss referendum blocked all attempts to introduce national health insurance and controls on doctors' fees. With these steps effectively precluded, more invasive government intervention became a non-issue.

Veto points and political influence

In each case, institutional rules established a distinct logic of decision making that set the parameters both for executive power and interest group influence. Institutional veto points comprised barriers to legislative action that served as useful tools for the interest groups that wished to block legislation. By making some courses of action more difficult and facilitating others, the institutions determined where the balance point between different interest group demands and the programmatic goals of the executive was to be found. As these institutional effects work via the action of interest groups and politicians, the argument of this book is not that organized interests are irrelevant to policy outcomes.[38] Rather, it argues that the *mechanisms* by which they become relevant are very different from those proposed by interest-centered theories of politics. Doctors associations, for instance, have influence over the political process not to the extent that one is more "professional" than another, but in proportion to the opportunities proffered by institutional veto points for blocking or challenging government policy decisions.

Interest-group power – and specifically medical dominance – thus depends on the veto points within political systems and not on the properties or organization of particular groups. In contrast to other views of institutions, the view presented here is not that institutions eliminate a set of policy ideas from the political agenda or hinder policy implementation; nor do they determine the ideas or actions of political actors. Instead, institutions merely provide incentives, opportunities, and constraints. Within these institutions, political actors are free to choose their own strategies, and even to make mistakes. By providing specific opportunities, the institutions change the rules of politics and therefore redefine the practical meaning of political power.

From this perspective, the view of the welfare state elaborated in this book departs from the macro-theories previously described. Welfare state programs, of which national health insurance is a good example, are not simply the product of long-term social and political trends; such programs have been introduced in steps, through discrete instances of legislative conflict. In order to understand the origins of social programs, one must examine the "micro-politics" of individual reforms. Formal political institutions changed the outcomes of these conflicts not by predetermining specific results, but by changing the rules of the game for politicians and interest groups. Over time, continuities in these political logics allow one to speak of differences in what has often been termed "political culture." This book argues, however, that these differences are not accounted for by differences in the mentalities of citizens or political elites in these nations; instead, these patterns of representation and conflict are understandable, if not necessarily predictable, from the structure of opportunities made possible by distinct institutions.

THE PLAN OF THE BOOK

The burden of the argument that follows is to show how these institutional mechanisms were established and why they continue to exert an impact on health policy making. Chapter 2 presents an overview of the policy choices that have been considered in a number of nations and compares the policy outcomes in the three cases chosen for this study. The chapter justifies the assertion that the health systems in these countries began from similar starting points and that similar policies were proposed in these nations. It also explains the logic of the case selection. Chapters 3, 4, and 5 look more closely at the politics of reform in France, Switzerland and Sweden. Each chapter presents an overview of the design of political institutions and explains why in practice they result in different decision-making mechanisms. The effects of these institutional mechanisms are then explored by examining the history of national health insurance politics in that particular case. Chapter 6 draws out the implications of this institutional analysis for studying health policy in other nations.

2

Doctors versus the state: The economic and political logic of national health insurance

To a surprisingly large extent, the role of the market versus the role of government has dominated public discussions of national health insurance. National health insurance programs have been viewed as an important step in the expansion of the role of government. Supporters of such programs have welcomed governmental assumption of responsibility for citizens' health care. Opponents have argued that these programs undermine individual responsibility, that they are too expensive, and that they impede the functioning of the private market in health. This clash between market and government underlies both the rational calculation of interests made by various health policy constituencies and the larger conflicts concerning partisan values that have been occasioned by national health insurance debates.

This chapter examines the significance of this reoccurring conflict over the role of the market versus the role of government. The impact of government health programs on medical markets will be used as a guide to understanding what is at stake in the political conflicts examined in subsequent chapters. First, the economic repercussions of government intervention in health for the medical profession are laid out. Next, the kinds of intervention undertaken by governments are classified according to the respective roles of market and government in the health system. After the policy alternatives have been presented, the chapter situates these alternatives within the political and historical context in which they developed. Finally, the cases selected for this study are discussed in terms of the broader framework of European health policies.

MARKET AND GOVERNMENT

Government health programs expanded the market for medical practice. Yet, despite this expansion, medical associations throughout Western Europe opposed such government programs. These doctors developed an ideology of "liberal medicine" and tried to defend the private market against state intervention. But why should medical professions oppose programs that would guarantee them a clientele? Why have so many political conflicts over government health programs centered around the role of the private market versus the role of government? And why have medical associations sought to defend the private market in these conflicts?

It is the premise of this book that these disputes about market and government are based on a very real conflict of interest between the buyers and sellers of medical services. As buyers of medical services, governments hope to reduce the price of these services. To the extent that payments for medical services become consolidated in the hands of government, governments can use their powers as payor to enforce price controls and other forms of public management of the health sector. Thus the position of government as a buyer is strengthened to the degree that the government becomes the sole buyer of services – that is, to the extent that government achieves a position of monopsony. This monopsony power of government is confronted, however, by the monopoly power of doctors, as they are the sole providers of medical services. The position of doctors is strengthened if they can sell their services not to a single buyer, but to many buyers.

Government health programs have two – contrary – implications for this confrontation. Government health programs comprise an entry point for governments into the health services market. Such programs are therefore a step toward monopsony. At the same time, government payment for medical services greatly expands the market for medical care by using government resources to purchase medical care for persons that otherwise could not afford it. Government health programs thus increase both the financial resources available for medical treatments, and at the same time such programs increase the leverage of governments over health care providers. Once governments pay for medical services, they are thus bound to try to lower the price of those services. And, further, if these government payments are centralized – for example, into a central budget – and if these payments are the sole source of financing for medical services, then the *pressure* on government to control costs as well as the *ability* of government to control costs is increased. At some point, the interest of government as payor in regulating service providers is bound to collide with the interests of doctors in maintaining a position as independent professionals. Because government health programs generally pay for hospital treatments and pharmaceuticals, similar conflicts between these providers and governments have also arisen. But here the focus will be on conflicts between governments and doctors.

Although in theory there have been many different ways in which governments and the medical profession might have resolved their differences, during the period of rapid expansion of government health programs in Europe (roughly 1930 to 1970), the medical profession in a number of different countries focused on one particular strategy. The liberal model of medicine looked to the free market as a realm of protection for the autonomy of the medical profession. Medical associations throughout Western Europe fought the entry of governments into the health insurance market; they fought subsequent government efforts to control medical costs by regulating doctors' fees and changing methods for paying doctors to more "collective" forms, such as salaries; and they fought prohibitions against private practice for doctors employed in the public sector.

In each case, a different aspect of the health market was labeled "private" and was defended by the profession. Although many of these proposed changes entailed increases in the absolute amount of government financing – even the fee regulations were often combined with increases in the total amounts governments were willing to pay – the medical profession took the position of defending the status quo against increases in government intervention to finance and regulate the health sector. Professional associations stressed the need for independent physicians to assure quality care. Financial independence, and in particular the right of doctors to receive payments directly from patients without intervening bodies such as government agencies or insurance companies, was incorporated into several medical codes of ethics on the grounds that economic independence was critical to the integrity of medical treatment.[1]

This defense of the private sector was not simply a defense of a foregone status. Nor did the private sector merely represent additional income. Instead, keeping some form of private practice open was economically rational as it prevented governments from achieving a position of monopsony. By maintaining different private forms of practice within health systems that became ever more dominated by government payment systems, these medical professions protected their ability to *exit* from the public sector.[2] This potential to leave the public sector forced government health authorities to compete with private buyers (private insurance companies, private patients, private hospitals), thereby strengthening the bargaining power of physicians. Even for the doctors that did not actually leave the public sector to go into private practice, the possibility that they might leave was an important strategic factor in negotiations on fees and salaries in the public sector. Indeed, it is important to note that it would not have been possible for all doctors to go into purely private practice. National health insurance programs expanded the demand for health services far beyond what patients could afford to pay out of their own pockets at the time of treatment. But by retaining small amounts of private practice, doctors nevertheless forced the buyers of health services to compete, thereby breaking up government monopsony.[3]

Thus, although medical associations initially fought the enactment of national health insurance because they feared that in the future governments would begin to interfere with physicians' economic and clinical autonomy once a program was in place, these associations adjusted to the influx of new resources. At this point, the associations turned their efforts to maintaining pluralistic financing, pockets of private practice, and to avoiding government regulation of fees and medical decisions. In short, the key goal of the liberal model of medicine was to avoid total financial dependence on government health authorities. For this specific period of time, a number of medical professions defined their interests in terms of the free market; economic autonomy became, in their eyes, the necessary condition for professional autonomy.

MONOPOLY, MONOPSONY, AND MEDICAL ORGANIZATION

This view of professional strategies deviates from the standard views of professional power discussed in Chapter 1, which emphasize functional needs, public legitimacy, technical autonomy, and the development of professional monopoly through medical licensing. Doctors fought the battles to consolidate medical knowledge into an officially recognized skill and for legal restraints on unqualified practitioners from the sixteenth to the nineteenth centuries. By the mid-nineteenth century, professional monopoly was an established fact in Europe, though interestingly enough not in the United States.[4] But efforts to establish collective financing for medical care in the late nineteenth century brought the issue of the private market versus government into professional politics as a new dimension.

It therefore makes sense to separate the "classical" issues of professionalism, such as the historical process by which medicine was established as a science – which established what we might call the "cognitive boundaries" of the profession – and the political efforts to establish a legal monopoly on medical practice – which set the "credentialing" boundaries of the profession – from later struggles over purely economic issues. In fact, some theorists of professionalism have explicitly distinguished the cognitive and credentialing aspects of professionalism from economic autonomy. For example, Eliot Freidson specifically says that technical autonomy should not be confused with economic autonomy: "[S]o long as a profession is free of the technical evaluation and control of other occupations in the division of labor, its lack of ultimate freedom from the state, and even its lack of control over the socio-economic terms of work do not significantly change its essential character as a profession. A profession need not be [an] entrepreneur in a free market to be free."[5]

Nevertheless, although one can distinguish analytically between "professionalism" and "entrepreneurship," entrepreneurship became a critical political issue for doctors. Although some writers have indeed discussed the classical professionalization process to establish medical licensing in terms of market monopoly, the late nineteenth and early twentieth centuries brought a new type of market issue into play. In addition to the idea that doctors as a group held a monopoly over practice, the role of doctors as entrepreneurs was central to national health insurance debates. Even among physicians with the same status as fully licensed practitioners, new subdivisions emerged between private office practitioners, doctors with insurance practices, full-time hospital practitioners, part-time hospital practitioners with private office hours, private doctors working in private clinics, doctors employed by local health centers, and public health officers. The goal of proponents of the liberal model of medicine was to ensure that these new forms of public employment for doctors did not eliminate private practice and to use these subdivisions to prevent government monopsony. They wished to prevent public employment from becoming the norm for all doctors.[6]

The conflicts over public programs in health stimulated a growth and restructuring of preexisting medical associations as they moved to defend the market interests of the profession. Whereas earlier medical associations can be described as learned societies that disseminated information and represented the academic elites of the profession in such matters as licensing, university policy, and public health matters, now the mid-to-lower stratum of the profession began to demand a form of economic representation. This unleashed a debate about the nature of professionalism: Should these associations take on a more "union-like" role? The older organizations either incorporated the general practitioners into their organizations, or were forced to compete with new associations that now promoted the economic interests of the mass of practitioners. For example, the British Medical Association was founded to represent general practitioners alongside the older Royal College of Physicians and Surgeons. The "Association for the Protection of the Economic Interests of German Doctors" (Verband für die Ärzte Deutschlands zur Wahrung ihrer wirtschaftlichen Interessen) was added to the corporatist Chamber of Physicians (Ärztekammer), membership in which was required by the state for licensing and ethical matters. In France, Sweden, and Switzerland, too, practitioner organizations (the French Union des Syndicats Médicaux Français, the Swedish Läkarförbund, and the Swiss Ärzteverein) were formed at the end of the nineteenth century to represent doctors in economic matters and in political lobbying efforts on government health programs.[7]

The conflicts over government monopsony were fought over three basic types of programs: government subsidies to voluntary mutual aid societies, compulsory national health insurance, national health services. The differences between these programs and their consequences for the economic autonomy of doctors will be discussed at greater length in the next section of this chapter. Briefly, these programs differ on the degree of government monopsony and the consequent role of government in health services delivery. Under programs of government subsidies to voluntary mutual aid societies, governments merely provide financial aid to privately organized health insurance carried by voluntary self-help organizations called mutual aid societies, friendly societies, or sickness funds. Under national health insurance, governments create their own public insurance programs in which citizens are required to participate by law. Under a national health service, governments bypass the insurance mechanism entirely, and provide health care directly to citizens, through nationalized hospitals and doctors in the employ of government. In the first case, the buyers of medical services are pluralistic movements of private insurers who receive some money from the government. In the second case, the buyers are consolidated into a single public insurance program. In the third case, the government itself buys medical services directly.

As stated in Chapter 1, this book compares the politics of enacting government health programs in three countries that all initially relied on the first type of program – government subsidies to voluntary mutual aid societies. Although politicians in all three nations proposed national health insurance and regulatory measures to control doctors' fees, the result of these political conflicts were three divergent health systems. Switzerland remains one of the few countries in Western Europe that still maintains government subsidies to voluntary mutual aid societies; France has enacted national health insurance; Sweden introduced national health insurance, then converted the system to a national health service.

Medical professions throughout Western Europe – and not just in the three cases selected for this book – fought each step toward greater government monopsony because they wished to avoid increasing government incentives and instruments for regulating the profession. They preferred programs subsidizing voluntary mutual aid societies to programs of national health insurance. In turn, they preferred programs of national health insurance to programs of national health services. Not only did doctors oppose the transition from one basic form of government program to the next, but micro-conflicts about the financing and administration of these programs, as well as the ways in which doctors would be paid, also reflect this basic conflict over monopsony. Indeed, in political negotiatons over new programs, these medical associations made limits on government monopsony and protection of the entrepreneurial status of doctors the quid pro quo for accepting an expansion of the role of government in the health care market.

Thus, the concept of monopsony allows one to understand the reaction of doctors to a wide variety of different, issues in the area of health policy. For any given reform proposal, one can predict the reaction of doctors by evaluating the impact of the reform on government monopsony, and hence on the economic autonomy of doctors. Whereas theories of professional power have been very interested in the concept of medical monopoly, and the creation and limitation of medical markets, they have neglected the issue of monopsony and its consequences for the economic autonomy of the profession.

ECONOMICS VERSUS POLITICS

To lay out the *economic* conflict engendered by government health insurance programs does not predict or explain the *politics* of enacting and modifying these programs, however. In the first place, we can conceive of many possible strategies for both doctors and governments even within the stark economic framework that has been set forth. Governments might have decided to rescind physicians' monopoly on medical treatment, opening up this market to anyone. This strategy has indeed been suggested by economists many times, and was in fact one of the grounds for the political debate that resulted in Britain's General Medical Act of 1858.[8] Nevertheless, this route has not been fully pursued. Although in some countries medical practice by unlicensed practitioners was never outlawed (notably in Britain, and in Germany from 1869 to 1939), official licensing procedures and restrictions of government posts to licensed physicians created de facto if not de jure monopolies; in the twentieth century, medical monopoly was maintained throughout Europe.

A second hypothetical strategy might have been a collectivist rather than a liberal movement among physicians. Rather than blocking government intervention, physicians might have focused on the absolute increase in resources permitted by government programs and elected to pursue a larger "economic pie" divided evenly among physicians rather than the intraprofessional inequalities and uncertainties implied by a market system. Again, this strategy was recognized by some medical leaders, and it is today seen by many as a fruitful strategy for physicians.[9] But the strategy is neither inevitable now, nor is it something new. For the last hundred years, it has been a potential professional strategy. Nevertheless, European medical associations insisted on the liberal route and not the collectivist route. Thus, many potential strategies can redress the same basic conflict of interests.

More importantly, conflicts over the role of governments and doctors in the health market were not fought out exclusively in market arenas. The decisions to enact national health insurance laws and to change them in ways that restrained the economic activities of physicians were made in legislative arenas. Here, governments and doctors faced one another not as buyer and seller, but as executive government versus interest group. Consequently, doctors had no choice but to rely on their ability to exert political pressure on politicians. Contrary to what is often believed, medical monopoly is not a key element in influencing legislative decisions. The exclusive right of doctors to treat patients was off-limits in these debates – and in that sense, professional autonomy was entirely successful in all of the countries studied – but this professional autonomy did not translate into political influence concerning the economic aspects of national health insurance.

The ability to call for a medical strike was equally irrelevant in this political context. Strikes may or may not be a useful weapon in administrative conflicts with government agencies; medical associations have launched both successful and unsuccessful strikes. But when it comes to making a law, none of these politicians let themselves be held hostage to a striking interest group, at least not by the medical profession. Instead, in the legislative arena what matters are votes by politicians. Even though we might hypothesize that a medical strike might inconvenience voters, and therefore discredit or pressure elected officials, the evidence assembled here does not support this hypothesis. Indeed, voters generally blame doctors and not politicians for medical strikes.[10] Systematic differences in the ability of medical professions in different countries to influence these legislative outcomes through pressure group tactics are analyzed in terms of systematic differences in the ways in which national political institutions are organized.

The purpose of elaborating the economic side of conflicts over national health insurance is to give a clear picture of what is at stake in these policy battles. This scheme allows us to make sense of the complex detail of many of these proposed reforms and gives a common dimension of comparison. The case studies that follow present a richly detailed political history of national health insurance politics, through which a single dimension of conflict is traced. In these cases, executive governments attempted to regulate the economic activities of physicians, while physicians' associations exerted political pressure to prevent these measures. We can compare the results of these conflicts to see how successful each government has been in regulating the economic activities of physicians. If there were no such dimension of comparison – that is, if the policy battles concerned completely unrelated issues and the goals of governments and physicians in different nations bore no apparent resemblance – it is not clear what there would be to compare. By selecting policy conflicts concerning the same basic issues of monopsony, the economic interests are held constant; the different outcomes of these political contests are then explained by the different opportunity structures established by nationally distinct political institutions.

This chapter establishes that there is indeed a comparable goal to health policies in Western Europe, and that the positions taken by governments and medical associations did follow a similar logic. However, whereas the respective points of view of governments and medical pro-

fessions have been set out in an extremely simplified form, the balance
of this chapter will refine this view. Neither governments nor medical
professions are unitary actors, of course. Nor are health policies complete
wholes. Government policies for regulating the economic activities of
physicians are part of complex sets of policies that address many goals
simultaneously.

The first section describes three basic approaches to government health
policies and explains how they differ with regard to the respective roles of
market and government along a number of dimensions. The next section
provides an overview of the history of national health insurance politics in
Western Europe. It shows how health policies fit into and were shaped by
political goals that often had very little to do with health care. The
historic events left particular health policies in place, but they were
also significant for the creation of the basic interest group and political
cleavages that would play a role in future health policy conflicts. Finally,
the cases chosen for this study are discussed in relation to this policy
typology and in relation to these political histories.

The chapter locates the basic conflict between the buyers and sellers of
medical services that has been sketched out here within a policy context,
within a historical and political context, and within a national context.
The economic autonomy of doctors is the common thread that runs
through these national histories; it serves to orient this study and to keep
the comparison on track.

THREE TYPES OF GOVERNMENT PROGRAMS

It is traditional to divide European health systems into three ideal
types.[11] These are based on the role of government in financing medical
services within the health system. This role is only one of many aspects of
health policy. A full treatment might include public health measures,
regulatory policies for pharmaceuticals and medical technology, and
public funding for medical research, hospitals, and other health facilities.
The *financial* role of government for medical services, however, has
implications as well for governmental *regulatory* capacity over the health
system. In addition, these financial mechanisms have implications for the
role of government as an *owner* of health facilities and as an *employer* of
doctors. From least interventionist to most interventionist, the financial
role of government for medical services encompasses government subsidies for private health insurance, national health insurance, and national
health services (Table 1). Each type of financing entails different regulatory, ownership, and employment roles for government. In turn, these
dimensions of government intervention affect the main providers of
health care – doctors, hospitals, and insurers – to different extents. In the
first type of program, governments simply subsidize private arrange-

Table 1. *Role of government in financing medical services*

Program	Financing	Regulation	Ownership of facilities	Employment of doctors
Mutual fund subsidies	Government subsidies to private organizations	a) Insurers: yes (if wish to receive subsidy) b) Patients: no (not compulsory) c) Doctors: no d) Hospitals: no	No: public ownership of hospitals possible, but unrelated to mutual society legislation	No: program of public health officers or other public employment possible, but unrelated to mutual society legislation
National health insurance	Government levies payroll tax to pay for public insurance	a) Insurers: now part of government or highly regulated b) Patients: yes, compulsory membership; voluntary for portions of the population c) Doctors: yes, usually efforts to regulate doctors' fees d) Hospitals: yes, usually efforts to limit payments to hospitals	No: possible, but unrelated to NHI legislation	No: possible, but unrelated to NHI legislation
National health service	Government tax revenues pay for all health expenditures	a) Insurers: NHS obviates need for insurance; insurance possible on purely private and voluntary basis, although may remain subject to government regulations completely unrelated to NHS b) Patients: yes, compulsory for all citizens c) Doctors: yes, efforts to establish full-time employment and salaries d) Hospitals: yes, efforts to establish public ownership or place hospitals under contract to public sector	Yes: although contracts with private facilities may substitute for direct public ownership	Yes: although contracts with private doctors may substitute for direct public employment

ments. In the second, governments create public health insurance programs that citizens are required to join. In the third, governments provide health services directly through nationalized hospitals and publicly employed doctors.

MUTUAL AID SOCIETY LEGISLATION

Government subsidies to voluntary mutual aid societies comprise the most limited form of intervention. Governments provide funding or various financial and tax advantages to voluntary organizations called mutual aid societies or sickness funds that insure their members for medical care, death benefits, and, occasionally, some form of old-age assistance. Governments exchange this funding for the right to regulate the mutual societies. Various aspects of the activities of the mutual societies, such as the conditions for membership, the financial practices of the societies, the types of benefits they are required to provide, as well as competition among the societies, are regulated by government.

This form of government intervention in health care provision can be viewed as relatively limited, however. First, the absolute amount of government spending is generally minimal. The subsidies do not necessarily – and in fact only rarely – cover the full cost of mutual fund insurance. Second, membership in the mutuals is voluntary; the role of government is restricted to reducing the cost of membership through subsidies, but does not go so far as to compel membership. The consumers of medical care are thus not regulated by mutual aid society legislation. Third, these laws do not directly address the delivery of medical care. The mutual societies make their own arrangements with physicians for providing health care to their members. Governments do not interfere with the fees that doctors charge or with the contracts signed between mutual societies and doctors. Thus, programs for government subsidies to mutual aid societies do not entail a direct relationship between governments and doctors. Governments pay the mutual aid societies and the mutual aid societies pay the doctors. Conflicts over the working conditions and economic autonomy of doctors are strictly between the mutual aid societies and the doctors.

In sum, laws that subsidize private mutual societies increase insurance coverage by reducing the costs of membership. In some cases they provide incentives for the restructuring of voluntary health insurance. But they stop short of interfering with the provision of medical services. If we divide the role of government into that of payor, regulator, owner, and employer, mutual society legislation increases the role of government as payor for services, somewhat increases its role as regulator, and does not necessarily entail a new role as owner of health facilities or as employer of physicians. If a particular national government already owns some hospitals and enacts mutual society legislation, the legislation would affect only the mutual societies but not the pattern of hospital ownership.

Mutual aid societies and doctors

Given the limited increase in government intervention implied by mutual society legislation, it is not surprising that medical associations did not object to this form of government financing for medical services, and in fact preferred it to more invasive forms. Nevertheless, issues of economic autonomy and working conditions were occasionally discussed within the framework of mutual aid society legislation, as both mutual aid societies and medical associations took the opportunity to lobby for provisions to improve their relative bargaining positions in conflicts over payment to doctors. Relations between the mutual aid societies (*mutuelles*, friendly societies, or sickness funds, as they were variously called in different countries) and doctors had generally been far from friendly. In order to economize, the funds hired doctors at a discount on a contract basis. They often paid doctors at a flat rate per fund member (capitation) and limited fund practice to a "closed panel" of doctors that agreed to these bargain rates.

Doctors did not want the funds to have the power to exclude doctors who refused to work for lower rates from fund practice. They wished to force the mutual aid societies to compete for doctors, rather than being able to form a payor cartel that could dictate the rates of payment to doctors. Medical associations fought for guarantees that would protect them from the monopsony power of the mutual aid societies. Therefore, they campaigned for a "free choice of doctor." Patients should be able, in the eyes of the doctors, to go to any physician that they wished. Furthermore, doctors should be able to boycott the sickness funds if their fees were unacceptable. Medical associations fought attempts by sickness funds to demand legislation to force doctors to treat sickness fund patients. Doctors with sickness fund practices began to organize themselves to present a unified front against the funds.

Disagreements over the fund practices were one (but not the only) stimulus for the transformation of preexisting medical associations. Leaders in these associations complained that contract practices turned physicians into employees of the sickness funds, and took steps to prohibit the signing of contracts or to improve the conditions set forth in the contracts. These doctors attempted to decide on the minimum acceptable rates for medical treatment and to police themselves to be sure that no doctor agreed to treat patients at lower rates. This, of course, meant penalizing doctors who agreed to fund demands. When mutual aid society legislation was debated, these new medical organizations demanded that the provisions for which they had fought through collective bargaining be made part of the regulatory framework for the mutual societies. But as mutual aid society legislation did not entail direct government payments to doctors, issues of medical payment tended to be a side issue in these debates.[12]

NATIONAL HEALTH INSURANCE

National health insurance, the second type of program, implies a more active role for government. Rather than subsidizing private arrangements, governments create public insurance programs that citizens are required to join and to which employers are required to contribute. The extent of government monopsony under national health insurance depends upon four factors, each of which had been politically contested: the financing of the program, the administration of the program, the percentage of the population covered by the program, and the type of benefits provided.

National health insurance programs tend to be financed by payroll taxes, although governments often provide some supplemental financing from general tax revenues. As these are public programs required by government, governments are politically responsible for financing, but the monies collected are usually separate from general tax revenues, and hence, considered "parafiscal." In most nations with national health insurance, the payroll tax rate is set by central governmental authorities at the national level, but in some, the health insurance administration may set the payroll tax rates independently. (In Germany, for example, they vary by region and by type of insurance fund.) In comparison with mutual society legislation, the financial role of government is increased, but the financial pressure is somewhat attenuated by its parafiscal nature.

National health insurance programs are public, yet the administration of the programs has often been delegated to organizations on the border of the public and private realms. Many nations simply converted the old, independent mutual aid societies into quasipublic carriers that were highly regulated by the government. Important administrative issues have concerned the degree to which national health insurance carriers should be centralized – that is, covering all occupational groups together or separately, and whether different insurance risks, such as health, old-age, invalidity, unemployment and family allowances, should be covered by the same program or separate ones. In addition, the degree to which the insurance carriers should retain their former independence as representatives of the insured, maintaining social insurance elections and other forms of "self-administration," has been a political issue.

Government regulation under national health insurance affects consumers as well as the insurance carriers. National health insurance programs are compulsory, not voluntary. Governments decide which groups are to be covered by public insurance. Early health insurance programs were generally earmarked for low-income wage earners. Later programs, especially those enacted after the Second World War, tended to include all salaried employees. Farmers and other self-employed groups were often added in the 1950s. The compulsory health insurance of the United States – Medicaid and Medicare – can be considered as a form of national health insurance. However, these programs are unusual in that they cover only the aged and those falling below an income limit. Today, the term "national" health insurance generally connotes universal programs that cover entire populations at all ages for medical care. To the extent that these government programs compel citizens to insure themselves, they cut into the available clientele for private insurance policies. Depending upon who is compulsorily insured and what types of health benefits are covered, the public programs determine how much scope there will be for supplemental, private insurance.

The increased role of government as payor under national health insurance creates pressures to control the costs engendered by providers such as doctors, hospitals, and manufacturers of pharmaceuticals and medical technology. Depending on the financing and administration of the program, however, the incentive to control the price and supply of services will affect different actors. National health insurance introduces collective payment for health services, but the type of monopsony that ensues depends upon how extensive the portion of the population covered by the program is, how centralized the administration is, and whether the government itself or an administrative authority at one remove from the government is in charge of payment.

Thus, national health insurance inevitably raises the issue of controlling payments to providers, but these economic incentives are filtered through different financial and administrative arrangements. Of course, collective payment through private insurers will raise the same issues. To the extent that private insurers band together in a payor cartel, their ability to dictate terms of payment to providers will increase, as there will be fewer alternative buyers. If, however, the collective payor is a government health insurance agency, political resources are added to economic power and the threat of regulation is more imminent.

Nevertheless, simply because the idea of controlling costs is bound to come up when governments pay for and administer public health insurance programs does not mean that regulation follows automatically. Separate political conflicts have been fought over, first, the decision to enact a national health insurance program to begin with, and second, the types of controls over providers that governments hope will reduce the costs of these programs. Depending upon how these conflicts have been resolved, and also on practices that existed prior to the enactment of these regulatory measures, national health insurance programs in different countries vary widely in the ways they affect providers.

Professional interests

To medical professions, compulsory health insurance laws represented both a potential liberation from the sickness funds and a future subordination to governmental authorities. National health insurance was viewed differently by doctors depending on their market position. For the doctors who treated poorer patients, insurance practice was an economic necessity, and national health insurance might free these doctors from the control of the sickness funds, and better guarantee their incomes. The doctors who had a private clientele, on the other hand, viewed national health insurance as a threat to their private practices and were concerned about the advent of future governmental controls on the profession. These were the advocates of the "liberal model," who wished at all costs to avoid dependence on the state.

Medical association leaders juggled the interests of these two groups and, simultaneously, as oligarchs they worried about the effects of medical policies on their associations. These leaders were extremely sensitive to political constraints and strategic opportunities for enforcing a medical veto. Their assessments of the views of other interest groups and the access of these groups to political decision making weighed heavily in their calculation of professional interest. The decisions of these leaders to back down and seek small concessions or to fight to the ultimate moment were thus made with an awareness of the system of interest representation and the design of national political institutions.

In political negotiations over national health insurance programs, three issues concerned medical associations: the percentage of the population covered by the program, the administrative structure, and the form and means of payment to doctors. Promoters of the liberal model of medicine preferred to keep as large a portion of the population as possible available for private insurance, and therefore argued for restricting compulsory coverage in public health insurance to those with lower incomes. Similarly, to avoid monopsony, these doctors preferred as pluralistic an administrative structure as possible. But perhaps the most intense political conflicts were fought over the issue of doctors' fees.

These disputes have concerned both the method and amount of payment. Payments to individual doctors can be calculated on a fee-for-service basis, case basis (based on episode of illness), capitation basis (annual fee per patient), or salary basis. Fee-for-service payment is the most directly affected by the activities of the individual doctor; salary the least. Most medical associations have fought for fee-for-service payment, and have tended to accept the other forms only when they predated the national health insurance program (as in Britain), or when they lost in political conflicts.

In addition to the form of payment, cash flow has also been important to doctors. Medical associations have preferred reimbursement systems of payment, under which patients themselves pay doctors and later receive reimbursement from health insurance authorities. Most insurance authorities, on the other hand, preferred direct third-party payment, so that they could pay doctors directly and resolve any fee disputes directly with the doctors.

Aside from the method of payment, efforts to introduce controls on doctors' fees have been the subject of dispute. One common mechanism for controlling doctors' fees has been the introduction of fee schedules – lists of standard fees that are usually negotiated between representatives of the medical profession and government insurance agencies. Among the standard problems that have arisen are what to do if the negotiations fail, and whether doctors may charge patients more than the fee listed in the schedule, and on what grounds. Some medical associations, as we will see in the French and Swiss cases, argued that exemptions from the fee schedule were warranted in difficult cases or for wealthy patients. In Canada, as well, doctors have fought for the right to "extra-bill" – that is, to charge patients willing to pay more an extra fee, over and above the amount that would be paid (directly or through reimbursement) by national health insurance. The right of doctors to charge publicly insured patients a supplemental fee can be viewed as a partial "exit" from public insurance practice. When doctors are dissatisfied with the official fees, they can bypass fee controls through extra-billing and refuse to treat patients who will not pay these private fees. Extra-billing has been opposed by insurers as being inegalitarian, and because they have feared that these private fees would produce inflationary pressures, driving up the standard fees in the publicly negotiated fee schedules. Extra-billing devalues public health insurance – as it no longer covers the full fee – thereby creating incentives for voluntarily insured patients to leave the public insurance system and for discontent among the compulsorily insured. Thus, these fee issues affect the actual benefits that patients receive from their insurance policies.[13]

Although the issue of doctors' fees can be divided into many detailed subareas, the common logic is that doctors have fought for forms of private payment – fee-for-service, direct payment from patients, extra-billing – that maintain the direct financial relationship between doctor and patient, and hence offset the consolidation of payment in the hands of governmental authorities. These authorities, by contrast, have argued for national, standard payments to be made directly from insurers to doctors, with adequate means to sanction doctors who overtreat or override the standard fees. As Sandier argues, "Generally speaking, the smaller the proportion of the cost borne by the patients themselves is, the greater are the power and influence of third-party payors . . . full and direct payment by health insurance agencies means that they have greater control over the physician's activity and remuneration."[14]

Depending upon how these conflicts have been resolved, payment systems under national health insurance programs vary widely. In the (former) Federal Republic of Germany, for instance, medical associations and public health insurance authorities negotiate a total lump sum that is then distributed to doctors according to the number and type of services they have performed within a given period. If doctors increase the number of services, the fee they receive for each service is correspondingly decreased. This system is considered to be quite successful in containing costs for physician services. In France on the other hand, the medical profession has vehemently opposed all attempts to "collectivize" payments to doctors in this manner. The profession has insisted that patients pay doctors directly. These patients are then reimbursed by national health insurance. Since 1970, a national fee schedule has been negotiated between the French medical association and national health insurance authorities. Not all physicians who treat publicly insured patients are required to abide by this fee schedule. Thus, even though France and the Federal Republic both rely on national health insurance to finance medical care, the regulations for doctors' fees are different. These differences may be traced to specific political conflicts. Analogous conflicts have taken place over government insurance payments for hospital treatments, and for drugs and technology.[15]

National health insurance, in sum, entails a greatly expanded role for government as the payor for medical care. This in turn creates pressures for government regulation of the price and availability of services. Nevertheless, the mode of regulation may vary from country to country. Under national health insurance, governments do not directly provide medical services themselves through government facilities or publicly employed doctors. As in the case of mutual society legislation, if public facilities and publicly employed doctors predate the legislation, national health insurance neither eliminates nor extends public ownership or employment; it merely creates financial incentives for governments to regulate public insurance payments to health facilities and doctors.

NATIONAL HEALTH SERVICES

The national health service, the third type of program, is based on yet a different mode of intervention. Rather than subsidizing private insurance or introducing public insurance, governments directly provide medical care to all citizens through nationalized hospitals and publicly paid doctors. Fully "socialized" medicine might entail government ownership of all hospitals *and* doctors' offices, with full-time employment for doctors as government civil servants. This has been the thinking behind government-run health systems in Eastern Europe, the Soviet Union, China and Cuba.[16] In other words, the idea of a national health service is that health care is fully provided through the public sector – through public financing, public facilities, and public doctors. Nowhere in Western Europe is this the case, however. Instead, many political conflicts have concerned the preferred mix of public and private health care provision within national health services. Some national health services rely on contracts with private facilities and with private doctors in order to provide these services.

The British National Health Service (NHS), introduced in 1948, is the most commonly cited example of this approach. According to William Beveridge, the direct provision of health services is more egalitarian than an insurance system, under which contributions establish an actuarially earned right to the benefit. The NHS embodies the ideal that social protection should be a right of citizenship and that these social benefits should be equally distributed regardless of one's ability to pay. Under this system, government tax revenues finance nearly all health expenditures, whether for visits to doctors' offices, for hospital treatments, or for pharmaceuticals. Patients do not pay for services at the time of treatment. To the extent that a central source must approve the total health budget, the budgetary process affords a powerful mechanism for containing costs, as health expenditures must compete with other government outlays.[17] Whereas the NHS relies on such budgetary centralization, other health services, such as the Swedish and the Italian, relegate greater spending authority to local governmental units, perhaps explaining why these health services are correspondingly more expensive than the British. But whereas local autonomy over financing or spending decisions has often resulted in greater fiscal laxity, the interference of local political authorities in the daily running of the health system seems to be greater than for central authorities.[18]

National health services were the form of government most disliked by doctors. They preferred the more diluted financial relationships engendered by programs of subsidies to mutual aid societies and national health insurance. Doctors did not contest public ownership per se, but the employment status of doctors and threats to their right to a private practice. Doctors preferred to work for national health services as subcontractors rather than full-time salaried employees, and to maintain the right to a part-time private practice. The status that doctors seemed to have worked hardest to avoid is salaried employment, and especially salaried employment by local health centers. Even in countries with national health insurance or mutual aid society legislation, doctors made eliminating the possibility for health insurance carriers to form local

health centers with salaried doctors the number one priority, even higher
than avoiding fee controls or blocking the introduction of national health
insurance.

Effects of national health services

Under a national health service, the government becomes the dominant
payor for health services, even though in practice pockets of private
medicine remain. The government comes close to achieving a monopsony. This increases both the incentives and instruments for greater
government regulation of health care consumers and providers. In comparison to either mutual society legislation or national health insurance, a
health service places greater obligations on patients and providers.
Whereas some national health *insurance* systems allow for voluntary
participation for citizens with incomes above certain limits (for example,
in Germany or the Netherlands), national health *service* taxes are usually
obligatory. For those who choose to purchase a private insurance policy
or attend a private clinic outside the national health service, these private
payments are an extra cost over and above the health service taxes that
have already been paid. The health service is viewed as a collective
expense, not as an individual policy.

Doctors. Direct government provision of services politicizes the relationship between doctors and government health authorities. Under national
health insurance, doctors' fees might be regulated, or the insurance might
cover only a standard fee, with the patient left to pay the remainder. If
governments rather than private patients or different public and private
insurance carriers are to pay doctors, however, the employment conditions for doctors become the subject of more far-reaching regulation.

One issue has been the time commitment of doctors to the public
system. Should doctors be considered as government employees or as
private contractors to the public system? Can the government demand a
full-time commitment, or may doctors in public hospitals and public
offices receive private patients as well? These questions of employment
relations have also provoked conflicts over the form of payment for
doctors. Particularly as a consequence of widespread disputes over doctors' fees, and the difficulty of controlling the number of services performed as opposed to the price per service, many planners have argued
that doctors should be paid a salary rather than on the customary fee-for-
service basis. Similarly, as employers of doctors, governments become
even more directly concerned with the availability of doctors, and often
interfere with medical education. They have increased the number of
doctors, and have attempted to steer physicians to choose some of the
less popular areas of medical specialization and to practice in regions

where there are shortages of doctors. Even in nations lacking a national health service, governments have come to be concerned with these issues.

However, as these governments do not directly employ doctors, they encounter (1) less pressure to solve these problems, because they are not directly responsible for the nation's health system, and (2) greater difficulties in solving them, because as they are not the direct employers of doctors they cannot easily steer doctors to new regional locations. And this, precisely, is where "exit" comes in. If a doctor who works for a national health service is dissatisfied, then the possibility of private practice, either in a private hospital or a private office, makes a tremendous difference. The private market allows the doctors to leave the public sector entirely, or, more conveniently, to *threaten* to leave the public sector unless the grievance is redressed.

Hospital ownership. The national health service affects the relationship between governments and hospitals as well. In Britain, introduction of the national health service entailed a transfer of hospitals from private to public ownership. In other health services, like the Italian or the Spanish, the government provides health services through both public hospitals and private clinics under contract to the public system. Even in countries without a national health service, such as France, efforts have been made to integrate public hospitals and private clinics into what they have called a "public health service" for *planning* purposes. The French idea is to include *total* health care resources and not just *public* sector resources in plans aimed at promoting a better distribution of hospital beds and medical technology. At the same time, the private clinics retain their independent status both legally and financially. This independence, and in particular the different financing system for the private sector, has hampered the coordination effort, however.[19]

This aspect of the French case makes a point that bears repeating. Public financing, public regulation, public ownership, and public employment are four distinct aspects of a health care system. In the French case, the increased financial responsibility of government for health care, public ownership of hospitals, and political pressures on government to ensure citizens' access to high quality health care have influenced the development of a policy aimed at regulating the provision of both public and private hospital services. At the same time, because financing and ownership are not as centralized as they are in a national health service, increasing the regulatory capacity of government through planning policies is more difficult.

Hospital financing. The brief overview has focused on the main public programs that aim to provide access to treatment to the general population. Governments also provide significant financing to the hospital sector, often by underwriting hospital deficits. This form of financing tends to be less visible to the public than a social program such as national health insurance, but it is nevertheless a critical component of the extent of government involvement in the health sector. This participation of government in the hospital sector should be added to the analysis of financing, regulation, ownership, and employment for any specific health system.

Nevertheless, although many governments provide significant financing to hospitals, the role of government implied by a national health service remains distinct. For government financial responsibility for the hospital sector is embodied in the concept of a national health service, and it is provided as part of a coherent plan.

In countries with mutual society or national health insurance legislation, on the other hand, government financing of hospitals tends to be carried out under separate auspices from the insurance program. In fact, these "dual" payment systems tend to result in complicated payments between different branches of government, or between private insurers and government. Consequently, the role of government in financing is fragmented, and hence the power of government as a single or dominant payor is diluted. In turn, the regulatory capacity of government may be reduced. The role of government as an owner becomes complicated because there may be private hospitals that receive such extensive public payments that the meaning of the word private is unclear (as in the Swiss case). Similarly, to determine to what extent this form of ownership affects the role of government as an employer of doctors, we need to look at a specific health system. In the Swedish case, for example (see Chapter 5), although most hospitals were publicly owned by local units of government, hospital doctors were paid for outpatient care on a fee-for-service basis by national health insurance and private patients.

Another issue worth mentioning, although it will not be taken up in this book, is the role of government as an employer not just of doctors, but of other employees. Health systems are now a major source of employment – most often highly unionized employment. As governments have sought to cut back health spending during the 1970s and 1980s, the jobs that might be lost in the health sector, as well as the wage-levels in the health sector, have emerged as highly politicized issues. These factors have been very important to the ability of governments to effect savings in the hospital sector.[20]

DIMENSIONS OF GOVERNMENT INTERVENTION

To reiterate, the three ideal-type health programs – mutual aid society legislation, national health insurance, and national health services – vary in four discrete dimensions of government intervention in the health sector. One fruitful dimension of comparison between health systems is the extent and type of government financing of the health system. A second dimension is the type of government regulation of the health sector that this financing structure may encourage or facilitate. A third dimension is government ownership; a fourth, government employment of doctors. These interconnected dimensions are the concrete policy consequences of the political debate about market and government. Together, the four dimensions affect the ability of governments to govern the health sector; they provide a more meaningful definition of the "public" versus the "private" than the more traditional dimension of public ownership.

Just as one would not want to describe a complex modern economy solely in terms of nationalized versus privately owned industries, government intervention in health does not merely mean "nationalizing" or "socializing" health facilities. Indeed, current health policy researchers are beginning to concur that government ownership of health facilities or the size of the public sector in itself is not especially critical as a variable. Not only are the lines between the public and the private sectors blurred, with the same doctors dividing their time between the two and with the same patient dividing his or her medical bill between public and private payors, but the consequences of public ownership per se do not by themselves appear significant. Instead, it is the ability of governments to regulate directly various parts of the health sector that is critical for planning, for the efficiency of the health sector in providing medical treatment to more persons at a given cost, and for overall health care costs.[21] These regulatory measures affect who is to be insured, how patients will receive medical treatment, how doctors will be paid, and how health resources will be distributed. Furthermore, this governmental regulation does not necessarily imply regulation by a "command-and-control" approach. For example, in the Swedish case, the social democratic government used market incentives to readjust the balance between ambulatory and hospital care, and to pressure doctors to agree to changes in the payment system.

As government financing is a key lever for introducing successful regulatory measures, the three forms of government financing give us a first approximation for the extent of government intervention in the health system. The financing system provides incentives for further regulation of health care providers and, at the same time, the mode of financing may facilitate certain forms of regulation. Notwithstanding, both the decisions to change the financial role of government in the health care sector and the subsequent decisions to increase government regulation have been the subject of extensive political conflicts. Systems of government subsidies to voluntary mutual funds, national health insurance, and national health services are not monoliths. These systems do not come ready-made; nor are they introduced at any one time as integrated wholes. To analyze a particular health system, we must look at the specific features of public financing, regulation, ownership, and employment. To understand the origins of these specific details, we must look into the specific political conflicts responsible for each law.

POLITICAL ORIGINS OF GOVERNMENT HEALTH PROGRAMS

Although we can classify different health systems according to the logic of government intervention, the health system in any one nation is the product of many years of historical development. As one Swiss politician put it, "Were it necessary to draft a health insurance bill today, I would never come up with the insane idea of proposing our current system. No one would design such a complicated system from scratch."[22] Instead, the organizational features of public and private health insurance as well as public and private hospitals and doctors' offices have been patched together by unconnected pieces of legislation, whose effects have interacted with private initiatives by a diverse group of actors. Just as some analysts describe political systems in terms of an archaeology of development, so too can health systems be described with reference to layers that reflect the political and social circumstances of different historical periods. If we want to know why governments decided to finance medical programs or why the programs took the particular form that they did, we must dig into the archives that record the political motivations and the political struggles that explain each individual reform.

Although there are policy motivations for these legislative initiatives, such as providing access to health care or controlling costs, these were rarely the sole impetus for legislation. Indeed, those directly concerned with managing public health care programs often had tremendous difficulties in convincing heads of governments or their ministers that health administration was of any interest. Health policy reforms were nearly always linked to larger political questions – it was the main opportunity for health administrators to capture the attention of those in the political, as opposed to the administrative, wing of the executive.[23]

The pattern of hospital ownership, for example, has been highly influenced by conflicts between church and state. Originally built by religious orders in the Middle Ages, hospitals became a prize in struggles to establish secular power. In Northern Europe, hospitals were taken over by public authorities through the seizure of church property during the Reformation or, as in France, during anticlerical revolutions. In Southern Europe, where the Catholic Church maintained a stronger role in hospitals, ownership was later transferred voluntarily to the state, as in Spain and Italy. William Glaser points out that it is only in countries with several religions, such as the Netherlands, Germany, and Switzerland, that government ownership of hospitals was viewed as a "loss of a highly visible evidence of good works," and, consequently, religious leaders fought to maintain private hospitals.[24] The practical meaning of public versus private ownership has of course changed significantly as public funding has gradually come to be responsible for large portions of hospital expenditures in both sectors. Nevertheless, even though the significance may change over time, these enduring patterns do affect contemporary health policies because they affect the basic structure and organization of national health systems.

Political factors have left their imprint on systems of health insurance, as well. The roots of health insurance lie in popular movements of the nineteenth century. Unions, political parties, and social movements founded self-help associations called "mutual aid societies," "friendly societies," or "sickness funds" that provided financial aid to sick members. These resembled the voluntary associations initiated by guilds and religious orders during the Middle Ages – although some societies claim to trace their origins back to religious cults of the Romans.[25] In some countries, as in Prussia, the societies were not voluntary, but required by legislation establishing a new form of guilds for skilled workers, as well as by municipal and local statutes.[26]

These societies provided a useful organizational base for the nascent popular movements. Sickness funds served as a selective incentive to attract members. The monies they collected were sometimes diverted to other ends, such as strikes. In some countries – for example, France – these associations initially had a clear political purpose, and were often quite radical. In others, the mutuals were viewed by governmental authorities as a tame alternative to other forms of working-class organization that was to be encouraged. The earliest government initiatives in the health insurance area were laws that regulated the activities of these mutual societies. Depending upon the interplay between these popular movements and these early efforts at government intervention, the mutualist movement acquired a nationally distinct political character.

These political links changed the dynamics of health insurance policy-making in different nations. Although these early conflicts concerned similar health programs, the different connections between popular democratic movements and sickness funds affected the political meaning of the programs. It might be tempting to label mutual fund legislation as a "conservative" approach to health insurance, national health insurance as "liberal," and national health services as "socialist." Current political categories do not fit the historical facts, however. Partisan politics over the sickness funds are better understood through a relational approach; party stances depended on the allegiances of the parties to different branches of the sickness fund movement and on the ties between the sickness funds and other popular movements. In a general sense, the growth of government financing for health insurance was indeed a response to the threat of working-class unrest. But the specific political reactions are more complex; the political history of health insurance is not simply the history of socialism.

Comparative development of health systems

From this complicated pattern of historical events, we can extract some generalizations about the development of national health insurance. The basic programs that were considered are similar in many ways. Many nations enacted government subsidies in the nineteenth century, then converted these programs to compulsory health insurance for low-income earners in the period before and after the First World War. A wave of reform also took place after the Second World War, with many countries extending older programs to entire populations, or enacting new universal insurance programs. As health care increasingly became a right of citizenship, many governments turned to addressing problems of health care delivery through plans for hospital construction and health care planning. Thus, we can identify an ideotypical pattern of development that can serve as a baseline; as a kind of "null hypothesis," we can assume a developmental sequence from mutual aid society legislation to national health insurance to national health services. The research problem is then to explain why nations deviate from the ideotypical pattern of development.

Table 2 shows that the same policies have been proposed in a number of European countries. Nearly every country listed in the table enacted laws regulating the mutual societies, and most provided subsidies to the mutual societies as well. All the countries examined other than Switzerland enacted national health insurance. National health insurance was proposed in Switzerland many times (1900, 1920, 1947, 1972, 1986), but each law failed. National health services are more rare – they were enacted only in Britain, Spain, and Italy. In Sweden, a proposal for a national health service failed in 1948, but the national health system has since been modified so that it is now a de facto national health service. In France, too, the idea of a national health service was discussed after the Second World War, but it was never pursued. Thus, the ideas for reform are comparable, but the legislative results differ.

In order to explain these different results, we must examine the political conflicts over specific government legislative proposals. For there is no general model that can explain the results. In every case, a look at the legislative process reveals an imbroglio of political parties, executive governments, and organized interest groups. The partisan impulse for national health insurance legislation varied widely and depended on interrelations between the mutual aid society movements and unions and other political movements. Furthermore, motivations for enacting health

Table 2. *Introduction of major health care programs in Western Europe*

Country	Failed legislation (incomplete)	Mutual aid society legislation	National health insurance	National health service
Britain		1793, 1815, 1850, 1898	1911	1946
Italy	1919	1886	1944	1978
Spain	1931	1839, 1859	1942	1986
Sweden	1919, 1948	1891, 1910, 1931	1946	(1969)
Norway	1893–6		1909, 1953, 1956	
Denmark	1919	1892	1971	
Germany		Municipal legislation	1883	
Austria			1888, 1939	
France	1928	1834, 1852, 1898	1930, 1945	
Belgium		1849, 1898	1944	
Netherlands		na	1913/1929, 1943	
Switzerland	1900, 1920, 1947, 1972, 1986	1911, 1964		

insurance legislation changed over time. The early sickness fund laws were part of the process of modern nation-building; enmeshed in these political conflicts were questions of nationalism, the role of the state, freedom of association, and the public household. Compulsory health insurance laws tended to be more directly concerned with class issues, and, unlike the government subsidies, which were directed at the artisanal constituency of the mutual societies, these laws targeted the core of the impoverished industrial workforce. The German legislation of 1883 was an early example of such "class" legislation; in most European countries, compulsory health insurance laws were proposed between 1910 (when a series of general strikes broke out in several countries) and 1919 (when the political effects of the First World War brought voting rights and social insurance to the forefront of legislative debates), although these laws were not always enacted.

Conflicts over industrial relations pervaded national health insurance debates; unions and employer associations were at the center of discussions about compulsory contributions and fund administration. Sickness funds, private insurance companies, and medical associations were equally concerned. Both voluntary mutual aid societies and the private insurance industry combated proposals that sought to dislodge them from their market niches. The dynamics of these conflicts were colored, as might be expected, by the previously described political relations between parties, funds, and popular movements. Furthermore, early government intervention had shaped the development of the insurance market, affecting the extent of mutualist and private insurance. We can see the effects of these various political relationship on the development of government health programs by examining some examples from the history of these programs.

Politics of mutual aid

Early sickness fund laws were motivated by the wish of executive governments – in this period often a monarch or a "state-builder" – to control associational life.[27] The laws dating from the end of the eighteenth century and the beginning of the nineteenth century concerned the right to exist and the legal status of these societies. Government recognition of the societies was a means of supervising the societies, in return for which the societies received some legal advantages. Or, where free association was illegal, registration was enforced by the threat of criminal penalties. Later laws added financial inducements for registration and regulated the financial practices of the societies. In some cases, the funds were allowed to make deposits at national banks at favorable interest rates; in others, they received direct government subsidies. Typically, the subsidies were set at a flat rate per enrolled member. In return, the funds were required to register with government agencies and to comply with government regulations. These regulations stipulated conditions for membership, sound financial practices, and minimum benefits the funds were required to provide, and regulated competition among the funds – for example, by limiting the number of officially recognized funds within a given geographical area.

Government policies for the sickness funds thus had several aims. First, they provided a means for governments to monitor these popular associations. In some cases, the policies went further and directly intervened to derail the political activities of the funds. Only as a later goal did the laws strive to protect and improve the benefits of the insured and to improve health insurance coverage. Under the latter laws, governments provided subsidies to the funds to encourage the expansion of fund membership, and, hence, health insurance coverage. By linking these subsidies to new regulations, these policies aimed to guarantee benefits to the insured and to stabilize the financial situation of the funds.

National sickness fund laws were enacted for the first time in 1793 in

Britain, 1839 in Spain, 1849 in Belgium, 1834 in France, 1886 in Italy, 1891 in Sweden, 1892 in Denmark, and 1911 in Switzerland.[28] Generally speaking, laws passed before 1850 emphasized the registration and monitoring of the sickness funds. Beginning in 1850, subsidies became more common, and the rate of growth of the mutuals began to increase. The laws of the late nineteenth century and early twentieth century aimed at improving insurance coverage and benefits.

The position of political parties on these questions depended more on specific political circumstances than on party ideology. To liberals, for example, the principle of self-help endorsed by the funds resonated well with their ideals, but an expansion of the role of government did not. French and German liberals opposed conservative efforts to coopt the mutuals, whereas in Sweden and Switzerland, it was the liberals that championed government support to the funds in opposition to conservatives arguing for fiscal prudence. In Britain, partisan interest in the friendly societies passed from a conservative to a liberal political interest during the course of the nineteenth century.

In Britain, the country with the earliest sickness fund law (dating from 1793), friendly societies legislation emphasized the registration of the societies and guidance on their actuarial practices; government funding and political interference with the funds was minimal. The early societies, like the Oddfellows and the Ancient Order of Foresters, were founded as social clubs that often held their meetings in taverns. Insurance benefits were added much later. According to the Webbs, the early history of British trade unions was intertwined with the development of the friendly societies, with many unions having their origins in a friendly society and vice versa. However, union leaders never made the provision of benefits their first priority; they felt free to use these funds for strikes or other (in their view) more pressing ends. Registration as a friendly society, however, provided a convenient means of avoiding the Combination Acts (which prohibited trade unions) until the courts ruled that a trade union was not a friendly society. In 1871, the Trades Unions Act introduced provisions for registering a trade union similar to those for friendly societies, and the trade unions and the friendly societies went their separate ways.[29]

In sharp contrast to the British pattern of tolerance, the Continental model was based on more interventionist legislation. Notably in France, mutual society legislation included provisions concerning the political activities of the funds. Banned after the Revolution, mutual aid societies – like other voluntary associations, including medical guilds – crept back during the Restoration. The French mutuals were workingmen's associations with a clear political purpose, in the tradition of the *sans culottes*. Held responsible for some of the activities of the 1830 Revolution, unauthorized mutual societies were banned by an 1834 law that strengthened the provisions of the 1810 penal code against associations of more than twenty persons. The fortunes of the mutuals rose and fell with France's sequence of political regimes. With the birth of the Second Republic in 1848, the mutuals were legalized. As the Republic drifted toward the right, however, restrictions on the mutuals were added, coupled with direct government subsidies for the funds.

This approach reached its culmination in the Second Empire with Napoleon III's decrees of 26 March 1852. These decrees permitted only mayors and *curés* to form mutual societies. The statutes were to be registered with the Minister of the Interior, the president of the society was chosen by the president of the Republic, and the funds were required to accept a certain percentage of "honorary" members. The latter were wealthy patrons who paid large contributions but did not draw benefits. In return, these members were entitled to a disproportionate number of votes on the fund governing boards. Supervision by representatives of the executive, the clergy, and local notables, as well as forced bourgeois membership in the mutuals, was intended to quench class conflict. Control over the mutuals was a means for the executive to enforce social order; conversely, greater political freedom for the mutuals became a sign of Republican liberalization.

With the formation of the Third Republic in 1870, the mutuals were allowed to elect their own presidents, but it took until the law of 1 April 1898 for the mutuals to become completely independent from political supervision by the state. By this time, however, the relationship between the mutual societies and the working class had been completely severed. Leftist unions maintained a hostile relationship to the mutuals, and a negative stance toward government intervention in this area that was to color future health insurance debates.[30]

In other countries, as well, the specific ties between the sickness funds and popular movements, as well as the attitudes of public authorities, varied. In Sweden, the Temperance movement and the Free Church movement were active in the funds. In Belgium, they were considered the terrain of the Catholic, socialist, and liberal political parties, and even today, they have been attacked as the "bankers" of the parties. In the Netherlands, many funds were founded by doctors in order to provide collective financing to their patients.

The German breakthrough

The introduction of compulsory health insurance by the German Reich in 1883 marks the beginning of a dramatic shift in the history of health insurance. Chancellor Bismarck announced his intention to enact health insurance, accident insurance, and old-age and invalidity insurance through the "Royal Message" (*Kaiserliche Botschaft*) of 1881. Bismarck was clearly concerned about class unrest and the formation of a social democratic party in 1869. The social insurance laws, which aimed to ameliorate the material needs of the growing industrial proletariat and foster their loyalty to the state, were accompanied by the suppression of the Social Democratic Party organization (although socialists could still run for office and hold parliamentary seats). Yet, although health insurance was indeed a class issue, the passage of this legislation can only be understood by examining other political and institutional factors as well.

For Bismarck, health insurance was part of his strategy of establishing a strong executive government. Although social insurance had been discussed since the 1840s, it was only when he forged the famous coalition of "iron and rye," composed of protectionist Catholics and conservatives, that he was able to marshall the parliamentary votes needed to outweigh liberal opposition to his plans. Such political factors also influenced the provisions of the law. During the negotiations over health insurance, Bismarck was able to maintain the principle of compulsory insurance. Plans for substantial government financing and a government insurance bureaucracy were blocked by the liberals and the Catholics, however. Consequently, the German compulsory health insurance legislation was financed solely by employer and worker contributions, and left the administration to the preexisting range of private sickness funds: the miners' *Knappschaften*, guild funds, factory funds, workers' *Hilfskassen*, as well as a newly created "territorial" sickness fund (*Ortskrankenkasse*). Some of these funds had been administered by representatives of the insured and of the employers. The principle of "self-administration" was not controversial, and in fact fit both the Catholic and conservative views on corporatist self-regulation.

Thus, many of the features of social insurance that were later copied by other nations – payroll tax financing, independent administration, and representation of the insured – stemmed from peculiarities of the German political situation. After these compromises, the socialists and the progressives were the only members of parliament who voted against the health insurance law. Ironically, the socialists later turned the legislation against Bismarck by infiltrating the territorially based funds. This created a German tradition of close ties between the unions and the sickness funds. Many funds were founded by unions, and the elections for positions within the fund administration served as an important political training ground for future union and party leaders.[31]

The German example provoked increased discussion of social insurance throughout Europe. Interest in the "social question" was a central concern everywhere, yet in each country political bargains and preexisting patterns of sickness funds left their mark on the legislation. In fact, the sickness funds were often even more opposed to compulsory health insurance legislation than medical associations, and many such laws could be passed only when the funds were guaranteed a role in insurance administration.

Austria and Switzerland moved almost immediately to enact legislation along the German lines. The Austrian compulsory health insurance law was enacted by a conservative government in 1888; thereafter it was extended in steps, including the extension to family members and dependents after the *Anschluss* in 1939. In Switzerland, on the other hand, liberals successfully enacted a compulsory insurance law in 1900, only to see it felled by a national referendum. In Britain, national health insurance was enacted by the Liberals in 1911. From an institutional perspective, it is interesting to note that its enactment in Britain was linked to a controversy concerning the House of Lords, which ultimately led to a reduction of its powers through the Parliament Bill of 1911.[32] In France, a succession of coalition governments prepared social insurance legislation, until it was finally passed in 1928; the system was expanded by ordinances legislated directly by General de Gaulle after the Second World War. In the Scandinavian nations, despite a common history of significant Social Democratic representation, only Norway passed national health insurance before the Second World War. Sweden enacted national health insurance in 1946 and Denmark relied on subsidies to voluntary mutual funds until 1971.[33]

In other countries as well, political conflicts and nationally distinct constellations of interest groups and parties were responsible for early health insurance legislation. In Belgium, the sickness fund movement that developed had strong ties to the political parties. Perhaps as a consequence of this party interest in an independent fund administration, national health insurance was delayed until 1943. In the Netherlands, health insurance was debated by a constellation of interest groups and parties that had been forged by the school issue: Catholics, Protestants, and secular (liberal and social democratic). A law compelling compulsory insurance for low-income earners for *cash* benefits only was enacted in 1913, but implemented first in 1930. Under the German occupation, compulsory health insurance was extended in 1941 to include medical and hospital care, and to cover a larger proportion of the population. Income limits on the public insurance system in the Netherlands have reserved approximately 30 percent of the population for private insurance. In the late 1960s, the sickness funds were regulated by new legislation, and catastrophic health insurance was introduced for the entire population. Proposals to replace the current system of public and private insurance with universal national health insurance were rejected in the 1970s.[34]

After the Second World War

Just as the German compulsory health insurance influenced the set of policy alternatives in other nations, the introduction of the British national health service after the Second World War established a new policy model. Although the idea of a national health service, and particularly the concept of national planning to meet health care needs, has been influential, few countries have actually introduced national health services. Britain's national health service was based on nationalized hospitals, whereas general practitioners were brought in as private contractors, paid on a capitation basis. Although the national health service legislation was enacted by a Labour government, preliminary steps in preparing the reform had been taken by an all-party government, and all of the British parties could agree on the NHS.

By contrast, a Swedish attempt to introduce a national health service in 1948 was considered too "socialist," despite a large Social Democratic parliamentary majority and despite the fact that hospitals had been almost exclusively public institutions, since the appropriation of church lands during the Reformation. Protests from doctors, employers, the Farmers' Party, and units of local governments blocked the plan. Nevertheless, in 1969, the Swedish Social Democrats eliminated private practice from public hospitals and placed all hospital doctors on full-time salaries. Thus, without formally introducing a national health service law, the Swedish system was transformed into a de facto national health service.

In Spain and Italy, the mutualist movement developed slowly as restrictions on association were lifted and small government subsidies added. By the end of the nineteenth century, the mutual societies were mixed between liberal and (predominantly) Catholic funds. In Spain, the Republican constitution of 1931 committed the state to a complete program of social security including health, but compulsory health insurance was first introduced by the Francoist state in 1942. In Italy, liberals, socialists, and conservatives had debated converting the mutualist based system into a compulsory national health and social insurance scheme from 1917 to 1919, but it was only under a fascist regime that this legislation was enacted in 1943.

The transition to democracy brought with it renewed discussion of the health system in both countries. In Italy, no parliamentary coalition was able to agree to health insurance reform until a pact between the Italian Communist Party and the Christian Democrats in 1978 established the Italian National Health Service. Spain also converted its social security system to a national health service in 1986, this time under a socialist government. In both countries, the private sector is large, with public and private medical practice related by a complex system of contracts and part-time work.[35]

The United States and Canada

Even in North America, proposals for government health programs have much in common with the European examples. In the United States, mutual funds were introduced by fraternal orders and ethnic associations. Possibly because these mutual aid societies never received government subsidies, as in Europe, the mutualist movement was eventually supplanted by employer health insurance programs. National health insurance was proposed in the United States by the Progressives in 1919 and by the Democratic Party in 1948, but both attempts failed. Government health insurance has been limited to the Medicare and Medicaid programs introduced by the Democrats in 1965.[36]

In Canada, national health insurance was introduced in steps, each of which was politically controversial. In 1947, the socialist Co-operative Commonwealth Federation government of Saskatchewan introduced compulsory hospital insurance for all residents. After several other provinces followed this example, the federal government introduced government subsidies to cover 50 percent of the costs of provincial hospital insurance in 1957. A similar cycle began in 1961, when Saskatchewan introduced universal, compulsory medical insurance to cover physicians' services in 1961, despite a doctors' strike. A national health insurance program, which followed the previous model of providing federal subsidies to provincial plans that met standard requirements, was introduced in 1966, as a result of liberal and conservative competition.[36a]

Political similarities and differences

In sum, proposals for government health programs throughout Western Europe, and to some extent in North America, have been similar. Government subsidies to mutual aid societies, national health insurance, and national health services have been proposed or at least mentioned in nearly every country reviewed. Because these programs affect doctors in similar ways – specifically because they alter the economic autonomy of the profession in similar ways – the same issues of medical payment, private practice, and professional freedom were at stake in each country. But the political motivations for enacting these programs and the political factors that decided whether the programs would indeed be enacted varied enormously. Furthermore, these programs had implications for and were affected by political, social, cultural, and economic factors well beyond the realm of professional issues. Freedom of association, industrial relations, national security, and changing conceptions of social equality were as important, if not more so, than the autonomy of the medical profession. Thus, although an understanding of monopsony and its implications for professional economic autonomy can usefully be added to the theories of professionalization, which have generally focused more exclusively on medical monopoly, the political logic of government health programs is independent of the economic logic of these programs. Not only are the political factors and policy results not reducible to economic interest, but there is no single political logic that can explain this wide variety of policy results.

THE CASES IN CONTEXT: POLICY RESULTS

The chapters that follow take a narrow look at the complicated problem of understanding the politics of national health insurance. I say "narrow" because rather than covering many different aspects of health policy or the ensemble of welfare state programs in a given country, I focus on the legislative politics of a specific issue: collective payment for physician services and the conflicts about the economic autonomy of doctors that such collective payments have unleashed. The idea of the study was to compare legislative conflicts that made a difference. I chose three cases where the results of these political conflicts were three health systems that comprise the two extremes and the center of government intervention in the private market for medical care. As Table 2 indicates, although Switzerland, France, and Sweden all initially relied on government subsidies to voluntary mutual aid societies, subsequent legislation determined the future extent of collective payment for medical services, the administrative consolidation of these payments, and the restrictions placed on doctors. The final section of this chapter compares these policy results.

The Swiss health care system

In Switzerland, efforts to enact national health insurance were blocked. As a result, government health insurance remained restricted to subsidies to voluntary sickness funds. The consequence of past legislative failure is a private insurance system that, although highly regulated, is fragmented, pluralistic, and decentralized. The government pays for a relatively small share of health care costs, and has a comparatively minor role in the administration and regulation of the system. Furthermore, individuals pay directly for a larger percentage of health care costs than in other European nations. Nevertheless, despite the fact that most Swiss citizens take out health insurance on a voluntary basis, nearly the entire population is insured.

Table 3 shows the proportion of public and private financing for health care in 1975, reflecting the extent and type of monopsony in each of the three countries shortly after the period analyzed in the case studies (1930–1970). The table shows that Swiss health care expenditures are

Table 3. *Health care consumption by financing sector 1975 [%]*

	Sweden	France	Switzerland
Public			
General taxation	77.5	7	31.6
Public insurance and social security	12.8	69	34.9
Private			
Private insurance	–	3	⎱ 33.5
Direct payment	9.7	19.6	⎰

Source: Robert J. Maxwell, *Health and Wealth. An International Study of Health Care Spending* (Lexington, MA: Lexington Books, D. C. Heath and Company for Sandoz Institute for Health and Socio-Economic Studies, 1981), pp. 130, 148, 151.

divided about equally between the government, government-subsidized private insurance, and direct costs paid by patients.[37] The figure for the government share is composed mainly of payments to hospitals from the provincial governments – the cantons as opposed to the federal government – which pay for hospital operating deficits. Government-subsidized private insurance (carried by sickness funds) is mainly paid for by patients: patients pay for 71 percent in the form of premiums and an additional 6.5 percent in the form of cost-sharing; the federal government contributes 13.3 percent, the cantons 4.7 percent, and employers 1 percent.[38] The 33.5 percent direct costs borne by patients includes unreimbursed doctors' fees and supplemental private insurance. Thus, one-third of the payments are private payments.[39] As these financing figures show, the degree of monopsony payment in Switzerland is relatively low; payments are divided among a number of payors. In addition, each payment source is subdivided further: government payments are divided among the 26 cantons and the federal government; sickness fund payments are divided among the 346 independent sickness funds; and patient payments, obviously, are paid by millions of individuals.[40]

The limited financial role of the Swiss government has implications for its regulatory role vis-à-vis insurers, patients, and doctors. The payment of government subsidies to the private sickness funds has been linked to regulation of the sickness funds. Only "publicly recognized" funds may receive subsidies. These insurance carriers must be nonprofit, and they must accept all applicants for insurance coverage. The funds may set their own premiums, but they must calculate the premium based on the age of insured persons when they *joined* the fund (as in many life insurance companies), and not according to their current age or health status. Different premiums may be charged for men, women, and children, but the government limits the differential that may be charged. Finally, the government has established the standard benefits (outpatient care and hospitalization) that must be covered by the subsidized health insurance policies. Although initially founded by unions, employers, political movements, and philanthropists, the funds have lost their political character. In fact, many private insurance companies have simply opened nonprofit divisions in order to take advantage of the government subsidies.[41]

In a sense, the Swiss system works like a voucher system, although the government payments are paid to the sickness funds rather than directly to patients. The cantons may enact compulsory membership for all or part of their populations. Few, however have done so. Nevertheless, whereas only 20 percent of the population is compulsorily insured by the cantons, an additional 75 percent have taken out voluntary coverage through the publicly recognized sickness funds. The insured are free to supplement the basic coverage of the government-subsidized health insurance with extra coverage – for example, insuring themselves as "first class" patients for hospitalization, which entails a priavate room and treatment by the hospital chief-of-staff. The same sickness funds can provide both types of benefit; they simply calculate a total premium based on the coverage chosen.

In comparison to European national health insurance schemes, the Swiss system allows for more flexibility in coverage, which in practice means that insurance benefits vary, but everyone is insured by the same carriers. Because a separate premium is paid for each family member, Swiss insurance does not redistribute costs in favor of families, as do most national health insurance schemes. Because the premiums are linked to age of entry, there is significant redistribution from the young to the old. This, however, has created incentives for insurers to found new sickness funds with special offers to attract younger members, whereas older persons are financially "locked-in" to their initial funds. As the composition of a particular fund becomes dominated by older members, the premiums may become extremely high. However, some cantons use their social assistance programs to pay the premiums of older persons. In sum, the Swiss system of voluntary insurance has solved the problem of access to health care. Coverage is universal, but the direct costs of the insurance to consumers are high, premiums vary widely, and private payment is used to buy privileged treatment, although of course it is not clear whether the treatment of "first class" patients is medically superior or merely more expensive.

Swiss doctors. Swiss doctors are subject to weaker fee controls and have more opportunities for private practice than French or Swedish doctors. As Table 4 shows, we can measure private practice either in terms of

Table 4. *Limits on private health care provision*

Country	Private payment (% paid by private patients and private insurance)	Publicly insured (% of population)	Doctors' fees	Hospital ownership (% of beds)	Government employment (% of doctors in private practice)
Switzerland	33.5%	20% compulsorily insured 75% voluntarily insured by private, publicly recognized, sickness funds	Office doctors: Locally negotiated fee schedules, with extra-billing for higher-income patients, predominantly fee-for-service, reimbursement payment. Hospital doctors: Full and part-time salary, plus private practice. Unrestricted, fee-for-service payment with reimbursement for private patients in hospitals.	Public: 60% Private, non-profit: 33% Private, non-profit: 6.9%	48% of doctors in full or part-time private practice (88% full or part-time above assistant level)
France	22.6%	99% compulsorily insured by public sickness funds	Office doctors: Nationally negotiated fee schedules, binding for 72.5% of doctors, others may extra-bill. Hospital doctors: Full and part-time salary, but may receive limited private patients, same fee schedules and extra-billing rules apply to those hospital patients, those in private clinics, and those in private offices.	Public: 80% Private, for-profit: 20%	69% full or part-time private practice 43% full-time
Sweden	9.7%	100% compulsorily insured by public sickness funds	Office doctors: Direct third-party payment limited by fee schedule. Hospital doctors: Full-time salary for inpatient and ambulatory services. No private practice allowed within public hospitals.	Public: virtually 100%	13.4% full or part-time private practice 5.7% full-time private practice

Sources: Provided in text.

private payments to doctors, which would include extra-billing as private practice, or as the number of doctors who receive private patients outside of salaried hospital practice (whose fees are partially or fully covered by sickness funds). By both indicators, private practice in Switzerland is extensive. Private payments comprise one-third of health care expenditures. Almost half (48 percent) of active doctors have at least a part-time if not a full-time private practice; the figure is as high as 88 percent of doctors above the assistant level. Specialization is also high; 62 percent of doctors with a full or part-time private practice are specialists. These figures reflect the limited regulations on providers. Private office practice takes place in private doctors' offices, within both public and private hospitals, and to a small extent, in private clinics. Private office practitioners are required to abide by locally negotiated fee schedules, but may extra-bill for patients in "good economic circumstances," a group that is defined by the cantons. If negotiations are unsuccessful, the cantons establish fee schedules. Because the negotiations take place at the local level, doctors practicing in localities with the highest fee schedules are allowed to charge double the amount for a standard consultation that is allowed in localities with the lowest fee schedules. The number of different procedures listed in the local fee schedules varies from 370 to 1,180. Thus, the fee schedules are not uniform, nor are there mechanisms for limiting increases in the fee schedules or the number of services performed by doctors. Hospital doctors are paid a basic salary, but may receive private patients. The fee schedules do not apply to these patients.[42]

Swiss hospitals. Except for the small number of private for-profit clinics, hospital ownership is largely a legal matter, having little bearing on hospital policy, reputation, or even financing. Senior doctors in both public and private hospitals may treat private patients on an unrestricted basis. Both types of hospitals contain general wards where patients (or their sickness funds) pay a flat-fee per day of hospitalization. In both sectors, the cantons play a predominant role in hospital planning, financing, and administration. The majority of Swiss hospitals are private, but because the public hospitals are bigger, the majority of the hospital beds are found in the public sector. Even in the public sector, moreover, 15–20 percent of the beds are private.[43]

Unlike Sweden and France, no national plans are drawn up for the distribution of hospitals, medical technology, medical schools, or physicians. Hospital planning is strictly in the hands of the cantonal governments. Consequently, regionalization, or the reallocation of resources based on standards of efficiency rather than according to traditional political boundaries – long a goal of other European polities – would be rather difficult to implement in Switzerland.[44]

The French health care system

France, like Switzerland, began with a system of government subsidies to voluntary mutual aid societies. Subsequent legislation modified the system, however. In 1930, compulsory health insurance for low-income earners was introduced. Immediately after the Second World War, a universal system for all salaried employees was added. A series of political conflicts prevented the extension of this system to the entire population. Instead, special insurance schemes have been introduced for groups such as farmers, artisans, white-collar employees, and the self-employed. For thirty years, political opposition prevented efforts to regulate doctors' fees. Such regulations were finally introduced in 1960, along with regulations on hospital doctors' hours and their access to a private practice. The result of these political conflicts is a national health insurance system with regulated doctors' fees, and some planning mechanisms for regulating hospital ownership and employment of doctors.

The French health system is mainly financed by national health insurance (69%), which in turn is part of social security (see Table 3). In 1983, employers contributed 71 percent of national health insurance receipts, the insured 25 percent, and the national government 4 percent. In addition, the insured paid for 20 percent of medical fees in hospitals and 25 percent of fees in office practice.[45] As a result of this cost sharing, as well as the significant number of doctors that may extra-bill, direct payments by the insured financed 19.6 percent of expenditures in 1975, and supplementary private insurance (carried by the mutual aid societies that predated the public scheme) paid for 3 percent – a total of 22.6 percent private payment. The French financing system can thus be characterized as one of public health insurance monopsony, although private payment sources remain.[46]

French national health insurance is compulsory. When the Social Security Ordinances were enacted in 1945, 65 percent of the population was covered; 99 percent is now compulsorily covered. The national health insurance component of social security is administered by public sickness funds, but separate schemes exist for salaried employees (75 percent of the population), agricultural workers (8 percent), the self-employed (7 percent), and special interests, such as public employees, miners, railway workers, and veterans (together, 9 percent).[47] French health insurance is thus less pluralistically financed and administered than the Swiss system, but more so than the Swedish. National health insurance covers all forms of medical treatment. For medical consultations outside salaried hospital practice – in private offices, in private clinics, and private consultations or private inpatient care in public hospitals – patients pay doctors' fees and are then reimbursed for the portion covered by national health insurance. Private supplemental coverage can be taken out for medical charges paid by patients – the standard cost-sharing component and extra-billing by physicians.

Economic autonomy of French doctors. French national health insurance has been used to regulate doctors' fees and conditions for private practice, but opportunities for unrestricted fees and private practice remain. Private payments comprise about 23 percent of health care expenditures. In 1979, 43 percent of doctors were in full-time private practice and 69 percent were in either a full-time or part-time private practice. (In 1988, 56 percent of French doctors were GPs and 44 percent were specialists.)[48]

As in Switzerland, private practice takes place in private offices, in public hospitals, and in private clinics. For each type of private practice, however, some restrictions have been introduced. These restrictions include controls on private fees, controls on the private sector within public hospitals, and controls on the private clinics. For all forms of private practice, a nationally negotiated fee schedule is in place. In conjunction with the fee schedule, insurance authorities monitor doctors' activities by compiling statistical averages or "profiles" of treatment practices. Nevertheless, a significant number of these doctors (28 percent) may override the fee schedule, although their patients are reimbursed for only 75 percent of the official fees.[49]

In addition to controls on fees, French policy has addressed the issue of public employment of doctors. Hospital doctors that worked on a part-time basis could divide their time between the hospital and private offices and clinics; private consultations and private beds were also found within the public hospitals. In 1958, efforts were made to increase the number of full-time, salaried hospital posts for doctors, thereby decreasing the number of doctors that would leave the hospitals daily for private offices and clinics. As a transitional measure, these doctors were allowed to receive private patients. In 1982, under the Mitterand government, private hospital beds were eliminated from public hospitals, and private consultations were scheduled to stop in 1987, but this policy has since been reversed.

Private clinics. Government ownership of health facilities and public planning have also been grounds for controversy. Hospital planning has been part of the French five-year economic plans during the entire postwar period. Since the 1970s, efforts have been made to integrate planning for both the public and the private hospital sectors, and to regulate the growth of both sectors. In comparison to Switzerland, where private inpatient care takes place within both public and private hospitals without much distinction between the two, private practice in France within public hospitals is more restricted, but the role of private clinics is more important.[50]

The Swedish health care system

In Sweden, also, early health insurance legislation was limited to subsidies to voluntary sickness funds. A national health insurance program was first enacted in 1946, after early efforts had failed, but did not go into effect until 1955. This delay was caused by political conflicts – including those over a plan for a national health service that was rejected. Nevertheless, many features of a national health service were subsequently introduced. Outpatient clinics in public hospitals were expanded, thereby competing with private office practice. As in France, conflicts over doctors' fees resulted in regulation by a fee schedule. Then, in 1969, fees were eliminated entirely for hospital doctors and full-time salaries were introduced. This was the decisive step to converting the system to a de facto national health service.

This legislative pattern produced a centrally regulated but locally financed and administered health system. Health expenditures are overwhelmingly financed (77.5 percent) by local tax revenues, which are levied by the local units of government, the county councils (see Table 3). National health insurance provides supplementary financing, paying for doctors' visits and reimbursing the county councils for a portion of hospital costs. Employers contribute 85 percent of national health insurance receipts, the national government 15 percent. In addition, the insured subsidize a portion of the costs through patient fees, paid at the time of treatment (9.7 percent).[51] Thus, health care financing is largely a local-government monopsony.

Swedish national health insurance is compulsory for 100 percent of the population. It is carried by a national network of public sickness funds – the remains of the old voluntary sickness funds, which were consolidated and placed under the supervision of a national health insurance administration when the public insurance system went into effect in 1955. National health insurance covers the entire population for medical care and sickness cash benefits, leaving few market opportunities for supplementary, private insurance.

As in Switzerland, hospitals are largely owned, financed, and administered by local governments, but to a much greater extent. The national government regionalized the health system in the 1950s and 1960s, drawing up plans for the distribution of hospital resources and technology, and using its power to approve investment expenditures to ensure implementation. Medical services (both ambulatory and inpatient) are concentrated in the hospital sector, with 71 percent of health care expenditures in 1975 going to services provided in hospitals, compared with 38 percent in France and 44.9 percent in Switzerland.[52]

For patients, the Swedish system guarantees access to health care as a right of citizenship, with medical services predominantly financed through taxes and predominantly provided through public hospitals. The cost of health care, and therefore the sharing of risk, is spread over the entire population. Economic privilege in health care has been virtually eliminated; it is not possible to buy a better class of care, although people in urban areas and those with higher levels of education use available services at higher rates. The costs of the system, however, are high tax rates, lower disposable incomes, and less choice to patients about the form of health care they wish to purchase.

Limits on private practice. The combination of national health insurance and public hospital provision has been sued to restrict doctors' fees and to limit opportunities for private practice. Private payments represent only 9.7 percent of expenditures. In 1975, only 5.7 percent of doctors carried out a full-time private office practice; only 13.4 percent had either a full or a part-time private practice.[53] At the same time, it should be noted that Swedish doctors are highly specialized (56 percent).[54]

The low level of private practice is the result of regulatory restrictions placed on the private sector. Although, in the past, Swedish doctors had extensive opportunities for private practice within public hospitals, in a few private clinics, and in both private offices and offices provided by the government (and could charge unlimited fees), these possibilities have been curtailed. No private practice is permitted in public hospitals. For hospital doctors, fees have been replaced by full-time salaries, even for ambulatory consultations, the majority of which take place within hospital outpatient clinics. Hospital doctors may practice privately in their spare time, but for this privilege, they must apply to their county council for permission.

Private office practice is allowed, and is covered by national health insurance if doctors register with the national health insurance authorities and agree to abide by a fee schedule. Even then, direct third-party payment is in force. Patients pay a small fee, and the doctor applies to the health insurance authorities for the balance of the payment. Compared with fee schedules in other nations, the Swedish fee schedules are extremely simple, divided into only three procedures and three levels of difficulty, thereby reducing the possibilities for multiplying the procedures or increasing the proportion of more expensive procedures. Further, the insurance authorities monitor the activities of the private practitioners.

Salaried practice for hospital doctors has eliminated the need for such direct monitoring of economic activities (though not of quality of care), as salaries are determined by collective negotiations and do not vary according to the number of services performed. For doctors, the effect of Swedish health programs has been to convert the majority of physicians into salaried employees of the government, with more restrictions on the private sector than even in Britain.

Political choice and policy results

As Table 4 shows, many years of political conflict have produced three health systems that are based on different degrees and types of monopsony payment and that restrict private medical practice to different extents. Switzerland, France, and Sweden differ with respect to the portion of the population available for private insurance coverage, controls on doctors' fees, public ownership of health facilities, government employment of doctors, and the restrictions placed on private practice. Consequently, the economic autonomy of doctors has been least reduced in Switzerland, and most reduced in Sweden.

The three health systems represent three different political choices. The Swiss have chosen the route of minimal government intervention, the Swedes the maximum. These different routes to the financing and provision of medical services have very different consequences for the security and choice available to patients, the equality of care, the distribution of costs, the economic freedom of physicians, and the regulatory capacities of governmental authorities. The choices were not made at one time, however; they emerged from a series of individual political conflicts. Nor could we assert that these choices reflect different levels of rational thinking, that one system is technically superior to the others. Indeed, the ultimate effect of these organizational arrangements on levels of health and health care costs is difficult to assess.[55]

Health indicators such as infant mortality and life expectancy do not provide information on the quality of health of populations, but these health outcomes are more favorable for Switzerland and Sweden than for France (Table 5). All three systems deliver high-quality care. All three nations have solved the problem of access to health care; none suffers from the problems of large uninsured or underinsured population groups, as is the case in the United States. The differences in the proportion of direct costs paid by patients have distributional consequences, but they do not seem to impede utilization of services for medical care; for dental care, however, there seem to be bigger differences. If we compare the costs of the systems, the Swedish system is most expensive when measured as a proportion of Gross Domestic Product, but in per capita terms, Sweden and Switzerland spend about the same.[56] Even the distributional consequences are difficult to assess, because whether paid for by direct payments, public insurance, or taxes, health care is not free; the final cost depends on total tax programs and their repercussions on economic growth. All three systems are significantly less expensive than the U.S. system (although the gap in costs widened rapidly during the 1980s). According to aggregate figures on doctors' incomes, which may not reflect real incomes or their distribution, Swiss doctors are paid the most, and Swedish doctors the least. Aggregate income levels thus correspond well with government monopsony and economic autonomy, but as Table 5 shows, the German case is an exception as far as this relationship is concerned, with high monopsony and high incomes.

Thus, each health system constitutes an alternative path to solving similar problems. Evaluation of the most preferable route is a matter of political values. These systems have solved some common problems, but in order to do so, each offers different burdens and different advantages to governments, doctors, insurers, and patients. The Swiss system comes at a high direct cost to individuals, but affords more individual choice, the French system is costly to employers and mixed in terms of its effect on patients and doctors, and the Swedish system has severely limited the economic autonomy of doctors.

METHOD OF STUDY

The next three chapters of this book consider the politics of making these policy choices. Behind each of the legislative acts depicted in Table 2 lies a different political story. The case studies investigate the politics of the legislative proposals critical to the emergence of the Swiss, French, and Swedish health systems. For each reform, I trace the legislative proceedings that led to each law, and pay a great deal of attention to interest group opinions and lobby efforts. This methodology bridges the case study method used to understand interest group politics and more structured comparisons. The focus on individual political decisions – on micropolitics – allows us to take advantage of the wealth of primary source materials and archival records that are available.

By examining individual political conflicts, the book presents the actual views of the various social and political actors engaged in these struggles. Insofar as I emphasize interest-group conflict, this approach comes close to the standard pluralist methodology for studying politics. The views of the interested parties are examined and compared with the resulting political outcomes. What distinguishes this method from pluralism, however, is the historical and comparative perspective.

When set against a comparative backdrop, different aspects of political decisions stand out than when these same decisions are viewed as self-contained events. The survey of health policies in this chapter provides a comparative yardstick by which the policy outcomes in Switzerland, France, and Sweden can be measured. This eliminates the risk that we are studying a great deal of political noise, but little of political consequence. The comparative perspective allows us to consider the non-decisions – the issues that never came up or the groups that failed to mobilize. By following an issue over time and in different countries, we can make a distinction between the basic goals of political actors and the strategies they use to pursue those goals.[57]

Table 5. *Health system outcomes: Costs, number of doctors, doctors' incomes, infant mortality*

Health system	Country	% public payment 1984	Total health expenditure (as % GDP) 1987	Per capita health spending (in US$) 1987	Number of doctors (per 1000 population) 1985	Doctors' incomes (ratio to average employee compensation) 1979	Infant mortality (percent of live births) 1986
NHS	Sweden	92.0	9.0	1233	2.58	2.14	0.59
	United Kingdom	90.4	6.1	758	1.33	2.32	0.95
NHI	France	72.0	8.6	1105	2.19	3.27	0.80
	Germany	79.3	8.2	1093	2.64	5.02	0.87
	Canada	74.4	8.6	1483	2.05	3.47	0.79
Subsidies	Switzerland	65.4	7.7	1225	2.85	4.49	0.68
Private Medicare/ Medicaid	United States	42.5	11.2	2051	2.14	5.08	1.04

Sources:
Organization for Economic Cooperation and Development (OECD), *Financing and Delivering Health Care. A Comparative Analysis of OECD Countries.* OECD Social Policy Studies No. 4 (Paris: OECD, 1987), p. 55.
OECD, *Health Care Systems in Transition. The Search for Efficiency.* OECD Social Policy Studies No. 7 (Paris: OECD, 1990), pp. 10, 12, 142, 193, 200.
Markus Schneider et al., *Gesundheitssysteme im Internationalen Vergleich* (Bonn: Bundesminister für Arbeit und Sozialordnung, 1989), p. 379.

Nevertheless, despite these methodological safeguards, the surprise of the study was not that certain issues of policy ideas were excluded in one country but acceptable in another. Nor was it the case that select interests were able to organize in one country but not in another. Instead, from the vantage point of comparison, political institutions, normally part of the accepted landscape for political decision making, emerged into the foreground, while the intricacies of new policy plans, interest group demands, and organizational intrigues receded into the background.

Although this chapter has outlined some common problems, issues, and policy alternatives, as well as the ways in which the economics of the health market were embedded in different political contexts, the next chapters will build on this comparative background to show what is specific and distinct about each national case. We will see the same issues of monopsony and professional freedom throughout the cases. In each country it is also important to be aware of the initial role of the sickness funds as social movements, and their unique relationship to political parties and unions. But against this comparative setting, the cases make clear that the specifics of policy proposals, the ideas for reform, the stances of various interest groups, and the political traditions of different sickness fund movements do not hold the key to understanding what ultimately happened in each country.

In each case, political institutions affected the ability of politicians to introduce policies and the potential for interest groups to influence these legislative outcomes. The institutions did not affect the goals of these actors or their subjective perceptions of their own interests. Nor did they force these actors into certain courses of action. Rather, the initial aims of policy makers and interest groups were quite similar across the cases, but because they pursued these goals within different institutional frameworks, they had different chances for success, and different political strategies made sense.

The next chapter develops this argument using the French case. Although the policy results are intermediate in relation to the Swiss and Swedish cases, this case will be taken first. The institutional argument of this book is dramatically illustrated by changes in French political institutions through constitutional reform. These institutional changes, in turn, permitted the introduction of health policies that had been debated for many years but had been blocked by institutional constraints.

3

The French case: Parliament versus executive

French health care policy making was shaped by a dynamic of jurisdictional contestation between parliament and executive. Both the ability of executive governments to enact legislation and the ability of interest groups to block legislation depended upon the relative autonomy of parliament and executive. When parliament had the upper hand, the passage of legislation was nearly not possible. The division of parliamentary majorities into infinitesimal warring factions was responsible for parliamentary stalemate. Legislative proposals supported by one parliamentary majority were almost immediately toppled by counterproposals supported by different majorities. Most often, the parliamentary majorities disintegrated before legislation moved through every phase of the policy process. Only in exceptional periods – for temporary, conjunctural reasons or because of constitutional innovation, when the executive dominated the parliament – did we see successful initiatives in health policy. The result of the French political pattern was a mixed health system. National health insurance was introduced in 1928 and expanded in 1946. But regulation of medical fees and salaried employment for hospital doctors was delayed for many years, until the constitution of the Fifth Republic enabled the executive government to impose these changes in the health system on an incalcitrant medical profession.

INSTITUTIONAL DESIGN

The French national health insurance system was established by reforms that spanned the Third Republic (1871–1940), the Fourth Republic (1946–1958), and the Fifth Republic (1958–). As the constitutional changes make evident, French political institutions were redesigned in this period. Several features of the political system, however, remained constant. One fundamental problem provides the key to understanding these efforts to redesign institutions, and also the dynamics of French health insurance policymaking during these years: a constitutional stalemate between the executive and legislative branches of government. Each successive constitution sought to ameliorate this institutional defect, and each constitutional regime fell through political crises that although not caused by this constitutional weakness, were exacerbated by the difficulties of political decision making stemming from this problematic separation of powers.

The heart of the problem was how to achieve a consensus for decisions. The executive of the Third and Fourth Republics was formally dependent on parliament. The tension in the relationship came from the fact that in practice parliament was fractionated into many different parties that were in turn divided into warring subfractions. Because the electoral system did not produce clear parliamentary majorities, a certain measure of decision-making power reverted to the executive; the executive could choose cabinet ministers with wide discretion. This was rarely sufficient, however, for the executive to dominate parliament in order to make decisions, and when executive action went too far, parliamentary representatives could strike back by ousting the executive government.

Analytically, we can divide the problems of French political representation into two parts. The executive government was to rest on parliamentary majorities; because these majorities were neither decisive nor stable, however, the executive government rested instead on fragile parliamentary bargains. The fragility of the parliamentary agreements can be traced back to the preceding step in the process of representation: Parliamentary majorities were detached from electoral majorities.

The French electoral system, although modified at several points, tended to be organized around two rounds of voting. The first round established a rank order of parties; during the second, these parties could enter into electoral alliances to compete for majorities. Once in parliament, however, members of parliament (MPs) were not bound by the electoral alliances, the parties retained their separate identities, and representatives could decide independently about the parliamentary coalition that would choose the executive. Thus, the two rounds of voting kept the smaller parties alive, and a single election could provide a mandate for a wide range of parliamentary coalitions. In the event of a governmental crisis, the practice in the Third and the Fourth Republics was to disband the cabinet and renegotiate the parliamentary coalition without calling for new elections, which further increased the possibilities for maneuver.

In sum, although the ideal view of a parliamentary system is that elections establish a distribution of parliamentary seats, and that this distribution is then used to invest an executive, in France these different political arenas – the electoral, the parliamentary, and the executive – were disarticulated. This freed parliamentary representatives from the constraints of limited majorities; policy choices were relatively unrestrained either by electoral results or by the executive. Thus, we can view the French parliament as a "weak link" or a "bottleneck" in the political system that accounts for the coincidence of instability and immobility to which many commentators have pointed. Almost any policy proposal could be countered by a second proposal that attracted a different parliamentary majority. Critics of policy proposals could not only vote against a particular proposal, but could threaten to withdraw their support for the governing coalition.[1]

Interest-group power

The instability of parliamentary majorities constituted a "strategic opening" that could be exploited by interest groups that wished to block government intervention. There were several points of access to political decision making available to these groups. The fragmented political parties were open for influence by even small groups with particular interest in a given policy. The lack of party discipline and the personalized bargaining that characterized parliamentary activity was rife with opportunities for any interest group – or individuals within these interest groups – that could sway individual politicians. The most important MPs for this purpose were the swing voters in the center parties that were critical to the parliamentary coalitions. The division of parliament into two chambers, where the Senate contained a crushing majority of rural representatives, offered a second, related, vehicle for these interest groups; influence with senators was often sufficient to put a stop to legislation, and as a consequence the conference committee between the two chambers of the Third Republic was recognized as a decisive veto point for legislation. The parliamentary commissions of both the Chamber and the Senate were similarly conducive to interest group influence; the selection of commission representatives reduced the range and number of opinions that needed to be persuaded.[2] Local interests achieved political influence because the parties were organized around local notables, and the simultaneous holding of several posts (*cumul des mandats*) often meant that the same politician was a mayor, a parliamentary deputy, and a cabinet minister; those with local influence could use this route to achieve national influence. This was a political system with many access points for interest groups, and the result was that those with the ability to disrupt the parliamentary majority could call the shots.[3]

French physicians were in an extremely favorable position in this political system. A well-known doctor was the archetypical "local notable" for which both the Third and Fourth Republics were famous. A surprisingly large number of physicians made careers for themselves in politics. Studies of the occupational origins of French members of parliament show that doctors held a significantly larger percentage of parliamentary seats in France than in other European nations. The percentage of physicians and pharmacists holding seats in parliament ranged from 10.4 percent in the latter part of the Third Republic (1898–1940), to 5.8 percent in the Fourth Republic (1945–1958) and 11.3 percent (for physicians alone) in the early Fifth Republic (1958–1973). In 1973, doctors held 12.2 percent of French parliamentary seats, compared with the European average of 3.9 percent (see Table 6).

Furthermore, the impact of this parliamentary representation was amplified by the concentration of these physicians within the parties that were critical for building a governing coalition. In the Third Republic, doctors comprised 16.4 percent of the Radical parliamentarians, 12.8 percent of the center-left (Républicains de Gauche, Gauche Démocratique, Gauche Républicaine), 8.6 percent of the moderates (Union Républicaine, Union Démocratique, and Républicains d'Action Sociale), 8.3 percent of the Independent Socialists (Socialistes Indépendents), and even 7.8 percent of the Socialists (SFIO, or Section Française de l'Internationale Ouvrière). In the Fourth Republic the figures were 10.5 percent of the Radicals, 6.9 percent of the Catholic left (Mouvement Républicain Populaire, or MRP), and 6.5 percent of the SFIO. Indeed, this strategic positioning was more important than the total proportion of physician-politicians. For it was not parliamentary representation per se that was critical, but rather what those parliamentary representatives could achieve within the French political system. Consequently, we cannot assume a direct relationship between the number of doctors in parliament and the influence of doctors on public policy. For example, the influence of physicians under the Fourth Republic was not significantly less than under the Third Republic – even though parliamentary representation decreased – because doctors remained important for creating parliamentary majorities. Similarly, the comparative influence of different European medical professions does not directly vary with their representation in parliament. With the highest proportion of parliamentary representation in Europe (Table 6), French doctors are indeed more influential than Swedish doctors but less so than Swiss doctors – or American doctors.

Thus, in France, the key to interest group influence was the ability to disrupt the parliamentary majority, and doctors controlled the levers to this majority.[4]

Not only were doctors critical to the parliamentary majorities, physician-politicians were also active as mayors, a skew in representation that was to become especially important in conflicts over whether local municipal councils and mayors rather than authorities of the political center, such as the prefects and the Minister of Health, should determine hospital policy. Because these physician-mayors also held parliamentary seats, their political influence was felt at both the local and the national levels.

In addition, physicians were often aided in political campaigns by

Table 6. *Physician representation in society, in medical associations, in parliament*

Year	Sweden	France	Switzerland
Doctors per 100,000 population			
1958	89.2	106.7	140.6
1975	171.5	146.3	185.8
1985	258	219	285
Membership in medical associations			
1930	76%	63%	–
1970	92.2%	60–65%	97%
Doctors in parliament			
1970	1%	12.2%	3%
Belgium (1974)		4.3%	
Italy (1976)		4.7%	
Great Britain (1974)		1.5%	
USA (1974)		1.5%	
European average		3.9%	

Sources:
Number of Doctors. James Hogarth, *The Payment of the Physician. Some European Comparisons* (NY: Macmillan, Pergamon Press, 1963), pp. 60, 139, 281; R. J. Maxwell, *Health and Wealth. An International Study of Health Care Spending* (Lexington, MA: Lexington Books, D. C. Heath and Company for Sandoz Institute for Health and Socio-Economic Studies, 1981), pp. 148–9, 130–1, 151–2; Markus Schneider et al., *Gesundheitssysteme im Internationalen Vergleich* (Bonn: Bundesminister für Arbeit und Sozialordnung, 1989), p. 379.

Memberships. *Läkartidningen* (Journal of the Swedish Medical Association), 19 April 1930, p. 516; Swedish Medical Association membership figures; Jean Meynaud, *Les Groupes de Pression en France*. Cahiers de la Fondation Nationale des Sciences Politiques No. 95 (Paris: Librairie Armand Colin, 1958), p. 66; Jean-Claude Stephan, *Economie et Pouvoir Médical* (Paris: Economica, 1978), pp. 38–9; Gerhard Kocher, *Verbandseinfluss auf die Gesetzgebung. Aezrteverbindung, Krankenkassenverbände und die Teilrevision 1964 des Kranken- und Unfallversicherungsgesetzes, 2nd ed* (Bern: Francke Verlag, 1972), p. 25.

Parliamentarians. Swedish figures for 1960, Lars Sköld and Arne Halvarson, "Riksdagens Sociala Sammansättning under Hundra År," in *Samhälle och Riksdag. Del I* (Stockholm: Almqvist & Wicksell, 1966), pp. 444, 465; H. Kerr, *Parlement et Société en Suisse* (St Saphorin: Editions Georgi, 1981), p. 280.

interest groups that objected to government health insurance. Groups that could be labeled *"petit bourgeois"* – for example, farmers and small employers – inadvertently improved the strategic position of doctors because they too opposed compulsory health insurance. Indeed, it is important to note that the issues of national health insurance and payment to doctors were fought out within the context of broader questions of social policy that involved interest groups and government agencies

quite separate from the profession. Religious issues, trade union pluralism, and the fate of small enterprises in a modernizing economy were
some of the political conflicts that coincided with national health insurance debates and that affected the resolution of these debates. These
other conflicts and the interest groups that took part in them were nonetheless affected by the same features of the political system that tipped
the balance of power between doctors and the executive.

The political clout of these groups was exercised in two directions. Like
the doctors, the groups depended on access to members of parliament
who were essential to the governing coalition. In addition, as groups with
a greater electoral significance than physicians, they profited from the
unbridled electoral competition in France. Members of the parliamentary
parties were constantly looking for new voters, and this dynamic was to
affect health insurance politics. Party competition was a motivation to
expand health insurance benefits, but it also made some parliamentarians
especially sensitive to the constituents who might switch allegiance from
one party to another, or to the short-lived "surge" parties of the Fourth
Republic.

Professionalization and organization-building

The political resources available to French doctors stand in sharp contrast
to their professional and organizational resources. The classical professionalization process was interrupted by the French Revolution.
Medical associations were outlawed by the Loi le Chapelier of 1791, and
in the name of scientific freedom, the university medical faculties were
abolished; anyone who wished could practice medicine. Even under the
old regime, moreover, the profession was split between the elite doctors
in universities and provincial doctors, the latter undergoing an artisanal
training that led to a public health officer's diploma rather than a doctorate in medicine.[5] A law of 1803 reestablished the system of medical
training and restricted legal medical practice to those with a university
doctorate in medicine or a public health officer's diploma. Nevertheless,
illegal practice continued in the countryside, in particular by monks and
nuns who were encouraged to return during the Restoration.

The medical societies that had formed from the 1820s on were organ-
izationally weak and ideologically split. A group of elite Paris doctors –
the Association Générale des Médecins de Paris – produced a legislative
proposal to fight quackery and to reduce the number of doctors, but
without success. The first national association of physicians – the Association Générale des Médécins de France – was formed in 1858 to represent
the middle stratum of the profession. It failed in its efforts to build a
unified organization to bargain with the mutual aid societies, however. Its
leaders were willing to support legislation for improved public health

measures, but wished to eliminate the public health officer diploma as an alternate training route and to suppress illegal practice. It could not gain support among doctors, however, for its plans to create a corporatist organization, the Ordre des Médécins, to which doctors would be required to belong. Nor did it receive support for drafting an official code of medical ethics (*Code de Déontologie*). Parisian practitioners, Catholic doctors, and physician-politicians were particularly opposed to these efforts; according to Steffen, these members of the profession feared centralization.[6]

It was not until the end of the nineteenth century that the decisive steps to professionalization and building medical organizations were taken. Notably, these steps were taken in different arenas by different groups of physicians. Further, French scholars have stressed the importance of general political and cultural developments in the period of the Third Republic for these steps, and have argued that the credit for these actions cannot be attributed solely to physicians. The Chevandrier Act of 1892 decisively established a medical monopoly. The law eliminated the public health officers, and made legal monopoly effective for the first time by allowing medical associations, which were legally recognized for the first time under the same act, to bring offenders before the courts. The legislation was pushed through the parliament by physician-politicians, but also owed its support, to the growing political currents of anticlericalism, urbanism, and republicanism, all of which found expression in a movement for scientific medicine. The law codified the new cognitive unity of the profession, left credentialing to the medical professors in the universities, and buttressed the legal monopoly of holders of university degrees with state power through the judiciary. The movement for medical unionization, on the other hand, was effected by non-elite physicians, with more narrowly economic concerns. In 1884 these doctors established the Union of French Medical Unions (Union des Syndicats Médicaux Français, or USMF), which was a national federation of local unions. These local unions and the national federation wished to establish a collective front against the mutual aid societies, and to divide medical practice fairly among practitioners. The Union supported compulsory health insurance, a position, as we will see, that put it at odds with the elite Paris doctors.

Thus, the French professionalization process was slow and in some ways incomplete. It did not produce a unified professional organization in control of medical licensing, education, or a code of medical ethics. Middle and lower class doctors were organized into local medical societies and a national federation. Education was under the control of university patrons. Paris practitioners formed their own local organizations, such as the medical union of the Seine, and relied on separate channels of influence. These doctors, joined by those in other large cities, such as

Lyon, regularly promoted their political views through their connections with "scientific personalities" in parliament in order to "short circuit" the more moderate views of the USMF. A second important elite channel of communication was the medical journal *Concours Médical*, which was founded in 1879.[7] As shown in Table 6, French medical associations had lower memberships than those in Sweden or Switzerland. During the late 1950s, French medical associations estimated their memberships at 66 percent of physicians, compared with about 90 percent in Sweden and Switzerland.[8] Moreover, in place of the centralized professional organizations that existed elsewhere, French medical unions continued the nineteenth-century pattern of competing organizations engaged in open political conflicts.

The liberal model of medicine

As discussed in Chapter 2, the opinions of French doctors on the conflict between private medical practice and national health insurance depended upon the market position of individual doctors. Rural doctors, who treated poorer patients, were predisposed to accept national health insurance and even controls on doctors' fees. Urban elite physicians, on the other hand, wished to protect private medical practice from government monopsony. These doctors developed an ideology of "liberal medicine" (*la médecine libérale*), which was elaborated in a medical charter of 1927. The practice of medicine, it was argued, was a highly individual art that required a direct and private relationship between doctors and their patients. Set forth as ethical principles, the tenets of liberal medicine protected several aspects of the doctor-patient relationship: First, patients were to be free to choose their own doctor; second, the doctor-patient relationship was to be subject to the strictest secrecy; third, physicians required complete liberty with regard to the choice of medical treatment; fourth, all financial matters ought to be decided by a "direct understanding" (*entente directe*) between doctors and their patients – that is, fees should be discussed individually with patients, and payment should be made directly to doctors, without the interference of a third party. The integrity of treatment was thus to be guaranteed by an individual relationship between doctor and patient that – by analogy with the French-liberal concept of plebiscitarian citizenship – was to remain uncontaminated by intermediate bodies.

The ideology of liberal medicine gave a certain coherence to the campaigns of doctors and provided a common language for communication with potential allies, but this philosophy does not explain the ability of the profession to impede increased government regulation. For the views of the liberal physicians were similar to those of Swedish and Swiss physicians; the liberal model of medicine was simply a codification of the defense of doctors' economic autonomy, common to elite physicians throughout Western Europe. The context of French political institutions explains why the liberal faction was able to dominate medical politics, and also the extent to which these doctors were able to lobby successfully for the incorporation of their demands into French health insurance legislation.[9]

OVERVIEW OF FRENCH HEALTH POLICY

This chapter argues that in order to understand the pattern of national health insurance policy-making in France, we must focus on French political institutions. The parliament of the Third and Fourth Republics provided an access point for physicians – and for the select interest groups that could threaten the parliamentary majority – to veto health insurance legislation. This route of political influence was so effective that the only way to bypass the veto power of the profession was to bypass parliament entirely. As William Glaser points out, "The ability of the medical profession to obstruct any unacceptable legislation in a democratic system is illustrated by the history of national health insurance in France. Basic reforms could be enacted only when the Parliament was suspended and when the executive ruled by decree."[10] When parliament was in session, the liberal faction of the French medical profession was able to block efforts to control doctors' fees. But because this power of the medical profession, as well as that of other interest groups, depended on the design of political institutions, the redesign of these institutions permitted the executive to override parliament. The most important constitutional revision was the creation of the Fifth Republic.

Despite the continued resistance of interest groups – such as doctors and small businessmen – that had been able to block parliamentary changes through their parliamentary influence, direct legislation by the executive without parliamentary ratification allowed the executive to circumvent the parliamentary veto point in the Fifth Republic. Indeed, all major initiatives in French health policy, even in the Third and Fourth Republics, were related to questions of executive power, and in each case, there were either ad hoc conjunctural reasons or specific institutional innovations that account for the ability of the executive to overcome parliamentary stalemate. The first compulsory health insurance law was introduced after the First World War when it was necessary to reintegrate the population of Alsace-Lorraine into France; this unique situation created a short-lived parliamentary unity, as MPs put aside electoral competition when faced with a threat to the nation-state. The system was expanded following the Second World War during a period of direct rule by de Gaulle and "dictatorship by consent." Regulatory measures to control doctors' fees and administrative reorganization were imposed shortly after the founding of the Fifth Republic.

Even in the nineteenth century, the laws regulating the voluntary mutual societies had been closely linked to the vicissitudes of France's many constitutional regimes. The July Monarchy, the Second Republic, the Second Empire, and the Third Republic each developed its own policy toward the mutual societies, so that the oscillations between imperial and republican rule were matched with alternations between stringent government controls and freedom of association for the mutuals.[11] Whereas previous opportunities for executive legislation had been temporary, under the Fifth Republic this policy-making independence of the executive became permanent. The key to this synchrony between constitutional regimes and policy is the relationship between parliament and executive and the opportunities for interest group veto that arose from these political institutions.

EXECUTIVE POWER VERSUS INTEREST-GROUP PRIVILEGE: EARLY LEGISLATION

Although a broad range of social insurance proposals had been debated in France since the late nineteenth century, progress had been relatively slow. An eighteen-year "parliamentary marathon" established employer liability for industrial accidents on 9 April 1898, but not the compulsory insurance for work accidents passed in many European nations in the 1880s. In 1910, parliamentary representatives braved the opposition of employers, unions, and farmers to introduce old-age pensions for workers and peasants. The law was a failure because it proved to be very easy for both employers and employees to avoid paying contributions, and high rates of inflation during the First World War rendered the funded pensions practically worthless. Health insurance was not specifically discussed. Rather the early debates on compulsory social insurance were dominated by philosophical discussions of the need for legal compulsion versus the virtues of voluntarism. Social scientists have explained this delay by referring to the strong liberal ideology of French parliamentarians, the autonomy of the individual will as the basis of French law, France's slow industrialization and the prevalence of small, family enterprises, and the complete opposition of farmers and employers to social insurance. The process of prolonged parliamentary debate on philosophical grounds by representatives more loyal to their political class than to specific constituencies is typical of most accounts of policy making during the Third Republic, however.[12]

This deadlock was broken by the First World War. An unusual set of circumstances led to a political consensus on social insurance for the first time in France. As in many other countries, the war brought with it new levels of unionization and an increased electoral popularity of the left that created pressures for social legislation. But the ways in which these pressures were channeled by the political system produced a consensus within the political elite that survived radical political fluctuations, at the same time that the political process allowed selected interest groups to revise the content of the legislation. Two factors motivated the members of parliament: a shared assumption that something had to be done about the provinces of Alsace and Lorraine, and a new opportunity for electoral gains.

The 1928 Social Insurance Law

Every historian writing on French social legislation stresses the importance of the return of the provinces of Alsace and Lorraine to France.[13] Because the population in these provinces had benefited from German social insurance for more than thirty years, political authorities found it imperative to equalize insurance benefits throughout France. Although they might have deprived Alsatians and Lorrainers of their benefits, or allowed the region to remain privileged by a benefit not available to other French citizens, no politician considered these alternatives as politically acceptable. This is one of the rare instances where, although the idea of a national interest may be theoretically suspect, the political elite was convinced that social insurance was a matter of the survival of the nation-state. This parliamentary consensus was translated into action by the appointment of Alexandre Millerand, former High Commissioner of the Republic in Alsace-Lorraine, as President of the Council of Ministers. Millerand, in turn, signaled that social insurance was to be a priority of his administration by appointing an Alsatian, Jordain, as Minister of Labor, and authorizing Jourdain to prepare a legislative proposal.[14] Thus, the tendency of the French parliament toward stalemate was overcome by a conjunctural ad hoc factor: Regardless of partisan differences and problems of coalition-building, French politicians were agreed that compulsory health insurance was to be introduced.

The electoral factor was related to successive electoral victories for the socialists, who polled more than 20 percent of the vote by 1919. Centrist politicians, like the Radicals, could not survive elections without making alliances with the left, and viewed social insurance as an electoral advantage. The right countered by claiming credit for the same programs. Each vote on social insurance in the Chamber of Deputies and the Senate was carried out shortly before elections, and the legislative proposals were passed by large majorities.[15]

Despite the consensus for social insurance, the parliamentary negotiations did not go smoothly. Instead, rapid changes in the parliamentary coalitions oscillating between center-left and center-right alliances, combined with maneuvering in the parliamentary committees, created opportunities for interest groups. The Social Insurance Law of 1928 took eight years to prepare. At each phase of the legislative process, interest groups demanded significant changes within the law. Even after the law was enacted, interest-group protests caused the law to be rescinded, but it was reenacted in 1930.

The 1928 law was based on three successive legislative proposals: the Vincent project of 1921, the Grinda project of 1923, and the Chauveau project of 1924. The original Vincent project provided for old-age, disability, health, unemployment, and maternity insurance that would be carried by regional social insurance funds under the supervision of elected administrative boards. This proposal was more universalistic in outlook, and in fact more administratively centralized than comparable legislation in Germany, England, or Scandinavia. Many types of insurance risks were to be unified under a single scheme; government-organized agencies would replace the scattered pattern of voluntary mutual societies. But the plan would not be enacted intact. Parliamentary loopholes – in particular, the parliamentary commissions of the Chamber of Deputies and the Senate – provided an access point for interest groups that demanded revisions. The parliamentary consensus was a vague consensus for action on social legislation, not a consensus worked out within and between different political parties for a particular plan. The parliamentary commissions were given almost complete autonomy over the legislative draft, and changes made in the commissions were not debated in the Senate and Chamber of Deputies.[16]

The Chamber of Deputies

In the Commission of the Chamber of Deputies, presided over by Dr. Edouard Grinda, a physician and mutualist, several changes were made in order to placate the voluntary mutual societies and farmers, the groups that, according to the commission's report, constituted the two most adamant opponents of the law.[17] The mutual funds had protested that the administration's proposal based on public "regional" funds was too "statist" (*étatiste*) and had the "["serious"] fault ... of making a *tabula rasa*, to ignore the efforts accomplished by the mutual aid societies for more than half a century, to sacrifice to a rigid mechanism organisms that are living and adapted to their end, to build social insurance on the ruins of liberal providence." In response to pressures from the mutualists, the proposed regional funds would be relegated to a secondary position, while the mutual societies would remain as the primary insurance carriers.[18] To please the farmers, agricultural workers would be given their own separate scheme that would be heavily subsidized by the state.[19] Whereas the administration's plan had established monopsony payment through centralized government administration, mutual aid society and farmer pressures forced a return to a more fragmented, pluralistic system. The project was unanimously approved by the Chamber of Deputies on 8 April 1924, shortly before the new elections.

Passage of the social insurance law by the Chamber was only the first step in this legislative process. When the law passed to the Senate, and specifically to the Commission of Hygiene, it moved into a more politically conservative arena, one more favorable to physicians and less receptive to the mutual aid societies. The legislative process was further complicated by conflicts between different factions within the profession. At issue were the principle of compulsory health insurance and the methods for paying doctors. The moderate USMF supported compulsory health insurance on condition that patients would be able to choose their own doctor; it accepted direct third-party payment from insurance authorities as long as it was calculated on a fee-for-service basis, and it preferred government administration to a plurality of mutual aid societies.[20] The "liberal" opposition, on the other hand, led by Dr. Paul Cibrie, a Paris physician who was head of the medical union of the Seine, was publishing articles in the *Concours Médical*, denouncing social insurance and calling it a "Trojan Horse" with which the Germans would ruin the French economy.[21]

The Chamber of Deputies' Commission had considered medical opposition when drafting the law, but did not consider it a threat. The resulting Chamber version (the Grinda project) recommended third-party payment with closed panels of doctors modeled on the German system. Doctors under contract to the mutual aid societies or regional insurance funds would provide treatments to patients and then present their bills to the insurance carriers; patients would not pay for medical treatments directly. This was the method preferred by the mutual aid societies.[22] And this was the version of the law approved by the Chamber.

The Senate

When the law passed to the Senate's Commission of Hygiene, professional considerations emerged as a more significant factor. Dr. Chauveau, the head of this commission, introduced several changes in the portions of the law that governed the relations between physicians and sickness funds, despite objections from the mutual societies. Chauveau was not by any means an official of a French medical association. He acted on his own, and represented the profession because he was a physician and member of parliament simultaneously, not because he had been delegated to this position by an official medical organization. This was typical in France. Chauveau, like Grinda, was involved in the mutualist movement, and his concessions to the profession were partly motivated by his desire to produce a workable scheme for social insurance in which doctors would willingly participate. Whereas the Chamber's commission had recommended direct third-party payment, Chauveau insisted on a reimbursement scheme. Further, he replaced the closed panels of doctors called for by the Chamber with a system of local contracts that would be negotiated between local sickness funds and medical unions, with the stipulation that these unions were required to belong to the national unions.[23]

These changes strengthened the negotiating position of physicians vis-à-vis the insurance funds. The switch to reimbursement meant that the sickness funds would be faced with a fait accompli as far as medical payments were concerned. In the case of a dispute, the funds would hold up reimbursement to their members rather than payment to a doctor. By making the panel lists a matter for negotiation rather than a unilateral decision of the funds, the Senate version deprived the funds of the main sanction at their disposal – removing doctors from insurance practice. The insistence on medical unions that belonged to the national unions would centralize the medical associations – to the benefit of the national unions that had been having trouble competing with the local unions – at the same time that the previous administrative changes had decentralized the sickness funds by replacing the regional funds with mutualist and pro-fessional funds. Though they had themselves been responsible for the decentralization, the mutual societies protested the Senate version, claim-ing that it would allow doctors to control the price of medical services. Fee-for-service payment would be difficult for their budgets, and the funds would be placed at a severe disadvantage if required to negotiate with the national medical unions.[24]

Professional conflicts

Despite the concessions made by the Senate Commission, the minority faction of liberal doctors objected to the social insurance law. Although the majority of delegates to the USMF's General Assembly of 1925 voted to support the social insurance law, the liberal minority insisted that the law did not protect the principle of direct payment (*entente directe*). Chauveau had established reimbursement, which entailed direct payment, as the financial mechanism, but allowed contracts between local sickness funds and local medical unions to propose third-party payment (*tiers payant*). For the liberals, this would entail an unwanted downward pressure on fees. This faction, comprising elite, urban practitioners, "defended direct agreement with the patient and direct payment, handing over the money directly, as a principle of medical usage, while admitting that this conservative ideal is not that of the majority of practitioners."[25]

The liberal doctors were forced to defend their position against charges of financial self-interest, indicating some public suspicion about their motives. A Dr. Duchesne wrote in the *Concours Médical*: "One has pretended that physicians hostile to *tiers payant* defend their material interests, that it is for them merely a question of monetary gain (*gros sous*). Nothing could be farther from the truth. One can affirm that with the regime of *tiers payant*, the doctor will receive larger fees than if he dealt directly with his patient."[26] Patients would flock to less expensive doctors, Duchesne claimed, so that direct payment would allow competition to force prices down.

The rift between the USMF and the liberal minority faction continued to deepen. The liberals split off from the Union to form the Federation of Medical Unions (Fédération des Syndicats Médicaux) in January 1926. Next, the liberals drafted a Medical Charter in January 1927, and convinced a joint session of the USMF and the new Federation to approve the Charter in November 1927. Finally, the USMF was disbanded and the Confederation of Medical Unions (Confédération des Syndicats Médicaux, or CSMF) was created in December 1928.[27] Thus, the liberal faction was able to break off from the main medical association, absorb the old association into the new one, and make the "idea of médecine libérale . . . the unifying principle, the emblem of the profession."[28]

The journal of the USMF was silent on the deliberations and the process that finally led the older leaders to join the liberal secession; this silence was justified on the grounds of professional unity.[29] The journal does, however, make clear the positions of different groups of doctors. The majority of doctors preferred compulsory health insurance, direct third-party payment, and fee-for-service (rather than capitation) payment. Because these doctors were familiar with mutual aid society practices and had collection problems with patients, they preferred guaranteed payments from government sickness funds, paid directly, but on a fee-for-service basis. The liberals, on the other hand, opposed compulsory insurance and direct third-party payment, but they too wanted fee-for-service payment. The policy compromise agreed upon when the groups fused was to adjust the liberal model to allow for compulsory health insurance (the majority preference) – which was inevitable given the question of national interest at stake – and to focus on the conditions of payment: direct payment from the patient (the liberal preference), fee-for-service, free choice of doctor. Nonetheless, this policy compromise does not satisfactorily explain why the liberal faction was first able to build a rival organization, then to swallow the more moderate and better organized USMF. Only the parliamentary contacts available to the liberal elite provide a plausible explanation for why the majority USMF was more dependent on the minority CSMF than vice versa.

Despite the opposition of both the mutual aid societies and the liberal doctors to the payment system, electoral pressures outweighed interest-group pressures on MPs. The Chauveau version of the law (reimbursement but allowance for third-party payment) was adopted by the Senate on 7 July 1927 by 269 votes to 2. The Chamber adopted the Senate version on 14 March 1928 by 477 votes to 2. Once through the committee, the principle of compulsory health insurance was accepted by an overwhelming majority. Nevertheless, for all of these machinations, the 1928 law was not to last long. Protests from employers and liberal doctors resulted in the repeal of the law. Not only was there massive opposition to the law, but the law's supposed beneficiaries, and the French labor movement in particular, were divided in their views.

Employer opposition

Even in the early 1920s, there had been evidence of employer opposition to the social insurance law. But employers were not united in their opposition nor did they campaign actively against the reform.[30] Although an employers' association had been formed in 1919 – the General Confederation of French Production (Confédération Générale de la Production Française, or CGPF) – no single organization spoke for employers at the time. Instead, government authorities received scattered comments from individual branch associations or employers' journals.[31] Employer opposition hardened after the law had been passed, when economic conditions began to deteriorate and the composition of parliament shifted to the right with the 1928 elections. Tactics ranged from inciting discontent among workers by insisting that workers pay their contributions directly and hinting that benefits would never be forthcoming, to legal commentaries that exaggerated the complexity of the law and pointed out various "escape" clauses, to a virulent press campaign and parliamentary initiatives.[32]

Hatzfeld argues that employer viewpoints were clearly divided, depending upon the size of the enterprise. Small employers were the most negative, and objected to the contributions, whereas the larger employers were more concerned with government spending and the financial equilibrium of the system, and displayed an interest in controlling the administration of social insurance benefits – as they eventually did for family allowances. Employers presented a counterproposal to the Chamber of Deputies that was signed by 77 deputies, including Claude Gignoux, future head of the CGPF. It called for the substitution of worker contributions with exclusive employer financing and exclusive employer administration.[33]

Medical opposition

Despite the advantages for the profession that the Chauveau Commission had introduced, the newly-formed Confédération des Syndicats Médicaux Français (CSMF) was not satisfied with the law either, and launched a campaign against it during the period when the administrative decrees for the implementation of the law were to be promulgated. Through a widespread publicity campaign and pressure on parliamentarians, the CSMF succeeded in obtaining a new law that specified that a reimbursement system would go into effect. The main point of contention had been the provisions in the 1928 law that allowed local contracts to deviate from the reimbursement system and that could introduce binding fee schedules through collective or individual contracts with doctors. Under the new law of 30 April 1930, the funds and local medical unions would negotiate local reimbursement fee schedules (*tarifs de responsabilité*). These schedules would not limit the fees that doctors could charge. They would merely set a maximum on the fees that the funds would be willing to reimburse. Furthermore, the idea of closed panels was eliminated entirely; any doctor could treat insurance patients. The CSMF was also able to insist that only medical unions approved by the national unions and the Government Council for Social Insurance (Conseil Supérieur d'Assurances Sociales) could negotiate agreements with the funds, thereby assuring its control over the system.

Divisions in the labor movement

For the previous seventy years, government policy had sought to undermine the class identity of the mutualist movement. Political control of the mutual societies through controls on the banking practices of the funds, as well as the insistence on wealthy "honorary members," had successfully counteracted the earlier radicalism of the mutuals. In fact, these measures had produced a hostile relationship between unions and the mutual societies. Consequently, French labor unions were very much opposed to the involvement of the mutuals in the Social Insurance Law. In 1910, the unions had gone so far as to oppose the 1910 Pension Law. Now, the Confédération Générale du Travail (CGT) – at the time socialist rather than Communist – was willing to support the principle of social insurance, but opposed the reliance on mutual societies. Instead, the CGT preferred state funds and even argued for the elimination of the employer contribution in order to keep employers out of fund administration. Employers had been particularly active in the administration of family allowances, which were used as a means to inspect the homes of workers and to control militants and strikers. In 1910, the CGT had feared that the contribution cards of employees would be used to establish a code for identifying the militants, as an extension of the workers' police identity card (*livret ouvrier*).

The insistence of the mutual societies on maintaining their own funds under the 1928 Social Insurance Law was viewed in this context: "it will be very dangerous for the workers who will be catalogued right away (affiliated to the red fund and affiliated to the white fund)." The Grinda report, for its part, did not hesitate to present the social insurance law as an element of the class struggle, asking, "Is it necessary to wait until the social peace is troubled before attempting to intervene with measures of appeasement? Is it when the battle has already begun that one should forge arms, invent explosives, reverse abuses?" More generally, the CGT, as well as other unions, complained about the decentralized administration, the huge number of tiny, inefficient funds, and the concessions made to employers that caused the separation of risks.[34]

The Communist labor union CGTU (Confédération Générale du Travail Unitaire), which had in fact only just split off from the CGT in 1920, was strongly opposed to the law and to worker contributions, as was the Communist Party. It argued that social insurance benefits would be used to fight strikes, that capitalists would simply pass on the costs of social insurance to the price of goods, and that the funds for old-age and invalidity insurance would generate a huge capital "from which French imperialism 'may serve itself for preparing new butcheries.'"[35] After the passage of the law, the CGTU organized strikes for increased wages to compensate workers for the cost of contributions – and a day of protest on 1 August 1930. Nevertheless, employer rather than union opposition was relevant to members of parliament, and none of the union demands were met.[36]

THE FRENCH POLITICAL PROCESS AND THE SOCIAL INSURANCE LAW OF 1930

Nearly nine years of parliamentary deliberation converted the initial plan for simple, rational administration and universal coverage into one of the most fragmented social insurance schemes in Europe. French social security has been called an

'unfinished cathedral' . . . [whose] edifice itself is of magnificent proportions and provides a wide variety of protection for nearly the entire population. But within the Church there are numerous altars, each collecting funds for different purposes and dispensing earthly benefits in different ways. Within the Cathedral grounds, an almost endless sprawl of cloistered groups obtain special comforts and privileges.[37]

The permeability of parliamentary deliberations to interest-group pressures was essential to this fragmentation process. The temporary parliamentary consensus for compulsory health insurance was insufficient as a barrier against interest-group influence. Although MPs were able to put aside party competition in order to pass the social insurance law of 1928, and even felt that support for social insurance might attract new voters to their party, fragile parliamentary coalitions could not withstand pressure from important constituencies. In particular, when decision making passed to parliamentary committees, whose representatives were drawn disproportionately from political parties with an interest in the votes of specific groups, concessions that undermined the rationale of the initial policy proposals were made. Had the French executive government been based on a firm parliamentary majority, composed of MPs bound by party discipline, such interest-group logrolling would not have been possible – no matter who was appointed to the committee. Thus, it is the political framework rather than access alone that explains this particular logic of interest-group influence.

In the Chamber of Deputies' committee, representatives reworked the administration's plan according to the wishes of farmers and the mutualists. In the Senate committee, the advantage switched to the medical profession – although the doctors themselves were divided and could not present a united lobbying front. Moreover, the rapid swings in the ruling parliamentary majority meant that no decision was cast in stone; interest groups had every incentive to protest, even after the 1928 law was to have been in force. The switch to a conservative government in 1928 provided an opportunity for employers and doctors to demand revisions in the payroll tax rates and the method of payment to doctors. The unions on the other hand were less important, as the socialists were now out of the coalition and the communists were not a potential coalition partner for the right and center parties. Thus, the fragmented nature of French political representation provided opportunities for interest-group influence that explain the specific outlines of the first French health insurance legislation.

The result of these interest-group battles was a law that differed radically from the original Vincent project of 1921. Bowing to pressures from the mutual aid societies and farmers in 1923, the centralized administration envisioned by the Vincent project was replaced by a decentralized system of voluntary mutual aid societies. The 1923 Chamber plan for mutual fund controls on doctors' fees through direct third-party payment and closed panels of doctors was replaced by, first, the 1924 plan for reimbursement, and then the 1930 law, which left fees to local collective agreements, without any mechanism to enforce the signing of these agreements. The right of mutual aid societies to create local health centers (free clinics paying doctors by salary) was curtailed.[38]

Finally, benefits were significantly cut. The risks that were covered were largely the same – sickness, maternity, invalidity, old-age, death – although the unemployment provisions had been virtually eliminated by the Senate. At the same time, the scheme was made less progressive by the replacement of income classes for contributions and benefits, with a flat-rate percentage for both. The law would cover all employees earning less than 18,000 francs per year, with contributions to be paid at the rate of 5 percent each for employers and employees on the first 15,000 francs of income. As a result of the employer protests following the enactment of the 1928 law, the contribution rates were lowered to 4 percent each for employers and employees, and the state subsidy was increased correspondingly.[39] Even with the decreased benefits, however, the 1930 Social Insurance Law did have a significant impact, particularly in expanding insurance coverage – fairly common in industry and mining – to new sectors of the salaried population. Membership increased from 5 million in 1923 to 8.2 million in 1930.[40]

The replacement of the Social Insurance Law of 1928 with the law of 1930 was an important victory for the French medical profession – at least for its liberal wing. Not only did the second law significantly increase the ability of the profession to set its own fees and remain fairly autonomous from the sickness fund administration, but the struggle established the CSMF as a political force – much as the American medical profession's struggle against national health insurance from 1915 to 1920 had a lasting impact on its own self-image, on its attitude toward national health insurance, and on public perceptions of the organization's political power.[41] But the ability of the liberal faction to obtain concessions is better explained by the access afforded by the parliamentary process than by peculiarities in the French process of professionalization or the organizational unity of the profession. Particular members of the medical profession were able to make political demands even at a time when the medical association was in organizational flux, with obvious differences of opinion within the membership. Furthermore, the concessions granted to doctors were analogous to those granted to other interest groups with parliamentary importance, such as the mutual aid societies and the farmers, demonstrating that parliamentary access and not professional power was the more important factor. Only the unions, despite their strikes, were not granted concessions. In the political sphere, electoral importance to the MPs critical to the governing coalition, and not economic organization, was the key to influence.

TEMPORARY EXECUTIVE DOMINANCE: THE SOCIAL SECURITY ORDINANCES OF 1945

October 1944. In liberated Paris, the Provisional Government emanating from the French Committee of the National Liberation assumes all responsibility for the political, economic and social life of the country. . . . The old social structures had been shaken, sometimes shattered. The workers' masses, which had taken an active part in the resistance against the enemy and in the battle against the Vichy regime, saw, in the already certain victory and in the overthrow of the regime, the result of their effort; in the new government, their government. In many regards, the climate of the moment resembles that of 1936 [the Popular Front]. Hope is born of a new social order. Social Security is an element of the response to this hope.[42]

Descriptions of the enactment of the French social security system are mythic. Social security has been viewed, then and now, as a symbol for the entire Liberation period. As in the period following the First World War, reform was expedited by concrete political and institutional factors that were specific to France. For a brief period, the executive government ruled directly. Although advised by a temporary legislative body – the Provisional Consultative Assembly – the executive could issue legislation directly by ordinance, without depending on parliamentary approval. This ability to issue legislation directly by decree was used to pass social security legislation, and thus to avoid parliamentary stalemate and concessions to interest groups.

Of course, we cannot overlook the other political factors of the period. Those who had participated in the resistance were now in power, whereas the old right was completely discredited. Many of the parties of the Third Republic, moreover, had been disbanded during the Occupation. Only one right-of-center political party, the Parti Républicain des Libertés (PRL), was represented in the Provisional Consultative Assembly, which was overwhelmingly composed of members of the socialist and communist parties and the MRP.

Moreover, the structure of interest representation had been reshaped by the Vichy regime and the subsequent Liberation. Under Vichy, many interest-group organizations had been dissolved and replaced by corporatist alternatives that were meant to work more closely with the state. These *comités d'organisation* had recreated the trade associations while eliminating union influence. The unions, however, which had gone underground and consolidated, quickly regrouped after the war, whereas the employer organizations suffered from their association with Vichy. The main employers' association was not reestablished as the Conseil National du Patronat Français (CNPF) until 1946, although the small business association, the Confédération Générale des Petites et Moyennes Entreprises (CGPME), was reconstituted in 1944 and took this opportunity to claim greater autonomy from the industrialists.[43]

Similarly, the French medical union – Confédération des Syndicats Médicaux Français (CSMF) – had been dismantled under Vichy and replaced by the Compulsory Order of Physicians (Ordre des Médecins). In April 1945, the CSMF was legally reconstituted, but the Ordre des Médecins was retained, with a revised structure outlined by the ordinance of 24 September 1945. In June 1946, the CSMF and the Ordre signed an accord that defined their different roles – the CSMF was responsible for collective agreements and other "trade union" functions, whereas the Ordre was responsible for moral conduct, licensing, and other "individual" aspects of professional self-supervision.[44]

The Social Security Ordinances of 4 and 19 October 1945 were enacted under the "dictatorship by consent." Strong executive leadership, political support from the Resistance parties, a parliament whose powers were restricted to consultation, and a chaotic mix of interest groups that, except for the CGT, were poorly organized and discredited, allowed the administration to enact its social security plan with a minimum of interest-group consultation and parliamentary bargaining.

These Ordinances were based on proposals that had been developed by Resistance leaders during the war and expressed in the economic and social program of the National Council of the Resistance in the spring of 1944 – although many of the ideas can be traced back to the prewar period. In June 1945, the administration presented a legislative draft to a special committee composed of interest-group, ministerial, and parliamentary representatives. Later in the summer, the plan was discussed in the Provisional Consultative Assembly. Despite objections from employers, the old mutual societies, and private insurance companies, as well as from Catholics represented by the MRP and the CFTC (Confédération Française des Travailleurs Chrétiens), the administration was able to steer clear of most obstacles to the law. Its own legislation was enacted largely intact and was to go into effect on 1 July 1946.[45]

The administration's plan called for a unified system of social security funds that would cover the risks of illness, old age, maternity, and work accidents, and provide family allowances. This system would unite risks covered previously by three separate pieces of legislation: the 1898 Act on Work Accidents, the 1930 Social Insurance Law, and the 1932 Act on Family Allowances. Further centralization would be accomplished by uniting the funds that were based on affiliation to mutuals and trade unions with the departmental funds, which already covered more than 50 percent of the insured. The displaced mutuals would be given a new status that would allow them to provide complementary schemes. The Ordinance of 19 October 1945 called them the "pioneers" of health insurance. Self-administration was not to be abandoned but strengthened by this centralization.[46] The social security funds were to be administered by boards of representatives delegated by the unions and employers' associations in a three-to-one ratio favoring the unions. The new plan would be financed almost exclusively through employee and employer contributions, with employers paying a considerably larger share (10 percent to the employee's 6 percent for social insurance, 16 percent for family allowances, and an average of 3 percent for work accidents, with no employee contributions for the latter two). The law extended social insurance coverage from low-income earners to *all* employees, and provided for a substantial increase in benefits, particularly for long-term illnesses and old-age pensions.[47]

Limited concessions to special interests

Given the circumstances under which the Social Security Ordinances were promulgated, it is not surprising that critics of the reform could not launch an open attack against the principles of the reform. Employers and private insurance companies, who had most at stake, limited their comments to criticism of the work accidents portion of the law during the meetings of the special commission, rather than taking a more public stance.[48] There was some criticism of the procedures by which the Ordinances had been enacted by groups such as CSMF, the mutualists, and the CFTC. Dr. Cibrie, president of the CSMF, stated that "important changes should not be legislated by ordinance but only after discussion by the elected representatives of the French people. To follow another route is to let oneself be inspired by totalitarian methods." M. Heller of the mutual societies also stressed his "worry about these social security reforms that have just been realized by route of ordinance and not by a Parliament reestablished by universal suffrage, incontestable basis of modern democracy."[49]

But the main controversies during the preparation of the law revolved around the idea of a unified social insurance fund (*caisse unique*) and representation on the administrative boards. In the special commission that met in June 1945, the employer representatives, the MRP, and the CFTC were opposed to unifying family allowances with the other risks. Because employers, Catholic mutualists, and the CFTC had been particularly influential in the family allowances funds, they did not wish to see this influence disappear through a merger of family allowances and social insurance.

The administrative structure of the social security funds had particularly important implications for the organizational survival of the CFTC. As one observer of the French labor movement wrote, "After having eliminated unified unionism at the Liberation, they saw pluralism menaced anew by the creation of the unified social insurance fund."[50] The CFTC also objected to the delegation of representatives on the administrative boards of the funds by unions. At this time, the communist CGT was by far the largest union. Hoping that it could obtain votes out of proportion to its membership, the CFTC pushed for a system of elections rather than delegated members.

The administration compromised by removing family allowances from the general scheme, but it insisted on the delegation of the representatives to the administrative councils. It did not concede to the demands of employers and insurance companies to remove the work accidents portion

of the scheme. Thus, the executive had the institutional means to introduce the legislation without fear of parliamentary opposition or concern
for the wishes of interest groups. But with the upcoming constitutional
ratification and parliamentary elections in mind, as well as the political
imperative to hold the resistance coalition together, the executive administration made concessions in the interests of political expediency. Thus,
the executive made good on its promise to the Socialists to push through
a program of social insurance; to the Communists, to hold firm on the
question of delegated representatives; and to the Catholics, to remove
family allowances to a separate and independent administrative agency.
Groups irrelevant to the political coalition, such as employers and private
insurers, were shut out completely from these decisions.

Return to democracy

The special conditions of the Liberation period were only temporary,
however. With the return to parliamentary democracy, political bargaining and party competition began to increase. Furthermore, the Resistance
coalition broke down, with both de Gaulle and the communists leaving
the government. The constitution of the Fourth Republic reestablished
many features of the Third Republic (despite the campaign of de Gaulle
against the new constitution); some changes even worked to the detri-
ment of the new regime. Like the Third Republic, the Fourth Republic
was based on the principle of direct parliamentary rule. In contrast to the
Third Republic, however, proportional representation with universal suffrage was introduced.

Although this measure eliminated the practice of electoral alliances
between parties, once the communists were excluded from the parliamentary coalitions, parliamentary majorities were worked out as fragile
bargains, virtually unlimited by the electoral results, as they were under
the Third Republic. For a few years, proportional representation resulted
in decisive majorities, providing that the three parties comprising the
majority – the Communists, the Socialists, and the MRP – could agree.
Even in this period of rule by left parties bound by party discipline,
however, electoral competition and differences of opinion over social
security resulted in major revisions in the legislation and concessions to
interest groups. When the communists became politically isolated in 1947,
majorities depended on coalitions with the old center parties, and the
Fourth Republic experienced the same instability as the Third.[51]

Legislation changes

Revisions were made in the Social Security Ordinances, even before the
ratification of the constitution, by the Constituent Assembly charged with
developing the constitution. Even at this early stage, electoral com-

petition provided a strategic opening for selected interest groups. The debate on social security was held by the Second Constituent Assembly in August 1946. Although the communists, socialists, and the MRP governed with a large majority, the coalition did not hold together against the efforts to court new constituents.

First, following the wishes of the Catholic union, the MRP succeeded in bringing up the issue of social security elections, and won an overwhelming victory in the parliamentary vote.[52] Next, managerial employees (newly organized in the Confédération Générale des Cadres, or CGC) refused to be included in the same scheme as workers. A compromise was reached that allowed employers to provide supplementary schemes for managers. Finally, when steps were taken to extend social security to the self-employed, employers threatened to block the system completely by withholding their contributions.

Under the law of 22 May 1946, the old-age provisions of social security[53] were to be extended to the self-employed as soon as the economy recovered to its 1938 levels. Encouraged by its success in the elections to the Second Constituent Assembly, the MRP proposed an immediate extension through the law of 13 September 1946. This expansion of benefits was part of its electoral strategy – the party hoped to strengthen its electoral standing with small Catholic employers, voters who had formerly voted for the right-wing parties that were now disbanded. But this electoral maneuver backfired.[54] The "independents" protested immediately. Led by the small business association (CGMPE), several associations of independents, notably including the CSMF, formed the Committee for Alliance and Coordination of the Middle Classes (Comité de Liaison et de Coordination des Classes Moyennes), whose goal was "to limit the growing ascendancy of the powers of the State that are likely to interfere with natural rights, with spiritual, moral and material interests, and with the family life of the middle classes."[55]

The self-employed considered it a matter of prestige not to be grouped together with industrial workers – prestige that increased in symbolic value in proportion to the declining economic importance of the small entrepreneur. They also objected to the pooling of risk with a population group with entirely different needs and financial assets, as well as to the high contribution rates of 9 percent. When faced with the outright refusal to pay contributions, the MRP rather opportunistically withdrew its law, and substituted the law of 17 January 1948, which introduced special retirement plans each for artisans, industrial and commercial professions, farmers, and liberal professions, such as doctors, lawyers, and architects.[56] Consequently, separate social security schemes were established for these groups, putting an end to the movement for universal coverage under a single scheme and fragmenting the national system of social insurance.

Regulating medical fees

During these preparations, doctors had also been able to wrest an important concession from the government. Medical fees were originally to be regulated by the Ministers of Labor, Health, and Finances. The CSMF, however, wanted to avoid direct ministerial supervision at all costs.[57] Therefore, it bargained for a system of fee schedules or conventions to be negotiated between medical unions and sickness funds at the local level, subject to the approval of a tripartite National Tariffs Commission, which was to be composed of representatives of the sickness funds, the medical profession and the administration in equal proportions.[58] Doctors were allowed three official exemptions from the schedule, depending on the wealth of the patient, the reputation of the doctor, and on "exceptional circumstances" based on the severity of the case or the need for time-consuming travel on the part of the physician.

The issue of doctors' fees had created problems for the insurance funds since 1930, when the social insurance law had gone into effect. Doctors could set their fees freely, but the sickness funds reimbursed patients only at official rates – a system that, as we saw, resulted from the political efforts of the CSMF, aided by employers, farmers, and mutual societies, each of whom was against the social insurance law for a different reason. The result of this payment scheme was that when doctors' fees went up, patients received lower and lower rates of reimbursement from the funds. Patient reimbursement averaged between 30 and 50 percent as opposed to the 80 percent provided for by law.[59] Foreseeing similar problems after the war, the new administrators of social security funds, many of whom had been recruited from the regional funds and the mutual aid societies, pressed for effective controls on doctors' fees. But eager to enact the legislation before elections to ratify the new constitution and to appoint the first parliament, the executive government bowed to CSMF demands, leaving fees to be regulated by freely negotiated conventions.[60]

After the Ordinances had been promulgated, when parliamentary and interest group conflicts opened up new strategic opportunities, some physicians enlarged their concerns beyond the details of the convention system and began to criticize the principle of social insurance itself. Warning of the "nationalization of medicine" and questioning "the Sovietization of French health care" (*la santé Française Soviétisée*), doctors, as well as supporters of the old mutual aid societies and social critics such as Raymond Aron, who all feared that a centralized social security scheme was a step toward a totalitarian society, argued for voluntary and pluralistic social insurance.[61]

At the same time, discussions of alternative forms of health care organization did not take place. Professor Robert Debré (who was responsible for the Debré reform discussed later) had presented a report to the Medical Committee of the Resistance in 1944 that advocated a national health service, local health centers, and more emphasis on preventative care.[62] These suggestions, of course, are very similar to the initial plans for the British NHS as well as to the Swedish Höjer reform (discussed in Chapter 5). But this reform proposal was not pursued. Debré, who had been president of the Resistance medical organization, the Front National des Médecins, and was already publicly at odds with many members of the profession, entered the debate on social security and direct payment (*entente directe*) by stating that "the specter of the bureaucratization (*fonctionnarisation*) of medicine" was based on ignorance or partisanship.[63]

Despite this lack of consideration of a national health service, the French Social Security Ordinances of 1945 should rightly be seen as a major reform. Acting decisively, the Provisional Government reshaped the preexisting social insurance scheme into a more universal and comprehensive plan. It is a widely held view that this enactment of the law was made possible by the unusual political circumstances of the immediate postwar period. As Henry Galant writes,

The pact concluded by the parties of the left in the immediate postwar period as well as the firm and precise projects of the administration left no place for backing off with regard to the principles of social security, but only for replies that were strategic and tactical. . . . The particular circumstances of the end of the war constituted an occasion without precedent and without future for reforming the social security system. This occasion was seized.[64]

With the return to more normal political relationships, however, special-interest claims on the government increased. For a second time, the rational plan proposed by the administration had been eroded by political pressures on parliament.

PARLIAMENTARY STALEMATE: THE INEFFECTIVE FOURTH
REPUBLIC

The concessions made to interest groups during the implementation of the 1945 Social Security Ordinances proved to be nearly fatal Achilles' heels for the system. The use of conventions to regulate doctors' fees did not work, the plethora of special schemes weakened the social security administration, and competition between various unions turned the social security elections into arenas of political competition that hampered unified leadership of the funds.

The convention system of the 1945 Ordinances did contain provisions meant to strengthen controls of doctors' fees. Whereas before the war, the funds and local medical unions were merely to negotiate minimum reimbursement rates (*tarifs de responsabilité*) for the funds, now there would be two tariffs. The National Tariff Commission (Commission Nationale de Tarifs, or CNT), composed of government, physician, and social security representatives, would negotiate official fees (*tarifs d'autorité*) that would constitute minimum rates. Doctors could charge above these rates, but patients would be reimbursed for only 80 percent of the official fee. The *tarifs d'autorité* could be overridden, however, by departmental conventions that were to be negotiated by the departmental social security fund and the local medical unions. The departmental commissions were to be binding. Physicians pledged not to charge above the convention fees, so that patients would be reimbursed for 80 percent of the fee actually paid.

This "double system," it was hoped, would provide stronger incentives for medical unions to sign the conventions. Patients would receive much higher rates of reimbursement in departments were the conventions were in effect than under the minimal *tarifs d'autorité*, which would presumably generate pressure on local doctors to agree to the conventions. Furthermore, despite the existence of special schemes, the social security administration had become more centralized (in comparison with the 1930s), so that members of the general scheme were represented in negotiations by a single departmental fund. These funds were organized into a national organization, the Federation of Social Security Organizations (Fédération Nationale des Organismes de la Sécurité Sociale, or FNOSS), which had been created in 1945. Initially, the Social Security Ordinance of 19 October 1945 had also included a provision that allowed the funds to sign individual conventions with doctors who were ready to agree to departmental tariffs (and whose patients would therefore receive substantially higher rates of reimbursement). But this provision was vetoed by the CSMF, as were plans to allow the social security funds to invest in local health centers.

Failed negotiations

The new system of conventions was to prove no better than the prewar system, however. Already in March 1946, the CSMF denounced the system and refused to participate. The FNOSS tried many strategies to induce the CSMF to negotiate, all without success. At several points, framework agreements were signed between the FNOSS and the CSMF, only to be denounced several weeks or even days later by the CSMF.[65] The result of these failed negotiations was that even in the late 1940s, when the convention system was at its most successful, it covered only 40 percent of the insured, with many patients paying 40 to 60 percent of fees as opposed to the 20 percent specified by law.[66]

There were several underlying causes for these failures. First, within the CSMF there were sharp conflicts between physicians who supported the conventions and those who were opposed. Despite his militancy in the late 1920s, Dr. Paul Cibrie was at this point a relatively moderate leader who promoted the conventions. Most rural doctors also supported the conventions as being advantageous for their patients. It was the physicians from large cities – Paris, Lyon, and Marseilles – who opposed the conventions and were responsible for the sudden denunciations of the agreements the CSMF signed with the FNOSS.[67] The convention debate thus reflected a split between the elite practitioners in the cities, who could demand high fees, versus those in rural areas, who did not charge much more than the rates of the conventions, but whose patients suffered from the low rates of the *tarifs d'autorité*. An indication of the magnitude of this rift is the estimate that in 1957, 10 percent of the medical profession received 50 percent of the income collected from fees.[68] Thus, there was virtually a class cleavage within the medical profession. Yet for many years the elite urban practitioners were able to dominate the politics of the association, which had crystallized around the concept of liberal medicine in the late 1920s.

A second factor in the failure of the negotiations was the competition among the unions represented on the fund administrative boards and in the FNOSS. The CGT, the CGT-FO, and the CFTC all believed that doctors' fees should be regulated in some fashion, but they disagreed as to the means. These disagreements were sharpened and exaggerated by union competition during social security elections. The 1950 election was a case in point. The CGT's Henri Reynaud campaigned for "free medical care" – which would eliminate direct payment and entail third-party payment, thereby eliminating reimbursement – and for removing the employer representatives from the social security boards. The CGT-FO proposed a national health service, while the CFTC pronounced itself in favor of the conventions system and asserted that eliminating employer representation on the funds would be the first step to a government takeover of the fund administration. After the election, Reynaud stepped down as president of the FNOSS and was replaced by a CFTC leader. This was the end of good relations between the social security administration and the CGT, even though the CGT retained its position as the largest union and still held the majority of seats on the boards.[69]

Parliamentary veto

When negotiations failed, the FNOSS attempted to push for legislation. But the anti-conventionist physicians were well placed to veto parliamentary initiatives. Visits to the main parliamentary groups resulted in many bills, but no party dared to oppose the medical profession by actually introducing the bill in the National Assembly. When the CSMF denounced the agreement of January 1950 only eleven days after signing it, the FNOSS prepared draft legislation calling for third-party payment and an independent administrative body to supervise adherence to the fee schedules. Legislative proposals were introduced in the National Assembly by the Communist group, the Socialist group, and two MRP politicians. But "despite all of the interventions made to the government, [both executive and parliament] abstained from taking a position in face of the reneging of the medical profession."

Later that year, hoping to force the government to intervene, the FNOSS decided to change its strategy by simply agreeing to use the actual rates charged by doctors as the basis for the conventions – that is, in the interests of guaranteeing patients 80 percent rates of reimbursement, and thereby enhancing the value of social security coverage, the social security funds would simply abandon efforts to negotiate fee schedules that would control costs. In the short run, patients would receive satisfactory reimbursement for the first time. In the long run, the FNOSS hoped that the increasing costs of the social security system would finally jolt the government into action, and the executive would take steps to regulate doctors' fees at the national level, rather than continuing to insist that the problems of fees could be solved by local negotiations. This about-face forced a reaction, but not one satisfactory to the FNOSS. By using a method that foreshadowed the institutional innovations of the Fifth Republic, the executive administration promulgated the decree of 20 December 1950 (also called the Bacon decree after Paul Bacon, MRP Minister of Labor and Social Security), which allowed the administration to veto any conventions that "jeopardized the financial equilibrium of the funds." The CSMF retaliated by boycotting the National Tariffs Commission, the only mechanism in existence – albeit an ineffective one – for addressing the issue of doctors' fees.[70]

Executive veto

In 1953, the FNOSS and the CSMF again tried to produce an accord. This time, the agreement called for replacing the National Tariffs Commission with a bipartite "Commission of Conciliation," allowing all locally negotiated conventions to take effect automatically unless either party called in the Commission of Conciliation, and granting all doctors the right to be exempt from the convention by placing their names on a list of doctors with the right to exemptions. This accord entailed a new shift in strategy for the funds. Rather than relying on government limits on maximum fees – which in practice meant that the government simply annulled the conventions without resolving the problems of reimbursement to the insured – the exemptions now provided a positive incentive for the signing of conventions that would increase reimbursement to the insured, while still allowing doctors to charge what they wanted.

An example will clarify the financial implications of these different payment systems. At the end of 1959, the official fee for a consultation was 320 francs in a city of more than 100,000 inhabitants. The average convention set the rate at about 600 francs. But doctors in the Seine Department charged between 1,000 and 1,200 francs. Thus, a Paris patient might pay 1,000 francs for a consultation, and be reimbursed 256 francs (80 percent of 320) under the official fee schedule, paying a total of 744 francs. A patient in an urban department covered by a convention, on the other hand, would pay 600 francs and be reimbursed 480 (80 percent of 600), a total of 120 francs. If, however, the Paris doctor was allowed an exemption from the fee schedule, his patient would also receive 480 francs rather tnan 120, thereby paying 520 francs (1,000 − 480), not 744.[71]

It is this discrepancy that made the issue of exemptions so central to the discussions over the conventions. Once again, however, the solution acceptable to the funds and the CSMF was not acceptable to the administration. Minister of Labor Bacon blocked the legislation needed to introduce these changes on the grounds that the revised system offered no effective controls on medical fees and that it would cost the social security funds an estimated 30–35 billion francs annually.[72] Consequently, by 1954, only 20 percent of the insured were covered by conventions, and patients were paying as much as 70 percent of doctors' bills.[73]

THE GAZIER PROPOSAL

The culmination of these struggles came in 1956 with the Gazier proposal, drawn up by socialist Albert Gazier, Minister of Social Affairs in the government of Guy Mollet. As part of the fiscal and price policies of the Mollet government, Gazier proposed to control doctors' fees by limiting fee increases to the rate of inflation. The proposal was no more popular than the other Mollet measures, which were attacked by all of the main producer organizations (CNPF, CGPME, CGC, CFTC, and CGT), and it was met by the same kind of public outcry and personal attacks on its author as the Swedish Höjer proposal, which will be discussed in Chapter 5.[74]

The project incorporated several points from the 1953 CSMF-FNOSS accord, but it also included several provisions meant to limit fees more effectively. The conventions would be limited by ceilings on fees set at the ministerial level and would be indexed to the cost of living and the minimum wage. Thus, there was a definite cap on the maximum fees that could be charged. Although a maximum of 15 percent of physicians would be allowed to charge above the convention fee schedule, the right to do so was to be based on "objective" rather than "subjective" conditions. The conditions were to be set out by law and to be approved in advance rather than being subject to the discretion of the individual physician.[75] Furthermore, patients of these doctors could not be reimbursed by social security, thereby adding a definite negative incentive to patients. Once the 15 percent limit was reached, moreover, the social security funds would be allowed to set up their own health centers or to sign individual conventions with doctors – provisions that the funds had demanded since the 1920s. In case of a breach of the conventions, the project's sanctions included a 1–6 month suspension for first offenders, 1–3 years for repeat offenders.

In effect, the Gazier proposal put to use the monopsony power of collective payments. Caps on fees would be set at the national level and indexed to inflation. Doctors who chose to ignore the fees would be excluded from social security practice (in a sense creating a closed panel). If too many doctors left the system, the social security funds would be free to establish forms of medical practice – local health centers and individual contracts – to which the profession was opposed.

Rural doctors were prepared to accept the Gazier proposal, whereas the urban elite, as so often before, was opposed. At the CSMF General Assembly of 14–16 December 1956, representatives of 13,264 doctors voted against the project and representatives of 12,616 doctors voted in support of continued negotiations. An analysis in the *Concours Médical* of 22 December 1956 showed that the vote was clearly split along urban-rural lines, with the urban delegates voting against the project and the rural delegates voting for negotiation.[76]

The Gazier proposal was adopted by the Cabinet (Conseil des Ministres) on 30 January 1957. On February 2, Dr. Cibrie left the governing board of the CSMF and was replaced by an anti-conventionist, Dr. Jonchères. At this point, the opposition of the medical association became more vigorous and the campaign in the press and in parliament more definite. Attacks on Gazier in the newspapers were extremely harsh. Particularly striking was a series of articles in the *Paris-Presse-Intransigent* that became notorious for their illustrations of "the brain of M. Gazier" – complete with diagrammed sections, such as "allergy to liberal medicine," "excessive admiration of the English system," "too fond a memory of Molière" – and the claim that Gazier was a CGT "militant."[77] The governing board of the CSMF announced its "absolute opposition to the Gazier project . . . without nuance nor attenuation . . . This proposal limits, in effect, the right of the sick to choose their doctor freely . . . and submits the exercise of a delicate profession to servitudes, controls and sanctions."[78]

The Ordre des Médecins and the Academy of Medicine announced that they were opposed to the reform. Doctors organized parliamentary opposition to the proposal, and the Independent deputies of the Seine announced that, "considering that the bureaucratization of the medical profession would be merely the prelude to the nationalization (*étatisation*) of all of the liberal professions . . . the Independent deputies of the Seine will demand that their group reconsider their positions vis-à-vis the government," and referred to the Gazier proposal as "a grave attack on the traditional liberal activities of the nation, and furthermore a supplementary cost that the ensemble of contributors are not in the position to support."[79] Thus, although the medical profession was in fact divided about evenly on the issue of doctors' fees, the liberal faction was able to use its contacts in the press and in parliament to put up resistance to the reform. Nevertheless, the project was approved by the Labor Committee of the National Assembly, with the Socialist, Communist, and MRP representatives voting for the project, the moderates, Poujadists, and Republican Socialists voting against, and the Radicals absent. In the end, however, the fate of the Gazier proposal was sealed when the Mollet government fell in May 1957.[80]

Politics of the Fourth Republic

With the unstable governments and parliamentary stalemate of the Fourth Republic, a little interest-group resistance could go a long way. Groups within parliament could be persuaded to take up the cause of interest groups in opposition to the ruling parties. Moreover, agreement on legislation was unnecessary. Interest groups opposed to legislation needed only to delay the process with negotiations, new proposals, and other maneuvers until the parliamentary coalition collapsed. For the duration of the Fourth Republic, the issue of doctors' fees proved irresolvable. Opponents of the conventions blocked both local conventions and national agreements between the FNOSS and the CSMF. Parliamentary recourse was ineffectual for the FNOSS. When agreements, heavily weighted to the advantage of the medical profession, were finally reached, they were squelched by the executive branch of government out of concern for the large cost increases that they would entail.

This impasse is a stereotypical example of the problems of the Fourth Republic. Weakened by a lack of party discipline and the access of a select number of interest groups to the "political class," where unstable parliamentary coalitions resulted in the fall of one government after another, the parliamentary rule of the Fourth Republic has been characterized as opportunistic at best and incapable of any action whatsoever at worst.[81] Without an effective parliamentary majority, members of parliament were free to propose or veto legislation based on personal bargains and constituency wishes. This created many opportunities for interest groups, particularly those that preferred that legislation not be enacted – that is, those that wished to preserve the status quo.

The politics of the Fourth Republic stymied hospital policy as well. Plans for more efficient hospital administration had been submitted to the National Assembly in 1954 and 1957, but political stalemate had precluded any action. These plans proposed the introduction of full-time positions for hospital physicians and stressed the need for "de-politicizing" the hospitals. Hospital administrative boards, according to reformers within the Ministry of Health and parliament, were made inefficient by their ties to local political structures. All decisions were said to be subject to "double" supervision, as they were required to be submitted to both the local municipal council and the departmental Prefect for approval.

The Barrot report of 1957 proposed that the power of professional administrators and the Prefect should be increased at the expense of the local municipal councils. The rationale behind these changes was that hospitals now served more than one local area and that decisions therefore should be made by a body with a larger frame of reference than a single commune. The Barrot report was presented as "a middle way between the partisans of immediate nationalisation and the defenders of local liberties . . . [that] sought a harmonious synthesis of projects of governmental origins with parliamentary propositions." Concretely, the project proposed that the administrative boards should no longer be presided over by the local mayor – who, not incidentally, was quite often a doctor. The deliberations of the administrative board should no longer be submitted to the municipal councils for approval, and hospital loans would no longer be required to be guaranteed by the communes.[82]

DIRECT EXECUTIVE RULE: THE DEBRÉ REFORM AND THE DECREES OF 12 MAY 1960

With the emergence of the Fifth Republic, the rules of the game were radically changed. The inability of the governments of the Fourth Republic to deal effectively with the Algerian crisis provided the opportunity for de Gaulle to take power once again, but this time, in contrast to the Liberation period, de Gaulle was successful in redesigning French political institutions. The thrust of the institutional reform was to create an independent and powerful executive, capable of governing despite the difficulty of achieving parliamentary majorities.

The constitution of the Fifth Republic effectively separated the executive and legislative powers – enhancing the powers of the executive while limiting those of the legislature. The President of the Republic would be elected – until 1962 by an electoral college, after 1962 by direct suffrage – rather than be appointed by parliament. The President would name the Prime Minister, but the executive government was nevertheless to be "responsible" to parliament. The system thus remained parliamentary rather than presidential, with dual leadership in place of direct parliamentary rule.[83]

As it was thought that MPs eligible for ministerial posts had an incentive to provoke governmental crises in order to vie for better portfolios –

a thesis that MacRae has since disproved – a greater cost both for entering the government and for dissolving it was added: Ministers would be required to give up their parliamentary seats, and if the government fell, they might be left without a parliamentary fallback.[83a] The respective roles of executive and parliament in drafting legislation were also revised. The executive was given expanded powers to issue legislation directly by decrees and ordinances and to put legislation before the public in referenda. The role of parliament, on the other hand, was restricted to legislation that was considered "law-making" rather than "rule-making," a distinction that would require legal interpretation.

Finally, the electoral system was changed from proportional representation (which had been gradually limited by changes in electoral laws during the Fourth Republic) to a majority system based on two rounds of voting, as under the Third Republic. In contrast to the Third Republic, however, limits were placed on participation in the second round that reduced the number of parties that could compete, thereby introducing a pressure for party consolidation and effectively changing the party system under the Fifth Republic.

It is important to separate the impact of these constitutional provisions on the political practices of the Fifth Republic in general from those that were relevant for health policy specifically. To introduce health policy reform, the executive government relied on its new prerogative to issue legislation directly by decree – thereby circumventing the parliamentary veto point. Not only was direct executive legislation by decree clearly and specifically related to these reforms, but the area of health policy was used as a test case for asserting the enlarged scope of the decree. (The decree method itself was not new. What was new was a clarification of the right of the executive to use the decree.)

The executive confirmed the formal powers granted in the constitution by immediately putting the decree to use – a good example of how policy issues can be utilized as vehicles for defining the practical meanings of institutions. The decree method has continued to be used during the Fifth Republic, and has become important for policy making generally. However, according to Duverger, the most important sources of long-term stability for the Fifth Republic are the changes in the electoral laws and the direct election of the President, which counteracted the tendency of the political parties toward unbridled electoral competition and organizational scission, and hence changed the behavior of politicians during parliamentary deliberations and the policy process.[84]

Health reform by executive fiat

Within two years of taking office, de Gaulle's government enacted reforms that reorganized the hospital system, introduced full-time salaried practice for hospital physicians, regulated doctors' fees, and expanded executive control over the social security administration. Repeating the pattern of the Liberation, the reforms were introduced through a series of ordinances and decrees, rather than by laws voted on in parliament. The reforms were thus issued directly by the executive without need for parliamentary approval, and in fact were issued over parliamentary and interest-group resistance. The reform proposals themselves were not based on new ideas or new analyses of the problems of French health care; they were, in fact, similar to the suggestions of the Gazier proposal, the Barrot report, and the administration's initial concept of the social security scheme in 1945. Nor can the changes be explained in terms of shifts in the opinions of the interest groups; comparison of the politics of the Fourth and Fifth Republics will show that the decisive shift was in the instruments of rule rather than a shift in interest-group opinion.

There is, however, a political shift in the transition from the Fourth Republic to the Fifth Republic that is worth making explicit. As in previous episodes of reform, institutional failure – and specifically the behavior of the political parties and parliamentary stalemate – resulted in political crisis and a widespread lack of legitimacy of the institutions. Foreign policy embarrassment, in particular, damaged the legitimacy of the Third and Fourth Republics. This intangible factor provided the political consensus for institutional reforms that allowed the executive to introduce either temporary or permanent procedural changes. These changes, in turn, concretely expanded the ability of the executive to act, in ways that outlived the particular crisis that had provided the impetus for institutional reform.

The political context of the Liberation period and the birth of the Fifth Republic explains why new institutional mechanisms could be introduced, and it affected the interpretation of the legitimate use of these mechanisms. As we will see, however, it was the institutional mechanisms themselves that allowed the passage of the new legislation. For despite the atmosphere of crisis and political consensus for strong executive leadership in these two periods, when it came time to introduce specific policies, all of the old actors reappeared and tried to use the old mechanisms to block the legislation. To the extent that the old institutional veto points remained effective, these groups successfully forced major revisions in the legislation, as in 1930 and 1946–7. But in the case of the Fifth Republic, constitutional reform made the executive independent of the parliamentary veto point, and the reforms withstood interest-group efforts to rely on the old institutions to undermine the reforms.

The Debré reform

The constitution of the Fifth Republic was ratified on 4 October 1958; only two months later the executive exercised its right to legislate by decree in the health area. The executive promulgated a series of decrees and ordinances in December 1958 that reformed the hospital system and set limits on doctors' fees. In May 1960, additional decrees were added to further regulate doctors' fees and to place the social security administration more directly under executive supervision. The hospital reform was prepared by a commission headed by Professor Robert Debré (father of Michel Debré, who as Minister of Justice drafted the 1958 constitution and later served as Prime Minister). The principles of the Debré reform were not new. Many of its elements came from previous proposals, and other elements were taken from Debré's ideas about the need for a French national health service that had been published in 1944.

Debré was a known but controversial figure within elite medical circles, having challenged the establishment during the debates in 1945 and 1946 about medical reforms and direct payment. The Debré commission had been appointed in 1956 by the Mollet government, and many of its concrete proposals – in particular the administrative changes – reiterated the recommendations of the Barrot reports of 1954 and 1957. Debré viewed the reform as a way to modernize the hospital system, reform medical education, and especially to improve the status of scientific medicine. Like other reformers put into a position of power by the change of regime, Debré saw the state as an agent of modernization, whereas older institutions and the political relationships of the Fourth Republic were, in his eyes, impediments to modernization. Pointing to "a veritable sclerosis of ancient institutions," Debré argued in his draft proposal that France was "[E]nslaved to an artisanal tradition poorly understood [and hence] considerably behind in the domain of medical research."[85] The public good was to be served by reforming medical agencies, and in order to do so a process was to be used that avoided the old barriers to reform.

Three ideas were central to the reform. First, health care needed to be organized in a more rational manner – using government to reorganize the hospital system on a regional basis, with distinctions made between different types of hospitals and the types of medical technology that were appropriate for each. This meant that governmental authorities should also be able to control the growth of the private hospital sector. Second, the practice of doctors of dividing their time between hospitals and private offices and clinics had to be rationalized. Private practice was creating incentives for doctors to devote their time to outside private patients, rather than encouraging them to carry out medical research. The Debré reform sought to create more full-time salaried posts for hospital physicians and to improve their ability to combine effectively clinical work, teaching and medical research. Third, and less publicized than the other two ideas of the reform, was an effort to ensure that hospital posts for assistant doctors were awarded on the basis of merit and not patronage, a patronage that was indeed often anti-Jewish.

The Ordinance of 30 December 1958 fused teaching hospitals and the biggest regional hospitals into a new system of Centres Hospitalo-Universitaires. These were to provide highly specialized medical treatment and a base for expanding the clinical portion of medical training. The new system established a rank-order among hospitals, important for coordinated planning because it established priorities for the distribution of medical equipment and defined more clearly the responsibilities of different types of hospitals. In the name of efficiency, hospital administrative boards were made more independent from local political entities, as suggested by the Barrot proposal, although the mayors were not removed from the presidency of the boards. Further departing from the Barrot project, the social security funds (and hence the unions) as well as hospital physicians were given a larger role on the administrative boards. In line with this effort, private hospitals or clinics could no longer be built or expanded without the approval of the Minister of Health. Further, the Ordinance of 30 December 1958 reformed the system of medical education so that hospital appointments would no longer be completely controlled by senior physicians – the *"grands patrons"* – of French medicine. Finally, the reform introduced full-time salaried practice for hospital doctors. As a transitional measure, senior doctors would be able to treat a limited number of private patients, but eventually all doctors were to be hired on a full-time salaried basis.[86]

In sum, relying on the mechanism of direct executive legislation, the de Gaulle government moved swiftly and decisively to introduce a series of measures that changed the role of the state in health care planning and revised the status of hospital doctors. The irrational mix of private and public hospital provision was to be rationalized, hospital doctors were to become full-time salaried employees of the government, and the prerogative of hospital chiefs of staff to chose their younger assistants unilaterally was to be curtailed by a competitive examination system. In terms of the economic autonomy of doctors, the reform aimed to restrict the ability of hospital doctors to choose their site of practice at will, thereby concentrating hospital practice within public hospitals, and separating this form of practice from that in private offices and private clinics. The role of hospital doctors as entrepreneurs would be reduced, but their status as scientists and their access to medical technology would be improved.

Decrees of 12 May

The same institutional mechanism and political understanding was used to introduce reforms of the ambulatory sector and social security administration. Again, the policy ideas themselves were ideas from the Fourth Republic, and the people who carried them out had been active during that period. The difference was the new political and institutional opportunity for translating the policy plans into legislation, without parliamentary veto, and hence without concessions to interest groups. For the reform of social security and doctors' fees, the counterpart to Debré was Minister of Labor Bacon. Like Debré, Bacon, a member of the MRP and long active in health insurance issues in his capacity as Minister of Labor during many years of the Fourth Republic, viewed an increased regulatory capacity for the executive government as critical for solving the problems of the social security system. Direct governmental control of doctors' fees and direct governmental management of the social security administration were to overcome the perceived irrationalities of health insurance. The convention system was not effectively limiting doctors' fees, and as a result, patients throughout France were receiving low and widely varying rates of reimbursement, even though they paid the same social security contributions. The administration of the funds was thought to be inefficient and not cost-effective, not only because of the problems of doctors' fees, but also because of the self-administration of the social security funds.

One current theory was that because the social security funds were themselves composed largely of representatives of unions, the administrative boards of the funds paid their employees at exorbitant rates. Legal decrees passed during the 1950s aimed to strengthen administrative control over the funds by the Minister of Labor, and by the regional directors responsible to him. Concretely, these resulted in more frequent vetoes of local administrative board decisions by the regional directors. These directors, responsible to the Minister of Labor, became increasingly involved in questions of detail, blocking relatively minor decisions, which resulted in aggravated relations between the elected administrative boards and the regional directors. As we saw, the Minister of Labor had also used decrees to annul overly costly conventions.[87]

Control of medical fees. The plan that was prepared to address these problems was, like the Debré reform, based on older proposals, and in fact consisted mainly of points that the executive administration had not been able to introduce at the Liberation. Now, the mechanism of direct executive legislation was used to expand the regulatory capacity of the executive over the protests of doctors and unions. In order to regulate doctors' fees, the executive administration would set maximum fees, and drafted a standard convention to which departmental negotiations were required to conform. In addition, a market incentive for the signing of conventions was now added; the highly contested individual convention was finally introduced. The ordinance of 30 December 1958 temporarily solved the problem of the conventions by setting a maximum tariff that could not be superseded through negotiations. The government was given the power to establish a standard convention to be used as a model for departmental conventions.

Within another seventeen months, the decrees of 12 May 1960 established a more permanent solution. First, the decrees replaced the tripartite National Tariffs Commission with an Interministerial Tariffs Commission composed of representatives of the Ministers of Health, Labor, and Finances. This step transferred ultimate authority over the conventions from a tripartite commission that included representatives of the medical profession to an exclusively governmental committee. This committee would set maximum tariff ceilings for the negotiated conventions, as well as *tarifs d'autorité*. All conventions would require the approval of this committee. Second, the decrees established a model convention for departmental negotiations. Third, and possibly most important, the decrees allowed doctors in departments where no conventions had been concluded to sign individual contracts with the regional social security funds. Patients of these doctors would be reimbursed at more favorable rates than would patients who sought care from doctors who refused to sign. Doctors adhering to conventions would also be given tax advantages and social benefits. These provisions, it will be recalled, were all part of the first draft of the 1945 Social Security Ordinances, which had been removed at the insistence of the CSMF. Though milder than the Gazier proposal,[88] the reforms of 12 May 1960 unilaterally imposed a workable system of conventions that was rapidly extended to the majority of French doctors.

Administrative reform. The administrative reform increased the direct power of the regional social security directors – responsible to the Minister of Labor – at the expense of the elected administrative boards. Like doctors' fees, this was an old issue. Even in 1945, the relative powers of the regional social security directors and the administrative boards had been hotly debated. At that time, employers and the administration, arguing in the name of fiscal responsibility and efficient management, had urged a greater role for the regional directors, whereas the unions had been unified in their fight for the autonomy of the elected boards. Although the unions prevailed on this issue, the administration had given the regional directors the right to veto the decisions of the administrative boards and had cut short plans to grant the boards a larger role in social security administration. As concerns about the social security deficit increased, tensions between the elected boards and the regional administrators were aggravated, especially as the deficit was blamed on mismanagement and waste.

Not only was the mechanism for the introduction of the reforms directly related to the new constitution, but the political rationale for the reforms was based on the need to solidify the new regime. Health policy provided an opportunity to show that the Fifth Republic could distinguish itself from the stalemate politics of the Fourth Republic, a regime characterized by its inability to do anything.[89] The reforms were part of a political program of creating a more important role for the executive and of a policy agenda of modernizing the economy and improving the governmental capacity to regulate the economy. Health care became a test case for this executive vision. Both the social security reform and the hospital reform aimed to isolate health care agencies from political interests and to move decision making into the sphere of technical rationality. Bacon explicitly viewed the social security reform as a means, "to restore the authority of the State." Indeed, it was his interest in the administrative reform that broke the logjam on doctors' fees. By tying the administrative reform to the controls on fees – for so many years a demand of the funds – Bacon hoped to force the funds to accept a reduction in their administrative autonomy. He counted on the fact that the public would be more interested in the increase in social security benefits than in administrative changes, so that the funds would have trouble protesting the decrees.[90] The same motivations help to explain the Debré reform. The health-care planning aspects were certainly important, but from the point of view of the administration this reform fitted neatly with its efforts to enhance the power of the executive and of its regional representatives, while weakening the power of local elites represented by municipal councils and mayors.[91]

VETO EFFORTS

During the preparation of both the Debré reform and the social security reform, opportunities for interest-group influence were sharply curtailed. The reforms were prepared at the highest ministerial levels, and interministerial cooperation was used so that the Ministers of Education, Finance, and Justice could counterbalance any efforts by the medical profession to intervene through the Ministry of Health.[92] Despite these precautions and the use of the decree mechanism, interest-group protests erupted.

Charging that the executive was carrying out a "politics of fait accompli," the CSMF General Assembly of 4–6 December 1959 announced that it was "indignant that the medical profession had not been consulted regarding the principles and the text of this convention . . . [and] rejects a priori all regulatory or legal texts that have not been submitted previously to the medical profession."[93] When the reform was announced in February 1960, the CSMF stated:

The Confederation of French Medical Unions cannot accept that the problems posed by the reimbursement of medical fees cannot be solved in a manner comparable to that used to resolve problems of labor: mediation. . . . The introduction of individual conventions constitutes an inadmissible attack on the principles of unionism. . . . In other words, medical fees will become an affair of the

State, and, at the same time, the profession will cease, in our point of view, to be a liberal profession, because it will lose, definitively, its economic independence.[94]

The French hospital elite, represented by the Paris medical press and the prestigious Academy of Medicine, opposed the Debré reform – and particularly the salary issue. Younger doctors, on the other hand, were ready for a reform of the rigid hierarchy of the hospital. Provincial doctors also were more receptive to the hospital reform; private practice was simply not as prevalent nor as lucrative.[95] As in previous attempts at reform, the medical opinion was split along rural-urban and age lines. And once again, the elite of the profession attempted to use its political contacts to veto the reform.

French doctors fought the decrees in the courts, in parliament, and in the market. In each case, however, the new institutional independence of the executive protected the administration from these old weapons. The hospital elite challenged the Debré reform in court. But the Constitutional Council, which had been created by the 1958 constitution, upheld the reform in January 1960 as consistent with executive power as defined by the new constitution. A group of well-known doctors who had taken part in the Resistance attempted to approach de Gaulle directly about the reform, but met with a singular lack of success. De Gaulle is reported to have said, "I saved France on the salary of a colonel. With the billions I give you, make me good medicine."[96]

In the legislature, an absolute majority in the Senate (155 senators belonging to the Independents, the Gauche Démocratique, the Peasants, or unaffiliated, and three former Ministers of Health) and an absolute majority in the National Assembly (241 deputies, including about half of the Gaullist UNR deputies) presented propositions for new laws to regulate relations between the medical profession and the social insurance funds. Nevertheless, although members of parliament remained loyal to the doctors – conceivably in order to reassert parliamentary control over legislation – the executive refused to consider revoking or amending the decrees.[97] Symbolically, these refusals to depart from authoritarian decrees signaled that the era of the local notable and the "Old Boys' Republic" (*République des Camarades*) was at an end.

Efforts to block the new system through the market arena proved equally unsuccessful. On 15 May, the Medical Union of the Seine called for an administrative strike, which was carried out by the CSMF on 17 May 1960. Doctors continued to treat patients, but they refused to fill out any of the forms required for the social security funds. Medical unions claimed that 80 percent of doctors in the Seine Department participated in the strike, as well as doctors belonging to the Union of Hospital Physicians (Intersyndicat des Hôpitaux). But the administration simply refused to negotiate. Although there is a widespread assumption that medical strikes can paralyze governments, this strike was ineffective as a political weapon, even though the participation of doctors was high. The strike continued in the Seine until 25 October 1960, when it was finally abandoned. The momentum for the strike was broken by the refusal of the administration to back down and the incentive for individual doctors to defect from the medical unions by signing individual conventions.[98]

Realizing that its chances of intervention had been "singularly reduced in the political context of the Fifth Republic,"[99] the CSMF decided to accept the idea of the model convention, and even the individual convention. The changed institutional context thus changed the balance of power within the profession. Faced with an executive fiat, the CSMF ignored the urban practitioners, who continued the strike, and went with the provincial doctors who had supported the conventions since 1945.[100] On 19 July 1960 the CSMF signed a supplementary agreement with the FNOSS that was to start the process of negotiation at the departmental level.[101] Some doctors were not as willing to compromise, however, and a group of hardliners broke away from the CSMF, forming a rival union, the Union for the Reform of the Decrees of 12 May (Union Syndicale pour la Réforme des Décrets du 12 Mai, or USR). After successive scissions and fusions, this organization became the Union of French Physicians (Union Syndicale des Médecins de France, or USMF), which eventually merged with two other medical unions, the Association of Physicians for Medical Union (Association des Médecins pour la Recherche de l'Union Syndicale, or AMRUS) and the National Federation of French General Practitioners (Fédération Nationale des Médecins Généralistes Français, or FNMG), to form the Federation of French Physicians (Fédération des Médecins de France, or FMF).[102]

Union and small business protests

Doctors were not the only group to oppose the government. The organization of sickness funds (FNOSS), as well as the individual unions – CFTC, CGT, and CGT-FO – were adamantly opposed to the administrative takeover of the funds, which the CGT called "a serious attack upon the democratic principles of the administrative boards." All unions were united in their opposition to the "nationalization" of the funds, as they called it – as were the local insurance funds. Both the FNOSS and the Government Council on Social Insurance (Conseil Supérieur d'Assurances Sociales) publicly stated that they opposed the decrees.[103] As Bacon had calculated when he insisted upon cementing the administrative reform to the controls on fees, the unions backed down in light of the benefits increase to their members.

Small employers, too, opposed the decrees on the grounds that they interfered with the freedom of the medical profession, and because they were concerned with the absorption of the special schemes for the self-employed under a "public service of social security."[104] After the passage of the reform, the newspaper of the CGPME, *Volonté* urged, "for the defense of liberties, solidarity with the doctors." The Executive Committee of the CGPME stated that it was

concerned to see, little by little, the different professional activities that depend upon the freedom of entrepreneurship struck down by measures seeking to limit their rights, to put a brake on their initiatives and to impose on them regulation subordinating them to the good will of the public authorities . . . [it] sees in the reactions of the medical profession to these measures, reactions identical to those of other professional categories each time that they find themselves faced with dispositions that entail their bureaucratization.[105]

Nevertheless, the alliance between the small businessmen and the doctors remained theoretical. Without the route of independent parliamentary disruption, these groups had lost their political leverage. The only interest group that favored the reforms was the association of employers (Conseil National du Patronat Français, or CNPF), which was dominated by industrialists. Large employers supported both the controls on doctors' fees and the administrative reorganization as cost-cutting measures, in line with their demands that the state take firmer steps in controlling the economy. This employer opinion, however, was not a sudden shift; the CNPF had voiced its concern with cost-cutting during the preparation of the Gazier proposal.[106]

Regime change and reform

We could look at the remarkable number of changes made in French health care between 1958 and 1960 as an inevitable result of the modernization of medicine. Or we could attribute the transformation to changes in the leadership of the CSMF, to pressures on the leadership from younger doctors and from provincial doctors, and to a decrease in the importance of an organization of private office practitioners as modern technology made the hospital the focus of medical practice. And it is indeed true that there were such pressures on the CSMF. Provincial doctors were pushing for a change. Hospital doctors were set apart from the CSMF, in a separate organization that no longer cooperated with the CSMF leadership. There were younger, more far-sighted doctors clamoring for reform. Much has also been made of the fact that the CSMF leadership changed in 1961 to the more moderate Dr. Monier. However, this change in leadership occurred after the debacle.

Explanations based on the modernization of medicine and changes within the medical profession are not convincing, because all of these conditions existed prior to the regime shift. Since 1945, the CSMF had been pressured by provincial doctors, yet the leadership consistently pursued policies that benefited only the elite practitioners in the big cities, rather than the majority of the membership. Nor could it be claimed that the medical profession had suddenly lost public credibility; for years, there had been charges that the issue of doctors' fees was merely one of monetary gain. Instead, the abrupt shift in the ability of the CSMF to block controls on doctors' fees is better accounted for by the shift in political opportunities available to doctors under the changed political circumstances of the Fifth Republic.

Social explanations emphasizing the demands of other interest groups are similarly incapable of explaining the health reforms. The social security funds and the unions had demanded controls on doctors' fees for 30 years. There is simply no evidence that the interest of these groups in fee controls or their ability to pressure the government suddenly increased in 1958. Indeed, given the fact that the funds and the unions lost on the issue of administrative change, the opposite seems true – the power of the unions was reduced under the Fifth Republic. The only social impetus for the health and social security reforms was the continued pressure from the CNPF for cost controls.

The abrupt shift in French health policy in 1958 to 1960 is best explained by institutional change. The overall logic of the health reform, consistent with the CNPF demands, was one of redefining the role of the executive by expanding its functions and its jurisdictional domain. The executive took the opportunity presented by the change in constitutional regime as a chance to restructure the social security system and the relationship between the medical profession and the state. The institutional changes allowed the executive to impose reforms unimpeded by parliament and the opportunities for interest-group influence that it permitted. Health policy was used as one of several vehicles for enlarging the powers of the executive government and solidifying the public support for this regime shift.

RESULTS AND AFTERMATH OF REFORM

From the point of view of encouraging the signing of conventions, the decrees of 12 May 1960 were an unqualified success. By October 1960, 65 conventions had been signed, covering roughly 7 out of 13 million insured people (54 percent). In departments without conventions, about 40 percent of the doctors signed individual conventions, so that by 1962, nearly 80 percent of all doctors in private practice had agreed to abide by the conventions.[107] The reform increased social security benefits (and expenditures) considerably.[108] Although the system did provide for exemptions from the fee schedule, with the competition from doctors adhering to conventions, the frequency of extra-billing was lower than originally feared by the funds.[109] The medical profession also demanded that the interministerial tarifs commission be changed back to a tripartite commission, through its participation on a commission set up by the decrees of 12 May to evaluate the reform.[110] Nevertheless, in contrast to the situation in the Fourth Republic where each change in the negotiating framework further incapacitated the conventions system, a new regime was permanently introduced.

The constitution of the Fifth Republic thus permitted the executive to introduce permanent changes in French social security, hospitals, and the conditions of practice for doctors. Both the changes in the political institutions and the changes in the organization of the health care system were to influence the subsequent development of health reforms. The convention system spread first at the departmental level, then later extended to the national level in 1971. The new national convention covered all physicians, but they were able to opt out. Thus, the burden was no longer on each departmental social security fund and medical union to negotiate a new convention. Instead, those doctors who did not wish to be covered needed to take the step of disengaging from the convention. As of 1976, only 4 percent had opted out, leaving 96 percent of physicians covered by the conventions. Of these conventioned doctors, 13 percent had the right to override the tariffs. When increased numbers of hospital physicians entered, the percentage grew to 18 percent.[111] At the same time, although the conventions provided for a certain number of physicians to override the tariffs, the conventions introduced mechanisms for controlling the practices of physicians through statistical checks. In fact, one of the problems with fee schedules was that they controlled only the price per service and not the total number of services performed. In 1979, an effort was made to link the total amount spent by social security on doctors' fees to the growth of the GNP, similar to what Gazier proposed in 1956. Although this idea of a cap or envelope on total fees was opposed by doctors, efforts by the government to pursue the cap informally rather than by government fiat in the late 1980s met with some success.[112]

Similarly, the administrative reforms of 12 May 1960 were the first step in a restructuring of the social security organization that was later extended. The Ordinance of 21 August 1967 – also unilaterally imposed by the executive government – eliminated the social security elections, revised the ratio of employer to employee delegates from 1:2 to 1:1, and separated the risks of old-age, illness, and family allowances into three separate schemes.[113] As in the nineteenth century, executive intervention was used to limit political representation in the sickness funds.

For the hospital sector, the Debré reform, though slow to be implemented, was eventually responsible for the addition of a large number of salaried, full-time hospital posts.[114] The 1970 Hospital Law built on the preliminary discussions of the Debré committee on the relationship of the public and the private hospital sectors, establishing a national hospital service, and a national plan (*carte sanitaire*) that would govern the distribution of hospital beds and equipment throughout France.[115] In 1982, the socialist government eliminated private beds from public hospitals and provided for the phasing out of private consultations, as had been envisioned by the Debré reform.[116] Both reforms were introduced through parliamentary votes along party lines, although doctors availed themselves of declining attendance, which increased their relative percentage of votes in parliament, to add late changes.[117] The socialist policy of eliminating private practice from public hospitals, as well as efforts to change the internal structure of hospitals by fusing departments and reducing the independence of the hospital chiefs of staff, has since been reversed under more conservative governments. But a lasting change in hospital policy was the introduction of global hospital budgets in 1984.

CONSTITUTIONAL RULES AND HEALTH POLITICS

French political institutions are critical for explaining both the French pattern of interest-group behavior and the specific sets of health insurance policies that emerged from these episodes of legislative reform. Constitutional rules and electoral results (some of which can be traced back to electoral rules) established an institutional context that provided incentives, opportunities, and constraints to political and social actors engaged in health and other policy conflicts. Although policy making is sometimes considered as separate from electoral and legislative politics, the French case has shown that institutions affect the legislation that sets specific policies in motion and the interest-group bargaining that surrounds the legislative process. The institutions did not determine the range of policies considered or the interests of specific groups – that is, institutional constraints did not screen out particular ideas or interests. Rather, the institutions affected both the ability of executive governments to introduce new policies and the incentives to politicians in parliament to depart from the executive program.

As explained at the beginning of this chapter, the parliament of the Third and Fourth Republics constituted a veto point because the lack of electoral majorities and the lack of party discipline impeded the development of unified parliamentary coalitions. According to the constitutions of both Republics, the political executive was to carry out the wishes of the parliamentary majority. But because these majorities did not exist, the two branches of government functioned at cross-purposes. Indeed, by strengthening the principle of direct parliamentary rule and adding proportional representation, simultaneously increasing the importance of parliament and decreasing the probability of decisive majorities, the constitution of the Fourth Republic exacerbated these problems. Most often, when executive ministers proposed legislation, it stagnated in parliament until the government fell through ministerial crises. The underlying electoral competition and the fact that MPs were not bound to follow a particular majority coalition allowed parliamentary decision making to be pulled in a number of directions at once, rather than being limited by a single electoral result and the establishment of a ruling party or coalition. This parliamentary behavior caused the legislative difficulties of the Third and Fourth Republics, and provided the impetus for the theory of the strong executive and the political consensus for modifying political institutions to establish routes for direct executive action.

This political and institutional framework set the terms for interest group influence. As long as MPs were unconstrained by adherence to an executive program, electoral ambitions and personalized bargaining made them open to influence. The key to influence, however, was to reach the MPs critical to the coalition; those outside the coalitions could not use the threat of defection to pull in the votes of fellow coalition partners necessary to pass or to veto legislation. Through their concentration in particular parliamentary committees, the effects of these MPs became even further pronounced. When the constitution of the Fifth Republic permitted the political executive, and in particular the cabinet ministers, to circumvent parliament, the parliamentary veto point became irrelevant, and although interest-group demands and their organizations remained unchanged, their political impact declined abruptly.

These institutional dynamics explain the impact of the French medical profession on health policy, as well as that of other groups. When parliament constituted the locus of decision making, elite medical practitioners had a direct source of access that was used to block controls on doctors' fees and other government incursions on private medical practice. Indeed, this parliamentary access point allowed the elite physicians to bypass the decisions made by medical association leaders and the more moderate provincial physicians, who were in fact in the majority. The Social Insurance Laws of 1928 and 1930 constitute a rare instance of successful legislation in the Third Republic. But even then, the legislation was enacted under the extremely unusual circumstance of the recovery of Alsace-Lorraine, and the legislation was not only rescinded, but emerged riddled with concessions to interest groups introduced by the parliamentary commissions. The same pattern was repeated after the Second World War. After a brief period of direct executive rule, parliamentary stalemate and opportunities for interest-group influence reemerged.

The medical profession was not the only group to avail itself of these opportunities – farmers, the mutualist movement, shopkeepers, employers, and the Catholic unions all gained concessions. The groups that were privileged by these institutions, however, were those of interest to members of the governing coalition. Furthermore, as the majority would have had to hold together to produce legislation, this route of influence was more conducive to negative demands than positive ones. The result was success for those who demanded to block changes in the status quo; exemptions from legislation or policy blockage were the prevalent policy results. Thus, it was not parliamentary access per se but importance (either personal or electoral) for MPs in the coalition that was the key to influence.

These conditions were changed by the constitution of the Fifth Republic. For many years, the liberal wing of the medical profession had been able to force concessions from parliament and the social security funds when confrontations took place at the level of local departmental negotiations or in the National Assembly. Now the executive government imposed reforms that undermined the market hegemony and syndical unity of the profession. At several points, doctors were able to ride the crest of more general protests against social security from employers and farmers. These allies, however, were weakened by the same factors that undermined the political power of doctors.[118] In addition, by the late 1950s, large employers were beginning to push for austerity measures. They became willing to sacrifice the interests of the medical profession in order to promote cost controls and to rationalize the social security system. Thus, the release of French technocrats from the political constraints of parliament permitted the introduction of reforms that had been debated for many years. In this way, the fear of executive power, which began as a reaction to the monarchy, resulted in institutions and political practices that so undermined the legitimacy of parliament that they produced the conditions for an authoritarian executive.

In the French frame of reference, some of these changes may appear as inevitable. The rhetoric of modernization and rationalization, in particular, that was the slogan of Gaullist reformers, lends itself to an interpretation based on modernization. The medical profession was increasingly composed of younger doctors less committed to the privilege of private practice and uncontested rule of senior doctors. Moreover, technological changes may have provided an imperative for change.

The most convincing argument against the modernization approach can be made from a comparative perspective. For, as the next chapter on the Swiss case shows, when doctors did not suddenly lose their main route of political influence, the medical profession did not compromise on health issues. Despite the increase in the number of younger doctors, changes in hospital technology, and increasing medical costs, the Swiss Medical Association continued to refuse more "socialized" forms of medical care. Through its recourse to the political weapon of the national referendum, the Association was able to block national health insurance, and to severely limit controls on doctors' fees and private practice in public hospitals. When the political veto point remained open, policy changes could be blocked indefinitely.

has proved to be a stumbling block to legislation. Voters view policy issues differently than do political and interest group representatives, and they depart from party lines in referendum votes. Further, for reasons that will be elaborated later, in referendum campaigns it is easier to mobilize the opponents of legislation than the proponents. Consequently, when laws are challenged by referenda, legislation is more frequently rejected than accepted.

Second, the tendency of referendum votes to be negative rather than positive has introduced a strong element of uncertainty into the Swiss policy process. Even after a number of political actors have agreed to a policy, the conditions for consensus may be shattered when the discussion enters the electoral arena. Given this uncertain outcome, risk-averse policy makers have sought to avoid referendum challenges. From the very moment that they begin to draft legislation, they anticipate potential sources of opposition and eliminate provisions that might offend. Although policy makers in many nations estimate or investigate the views of voters and interest groups as they prepare policy legislation, the threat of referenda makes Swiss policy makers more concerned with potential opponents than potential supporters. The immediate danger that opponents will block legislation through a referendum overshadows considerations of the potential electoral gains that popular legislation may bring; for if a law is never enacted, it cannot possibly influence the outcome of the next election.

Third, the strategic uncertainty created by the referendum has provided organized interest groups with an unusual route of political influence. Armed with the membership and financial resources necessary to call for referendum challenges, Swiss interest groups have wrested a niche for themselves as "gatekeepers" to the referendum process.[1] As intermediaries between political elites and the public, interest groups have exploited their pivotal position in the chain of decision making to demand extraordinary concessions during the policy process. This gatekeeper role has given a few electorally unimportant interest groups a disproportionate voice in health policy making, and, further, has placed interest groups at the center of Swiss policy making more generally.

However, as the ability to threaten legislation by calling for referenda is the key to interest-group power, it is only the groups that are willing to block legislation completely if their demands are not met that are privileged by this institutional mechanism. Groups such as doctors, farmers, and small employers that, as in the French case, opposed an expanded role for government in health insurance, profited from the referendum mechanism. Unions, women's and family associations, church organizations, and the sickness funds (mutual aid societies) found it difficult to use the referendum weapon because, as supporters of legislative efforts, they were unwilling to halt the legislative process entirely in

4

The Swiss case: Referendum politics

The popular referendum is the linchpin of the Swiss political system. As the core institution of direct democracy, the referendum provides the general public with an immediate voice in policy issues. Rather than waiting for periodic elections, the electorate can demand that a policy issue be considered by launching a popular initiative, or voters can veto legislation that has already been enacted by calling for a referendum challenge. As this chapter will show, the referendum had a significant impact in the course of Swiss health policy making. The referendum impeded efforts to enact national health insurance, and by providing organized interest groups with the means to veto policy initiatives, it enhanced the strategic bargaining power of interest groups opposed to an expansion of the role of government. Consequently, the health system that has emerged from referendum politics is based on the most minimal form of government intervention: subsidies to voluntary mutual aid societies.

The ability of voters to pull policy issues into the electoral arena is the key to the dynamic of referendum politics. Issues deliberated with one set of substantive criteria by policy experts and professional politicians in executive and parliamentary arenas are reconsidered according to different standards by individual voters in the electoral arena. In the electoral arena, issues are no longer limited by previously worked-out definitions of the problem at hand or by the promises of representatives to compromise on some of their demands in the interests of reaching a collective accord. Instead, each referendum voter may decide independently whether a proposed policy is consistent with his or her individual interests or world view. Thus, in contrast to the politics of representative democracy, which is characterized by political bargaining between representatives of political parties, the bureaucracy, and interest groups, the politics of direct democracy opens up a channel of individual participation that is unmediated by representative bodies and unconstrained by preexisting agreements. By providing a mechanism for switching the locus of decision making from the executive to the electoral arena, the referendum has altered the character of Swiss policy making.

In practice, the referendum has had three interrelated effects. First, it order to demand modifications in specific provisions of these laws. Hence, although the referendum is intended to insert the general public into politics, in practice it has been used as a tool of organized interests that wish to preserve the status quo.

This chapter will show how the dynamics of referendum politics blocked the introduction of national health insurance and the expansion of government regulation in the health area. It will also show why an institutional mechanism based on majority rule – the referendum – ended up working to the advantage of small, relatively privileged interest groups.

The result of nearly a century of referendum politics is a health insurance system based on the most limited form of government intervention: government subsidies to voluntary mutual aid societies or sickness funds. Contrary to what we might have expected, the broad political access afforded by the referendum did not generate popular pressures for programs such as national health insurance or a national health service. Instead, despite consensus among the political parties across the political spectrum, and despite the active lobbying of a number of large interest groups such as union, church, women's, and employee associations, proposals for expanding the program of government subsidies into national compulsory health insurance have been rejected. The same political dynamics have blocked proposals for controls on doctors' fees. With these first steps effectively precluded, the use of government health care financing as a tool for more extensive government intervention such as health planning and direct government employment of doctors has become a non-issue.

INSTITUTIONAL DESIGN

Swiss political institutions were designed to restrict the power of the national – federal – government through a series of institutional mechanisms. First, the jurisdiction of the federal government as opposed to the cantonal government was limited to areas specifically set forth in the constitution: In order to enlarge the scope of the federal government, a constitutional revision would be required. Second, the federal political executive was designed as a collegial executive, called the Federal Council, or Bundesrat. No political movement was to be able to take political control of the executive; this power would be shared (and divided) by seven persons elected by parliamentary representatives. Third, the bureaucracy responsible to the federal executive would not be directed by cabinet ministers. Instead, each member of the Federal Council would head an administrative department. Fourth, the legislative branch was divided into two chambers, one elected on a national basis and one elected by the cantons. This would divide power further, and ensure cantonal veto power. Fifth, legislation would be subject to direct popular veto through the referendum.

These formal institutions are marked by the political conflicts from which they emerged. During the course of the nineteenth century, the Swiss confederation of independent cantons had been transformed into a federal state as a result of foreign invasion and the rise of an internal nationalist and liberal political movement. The period from 1830 to 1880 – which began with the liberal "Regeneration" and lasted through the drafting of the constitution of 1848 and its total revision in 1874 – was characterized by severe religious and political conflicts between liberals, who promoted a strong national state and free trade, and Catholic conservatives, who fought for cantonal power and opposed free trade, industrialization, and the liberal ideology of progress. These conflicts came to a head in the Sonderbund War of 1847–1848, which erupted when the Catholics formed a separatist league. The 1848 constitution, which resulted from the victory of the liberals, created the first Swiss federal state, although Switzerland retains its earlier name, the "Swiss Confederation." Although the constitution was ratified by cantonal referenda, it was notably rejected in five and a half predominantly Catholic cantons, a sign of Catholic opposition that was not to disappear.[2]

The liberal-Catholic split influenced the institutional provisions of both the 1848 constitution and the 1874 revision. As in the United States, the 1848 constitution effected a compromise between centralist and localist tendencies, and it was in fact explicitly modeled on the American constitution. The 1848 constitution established the federal form of government, the divided legislature, and the collegial executive. At the behest of the liberals, the 1874 revision expanded the powers of the federal government, particularly in areas related to commerce. But, in return, the revision added two counterbalances by limiting federal powers to those explicitly named in the constitution and introducing the possibility of legislative recall through popular referenda.

At the cantonal level, however, the referendum has a much longer history, and is part of the Swiss tradition of direct democracy, called *Volksrechte* or "popular rights." As the purpose of the referendum is to allow minorities to block majority decisions, it has also been called a *Vetorecht* or "veto right." Despite this negative effect of the referendum, both the liberals and the Catholic-conservatives could agree on its introduction in 1874. To the liberals, the referendum's association with the Regeneration period made it a symbol of democratic progress, and the liberals preferred a veto mechanism based on individual rather than cantonal representation in order to avoid the reemergence of regional conflicts; for the Catholics, the referendum was a protection against the liberals. When it became evident, however, that the referendum was used effectively by the Catholics to block liberal reform efforts, the constitutional initiative was added in 1891. Again, however, the initiative – which could be proposed either from "above" by the executive government or from "below" through popular petitions – had a broader appeal, and was supported, as well, by the Catholics and the newly organized Social Democrats. Both groups were disadvantaged by the electoral system, which was based on majorities in multiple-member districts, and sought a greater political voice.[3]

Whereas the collegial executive, the weak federal bureaucracy, the bicameral parliament, and the constitutional constraints on the role of the federal government slowed the process of social legislation, however, it was the referendum that constituted the true veto point in the system. In contrast to the French case, the executive-legislative relationship was not problematical. The collegial executive buffered the effects of elections – as the winning party or coalition would not solely control the executive – but the partisan composition of the political executive nevertheless mirrored that of parliament. Therefore, although parliamentary discussion led to revisions in legislation, particularly as party discipline was not strict, parliament usually ratified executive proposals. In addition, although parliament elected the members of the executive Bundesrat, once elected the Bundesrat was not subject to parliamentary recall. Moreover, in contrast to France, the partisan composition of both Bundesrat and parliament was unusually stable. From 1874 to 1919, the electoral system was based on majorities in multiple-member districts, which benefited the liberal Radical-Democratic Party. Consequently, this period is known as one of liberal hegemony.

After the introduction of proportional representation in 1919 – partly as a consequence of the First World War and a general strike – there was an electoral realignment that benefited the Social Democrats and the Farmers' Party. However, since the 1919 election, Swiss electoral results have been astoundingly stable. Indeed since 1959, the Bundesrat has been elected by a "magic formula" that guarantees two seats each to the Radical-Democratic, Catholic-Conservative, and Social Democratic Parties, and one seat to the Farmers' Party, now called the Swiss People's Party. This extreme stability and proportional division of power has earned the Swiss system the name *Konkordanzdemokratie*, or "concordance democracy." Indeed, many observers of Swiss politics have stressed the way in which these multiple veto points and division of powers make consensus necessary for political decisions, and hence create political stability and integration in a nation composed of peoples of several religions and languages. Although these checks and balances have served to slow policy making, however, in practice it is the referendum that has provided the most important mechanism for blocking specific policies. Moreover, as the referendum places minorities in a position to veto decisions unilaterally, an observer will see legislation only in areas where all the actors who could potentially veto the legislation are willing to agree to the legislation. As this effect of referendum is counterintuitive, it bears exploring in greater detail.[4]

THE SWISS REFERENDUM

The referendum has had a dual impact on the dynamics of Swiss health care politics. The intended effect of the referendum is to give voters a direct voice in policy making; the unintended effect is that the referendum has given interest groups tremendous influence over policy making, at the expense of traditional policymakers, such as executive government department heads, civil servants, and members of political parties. The Swiss referendum differs from that in other European nations in that facultative referenda are called by voters and the results are binding. In Switzerland, voters do not follow partisan loyalties in referenda. Instead, referendum voters are influenced by specific issues; they tend to be "issue" or "pocketbook" voters rather than "partisan" or "identity" voters. In fact, Swiss voters deviate so much from party lines in referendum votes that although the legislative proposals considered by referenda have been previously approved by the political parties in the legislature, referendum votes are more often negative than positive. The rejection rate is 60 percent. The rate of passage of popular initiatives is even lower – 90 percent of popular initiatives have been rejected.[5]

The propensity of issue-specific referendum votes to be negative can be explained by the problems of collective action. Voters will participate more actively in referenda to the extent that they feel directly affected by the proposed legislation and to the extent that they feel that their individual vote will actually make a difference to the outcome. Because voters respond more strongly to perceived costs than to perceived benefits, those who view the legislation as a cost are more likely to vote than those who view it as a benefit. Further, members of smaller groups with relatively homogeneous interests are more likely to evaluate proposed legislation in similar ways and to feel that their individual votes are significant than are members of larger, more diverse groups. For voters who are threatened by the legislation, the costs of voting are balanced by a larger payoff than is the case for voters who will share in the public good produced by the legislation, whether or not they vote to support the law. Moreover, opponents of a law do not need to coordinate their action or to agree on what specific points of the legislation they dislike. Proponents of legislation, on the other hand, must be sure that each and every point in the legislation appeals to all potential supporters. Thus, voters affected by concentrated costs turn out to vote at higher rates than voters affected by diffuse potential benefits.

Two subsidiary factors exacerbate these effects of collective action. First, voter turnout for referenda is low in Switzerland. Selective participation means that the characteristics of voters may be significantly skewed, depending upon what fraction turns out to vote, in contrast to high participation rates, which would more closely approximate the general electorate. Indeed, recent studies of Swiss referenda show voter participation to be correlated to socioeconomic status, with higher rates of participation for individuals with higher incomes and higher levels of educational attainment. These voters, however, are those least likely to benefit from national health insurance or other forms of social legislation. In the area of social legislation, intended to benefit those of lower socioeconomic status, the combined effects of problems of collective action, low turnout, and a socioeconomic skew to participation make the referendum a retarding mechanism rather than a facilitating mechanism.[6]

The unintended consequences of the referendum go well beyond specific instances of defeat, however. Swiss policy makers are loath to see legislation subject to a referendum challenge after a lengthy process of executive and parliamentary deliberation. Not only is the outcome uncertain, but the probability of failure is greater than that of success. This is not unique to the Swiss system, but a more general feature of referenda. A study by the American Enterprise Institute concludes that throughout Western Europe and North America, not just in Switzerland,

politicians have been reluctant to call referendums. Referendums may go the wrong way. And referendums may undermine party solidarity. . . . It is usually easier to manage a parliament than to manage the electorate; a defeat in the Chamber can be more easily circumvented or reversed than a defeat at the polls. Referendums, too, cut across normal routines. The question referred to voters is not usually expressed as a party issue but is presented for each to judge independently.[7]

It is precisely the uncertain outcome of the referenda, and the greater probability of negative votes, that places power in the hands of interest groups. In order to avoid rejection of legislation through a referendum at the very last phase of the legislative process – that is, after legislation has already gone through the phases of executive preparation, parliamentary consideration, and parliamentary votes in two chambers – Swiss politicians work hard to prepare legislation that will not be subject to a referendum challenge. To achieve this end, they seek out sources of potential opposition to legislation and try to placate those opponents early on. As the general public has no mechanism for making its wishes entirely clear – the referendum votes are after all limited to "yes" or "no" votes – politicians question interest groups closely. In fact, the interest groups are in a pivotal position, because although they cannot control the outcomes of the referendum votes, they enroll sufficient numbers of members to guarantee that they can obtain the necessary 50,000 signatures to call for a referendum vote. Thus, the fear of referenda makes policy makers extremely attentive to interest-group opposition.

The small number of facultative referenda that have been called is a testimony to this caution of policy makers. Out of 1,200 laws and decrees that might have been subject to a referendum, 1,100 have not been challenged. "In other words, 1,100 of these 1,200 laws and decrees were so devised that it was not possible to find 50,000 people (formerly 30,000) to attack them – strong evidence of the prudence in parliament in not provoking opposition."[8] In his discussion of the referendum, Jean-François Aubert describes the link between Swiss referenda and interest-group power:

A common criticism of the referendum is that it increases the influence of pressure groups and gives them a particularly effective weapon. In a representative democracy pressure groups have only limited means of giving weight to their demands – financial promises and threats about the next elections. With referendums it is different. The big economic power blocs, which are consulted in the preparation of laws, let it be known that if their wishes are not met they will campaign against the law. The legislators are well aware that if the group has a large number of members, their votes cannot be ignored. In other words, the most successful referendums are those which do not take place. The circles which might have fought the law do not do so because it contains what they want. This is the explanation for the compromise character of a large part of federal legislation; parliament does not make laws in a sovereign way but always under the threat of a referendum.[9]

Although Aubert stresses the number of members in an interest group as being critical for the referendum threat posed by the group, the analysis presented here deviates from Aubert's on that score. The case of national health insurance policy making will show that group size was not the critical variable for referendum threats. Interest-group leaders could not guarantee that every one of their members would vote according to their directives. Moreover, many of the groups, such as doctors, were too small for the votes of the members to determine the electoral outcome. Rather, the important threat that could be made by interest groups was simply to launch a referendum. Once launched, referenda tended to produce negative results, without orchestration from interest-group leaders. Wishing to avoid the delays and uncertainties caused by the possibility of a referendum challenge at the end of a lengthy legislative process, legislators compromised with the groups prepared to risk electoral rejection of legislation by launching a challenge. As it happened, the groups that wished to prevent enactment of national health insurance legislation, or that successfully demanded legislative amendments, were small. They included doctors, artisans, and chiropractors. These groups were willing to block the legislation entirely if their demands were not met. For the groups that wished to promote legislation, on the other hand, the referendum challenge was a mixed blessing. Threatening to stop the process entirely if specific demands were not met worked against their primary demand, which was to see the legislation enacted.

Unions, employee associations, women's groups, and the sickness funds were far less successful in making demands than employers, chiropractors and doctors, even though their larger memberships should have been an advantage in the referendum campaigns. These groups were perplexed when they had trouble convincing their memberships to go out and vote. Even though they successfully organized constitutional initiatives to put a new issue on the political agenda at some points, they were far less successful at getting their members to vote to support the final legislative proposals. These failures will be explained in terms of the collective action problem of generating support for diffuse benefits. Furthermore, as we will see, by the time legislation was enacted, so many compromises had been made in the pre-parliamentary expert commissions and in the parliamentary committees that the benefits offered by the legislative proposals were rather diffuse indeed.

PROFESSIONAL DOMINANCE

As the remainder of this chapter will show, referendum politics stymied attempts by policy makers to enact national health insurance, to control doctor's fees, and to increase the scope of government in health planning. However, although the rejection of these proposals prevented the development of the government monoposony that medical professions throughout Europe strove to avoid, these policy results cannot be explained by theories of professional dominance. First, many of these policy proposals were eliminated by voters and interest groups that were not in any way influenced or directed by the Swiss medical profession. Second, to the extent that Swiss doctors were able to wrest concessions from the legislative process, their ability to do so was related to the referendum threat, and not to particular professional or organizational resources.

The Swiss process of professionalization was slower and less complete than in either France or Sweden. The licensing procedures that were introduced provided a less effective barrier to entry to the profession than in other countries. Consequently, the number of doctors produced in comparison to the population was higher, and nonlicensed practitioners were more widespread. In market terms, the profession was comparatively disadvantaged. Nevertheless, as a political lobbying group, Swiss doctors were extremely successful. The context of referendum politics explains this apparent paradox.

Professionalization

As in France, early professionalization under the old regime (including conflicts between the university-trained *Ärzte* and the artisanally trained *Wundeärzte*) was interrupted by the French Revolution and its aftermath. Subsequently, each canton decided independently how to regulate the medical profession. In many cantons, particularly in the French-speaking parts of Switzerland, medical practice was open to anyone; no licenses were required. Elsewhere, the prerequisites varied widely, from the requirement of a medical degree from a university to the obtainment of a license or "patent" from cantonal heath authorities. Cantonal disagreements over the issue of allowing doctors to move their practices from one canton to another finally resulted in national licensing requirements, first through an intercantonal agreement or *Konkordat* in 1867, and then through a national law in 1877. In contrast to France and Sweden, however, no central government bureaucracy was in charge of medical licensing or was made responsible for controlling the number of doctors. Nor were provisions made for sanctions against unlicensed medical practice. In order to practice medicine, Swiss doctors needed only to enter medical school and to pass a national examination (*Staatsexamen*).

Although the Department of the Interior formally supervises medical education, informal control over the content of education and the exams rests with the cantonal medical schools. Anyone who wishes may enter medical school; the number of doctors is regulated only by the failure rates in the examinations. Whereas bureaucratic regulation of the profession in France and Sweden kept the number of doctors low, entry to the profession in Switzerland was simpler and the number of doctors correspondingly higher. By 1958, the number of doctors reached a level of 141 per 100,000 population; in France and Sweden, the numbers were 107 and 89, respectively. Even after government policies in Sweden and France increased the numbers of doctors following the Second World War, Switzerland remained the country with the highest density of doctors – 285 per 100,000 population in 1985, as compared with 258 in Sweden and 219 in France (see Table 6, page 84).[10]

Not only did the limited federal bureaucracy not provide a mechanism for controlling the numbers of doctors, but controls against natural forms of healing and quackery were lax as well. Indeed, after national licensing was introduced, three cantons passed legislation to allow self-trained healers to practice medicine. This legislation was pushed through by popular initiatives, against the wishes of cantonal political authorities. As we will see, the institutions of direct democracy also provided a resource to chiropractors, who by threatening to block health insurance legislation succeeded – against the protests of the Swiss Medical Association – in being recognized as practitioners of equal status to licensed physicians

[Discussion of Table 7 is on page 150]

Table 7. *Union and employee association membership*

	Union membership as percentage of labor force				Union membership as percentage of non-agricultural wage and salary earners			Total union/employee association density
Year	**1913–1914**	**1935**	**1950**	**1970**	**1935**	**1950**	**1970**	**1960**
Switzerland	5	17	29	27	30	40	31	30.3%
France	5	7	22	15	21	47	20	19.8%
Sweden	6	24	51	75	44	69	87	73%

Sources: Union membership: John D. Stephens, *The Transition from Capitalism to Socialism* (London: Macmillan, 1979), pp. 115–116. Association membership: Jelle Visser, "Dimensions of Union Growth in Postwar Western Europe," *European University Institute Working Paper No. 89* (Badia Fiesolana, San Domenico (FI): European University Institute, 1984), pp. 29, 65, 77.

for health insurance purposes. Thus, the Swiss profession did achieve monopoly through the introduction of a state examination for medical practice. But the limited federal government did not provide a mechanism for controlling the number of doctors, and the institutions of direct democracy produced significant loopholes in the protection of licensed practice against forms of natural healing. The same political institutions that proved advantageous to doctors in blocking expanded government intervention in health insurance, proved disadvantageous when it came to errecting entry barriers to the profession.

Medical organization

Whereas medical monopoly was relatively weak, the Swiss profession can be ranked as intermediate or strong as far as organizational resources go. Swiss doctors were more much more highly organized than French doctors, but about equally as well organized as Swedish doctors. Membership density in the post-Second World War period was well over 90 percent for both Swiss and Swedish doctors, compared with the inflated estimates of 40–60 percent for French doctors. Both the Swiss and Swedish Medical Associations controlled specialty licensing (until 1960 in Sweden), which may account for this high membership rate. But, whereas Swedish doctors established a tightly disciplined national association, Swiss doctors were more beset by regional differences and left greater decision-making autonomy to the cantonal medical associations.

Regional and intracantonal political differences hampered the formation of a national Swiss medical association. The first national association, the Swiss Medical Association (Verbindung der Schweizer Ärzte), was founded in 1901, after a great deal of conflict, from a merger of the Société Médicale de la Suisse Romande and the Ärztlichen Centralverein, founded in 1867 and 1870, respectively, to represent medical societies in the French and German-speaking regions of Switzerland. The Swiss Medical Association is structured as an association of cantonal medical societies rather than as a national organization. Representatives of local medical societies meet in the legislative body of the Swiss Medical Association – the Ärztekammer – which elects an executive council. Although this organizational structure allowed regional conflicts to emerge quite clearly, the Medical Association was nonetheless successful. Its success in the political sphere, I will argue, was not caused by organizational factors or by a unique process of professionalization. Instead, the dynamics of the referendum placed the organization in a strategically powerful position.

SWISS NATIONAL HEALTH INSURANCE POLITICS:
AN OVERVIEW

The pattern of referendum politics has influenced each step in the development of Swiss health-care programs. The history may be divided into three phases. (1) Between the end of the nineteenth century and the First World War, the outlines of the current health insurance system were established. As in other nations, problems related to industrialization and the fear of worker unrest provided the impetus for reform. National health insurance was the preferred choice of the governing Radical-Democratic Party. But although national health insurance was indeed enacted into law in 1899, it was subsequently vetoed by a referendum challenge. Consequently, policy makers scaled back their plans and introduced a system of government subsidies to voluntary sickness funds.

(2) After the Second World War, under the influence of the wave of social policy reforms that swept Europe, the Swiss government again attempted to introduce national health insurance. Again, however, a referendum challenge blocked the pursuit of national health insurance, and policy makers were forced to reduce their ambitions, taking steps to improve the financing of government subsidies, which had failed to keep up with rising health care costs.

(3) Finally, in the 1970s, when other nations turned to planning and coordinating their hospital systems on a nationwide basis, the Swiss political debate was once again centered on the problem of health insurance. Hospital stays were not adequately covered, and insurance premiums and government subsidies could not meet rising health care costs. After lengthy preparation, two separate reform proposals were vetoed in a national referendum in 1974. A scaled-down version of these proposals, this time addressing cash benefits and maternity insurance, was vetoed in a 1987 referendum. Debate about these issues has continued, and new proposals for health insurance reform continue to be presented to the Swiss parliament.

The remainder of this chapter will look more closely at selected instances of health-policy reform critical to the development of the Swiss health-insurance system. It will show that the initial ideas of Swiss policy makers resembled those of policy makers in other nations. However, referendum politics forced retrenchment to more minimal programs. Not only did the referendum block a series of proposals for national health insurance, but the opportunities provided to interest groups by the referendum threat determined the specific policies adopted in the wake of referendum defeats.

The cases will show that the design of political institutions, and not a peculiar path of professionalization, explains the extent to which the medical profession was able to influence health policy outcomes. Similarly,

I will argue that the ability of unions to push for reforms was hampered, not by any preexisting organizational weakness of the union movement, but by referendum politics. The same argument applies to the strength of the Social Democratic Party. As we will see, the party achieved significant electoral gains but few policy results as a consequence of the institutional obstacles to expansion of the role of the federal government. Finally, the chapter argues that federalism, by itself, did not constitute a block to national health insurance. Rather, this program was precluded by national referenda, and *especially* by the more far-reaching effects of the referenda on the policy process.

INTEREST GROUPS AND THE EMERGENCE OF
REFERENDUM POLITICS

The rejection of an 1899 law for national health insurance is one of the first examples of the pattern of referendum politics. This example provides striking evidence that it is the referendum, and not the ideas of policy makers, the partisan composition of the legislature, federalism, or the organization of the labor movement, employers, or the medical profession that blocked the introduction of national health insurance in Switzerland. Members of the Radical-Democratic Party drafted a plan for compulsory national health insurance that was notable for its comprehensive coverage and universal financing and administration. These politicians, who had a dominant standing in both the executive and legislative branches of government, were able to garner overwhelming parliamentary support to enact their program, and, national health insurance was passed into law. Not only did political leaders and the members of opposition parties vote in favor of national health insurance, but the law had been preceded by a national referendum vote in favor of changing the constitution to allow for national health insurance legislation. Nevertheless, despite this apparent political consensus, the national health insurance law was subsequently rejected in a popular plebiscite. This defeat at the polls resulted in a reversal of policy. The Radical-Democrats withdrew their plans for comprehensive national health insurance and embarked on the more limited course of providing government subsidies to private voluntary mutual aid societies.

These early political conflicts over national health insurance in Switzerland not only established the future direction for government health programs, but they were instrumental in the emergence of the pattern of referendum politics generally. The rejection of national health insurance by the voters was only one of many instances when the referendum was used to challenge decisions made by political representatives in the executive and legislative branches. As voters launched one referendum challenge after another, legislators sought to avoid these challenges that so often ended in defeat. They drew the conclusion that no piece of legislation would be safe from the referendum threat unless it was fully supported by established interest groups. Interest groups, too, learned that they could bargain for concessions by threatening to launch referenda. Consequently, policy proposals were modified in accordance with the wishes of these interest groups – which, as will be seen, accounts for the specific organization of Swiss health care programs. At the same time, the policy-making process itself was adapted to accommodate the perceived referendum-based power of Swiss interest associations.[11]

Insurance reform

National health insurance was actually put on the political agenda by a related, but separate, issue – the problem of industrial accidents. Both employers and industrial workers – actually, the organizations that represented them – were dissatisfied with the liability laws established by the Factory Acts of 1877 and 1881. Large unpredictable liability settlements could bankrupt employers, at the same time that workers, forced to battle employers and insurance companies in the courts were not certain to receive compensation. Lawyers led the drive to reform the liability system, calling for legislation to establish compulsory insurance against industrial accidents (workmen's compensation) of the kind introduced in other nations. In 1885, a parliamentary motion was passed that called for obligatory accident insurance for workers as well as an extension of the liability laws to certain nonindustrial occupations.

Members of the Federal Council and Representative Forrer, a member of the Nationalrat, took this opportunity to prepare a more ambitious proposal. The main advocates of reform were progressive members of the Radical-Democratic Party who viewed social insurance as a critical part of the functions of a modern state. Like reformers in other nations, they hoped that by improving working conditions and providing social benefits, they could defuse worker radicalism amd create a regulatory framework favorable to economic growth. Although these politicians were inspired by Bismarck's social insurance laws, they were well aware of the ways in which the German legislation had unintentionally encouraged the growth of socialism. Therefore, they were intent on constructing a more universal scheme.

In terms of the persons covered, the benefits provided, and the financing and the administration of the scheme, the Swiss plan was more progressive than either German social insurance or contemporaneous legislation in France, Britain, and Scandinavia. In the latter three countries, late nineteenth-century legislation was limited to registering and subsidizing voluntary mutual aid societies. In Germany, compulsory health insurance had been introduced, but it was limited to industrial workers. Swiss policy makers decided to follow the German route of compulsory insurance, but in contrast to the German system, Swiss social insurance was to be a broadly based citizens' (*Volks*) insurance, rather than a "class" insurance. The Swiss plan would provide coverage for accidents, for income lost during illness, and for medical treatment. Whereas German social insurance was restricted to industrial workers, the Swiss plan included low-income earners in *all* occupational sectors, including agriculture, crafts, and small businesses. In line with this universalist approach, a network of public sickness funds, to be subsidized by the cantonal governments, would be created to administer the system, although preexisting factory funds and voluntary private funds would also be accepted as insurance carriers.

The financing of the system entailed a greater burden for both employers and the state than did the German plan, under which employers financed the accident insurance and one-third of the health insurance, while employees paid for two-thirds of the health insurance. In Switzerland, employers would cover 46 percent of the costs, the government 22 percent, and the insured 32 percent.[12] Thus, the ideas of Swiss policy makers were not more conservative or minimalist than the ideas of their foreign counterparts. As in the French case, the proposed Swiss legislation was relatively universal and comprehensive in terms of coverage, financing, and administration, particularly if we consider that the first French health insurance legislation was proposed in 1923 and a comparable Swiss plan in 1890.

The 1899 Lex Forrer

In contrast to the French case, however, the Swiss law moved smoothly through the legislative process, despite a number of institutional obstacles. As health insurance was a new area of competence for the federal government, the constitution would need to be amended before such legislation could be prepared. This process was successful. The necessary constitutional amendment was ratified on 26 October 1890 by 283,228 votes to 92,200 and by eighteen whole and five half cantons – a 75 percent majority with a voter turnout of 60 percent. Consequently, the Department of the Interior, under Forrer's direction, drafted a law known as the *Lex Forrer* of 1899, which established mandatory national health insurance for low-income earners, industrial accident insurance, and health and disability insurance for those in active military service. Next, the *Lex Forrer* was approved by both houses of parliament (unanimously in the Ständerat and by a vote of 113 to 1 in the Nationalrat).

Until this point, then, political proceedings indicated a consensus for national health insurance, the many veto points in the system notwithstanding. Proponents of national health insurance had the full support of the Bundesrat; they had managed to marshal the votes to change the Swiss constitution. And Representatives in both houses of parliament, even in the more conservative Ständerat, supported the decision. Whereas Bismarck had needed to forge the coalition of "iron and rye" to assemble the parliamentary votes to approve his social insurance program, and was required to make many concessions to parliamentary factions in order to enact his program, and French reformers were interrupted by many changes in government and countless revisions in the parliamentary committees, the Swiss Radical-Democrats did not face these problems. The Radical-Democratic Party was in a dominant position, holding 6 out of 7 seats in the collegial executive, 58 percent of seats in the Nationalrat, and 39 percent in the Ständerat. And, as the parliamentary votes demonstrate, the Catholic-Conservative opposition supported the national health insurance law.

In light of this favorable political position, and given the agreement of the minority opposition, in any other political system, passage of national health insurance would have been a fait accompli.[13] Consequently, it came as quite a shock when the *Lex Forrer* was subsequently rejected by a large majority of voters in a national referendum. The law was defeated by 341,914 to 148,035 votes, and passed in only one canton; with a 67 percent turnout, only 30 percent of the electorate voted for the law. Forrer, was so upset that he left his seat in the Nationalrat and returned to his private law practice for several years.[14] This defeat, coming only ten years after an overwhelming majority had voted in favor of sickness and accident legislation, had a traumatic impact on Swiss health-care politics. Even today, critics of national health insurance refer to the rejection of the *Lex Forrer* by the Swiss people. This referendum defeat brought the movement for universal national health insurance coverage to an abrupt halt.

Referendum dynamics

The causes for the referendum defeat remain a mystery, however. Although it is clear that large numbers of voters turned out to oppose the national health insurance law, it is not clear who voted against the law or why. There is no public opinion poll form that era that can shed light on the opposition of the voters to the law. The historical information simply does not exist. Without such empirical evidence, we do not know why the individual voters who participated in the referendum voted as they did.

The referendum was launched by a journalist from Bern who collected signatures via a printed form in the *Berner Volkszeitung*.[15] We do know that at the time, despite the existence of universal male suffrage, nearly one-fourth of those legally entitled to vote could not vote, on the grounds that they had not paid their taxes, had gone into bankruptcy, or were blind or otherwise physically or mentally handicapped. Further, many unemployed persons and low-income earners avoided registering to vote in order to avoid taxes.[16] Thus, we can assume a socioeconomic skew in the referendum participation. Nevertheless, the electorate that regularly participated in elections was electing the Radical-Democrats, with the next largest group voting for the Catholic Conservatives. So it is not immediately evident why the constituencies of these parties would turn around and block the policies proposed by these parties.

Searching for an explanation for this defeat, policy makers and other political actors, as well as historians, tried to understand the referendum defeat by examining interest-group opinions. As one admittedly partisan observer, Social Democrat Hermann Greulich, put it, "On May 20, 1900 [the date of the referendum] we learned something once again: No health insurance law that obligates employers to pay contributions has a chance of passage."[17] Not every account blames only the employers, however, but virtually all point to some aspect of the law that was disliked by a certain group as an explanation for its failure.[18] Farmers and craftsmen objected to paying social insurance contributions, as well as to the high cost of the new system. Industrialists, on the other hand, were divided; many were eager for a solution to the problems caused by the liability laws, but not all were in favor of the employer contributions.[19] Sickness funds – the voluntary mutual aid societies that provided health insurance to their members – opposed the introduction of public sickness funds.[20]

Criticism of the government's scheme was not restricted to those who preferred more limited forms of intervention. Equal opposition came from those who argued that the *Lex Forrer* did not go far enough. Strangely enough, both the liberal *Neue Züricher Zeitung* and the labor movement felt that the law should have been more extensive in terms of the risks covered and the benefits provided. The most ambitious counterproposal came from Nationalrat representative Greulich of the *Arbeiterpartei*, an early social democratic party. Greulich's scheme, which was presented as a petition for a constitutional initiative, consisted of three parts: free medical care for all citizens to be financed by the federal government (a national health service, in other words), *employer*-financed and administered industrial accident insurance, and *employee*-financed and administered cash benefits. The Greulich plan was motivated by the socialist idea that a national health service would better serve the interests of workers than privately provided health care financed by insurance. In addition, workers would be compelled to join worker-run cash benefits schemes, which would facilitate unionization. Although socialist organizers were briefly successful in interesting both secular and Catholic trade unionists in the plan, they obtained only 40,000 of the 100,000 signatures needed for an initiative. Nevertheless, Greulich supported national health insurance as a step in the right direction.[21]

Tempting as it may be to attribute the referendum defeat of the *Lex Forrer* to interest-group opposition, it is not clear that the voters in the referendum indeed followed the directives of interest group leaders. There are several indications, in fact, that referendum participants were unorganized individuals who had a wide variety of reasons for opposing the reform. For, although leaders of interest organizations voiced some criticisms of the *Lex Forrer*, they had not protested against the law during the parliamentary proceedings. In fact, according to Erich Wyss, the elites in these organizations were prepared to accept the law; but it was the rank-and-file that voted against the law in the referendum.[22]

Further, opinions within different organizations were not clear-cut. For example, when representatives of the medical profession, who were not yet organized into a national organization, discussed the issue of national health insurance, a variety of viewpoints emerged. French Swiss doctors were virulently opposed to national health insurance, whereas the German Swiss doctors were more favorable, on the grounds that insurance would solve the problem of uncollected payments from patients, although it would also entail a risk of control by the sickness funds. The *Ärztekommision*, a committee of representatives of cantonal medical societies, which was consulted by the government as no national association was available, concluded that the pros and cons of national health insurance were a toss-up and took no official position on the law. Thus, the hypothesis that members of specific interest groups constituted a well-organized front with well-defined interests, mobilized and ready to fight the national health insurance law, seems implausible, especially as there is evidence of voters completely unconnected to interest associations, such as French Swiss liberals, who opposed the law for ideological reasons.

Procedural factors are the key to understanding the defeat of national health insurance in Switzerland. In contrast to the parliamentary process in other nations, where parliamentary votes, and sometimes the agreement of interest-group leaders, were sufficient to guarantee the passage of a law, the Swiss referendum raised the barriers to legislative action. An affirmative referendum vote required the enthusiastic participation of a majority of voters, rather than a moderate willingness to compromise among a group of political professionals. This shift in what one could call the "burden of support" required for ratification made the difference to the outcome.

The *Lex Forrer* provided government subsidies to employer contributions for health insurance, but for the 600,000 potential beneficiaries it entailed government compulsion to insure themselves and to pay for one-third of the cost. If these intended beneficiaries had voted for the law, it would, of course, have remained in force. But it is not particularly surprising that individuals that had not bought private insurance policies did not go to the polls to submit themselves to a new tax. Whereas union leaders and socialists viewed the tradeoff between the costs of social insurance and the security the program would bring as worthwhile, for individual workers, who would not necessarily fall ill, the law entailed a definite cost, but not a definite benefit.

Similarly, on the employer side, the collective benefits perceptible to interest group leaders were not necessarily apparent to individual employers. Social insurance would raise labor costs but, in return, would protect firms from liability claims. Moreover, the extra costs would raise entry barriers, an advantage for larger, established firms. But for individual employers, who would not necessarily be sued for an industrial accident, the tax costs of the reform loomed larger than the potential benefits. After all, if individual employers had been willing to pay for industrial accident insurance, there would have been no need for legislation; the private insurance market could have handled this collective risk.

Indeed, the electoral behavior of Swiss voters corresponds with polling results from other countries: When national health insurance is presented as a general principle, levels of support are high, but when specific proposals including taxes and spelling out the role of government versus the role of the private insurance sector are mentioned, support drops precipitously, and differences of opinion on the preferred type of health insurance plan emerge.[23]

Thus, the outstanding feature of this episode in the history of Swiss health insurance policy is not the existence of disagreements and opposition to reform – which, given the diversity of interests, is inevitable for any policy proposal – but the institutional channel available for the expression of these disagreements. The referendum gave each individual who wanted to avoid the costs of the reform an opportunity to block the law, whereas for supporters of the law, the individual expression of interests was a disadvantage. In an area of market failure, the referendum mechanism, which reproduces the individual decision making of the market, albeit at a lower cost, is not conducive to market-corrective government intervention.

POLICY RETRENCHMENT: THE 1911 SICKNESS
AND ACCIDENT INSURANCE LAW

Faced with the defeat of the *Lex Forrer*, the Radical-Democrats were unsure as to how to proceed. There were no immediate plans for continued reforms. The issue of national health insurance reemerged only when lawyers again petitioned the Bundesrat to legislate on liability and workers' compensation. This time, however, the Bundesrat proposed a far more limited reform in place of the ambitious *Lex Forrer*. In its 1906 presentation, the Bundesrat announced that its proposal followed the "dual principle [of] compromise and incremental action [which is] the legislative policy of a referendum-State."[24]

But in deciding on which specific policy points to compromise, the Bundesrat made calculated guesses as to which groups would be likely to call for a referendum challenge. The Bundesrat politicians, including Forrer who was now back in politics and had been elected to the Bundesrat, eliminated all provisions that might have offended the majority of employers and the sickness funds, but disregarded the demands of both Social Democratic and Catholic unions, as well as the private insurance companies. Forrer avoided consulting interest groups extensively, and did not rely on an expert commission of interest-group representatives to prepare the proposal. Instead, his strategy was to provide legislative benefits to just enough groups to avoid referendum defeat, while keeping some important points in the proposal intact. Thus, the final legislative proposal was drafted with greater concern for the potential opponents of the law than for the potential supporters.

Rather than introducing mandatory national health insurance, the federal government would simply subsidize voluntary private health insurance carried by the preexisting sickness funds. The new proposal eliminated the requirement to insure oneself, eliminated the public funds, and eliminated the employer contributions. Instead, the insured would pay premiums to the sickness funds, as under any private insurance system. As before, the health insurance scheme was coupled with industrial accident insurance. In contrast to the health insurance portion of the scheme, however, accident insurance would be financed through employer and employee contributions and administered by an independent agency whose governing board would include representatives of employers and employees; private insurance carriers were excluded from the accident insurance. Thus, the legislative proposal of 1906 was tailored to accommodate those thought to be responsible for the failure of the *Lex Forrer*: Citizens who disliked the compulsory aspect of the insurance, the employers who objected to the employer contributions (in particular, small employers and farmers), and the sickness funds, who had objected to the public funds.[25]

Union demands

The concern of the Bundesrat for referendum threats, however, made these politicians quite impervious to the demands of interest groups that promoted government expansion. Although socialists, trade union leaders, Catholic organizations, and the sickness funds formed a coalition to press for changes in the legislation, the basic interest of these groups in legislation, as well as the clear financial interest of the funds in the government subsidies, allowed the Bundesrat to outflank the progressive opposition. Although these groups were well organized, the logic of referendum politics placed them in a disadvantageous bargaining position. By 1906, Catholic and secular unions had managed to organize 18 percent of the industrial workers.[26] Furthermore, although divided on religous issues, the unions stood united on health insurance issues. (In comparative terms, as Table 7 shows, Swiss unionization, calculated as a percentage of the labor force, as a percentage of nonagricultural wage and salary earners, and as a percentage of total employed as opposed to industrial workers, was not especially low at that date, and throughout the period studied, unionization levels remained higher than in France.)

Similarly, the sickness funds had increased their memberships from 260,000 in 1900 to 400,000 in 1905. The Swiss sickness fund movement was divided; but disparate groups had formed a united coalition. The Swiss sickness fund movement was composed of Catholic, trade union, craftsmens' and factory funds. The relationship between the Social Democratic unions, now united in the Workers' Alliance (Arbeiterbund), and the sickness funds was neither hostile, as in France, nor tightly coordinated, as in Germany. Rather in Eastern Switzerland, there was a concentration of Arbeiterbund funds that provided cash benefits only; otherwise, the sickness funds were a pluralistic group. Nevertheless, they had been able to cooperate, forming regional associations to represent funds in the German-speaking regions in 1891 and in the French-speaking regions in 1893.

In 1902, the sickness funds united behind a socialist plan that would allow the cantons the option of using the proposed federal subsidies either to provide free medical care through cantonal health services or to subsidize cash benefits insurance.[27] Thus, rather than pushing for federal subsidies for insurance to pay for medical treatments, the reform coalition preferred that cantons be given the choice of "socializing" medicine, which is what the socialists wanted, or promoting cash benefits insurance, which is what the trade unions and Catholic organizations preferred. These organizations, particularly the trade unions and Catholic groups – such as the Arbeiterbund, and the Associations of Agriculturalists, Metalworkers, Textile Workers, Wood Workers, and the Catholic Popular Association – all argued for complusory insurance for low-income earners. Even though the cost of insurance for these individuals would be reduced by the government subsidies, the organizational leaders argued that compulsory coverage was necessary to meet the needs of those who would not take the step of insuring themselves. These groups also asked for explicit inclusion of political and confessional sickness funds under the law.[28]

Despite this coalition, none of these demands was met, however. When faced with a parliamentary interpellation on the sickness fund initiative for free medical care, Federal Councilor Deucher charged that support for the initiative was not widespread.[29] Privately, however, at a meeting of the Bundesrat committee that drafted the law, he acknowledged the popularity of the initiative, calling it a "more dangerous" version of the Greulich proposals of 1893. Supporters of the Greulich proposals had collected only 40,000 signatures, but the compromise that allowed the cantons to make the choice between free medical care and cash benefits insurance had the support of the vast majority of funds and the trade unions. Nevertheless, the committee in its deliberations concluded that the alliance between the unions and the funds would break down as soon as the funds realized that they would receive substantial federal funding under the new law. The leadership, Forrer said, just want some money and to see some progress with their work; in his opinion, the funds would realize that socialist agitators were "an enemy in their backs."[30] The committee also decided that compulsory insurance was impossible for "political" reasons – that is, because of the referendum. The request for explicit inclusion of political and confessional sickness funds was ruled out by Nationalrat politicians, who refused to guarantee subsidies to such funds in light of the use of sickness funds in Germany as a "social democratic instrument of power."[31]

Regardless of their many members, the coalition of unions and sickness funds did not pose a credible threat to the legislation once the issue of public funds – the one point in the legislation that would make it worthwhile for the preexisting sickness funds to block the legislation regardless of the subsidies – was removed.

Medical interests

The rejection of the *Lex Forrer* also had an impact on the Swiss medical profession. The referendum campaign had prompted the regional medical associations to put aside their differences and to create a single organization in 1901, the Verbindung der Schweizer Ärzte. In its campaign for the 1911 law, the medical association's main concern was the relationship between doctors and the sickness funds. To prevent the German and Austrian sickness funds' practice of employing closed panels of doctors to treat fund patients at low rates, which rendered the physician entirely dependent upon fund managers, the medical association argued for a "free choice for doctor."

There was a parliamentary battle on the last point – with the Nationalrat voting to allow patients an absolutely free choice of doctor, and the Ständerat, with its rural bias, arguing that the sickness funds should have some means to control fees. Nevertheless, the medical profession won on every issue. Patients could be treated by any doctor, but the sickness funds would be liable only for charges within a fee schedule that was to be negotiated between the funds and cantonal medical associations.[32] Thus, it appears that although the profession did not play a role in blocking the first attempt to enact national health insurance in Switerland, by the time the 1911 law was about to go into effect, the profession was relatively successful in determining how relations between physicians and sickness funds would be regulated.

Referendum challenge

Despite such concessions to potential sources of opposition, however, the future of the law was not assured. Though approved with large majorities in both houses of parliament on 13 June 1911, the law was challenged by a petition for a referendum. This challenge was launched by insurance companies, who objected to the introduction of a government monopoly on industrial accident insurance. These insurance companies, which were members of the Swiss Association of Trade and Industry (the Vorort), had first demanded that the Vorort launch a referendum against the law. But the Vorort leadership, on the other hand, wished to cultivate a better relationship with the federal bureaucracy and felt that use of the referendum should be restricted.

Against the wishes of this leadership, insurance companies in Zürich were able to pressure the local chamber of commerce and a local trade association to launch a referendum. As in the case of the *Lex Forrer*, the referendum provided a mechanism for specific interests to bypass their association leadership, thus working against pressures for the aggregation of interests and the oligarchical factors that tend to make association leaders more cooperative than their members.[33]

In the end, the law withstood the referendum of 4 February 1912 – but barely, by 287,565 votes to 241,426. Two "coincidental" factors were held responsible for the fact that the 1911 law withstood this challenge: Railway workers were assured that they would not lose benefits under the new law, placating the 50,000 members of the Föderativeverband des Personals öffentlicher Verwaltungen und Betriebe, and Luzern was chosen as the site for the accident insurance, winning over the anti-insurance "inner" Switzerland. (Indeed, the referendum results show the highest levels of support for the 1911 law in Luzern and Solothurn, the seat of the association of sickness funds for the German-speaking regions, the Konkordat.) Thus, despite the concessions made to interest groups, this outcome was certainly in no way inevitable or predetermined; the Factory Acts, for example, withstood a referendum. The narrow approval of the 1911 law by the referendum served only to underscore the lesson of the *Lex Forrer*. When interest groups were not placated during the legislative process, they had the means to undo the work of government.[34]

Consultative procedures

The failure of the *Lex Forrer* and the passage of the 1911 Sickness and Accident Insurance Law illustrate the main characteristics of the Swiss pattern of policy making. The referendum tended to attract negative voters, whose individual definitions of interest contradicted the views of interest-group association leaders and politicians. Whereas organizational leaders thought in terms of policy packages and were willing to make compromises, the individual voters were not bound by these constraints. The uncertainty created by the rejection of the *Lex Forrer* shaped all of the provisions of the 1911 legislation. Great care was taken to eliminate all points to which potential opponents would object, although the views of interest groups that wished to see legislation enacted were not taken into account, even though the proponents represented groups in the population that were far more numerous than the opponents.

This meant that plans for national health insurance, compulsory membership, employer contributions, and public administration of the program were scrapped in favor of a minimal program of government subsidies for voluntary insurance. Not only was the government role in financing health insurance pared down, but alternative ideas about providing medical services through a national health service were rejected. Furthermore, suggestions for regulating doctors' fees under the program were also rejected. Thus, referendum politics eliminated several points of potential incursion on professional autonomy – direct government provision of services, centralized national health insurance, and controls on doctors' fees. Yet, it could not be claimed that the neglect of union demands and the incorporation of medical demands could be traced to the specific organization of either the medical profession or the labor movement. Instead, the bias of the referendum mechanism toward the opponents of legislation, and the strategic opportunities for interest groups that this bias afforded, explain which points were adopted.

These experiences – not only in the field of health insurance but also in other policy areas such as the Factory Acts – affected more than the specific provisions of particular legislative proposals, however. They spurred institutional changes in the relationship between interest groups and the Swiss federal executive. At the turn of the century, procedures for interest-group consultation were formalized and made an integral part of the policy-making process. Interest groups were represented on expert commissions charged with drafting legislation, and then consulted again when formulated proposals were distributed to a large number of groups for comment, a process known as *Vernehmlassung*. To compensate for its weak bureaucracy, the federal government decided to provide interest groups with annual subsidies of up to 15,000 Swiss francs. In return, these groups were to help in preparing and implementing legislation. This step increased the mutual dependence of the federal bureaucracy and interest groups. It also affected the importance of interest associations relative to competing representative institutions, such as the cantons and the political parties.[35] These institutional changes – changes that came about as interest groups and policy makers adapted themselves to one another – had a lasting impact on the course of health care politics in Switzerland.

CONFIRMATION OF THE REFERENDUM PATTERN

As in other Western European nations, the First and Second World Wars and the Depression created political pressures for social policy reform in Switzerland. The number of workers organized into unions and the number of votes for the Social Democratic Party rose significantly. Two political and institutional turning points were particularly critical for the incorporation of the social democratic forces into Swiss politics. Since the beginning of the century, the Swiss left had become increasingly militant. Gruner argues that the exclusion of the left was responsible for this growth in antisystem sentiment.[36] Despite universal manhood suffrage, the de facto income barriers to voting and the results of the multimember majority voting system meant that the Social Democratic Party was significantly underrepresented. Since 1900, the Social Democratic Party had steadily polled one-third of voters in Swiss elections, but in 1907 the party held less than 5 percent of the seats in parliament.

In addition, as the case of the *Lex Forrer* illustrated, the dynamics of referendum politics decimated the ability of the left to exert pressure for meaningful social reforms. As early as 1900, the Social Democrats had launched a double constitutional initiative to introduce proportional representation and direct election of the executive, but it failed. The increasing restiveness of the labor movement came to a head after the First World War, when the Social Democratic Party and the Swiss Trade Union Confederation cooperated in organizing a general strike. This challenge to the status quo was put down when the Bundesrat threatened to call out the military. A civil war was narrowly averted because the strike organizers backed off. But the confrontation caused a change in course by the Radical Democrats. Proportional representation was introduced in 1918, and the party announced plans for a number of social reforms, including the eight-hour day, old-age and survivors' insurance, and regulation of working conditions. Despite these institutional and political changes, however, the referendum set severe restraints on what was ultimately enacted.[36]

Political realignment

The first election after proportional representation caused an electoral realignment. Radical Democratic representation in the Nationalrat decreased from 105 to 60, while Social Democratic representation increased from 22 to 41 seats, and the Farmers' Party entered the Nationalrat for the first time with 29 seats. Between 1919 and 1935, the number of votes for the Social Democratic Party increased from 175,000 to 255,000, when the Social Democratic Party became the largest party in the Nationalrat. The party entered the executive in 1943 when it received its first seat on the Federal Council. Not only did the party become incorporated, in terms of votes and formal representation, but during the 1920's the party and the trade unions began using the referendum mechanism, blocking an increase in the number of working hours and a law providing for increased penalties against sedition. This demonstration of their veto power brought the trade unions into consultation procedures as equal partners, cooperating with the Farmers' Association in promoting protectionist legislation, and signing a corporatist bargaining agreement in the watch industry, the "Peace Agreement" of 1937. From enrolling 18 percent of industrial workers in 1906, Swiss unions enrolled 41 percent of industrial workers and 29 percent of the total labor force by 1950; by 1955, union membership reached 49 percent of industrial workers. Thus, in terms of many indicators of "working-class strength" – Social Democratic votes, union membership, corporatist agreements, strike threats, alliance with farmers – the Swiss labor movement emerged from the interwar period with substantial gains.[37]

Nevertheless, despite this shift in electoral and organizational power, the referendum continued to work against the political pressures for social policy expansion. Although preceded by a constitutional initiative, efforts to establish old age and survivors' insurance during the 1920s were blocked by a referendum in 1931. Paralleling the French case, the Swiss executive then turned to institutional change in order to bypass the relevant political veto point – in this case the referendum rather than the parliament. An emergency powers act, temporarily suspending the referendum and allowing the Bundesrat to enact legislation directly, was passed in 1939. This direct executive route was utilized to establish several pieces of social legislation: insurance to cover the salaries of military personnel, old-age and survivors' insurance, and disability insurance.[38]

After the Second World War, preparations began for national health insurance and maternity insurance. But a popular initiative for a "return to direct democracy" reestablished the referendum mechanism, and the logic of referendum politics was again reproduced, despite the changed social and political circumstances of the postwar period.[38a] Although the sickness funds, unions, women's, family, and church groups all demanded national health and national maternity insurance, the referendum again brought out negative voting. And again, the opponents of national health insurance were able to determine the course of action taken in the aftermath of the referendum defeat.

Problems of the sickness funds

Pressure for a new health insurance law came mainly from the sickness funds, which had lobbied continuously since the implementation of the 1911 law for legislation to correct what they perceived as the deficiencies of the law. Three issues were of concern to the funds: the financing of the system, the lack of compulsory coverage, and the regulation of doctors' fees. As will be recalled, all three areas had been politically contested during the drafting of the 1911 law, and there were political grounds for the particular provisions of the 1911 law on these points. As the Swiss health insurance system developed within the economic and regulatory framework set forth by the 1911 law, the same questions continued to trouble the funds.

After the introduction of the 1911 law, sickness fund membership grew rapidly. In fact, health insurance carried by government-subsidized sickness funds was slowly turning into middle-class insurance. Because the sickness funds were private, nonprofit organizations receiving government subsidies, the lines between sickness funds and private insurance companies had become blurred. Subsidies were paid to the funds on behalf of each member enrolled, no matter what his income, or what type of insurance policy he bought. Many private insurance companies simply opened nonprofit divisions so that they could receive the government subsidies. Patients were allowed to take out any kind of policy they wanted, the basic benefits required under the 1911 law, plus extras, such as hospital care in a private room rather than in a general ward. This flexibility and allowance for privileged treatment in the policies had the effect of unifying insurance carriers; there were no first and second class-insurance *carriers*, only first and second-class *policies*.

Between 1911 and 1950, the number of insured persons increased from 500,000 to 3 million, or from 11 percent to 65 percent of the population. Nevertheless, low-income earners – those most in need of health insurance – were not availing themselves of voluntary health insurance. In addition, the growth of voluntary coverage had increased the financial burdens on the funds. Enrollment of women and children, who were more expensive to insure, and greater numbers of policies covering medical, as opposed to cash benefits, had rapidly increased the average cost of health insurance. As the federal subsidies were only occasionally increased, the funds had to pay for these cost increases by raising the premiums of the insured. The funds argued that the increase in premiums was causing government-subsidized health insurance to lose its social character. Whereas the government subsidies had initially covered 40–60 percent of health insurance costs, by 1922 the subsidies covered only 20 percent of costs, pricing health insurance out of the reach of those who needed it most. Of course, as the funds competed with one another, there were market pressures against increasing the premiums, which gave the funds a self-interested reason as well as an altruistic reason for preferring additional government funding to premium increases.[39]

The spread of insurance coverage to the middle class also had repercussions for the issue of doctors' fees. Under the 1911 system, local medical associations were to negotiate fee schedules with individual sickness funds that were to be approved by the cantons. In addition, the cantons were to establish a schedule of minimum and maximum fees that were to provide a framework for these negotiations and to regulate fees in the event that no agreement had been reached. The method of paying doctors varied from fund to fund. Some relied on the French system of reimbursement (third-party guarantor, or *tiers garant*); others used the German method of direct third-party payment (*tiers payant*). In both cases, as in France, locally negotiated fee schedules did not effectively cap fees, however. Local medical associations had no incentive to negotiate the schedules, and few fee schedules were renegotiated. Although the cantonal fee schedules were intended to limit fees in "contractless" situations, and the funds were liable only for the fee listed in the cantonal schedule, the discrepancy between the actual fees charged by doctors and the cantonal fee schedules threatened the value of the insurance. The funds could stick to their legal obligation and pay only part of the actual fee charged, or they could pay for the actual fees charged and raise their premiums.

Many doctors took matters into their own hands, simply ignoring the cantonal tariffs, and charging patients the difference between these schedules and their own private rates (balance-billing). Particularly as middle-class patients joined the sickness funds, local medical associations objected to fee controls. The sickness funds complained about a movement of doctors (particularly the French Swiss) who wanted to free themselves from the sickness funds. Some sickness funds agreed to allow doctors to vary their fees according to patients' incomes, charging more for wealthier patients. (This was the controversial exemption from the French fee schedules (*fortune du malade*) at issue during the debate over the Gazier reform, which was eliminated by the Decrees of May 1960.) But this system of "class categories" – as it was called, or "sliding fees" as it would be referred to in the United States – was technically illegal under the 1911 law.[40]

The size of the federal subsidies to the funds, compulsory coverage, and controls on doctors' fees had been discussed in 1921, in conjunction with plans for old-age and survivors insurance, but these plans were shelved when a 1931 referendum blocked the proposal. Instead, in 1936, the government introduced obligatory cost-sharing measures to improve the financial situation of the funds. Patients would be required to pay deductibles of at least 10 percent and not more than 25 percent of health care costs, with the exact percentage left to the individual funds.

In sum, the funds preferred to solve their financial problems through increased government subsidies rather than damaging their competitive position vis-à-vis other funds by raising their premiums, which would also make it more difficult for poorer persons to insure themselves, and by reducing their costs by limiting the fees charged by physicians. The government, on the other hand, did not want to take on extra fiscal responsibility during the Depression. But with the changed political situation after the war, the Bundesrat now seemed prepared to enact more expansive social policy measures.[41]

The 1949 TB law

As in the late nineteenth century, a related policy issue, rather than health insurance itself, provided the opportunity for legislation. A constitutional amendment – the Family Protection Article of 25 November 1945 – declared that the federal government would introduce maternity insurance that could be compulsory for all or parts of the population. Viewing it as more rational to work out a comprehensive program, the Federal Department for Social Insurance drafted a proposal covering both national health insurance and maternity insurance for low-income earners in 1948. At the same time, it prepared a second proposal to combat tuberculosis that included obligatory x-rays for the entire population as well as compulsory health insurance for low-income earners.[42]

While the national health and maternity insurance law was still in draft form, however, the reform process was interrupted by conflicts that broke out over the new tuberculosis law.[43] The law had been unanimously approved by the cantonally elected Ständerat and by all but three votes in the proportionally elected Nationalrat in October 1948. Nevertheless, it was defeated in a heated referendum battle.

Although the referendum was initiated by French-Swiss liberals, doctors and employers were the most visible opponents of the law.[44] The Swiss Medical Association accused the government of trying to sneak national health insurance in under the guise of more popular measures to combat tuberculosis, and viewed compulsory health insurance for low-income earners as the first step to a universal scheme. Although the association had previously been willing to discuss compulsory national health insurance, as long as guarantees were made that only 30 percent of the population could be insured, now that an opportunity presented itself, the association declared itself against any compulsion whatsoever. In addition, the profession argued, the program of compulsory x-rays could not be recommended from a medical point of view; too much tuberculosis was imported to Switzerland via foreign workers, according to the doctors, for compulsory screening of the Swiss population to be effective.[45]

The Swiss Employers' Association, too, warned of the "bureaucratization" and "socialization" of medicine, stating that the law "threatens our individual liberties, that is to say, the right to dispose of one's physical being."[46] Employers' support for the medical profession was not entirely disinterested, however – for employers were also concerned about the portion of the law that allowed cantons to charge employers for costs of compulsory x-rays. Though the Swiss Farmers' Association and the Swiss Small Business Association did not openly oppose the law, their point of view was clearly negative and, like the Employers' Association, they linked national health insurance to the issue of government intervention per se. The Small Business Association noted, for example, that the "same authoritarian, police-state spirit is hidden in the TB law as in other recent governmental measures."[47]

On the other hand, the law was supported by unions, employee associations, some church organizations, and, of course, the sickness funds – groups whose large memberships should have counted heavily in a referendum campaign. The unions had organized 40 percent of non-agricultural wage and salary earners, or 29 percent of the total workforce.[48] And the sickness funds alone, with 3 million members, should have been able to determine the outcome, although, of course, many of these members – women and children – could not vote.[49] Now united in a single federation – Konkordat of Sickness Funds – the funds were also in a better position to organize a referendum campaign than they had been in 1900.[50]

Furthermore, the law was supported by the political parties. It had, after all, been approved virtually unanimously in parliament, and in preparation for the referendum the four largest Swiss parties had declared themselves either in favor of the law or neutral – the Social Democratic Party and the Catholic-Conservative parties supported the law (the latter, however, without binding its cantonal affiliates), whereas the Radical-Democrats and the Farmers, Artisans, and Citizens Party left this decision up to their individual members. In 1947, these four parties controlled 85 percent of the seats in the Nationalrat. The Social Democratic Party was now considered a fully incorporated party, with its first member of the Federal Council elected in 1943 and controlling 24.7 percent of the seats in the Nationalrat, compared with 26.8 percent for the Radical-Democrats and 22.7 percent for the Catholic-Conservatives. In the Ständerat, the situation was different, however, with the proportions at 9 percent, 25.6 percent and 41.9 percent, respectively, for the Social Democrats, the Radical-Democrats, and the Catholic-Conservatives. This difference had no impact on the TB law, however; in fact, the Ständerat had voted unanimously for the law.[51] Of the smaller parties, the Democratic Party supported the law, while the Liberal Party and the Party of Independents opposed the reform.[52]

Nevertheless, on 22 May 1949 the TB law was defeated by a three to one majority (614,000 votes to 203,000). It did not carry a single canton. Given the evident fact that the groups that supported this law had much larger memberships than those that opposed the law, how can we explain this defeat? Why did the individual voters enrolled in unions or sickness funds not support the TB law, with its concomitant national health insurance for low-income earners?

Obviously disappointed by these results, the sickness funds argued that the referendum resulted from the medical profession's ability to mobilize antistate sentiment, which was particularly high as a result of wartime restrictions, and from a general lack of understanding of social insurance among the public.[53] The TB referendum was part of a wave of referenda that followed the lifting of the executive's wartime emergency powers, lending support to this claim. In fact, a second law, concerning banking, was vetoed on the same day. Opponents of national health insurance, on the other hand, argued that the "overwhelming majority of the People wish neither for state socialism nor for centralizing policies; they prefer to remain with their approved, sound, free and Federal order."[54]

Negative voting

As with the *Lex Forrer*, however, the results can be explained simply by looking at the legislative proposal and considering how individual voters would be likely to react. Although policy makers, the sickness funds, and union organizations might have understood the collective benefits of national health insurance, and the role of the TB law as the first step in establishing national health insurance, the TB law had little appeal to the individual voters who participated in the referendum.

The law called for compulsory insurance for low-income earners. Anyone with a high income had no particular interest in this compulsion – unless for some reason he was concerned about the uninsured. For those with low incomes, the law required only that they insure themselves; it did not provide government financial aid. If they had not taken the step of insuring themselves, why would they vote for a law that would compel them to insure themselves? And who would bother to go out to vote for compulsory x-rays? Moreover, the initial impetus for the law was a popular plebiscite calling for maternity insurance. But the Federal Office of Social Insurance began its efforts with health insurance. It was not in the individual interests of voters to vote for a law that was to be the first step toward increased government funding and regulation, when the law proposed higher taxes with no increase in benefits for those that were already insured. Of course, in the long run, many of these individuals might have more children or become chronically ill, and they would certainly become old, in which case, spreading the risk of social insurance would be a more advantageous option.

But this kind of logic required adding many steps to the proposal. The law before the voters was so minimal that it is difficult to see how the unions and sickness funds could easily inspire their members to go out and vote. Thus, when the issue of national health insurance was moved from the executive and parliamentary arenas – where there was widespread agreement on the law – to the electoral arena, a different set of criteria became relevant. Whereas political elites were concerned with the percentage of the population covered by health insurance, preventive medicine, and their ability to control the overall costs of the system through collective financing and regulating doctors' fees, individual voters viewed the relative costs and benefits of the legislation in individual terms.

The referendum process did not end with this negative vote, however. Over the protests of the Swiss Trade Union Federation and the Konkordat of Sickness Funds, the opponents of the law – the Swiss Medical Association and the Employers' and Farmers' Associations, supported by the Small Business Association – petitioned the Federal Office of Social Insurance to withdraw its plans for health insurance reform in light of the referendum. Although it might have been possible to interpret the results of the plebiscite as a mandate for greater benefits, or sticking to maternity insurance rather than tuberculosis, interest groups were able to demand an end to social benefits expansion. Thus, for a second time, national health insurance was blocked by the results of a national referendum. And, once again, interest groups controlled the interpretation of the plebiscite.

UNANIMITY RULE: THE 1954 REFORM ATTEMPT

Although national health insurance had been removed from the political agenda, the problems that had motivated the Bundesrat in 1949 had not disappeared. The constitutional initiative for maternity insurance still stood. And the sickness funds continued to lobby for better federal subsidies and controls on doctors' fees. As in previous attempts at reform, the Bundesrat drafted a proposal that paid attention to possible referendum threats. However, when interest-group disagreements were voiced in the preparliamentary expert commission, the Bundesrat withdrew its reform. After years of referendum politics, the principle of unanimity rule had now become explicit.

The 1954 Bundesrat proposal specifically announced that while low-income earners lacked coverage, previous referenda had made it necessary to renounce compulsory health insurance. Instead, the Bundesrat proposed to enact compulsory maternity insurance and to double the size of the federal subsidies, which now covered about 10 percent of health insurance costs, as opposed to the 40 percent envisioned by the 1911 law.[55] This proposal made it as far as the expert commission stage, but interest-group responses to the commission report were "too divided" for the government to pursue reform.[56] The main points of contention were the increased federal subsidies, the compulsory aspect of the insurance, and a new issue, a provision that legalized the division of the insured into income classes. The 1954 proposal sought to establish a system of binding fee schedules for low and middle-income earners, in return for which doctors would be able to set their own fees for wealthy patients. This area of insurance law was referred to as "medical rights."

Although interest groups had participated in the expert commission that prepared the reform, they were then given a chance to comment on the reform before a final legislative proposal was drawn up. Significantly, the potential for a referendum allowed the opponents of government expansion to increase their demands; even points on which they had seemed willing to agree during the expert commission were raised again, and new suggestions were made.

Like the French interest groups of the Fourth Republic, who could disrupt the parliamentary coalition, the Swiss interest groups willing to use the referendum had no reason to compromise and could escalate their demands at any stage in the policy process. The Employers' Association, the Federation of Trade and Industry, the Farmers' Association, the Small Business Association, the Association of Private Insurance Companies, and the Swiss Medical Association all opposed the reform. They were against the increased federal subsidies, arguing that the premiums of the insured should be increased, and they objected to federal compulsory maternity insurance. On the division of the insured into income classes, employers appeared neutral. They acknowledged that income classes were unpopular, but did not consider it reasonable that doctors should be "forced to treat economically well-situated patients for low fees when these same people remunerate other free professions at their usual rates."[57] In contrast to French employers, who by the mid-1950s were paying large sums for compulsory health insurance, Swiss employers were not financially involved, and did not concern themselves with medical fees.

Although the medical profession agreed with these employer groups that the federal subsidies would be too costly and that compulsory maternity insurance was ill-advised, they differed from these allies in that they strongly supported the new system of sliding fees. In discussing the issue of compulsory national health insurance – which was not even proposed by the 1954 Expert Report – the Swiss Medical Association noted that the current system "corresponds to the Federal structure of our country and doubtless also to the wishes of the large majority of our people." And, rather pointedly, they added that "without indulging in historical reminiscences, we refer in this connection to the results of the popular plebiscites on the so-called Lex Forrer of 20 May 1900 and on the Supplementary Tuberculosis Law of 22 May 1949."[58]

The Konkordat of Sickness Funds also referred to the *Lex Forrer* referendum in its position paper, arguing that the law had been rejected for reasons completely unrelated to the compulsory nature of the insurance, such as the introduction of public sickness funds.[59] The funds were part of a reform coalition consisting of unions, employee associations, and women's and family groups.[60] These groups welcomed the increased federal subsidies and maternity insurance, but protested against the neglect of national health insurance, at least for low-income earners. Although official figures showed that 69 percent of the population was insured, these organizations argued that such figures were misleading. Members belonging to several funds were counted several times. The figures did not distinguish between members insured for medical benefits and those insured only for cash benefits. And they hid important regional differences. In fourteen cantons, less than three-quarters of the population was insured; in six cantons, less than half; and in one rural canton, less than one-third. Most important, it was precisely the population group that was uninsured – low-income earners – that most needed insurance. These groups were also opposed to the division of the insured into income classes. (The sickness funds were absolutely opposed and unwilling to accept income classes, but the unions stated that they were willing to go along with it.[61])

Even though this proposal resulted from an expert commission composed of interest-group representatives, no compromise appeared possible.[62] Employers, farmers, small businessmen, private insurers, and doctors opposed the increased subsidies and maternity insurance that the sickness funds, unions, family and women's groups supported. No group other than the Medical Association supported the system of income classes, although many were willing to accept the system, considering it inevitable. The sickness funds, on the other hand, would not concede this point. Given these differences of opinion, the Bundesrat refused to proceed; the risk of a referendum was simply too high.

REFERENDUM-BASED BARGAINING: THE 1964 PARTIAL REVISION

Each successive failed attempt at national health insurance reform had further limited the definition of what was politically feasible in Switzerland. Although the Second World War had returned the question of social citizenship rights to the political agenda, the failure of the 1949 tuberculosis law had ruled out compulsory national health insurance.

The failure of the 1954 proposal ruled out the issues of compulsory maternity insurance and regulation of doctors' fees. Nevertheless, health insurance reform was not abandoned. In 1958, the Federal Office for Social Insurance announced that it intended to pursue a partial reform of the health insurance system. As a total reform had been shown to be politically unfeasible, the new reform "must be designed in such a way so as to assure its prospects of acceptance without a referendum battle."[63] To this end, the reform would not include national compulsory health or maternity insurance. Instead, the Federal Council would focus on increasing the government subsidies. The executive was thus attempting to protect itself from the electoral arena, the veto point. As the referendum could not be circumvented in the way that the French executive had circumvented parliament, the risk of referendum was to be reduced by keeping certain issues off the agenda.

In 1959, the balance of political power in Switzerland shifted once again in favor of the Social Democrats. With the election of Hans-Peter Tschudi to the Federal Council, for the first time, two out of the seven members of the executive were chosen from the Social Democratic Party, a proportion that has been maintained ever since.[64] Professor of Labor and Social Insurance Law, as well as President of the Swiss Association for Social Policy, Tschudi took over the Department of the Interior, making the health insurance reform his personal project. Like his predecessor Federal Councilor Forrer, Federal Councilor Tschudi used the tactic of trying to eliminate controversial points in the legislation and trying to push the reform through as speedily as possible. As in 1949, however, referendum politics were to dampen the effects of increases in Social Democratic representation. Tschudi was ultimately successful in putting together a package to which no interest group was sufficiently opposed to call for a referendum challenge. However, along the way, so many compromises to interest groups had been made that the legislation was hardly recognizable.

Building consensus

Tschudi played an assertive role in pushing the reform through the legislative process. During previous reform efforts, interest groups willing to launch referenda had increased their demands at every phase in the policy process, making it extremely difficult to reach consensus. This time, Bundesrat politicians tried to streamline the process, minimizing the number of times that interest groups would review the proposal, and both the sickness funds and the medical profession were specifically asked to pledge themselves to refrain from reintroducing controversial issues into the reform debate. Generally, once the Federal Council had formally been invited by parliament to formulate a proposal, the government would appoint a commission of interest-group and government representatives to draft a legislative proposal, which would then in turn be submitted to interest groups for further comment. Only then would the Federal Council present its final proposal (*Botschaft*) to the parliament. In this case, however, the Department of the Interior drew up a list of general principles that were presented to interest groups for comment.[65]

Not only did the bureaucracy insist upon a very limited reform, engineered to improve health insurance finances and benefits quickly without generating political conflicts, but even after the release of its report, it continued its efforts to promote speedy passage of the reform. As a result of these meetings, the Konkordat and the Swiss Medical Association agreed to support the government's proposal for improved federal subsidies and insurance benefits without revision of the conflict-ridden "medical rights" portion of the law, which regulated the relationship between patients, doctors, and the funds.[66] This agreement – the "Geneva accord" of June 1960 – paved the way, it was assumed, for smooth passage of the law. In addition, Tschudi insisted upon an unusually short period for interest groups to return their written responses (*Vernehmlassungen*) to the government report, and was able to produce a legislative proposal only four months after the consultation procedure.[67] In order to increase the probability that an agreement could be reached, the Bundesrat reduced the range of issues covered, attempted to bind interest groups to stay away from these issues, and to limit the number of decision points.

In order to improve health insurance financing, the report proposed that the system of federal subsidies be revised. Previously, these subsidies had been set at a fixed rate – that is, a certain sum of money was paid on behalf of each sickness fund member. New legislation was required for any increase in these subsidies that might be made necessary by rising costs. Now the government proposed that the federal subsidies be calculated on the basis of actual health insurance costs. The Federal government would now pay 10, 15, and 25 percent of the average annual costs incurred by the sickness funds for men, women, and children, respectively. This would increase federal subsidies by about 25 million Swiss francs – from the 60 million paid annually to 85 million. No subsidies would be paid on behalf of members in "very good economic circumstances," a group that was to be defined by the individual cantons. The federal subsidies would thus be indexed to health insurance costs. At the same time, the minimum benefits required of the funds would be improved: The minimum coverage for hospitalization and cash benefits was increased, and coverage for ambulatory care would now be unlimited. The controversial issues that had undermined previous attempts at reform – national compulsory coverage, maternity insurance, and the issue of doctors' fees – would be completely left out of the reform.

Interest-group opinions

At first, Tschudi's strategy was relatively successful. As long as health insurance remained voluntary and not compulsory, the Swiss Employers' Association, the Federation of Trade and Industry, and the Small Business Association were willing to go along with the reform, although these groups argued that indexing the subsidies was inflationary and that they preferred that cost increases be met with increases in premiums and cost-sharing on the part of the insured.[68] The Swiss Medical Association also criticized the indexing as a "centralizing tendency" contrary to the principles of the decentralized Swiss system.

On the other hand, two traditional opponents to expanded government financing strongly supported the indexing of subsidies. On the grounds that the new federal subsidies would greatly improve rural health care, the Swiss Farmers' Association supported the proposal. The cantons also supported the new subsidies, and in their responses brought up a relatively new issue in Swiss health care policy: rising hospital costs. Because the cantons subsidized hospitals by paying large portions of their operating deficits, they were becoming increasingly concerned about the gap between hospital costs and health insurance coverage. According to the Swiss Hospital Association (VESKA) – to which, as hospital owners, most cantons belonged – payments by sickness funds comprised 22 percent of hospital receipts in 1958 but covered only 14 percent of costs.[69] Noting their concern for these rising deficits, virtually all of the cantons strongly supported the switch from flat-rate to indexed federal subsidies.[70]

Unions, employee associations, and the sickness funds also supported the system of indexing, although some of these groups were angry that the reform ignored the issue of compulsory insurance. Whereas the Swiss Trade Union Confederation limited its negative comments, simply noting its "regret" that a more far-reaching reform could not be undertaken, other groups were more critical. The Catholic Trade Union Federation, the Protestant (Evangelical) Confederation of Trade Unions and Employee Associations, women's groups, and the *Mouvement Populaire des Familles* (a family organization) all demanded national maternity insurance, and some also demanded national health insurance.[71] Catholic, employee, and women's groups thus seem to have been more concerned about health and maternity insurance than the unions, possibly because these groups represented greater numbers of women, whose insurance costs were higher than men's, as well as out of a commitment to family issues.

Thus, although not every interest group was completely satisfied, no group threatened to call for a referendum. Based on these responses from interest groups, the Federal Council drafted a legislative proposal that was presented to the Federal Assembly on 5 June 1961.[72] Arguing that the provisions of the reform had been discussed in previous expert commissions and that interest groups had already been given a chance to comment on the main points of the reform, the Federal Council decided that parliamentary consideration of the proposal should begin immediately, rather than being delayed by another round of interest-group consultation. Consequently, the proposal was sent directly to a committee of the Ständerat for discussion.[73]

Return to medical rights

Before the proposal could be discussed, however, a major setback for Federal Councilor Tschudi's strategy occurred. The executive council of the Swiss Medical Association informed Tschudi that because the proposal touched on the issue of medical rights, the association would not abide by its previous decision to refrain from demanding revisions in this area, but was instead reasserting its freedom to negotiate over medical rights.[74] This sudden about face was sharply criticized not only by the sickness funds, but also by parliamentarians and the press. At the first meeting of the Ständerat commission in August 1961, Federal Councilor Tschudi and the Director of the Federal Office for Social Insurance, Arnold Saxer, argued that the medical profession was simply using a pretext to renew its demands for legalizing the division of the insured into income classes, and that consideration of this difficult issue would block the reform process. Nevertheless, the commission voted unanimously to reintroduce the issue of medical rights into the debate.[75]

This decision, one that ultimately benefited the medical profession, should not be interpreted simply as a concession to the wishes of the Swiss Medical Association. Some members of the commission did promote the point of view of the profession. Others, however, argued that the committee had a duty to consider the issue of medical rights not in order to legalize sliding fees, as the physicians had demanded, but in order to assure effective regulation of doctors' fees, especially in the absence of contractual agreements between the funds and local medical societies.

During these deliberations, the committee members debated at length the possibilities for a referendum challenge to the reform. One proponent of regulation of doctors' fees argued that as the law provided greatly improved benefits, chances of a referendum defeat were slim. The committee should therefore seize this opportunity to settle the matter of doctors' fees. Supporters of the medical profession, on the other hand, used the same reasoning to argue that the sickness funds would not be able to launch a campaign against the law and that, consequently, the committee should not concern itself with appeasing the funds. Still other supporters of physicians argued that the results of the TB referendum of

1949 demonstrated that no health insurance reforms could be enacted without the approval of the medical profession. The committee finally ruled that the health insurance reform should include the issue of medical rights and that the bureaucracy should work out a suitable revision through further consultation with representatives of the medical profession and the sickness funds. At the same time, the committee discussed some preliminary ideas for the regulation of doctors' fees that had been drafted by the Federal Office for Social Insurance. Thus, the discussion centered on the referendum threat, yet even the participants disagreed as to the optimum political strategy to pursue given this institutional constraint.

Escalation of medical demands

As Federal Councilor Tschudi had feared, the inclusion of "medical rights" severely impeded the legislative process. Not only was it difficult to find a compromise position between the disputing parties, but, once the issue had been reopened, the demands of the medical profession began to increase. Originally, the profession simply asked that the portion of the 1911 Sickness and Accident Insurance Law that prohibited sliding fees be struck. Now, doctors in the western, French-speaking regions of Switzerland, who publicized their views in the journal *Médecine et Hygiène*, demanded absolute freedom to determine their own fees. In addition, all third-party payment should be replaced by a reimbursement system, as in France. That is, rather than sending doctors' bills to their sickness funds for payment, patients would be obliged to pay doctors' fees in full and would then submit these bills to the funds for reimbursement.

The 1911 law did not specify whether patients or sickness funds were directly liable for payments to doctors, and both *tiers payant* and *tiers garant* were found in practice. To the sickness funds, however, the reimbursement system was unacceptable. In the funds' view, third-party payment would allow the funds to enforce negotiated fee schedules, whereas under a reimbursement system, doctors would be able to charge more, demanding that their patients pay the difference between these fees and the official fee-schedules. The funds *were* willing to accept income classes, on the other hand, but only on the condition that adequate mechanisms were introduced to guarantee the availability of medical treatment at reasonable rates to fund members.[76]

The reintroduction of the issue of doctors' fees delayed the parliamentary procedings for more than two years. As Tschudi had predicted, opening up the agenda allowed conflicts between the doctors and the sickness funds to dominate the legislative discussions and created stalemate. The legislative proposal that finally went back to the Ständerat (after countless meetings between Tschudi, the Swiss Medical Associa-

:ion, and the Konkordat of sickness funds) divided the insured into two groupings. Doctors would be able to set their fees freely for patients in "very good economic circumstances." The fees charged to other patients would be regulated by negotiated fee schedules; when negotiations failed, doctors' fees would be regulated by cantonal fee schedules. The negotiated fee schedules could specify either direct third-party payment or reimbursement. If no fee schedules were negotiated, however, third-party payment would be used for the compulsorily insured, but reimbursement for the voluntarily insured. Finally, the cantons could force doctors to participate in insurance practice in areas where there were shortages of doctors available to fund members. Doctors who refused would be subject to six months in jail or a 10,000 franc fine. These provisions essentially codified the legal status quo, but with some changes to satisfy each of the parties. The doctors would get the income classes and the funds would be able to force doctors to treat patients. By restating the principle that the cantons would set fee schedules, it was hoped that enforcement of this provision would be improved.[77]

Referendum threats

Tschudi had hoped that this compromise proposal would be passed by the Ständerat and that the potential benefits to the insured and the indexing, which the cantons wanted, would be an incentive to push the law through. But the medical profession was in a position to hold up the debate. Like the French doctors who had no reason to compromise as long as parliament was the relevant political arena, Swiss doctors ready to grasp the referendum threat were in a veto position. As in France, the open channel of resistance allowed the economic liberal faction of the profession – the French-Swiss doctors – to push for a more hard-line solution.

The Swiss Medical Association charged that fee controls were "the first step towards socialized medicine."[78] Calling the proposal an example of "unnecessary statism . . . unworthy of a liberal profession and a democratic state," the medical profession launched a full-scale attack on the reform.[79] Increasing the dues of its 7,000 members from 40 to 70 Swiss francs, the Swiss Medical Association built up a "war chest" estimated at over 1 million francs and hired a professional public relations firm. This strategy self-consciously emulated the American Medical Association's successful campaign against national health insurance, in which its 140,000 members were each assessed $25 and an estimated $4.6 million was spent between 1948 and 1952. Most of this money was spent on a press campaign aimed at both the general public and other interest groups. Had a referendum battle been necessary in Switzerland, the profession would have spent even more.[80]

Swiss doctors were not the only group to warn politicians of the eventual referendum power, however. Swiss chiropractors dropped a bombshell. The chiropractors, who were not recognized by the Swiss Medical Association, collected nearly 400,000 signatures for a petition demanding that treatments by chiropractors be covered under health insurance policies on the same basis as treatments by licensed physicians. This, of course, created a dilemma. For the medical profession was adamnantly opposed to the inclusion of the chiropractors, but with such a large number of signatures, the chiropractors were clearly in a position to veto the reform by demanding a referendum.[81]

The Ständerat vote

During the progress of the law in both houses of parliament, the debate was dominated by the demands of groups that were perceived to be able to launch a referendum: doctors, chiropractors, and the sickness funds. Indeed, interest-group position rather than party affiliation constituted the main lines of cleavage; the main supporters of both the doctors and the sickness funds were to be found within the Catholic Conservative Party.

The main debate in the Ständerat took place on 21 March 1963. Although the behavior of the medical profession was severely criticized – with one admitted supporter of the physicians stating that the leadership had been "overrun by a more-or-less radicalized mass"[82] – the final vote constituted "a large and unequivocal victory" for the medical profession.[83] Income classes were accepted and could continue even if contracts between the funds and medical societies lapsed; the sanctions against doctors who refused to treat fund patients were dropped; the demand of the chiropractors was ignored; and it was decided that reimbursement rather than third-party payment would be the practice unless negotiated agreements specified otherwise. The debate focused on the medical profession, with the assurance that in Switzerland, no one wanted to turn the medical profession into civil servants, as was the case in England and Sweden, where the doctor was merely a functionary, "but no longer a doctor in our sense."[84] Defenders of the profession, appealing to liberal ideals, argued that only on "the soil of freedom" could one nurture the kind of physicians "that in practicing their profession unite a sense of ideals, social understanding, and human values . . . With the fettering of the freedom of its own citizens, begins the growth of bondage in the state."[85]

The points of view of other interest groups were also mentioned briefly. Several speakers noted that Swiss unions and employee associations were opposed to income classes, and that such classes would come across very poorly in a referendum campaign, but this seemed to have little effect. A number of articles by lawyers appearing in major newspapers, such as the *Neue Züricher Zeitung*, had questioned the constitutionality of the proposed measures for the regulation of doctors' fees.[86] These articles were discussed, and seemed to influence the votes.

Gerhard Kocher, the author of the main study of this reform, concludes that the vote in the Ständerat may be attributed to "the basic sympathy of the council majority for the medical profession, legal and constitutional considerations, and the physicians' propaganda and pressure-group activities."[87] What made these pressure-group activities so effective, however, was the possibility of veto through the referendum and, for the first time in Swiss health politics, through the courts.

The Nationalrat vote

The Konkordat of Sickness Funds reacted to the Ständerat vote with anger and demanded that the medical rights portion of the reform be removed. Some groups, such as the family organizations and the Protestant Union and Employee Association supported the funds. Most interest groups, however, including the Swiss Trade Union Confederation and the Association of Salaried Employees, were becoming increasingly impatient. The conflict over medical rights was simply holding up the long-awaited improvements in benefits; they demanded that the law be passed within a year. At the same time, the chiropractors made it clear that they were prepared to launch a referendum if the Nationalrat did not concede to their demands. The chiropractors offered to cooperate with the sickness funds, but the funds refused. The funds did not agree that chiropractors should be able to treat patients directly, without previous referral by a licensed physician. Moreover, they hesitated to oppose the Swiss Medical Association openly on an issue of professional licensing.

When the law moved to the Nationalrat, which had a much higher proportion of Social Democratic representatives, the politicians liberalized the health insurance proposal in several respects.[88] The Nationalrat decided to strengthen the provisions of the law concerning the protection of the insured in the event that contracts between the sickness funds and medical societies lapsed.[89] Third-party payment would be in force for low-income earners while reimbursement would be the assumed form of payment for those above a certain income limit – unless, of course, contractual agreements specified otherwise. The cantons would set these income limits, but in the discussion it was evident that generally these limits would apply to about 50 percent of the population in each canton. Though there was some controversy about the fact that 50 percent of the population was defined as low-income earners, this limit was generally accepted. The Nationalrat also voted to accept treatments by chiropractors on the same basis as treatments by physicians. In addition to these changes of concern to the medical profession, the Nationalrat amended the reform to benefit the insured. Federal subsidies would be increased from 102 million francs, as suggested by the Ständerat, to 130 million francs, with most of the increase coming from covering a greater portion of the costs incurred for female sickness fund members. The council also ruled that premiums for female members could be no more than 10 percent higher than men's contributions, compared with the 25 percent difference proposed by the Federal Council and the Ständerat.

Final compromises

When the reform went back to the Ständerat, it was quickly decided to accept the Nationalrat rulings on the protection of the insured in contract-less situations and on the maximum allowable difference between women's and men's insurance premiums. The question of liability for doctors' fees, third-party payment versus reimbursement, and the inclusion of chiropractors in sickness fund practice remained hotly contested, however. In subsequent parliamentary sessions, the Ständerat backed down on the issue of the chiropractors, and the Nationalrat give in on the question of doctors' payments. Unless otherwise specified, reimbursement would be the assumed method of payment.[90] On 13 March 1964, both houses of parliament voted unanimously for the 1964 Partial Revision of the Sickness and Accident Insurance Law of 1911.

During the final deliberations, the issue of a referendum challenge continued to reemerge, with the medical profession, the sickness funds, and the chiropractors singled out as the groups most likely to launch a referendum. Their calculations were so precise that the Ständerat committee even discussed the proportion of the signatories of the chiropractors' petition who were women and therefore not eligible to vote. The chairman of the Nationalrat committee explicitly stated that the committee had prepared a proposal that "could steer clear of the referendum 'cliff': One has to some extent satisfied the sickness funds (through the increases in subsidies), one has compromised with the doctors in the area of medical rights, and one has given the chiropractors more than the Bundesrat wishes to give them."[91] At this stage, commentary about the reform process was becoming ever more critical, with one politician summarizing the parliamentary behavior as "referendaphobia."[92]

Despite these criticisms of lobbying by special interests, these efforts were largely successful. The Swiss Medical Association had been able to make "medical rights" the central focus of debate, and it had achieved its main goals: income classes were legalized, reimbursement would be the method of payment unless collective agreements specified otherwise, and sanctions against doctors who refused to treat insurance patients were dropped. Chiropractors, too, were very successful. Over the protests of the Swiss Medical Association, chiropractors were incorporated into the system on the same basis as licensed physicians.

The sickness funds, on the other hand, were dissatisfied with the changes in medical rights. Physicians had been granted the right to charge the insured at rates that depended on patients' incomes, but the guarantees of low fees for low-income earners that were always viewed by the funds as the quid pro quo of income classes, were basically nonexistent.[93] Nevertheless, at a delegates' meeting of the Konkordat it was decided not to pursue a referendum challenge. As Konkordat president Hänggi explained, no party or union would be willing to fight the reform, and the chiropractors, delighted at the outcome, would constitute fierce competition in a referendum battle.

Better a little bit of progress with this revision than none at all. . . . For one must be clear about one thing: in a referendum battle, "medical rights" would not play a major role; instead, the talk would be of the improvements in benefits and Federal subsidies, that is, about the material improvements for the insured. The basic conflicts over medical rights, that are of interest to few, would remain obscure to most people; certainly, they would hardly unleash the groundswell of opposition that would be necessary to topple this law.[94]

After more than three years of debate, then, a reform process that was intended to be simple and uncontroversial had become protracted and ridden with conflict – without producing the kinds of structural changes needed to overhaul the system. As one critical account put it, "The public was treated to a ballet between, on the one hand, the commissions of the two parliamentary chambers and, on the other, doctors and sickness funds."[95]

The reform did bring about substantial improvements: The federal subsidies were more than doubled from a total of 61.5 million francs in 1963 to 129.6 million in 1964, as opposed to the 89.3 million proposed in the 1961 proposal.[96] More importantly, federal subsidies were now indexed to health-care costs. In addition, the minimum benefits required of the funds were increased.[97] The law also clarified the legal rights of the insured, specifying that disputes with sickness funds be settled by cantonal insurance courts, with appeals to the Federal Insurance Court.[98]

The law did not, however, provide a long-term solution to the financial troubles of the sickness funds, although it did clarify the obligation of the insured to pay between 10 and 25 percent of medical costs, except for hospital treatments and maternity care. Nor did it provide a satisfactory solution to the regulation of doctors' fees. National maternity insurance, a subject of debate since the constitutional initiative of 1945, had somehow gotten lost in the shuffle. Maternity benefits covered by the recognized sickness funds were increased, but all plans for compulsory insurance and better cash benefits for working women were dropped following the rejection of the 1954 Expert Commission proposal.

The ever-present possibility of forcing decisions into the electoral arena discouraged compromises and allowed even very narrow interests – for example, the chiropractors – to play a central role in the reform process. In the Swiss political system, the concept of power was defined by the referendum, and the rules of the game were set by an interpretation of how the referendum works. Just as in the French case, the logic of the system revolved around controlling the unpredictable parliament.

LATEST REFORM EFFORTS

The logic of referendum politics has continued to shape Swiss health policy since the 1964 partial revision, although that is the last reform that will be considered in detail. As health care costs have continued to rise, the executive has sought alternative financing sources for health insurance, but referendum challenges and interest-group resistance have blocked the proposals. In the early 1970s, a number of proposals were considered for national health insurance to cover hospitalization. The Social Democratic Party presented a popular initiative calling for compulsory national health insurance to be financed by federal contributions and a payroll tax. The insurance was to cover ambulatory and hospital care, sickness cash benefits, maternity care, dental care, and pharmaceuticals. In response, a government commission proposed compulsory hospital and sickness cash benefits insurance; insurance for ambulatory care and pharmaceuticals would remain voluntary. In addition, this plan, known as the Flimser model, also called for federal subsidies to hospitals that would be distributed according to a national plan, as well as a national fee schedule for doctors – thus outlining the beginnings of national regulation of doctors' fees and hospital construction found elsewhere in Western Europe.

These plans were met by a host of counterproposals by interest groups – including one jointly prepared by doctors and sickness funds, united in opposition to the separation of voluntary and compulsory insurance, that served as the basis for the final proposal presented by the Bundesrat. The Bundesrat's counterproposal combined some elements from both the Social Democratic initiative and the Flimser model, but, in contrast to both, hospital insurance would not be compulsory. Instead, insurance would be compulsory only for catastrophic illnesses and sickness cash benefits; everything else would be left to voluntary insurance. Compulsory payroll contributions would be levied; these would be used to subsidize hospital, maternity, preventive, and home care.

In the plebiscite of 8 December 1974 both plans were rejected – the Social Democratic plan by a ratio of five to two, the government's counterproposal by 880,000 votes to 450,000. Voter turnout was only 41 percent. The main result of this failure was that the federal government lowered its subsidies to health insurance by 10 percent, or 76.8 million francs. To compensate for this income loss, the patient deductible was increased from 20 francs per visit to 30 francs (50 francs for high-income patients).[99]

Even after the failure of these two plans, several new proposals have been put forth. In 1977, an expert commission proposed a payroll tax for hospital insurance, but interest-group opposition caused the withdrawal of the report. In 1981, a new proposal was published, this time covering mandatory sickness cash benefits to be provided for by employers, improved health and maternity benefits, and increased cost-sharing by the insured (coinsurance would be doubled from 10 percent to 20 percent of medical bills). However, interest-group resistance first caused the cash benefits insurance to be dropped; next, a referendum launched by the Small Business Association against the maternity insurance felled the proposal in 1987. Since that time, the sickness funds have presented a petition for a constitutional initiative for larger government subsidies, which has been met by a parliamentary increase in the subsidies, a move to reduce the support for the initiative.[100] Health policy debates, in sum, have continued to focus on compulsory versus voluntary insurance and the financing of the system.

HEALTH CARE POLITICS IN A DIRECT DEMOCRACY

This chapter has shown how the referendum, the core institution of direct democracy, established the "rules of the game" in Swiss health care politics. As Alfred Maurer, a Swiss social insurance expert states:

The facultative referendum has held the emergence and development of social insurance very much in check and has, in part, channelled it along lines which was not "programmed" by the authorities. . . . The referendum casts its shadow before it actually takes place. This is noticeable when boards of experts or the competent Department of the Federal Council prepare a legal bill. It is often apparent whether certain proposals will meet with opposition or not. This applies particularly if the competent Department submits its proposed solutions for a new bill to interested circles for comment. . . . The facultative referendum makes Swiss democracy a democracy of consensus, particularly in the sphere of social insurance; it is imperative that federal authorities have the approval of the most important groups in the population whenever decisive reforms are to be realized.[100a]

The referendum, as we have seen, has two separate effects. It provides the general public with a voice in policy making. And this public has not always agreed with politicians and interest organizations that the voters would be best served by an expansion of government. It is not at all clear that similar votes held in other countries would have yielded different results. For attempts to compare public attitudes to social programs do not show clear national trends. Wilensky does not find significant variation in public attitudes toward social programs, nor does Coughlin, nor do Shapiro and Young.[101] Moreover, we would expect problems of collective action and Pareto optimality to arise in any other country. The diversity of interests in the electorate and the pattern of negative voting causes the referendum to favor the status quo. In contrast to representative democracy, the semidirect democracy of the referendum does not provide a mechanism for reconciling interests, as the individual vote unbundles policy packages. It is therefore difficult to devise legislation that satisfies the wishes of a majority of voters, particularly in the area of protectionist legislation.

But referenda on Swiss national health insurance have only been held four times in the last hundred years. The effects of the potential of interest groups calling for a referendum are evident every day and have affected the entire policy process. Interest-group negotiations based on the unanimity rule of decision making (caused, in turn, by the referendum threat) have established limits to the policies that are proposed and enacted quite apart from actual referendum results. These interest groups have also been active in interpreting the public mandate of referendum results, which were not always entirely clear. Health care policy has been made by the Swiss Medical Association, employers, chiropractors, and to some extent the Konkordat of Sickness Funds, whereas unions and women's and family groups seem to fail systematically in their lobby efforts. The influence of these groups on health policy, like that of French interest groups, depends not on organizational or other resources, but on the opportunities provided by political institutions.

The Swiss health care system is thus not the only scheme imaginable to the Swiss; it is the product of years of political conflict. It was not the initial ideas about health policy proposed by civil servants, political parties, social movements, or interest groups that stand out as distinct from those in other countries, but rather Swiss political traditions, the specific institutional expression of those traditions, and the strategic opportunities for attaining and exploiting political power that these institutions made possible. Similarly, the fact that Switzerland is a federal state did not automatically preclude certain initiatives in health. It is not that it was unfeasible to construct a national health insurance system under the Swiss constitution or given Swiss political boundaries; it was not unfeasible, but it was politically impossible.

The referendum affected not only the outcomes of individual policy conflicts, but the organization of groups and the long-term pattern of political interests. Historically, recourse to the referendum was a countervailing force to pressures for centralization and aggregation of interests present in other political systems. The possibility for minority factions to go their own.ways without having to make compromises to organizations affected both the party system and the system of organized interest groups. Gruner stresses the effects of the referendum on the internal structure of political parties. They developed as loose alliances prepared to mount referendum campaigns. The continued importance of these local campaigns maintained the autonomy of local alliances within the party system. By analogy, the power of small groups to launch referendum challenges has kept small associations, such as the artisans, autonomous and free from the pressures that have led to interest-group consolidation in other countries. This fragmentation, in turn, made it more difficult to mobilize affirmative majorities in referendum campaigns. Further, because small groups wielded such influence, issues tended to be discussed in terms of minority interests rather than along other possible cleavages, such as party policy or class position.[102]

A conservative health system

It should be made clear, however, that the Swiss political process has not blocked the development of the health system or of health insurance. Instead, what has been precluded is the social democratic vision of what a health system should look like (or indeed, the Gaullist vision). The Swiss have achieved a conservative version of a health system. It is a system that has been called "ungovernable" but effective nevertheless.[103] Nearly the entire population is covered by government-subsidized private insurance. The financing of health insurance is less progressive than in other countries; individuals pay for a greater portion of health costs through individual premiums and out-of-pocket costs than in other nations; insurance coverage for low-income earners and the aged is not always adequate and is expensive.

The advantage of such a system is that it is fiscally sound and provides a high degree of individual choice. The sickness funds have been unable to expand benefits without raising insurance premiums, and individuals can decide for themselves what level of coverage they wish to take out and how much self-risk they wish to assume. The disadvantages are that regulation of medical fees is ineffective (it remains a political issue today), and other forms of national planning for health have been precluded. Proponents of planning argue that the Swiss system could produce better health outcomes with the resources that are spent if the system were made more socially efficient. Further, significant regional and urban-rural differences remain. It is not clear, however, whether planning solves these problems, and whether these Swiss inequalities are greater than those in countries with more extensive planning.

In comparison to the United States, the Swiss form of government intervention, although minimal, has produced a health insurance system that covers more persons at a lower cost.[104] Government subsidies have helped to expand insurance coverage, and have given the federal government an effective means to regulate insurers. Particularly since the expansion of subsidies and benefits in 1964, the adequacy of coverage has been assured by this limited form of government intervention. Although individual coverage varies according to individual insurance policies, the minimum benefits are set by law. This allowance for individual variation has had the unintended consequence of making the health system as a whole more universal. Patients are treated by the same doctors in the same hospitals and are covered by the same insurers, even if their policies may provide for treatment as first, second or third-class patients, and even if doctors may extra-bill for affluent patients.

The Swiss case is an interesting example of a system shaped by the principles of economic liberalism that should be of interest for reform efforts in the United States. However, differences in the distribution of income in Switzerland and the United States, as well as the public assistance provided by the cantons, would significantly alter the functioning of voluntary government subsidized health insurance in the United States. Any such plan would require conversion from corporate to broader voluntary plans, in any case.

Summary

To repeat the main argument of this chapter, the Swiss health system was created by specific episodes of reform, during which we can observe the intended and unintended effects of Swiss political institutions on the political behavior of interest groups, politicians, and policy makers. Liberal principles – and also the Catholic Conservative concern for cantonal autonomy – were very influential at the time that these institutions were introduced into the constitutions of 1848 and 1874. But their effects are reproduced because they create a strategic context in which political conflicts take place.

Emerging from conflicts between nationalizing liberals and more locally based Catholics, Swiss political institutions reflect both these centralist and localist tendencies. Severe constitutional constraints on the federal government, a weak party system cross-cut by linguistic, religious, and ethnic cleavages, as well as the referendum system, have produced a political system in which politics are dominated by interest groups. Interest groups, in turn, have actively worked to prevent the emergence of a more powerful central state by blocking specific legislative proposals that might entail a greater role for the federal government.[105] In the Swiss case, we have seen how the referendum and its unintended consequences blocked specific social policies, and, more broadly, a conception of politics and government based on social equality rather than political equality. In the Swedish case, we will see how institutions played precisely the opposite role, fostering social policies and a social democratic vision of society and politics.

5

The Swedish case: Executive dominance

Swedish political institutions allowed for a greater degree of policy change than in France and Switzerland. A coincidental combination of institutional design with unexpected electoral victories created a chain of decision making with no veto points. The executive government was able to introduce policy legislation unimpeded by parliamentary vetoes, as in France, or by electoral vetoes, as in Switzerland. This pattern of executive dominance was made possible by both de jure and de facto aspects of the political system.

For most of the period studied, the executive could count on stable parliamentary majorities bound by party discipline to ratify its proposals. Moreover, even at times when the majorities were unstable, institutional mechanisms developed to isolate policy-making procedures from both the executive and parliament allowed for continuous policy preparation despite fluctuations in the governing coalition. Paradoxically, institutional features introduced to preserve the power of the monarch and the Conservative Party during the transition to democracy ended up working to the benefit of the Social Democrats once they assumed control of the executive. Consequently, although these institutions were intended to ensure stability – that is, the status quo – they facilitated radical political change. This process was based on conciliation rather than conflict, however.

This chapter argues that the Swedish "politics of compromise" was not based on a preexisting consensus or absence of conflict; rather, compromise was forged by Swedish political institutions, which did not provide opportunities for minority interests to override the executive-level consensus. The result of the pattern of executive-induced conciliation was a health system that represents the public extreme of government financing and delivery of health services. The Swedish government introduced national health insurance and controls on doctors' fees and finally placed all doctors on full-time salary in conjunction with severe restrictions on the ability of doctors to practice privately, thereby converting the system to a de facto national health service. Because health reforms were not blocked by institutional brakes to change, the Swedish case provides a particularly interesting example of the use of monopsony payment to regulate the health system by changing market incentives to patients and doctors.

INSTITUTIONAL DESIGN

Political bargains worked out in the transition from monarchical rule in 1866 and in the subsequent extensions of the franchise in 1907 and 1918 established a system with some of the same institutional checks as in France and Switzerland. Parliament was to balance the power of the executive, while the indirectly elected First Chamber of the bicameral parliament was to restrain the effects of the expansion of the franchise. Whereas in France and Switzerland such institutions provided effective veto opportunities, in Sweden, mechanisms were developed to overcome these jurisdictional conflicts.

In reaction to the opposition between monarch and parliament and between the two chambers of the parliament, Swedish politicians increasingly relied on the institutions of Royal Committees (Kungliga Kommitévásendet), consultative bodies of interest group and political representatives appointed by the executive to draft legislative proposals. Interested parties were further invited to comment on the Committee proposals through written statements, called *remiss*. The committee and *remiss* system isolated policy making from the problem of conflicts between executive and parliament and from unstable majorities in the parliament. Policy preparations continued despite frequent changes in the governing coalitions and vetoes from the First Chamber.

When the Social Democrats effected a stable parliamentary majority by forming a coalition with the Farmers' Party in the 1930s, and obtained a majority in the First Chamber, the process was accelerated. The veto points were in a sense closed off, because they were filled with representatives of the party that governed the executive. That is, with a congruence of representation in the executive, the First Chamber, and the Second Chamber, neither parliament as a whole, nor the First Chamber specifically, threatened the decisions of the executive. The combination of constitutional rules and the electoral victories of the Social Democrats resulted in an institutional context for policy making that allowed the smooth passage of legislation. The lack of opportunities for abrupt interruption of executive decisions ushered in a period that we could call "executive dominance." This ability of the executive to introduce policies is the key to the Swedish pattern of cooperation among political parties and policy actors, and to the specific set of health policies that both Social Democratic and non-Social Democratic governments introduced between 1931 and 1969.

Political development

These political and institutional features were established by a series of unrelated steps. The Parliament Act of 1866 replaced representation based on four estates (nobles, clergy, burghers, farmers) with a bicameral parliament, whose powers vis-à-vis the monarch were expanded. The king would appoint the cabinet ministers, but was dependent upon parliamentary approval of legislation. The upper house, or First Chamber, was indirectly elected; the lower house, or Second Chamber, was elected by direct suffrage, but with a limited franchise. Between 1866 and 1917, parliament gradually increased in importance, as first a post of prime minister was added, and slowly the cabinet ministers came to be held responsible to parliament rather than to the king. Until 1917, the king chose the prime minister (initially an autonomous selection) based on party standings in one of the two chambers. But the appointment of a Social Democratic-Liberal coalition government in 1917 based on majorities in both chambers marks the final transition to a parliamentary system.[1]

The functioning of this institutional design in practice can be understood in terms of three different aspects of the system: the formal institutions, the distribution of political representatives within these institutions, and institutional practices that developed to overcome some of the weaknesses of these institutions. Formal constitutional changes established the bicameral parliament. The difference in methods for election of parliamentary representatives and the property qualifications, however, resulted in a class divide between the two chambers: The First Chamber was filled initially with nobles, industrialists, and landlords; the Second Chamber by farmers. The clergy, on the other hand, was effectively removed from parliamentary representation, but maintained its official representation through the state church. Thus, parliament reform maintained the clear link between socioeconomic groupings and political representation, although in a different form.

Royal Committees and remiss. In order to overcome these cleavages, however, institutional practices were developed to mediate these political and social conflicts. Policy making was increasingly delegated to Royal Committees and the associated *remiss* system. As Hesslén notes, these committees, as well as the *remiss* system, were established in order to submit the bureaucracy to greater parliamentary supervision and to reduce the royal administration. Parliamentary representatives regarded the committees as a substitute for the monarchical bureaucracy, and hence as a means to reduce royal power, whereas, from the point of view of the monarch, the committees could be used to avoid the parliament and perhaps minimize opposition to royal initiatives.[2] With the emergence of severe cleavages between the two chambers of the 1866 Riksdag, the committees were used increasingly to overcome political divisions – between the farmers that dominated the Second Chamber and the landlords and industrialists in the First, then later between the equally class-divided political parties.[3]

By removing policy making to an arena partially independent of both executive and parliament, the committee and *remiss* system protected decision making from conflicts between executive and parliament and from conflicts within the parliament. As a result, agreements on policies could be reached despite the class divisions between the two chambers and between the political parties, and also despite the unstable parliamentary majorities and consequent frequent shifts in government that characterized the period from 1866 to 1932, and particularly the 1920s. Even after the achievement of stable majorities, practices developed in this period continued, and promoted multipartisan collaboration on Swedish health legislation and conciliation among interest groups.[4]

The County Councils. The same conflicts over democratic political representation were responsible for a second institutional feature that was to influence health policy. Provincial-level government bodies, the County Councils, were introduced as a counterweight to monarchical rule. They were to serve as an organ of self-government at the provincial level in order to balance the power of the provincial governors, who were appointed by the king. In addition, the County Councils were given the responsibility of providing health care through hospitals.

The relegation of health care responsibilities to these new bodies appears merely coincidental to their political role, however. Odin Anderson refers to a Swedish government report that discusses the County Councils' assumption of responsibility for hospital care: "Recalling that the creation of the counties was really a method of distributing political power, aside from services to the people, the counties moved into a vacuum by assuming responsibilities in which other governmental units did not already have vested interests."[5] Later, the County Councils became the basis for indirect election to the First Chamber of parliament. This special political role allowed County Council politicians to shape health care reforms, not only in their capacity as hospital administrators but especially in their capacities as an informal interest group within the political parties. Moreover, although the County Councils were introduced in opposition to the executive, when the executive and County Councils were in agreement they proved to be a virtually insurmountable coalition.

The electoral laws. These two contrary tendencies – a politics of class conflict and a politics of conciliation – were further strengthened during the struggles over voting rights. Just as the negotiations for the transformation of the Estates Parliament into a bicameral parliament openly considered the effects of the rules of representation on nobles, farmers, and priests, so too do we observe a pattern of explicit class bargaining as working-class mobilization provoked gradual extensions of the franchise.[6] Each extension resulted in immediate political gains to the political parties representing the newly incorporated groups (other than women).

The 1866 Parliament Act had brought the farmers into the Second Chamber, where they formed the first political party, The Countryman's Party (Lantmannapartiet), and used their control of the Second Chamber to oppose the decisions of the First Chamber. The 1907 Reform Bill (ratified in 1909) established universal male suffrage for the Second Chamber, thereby doubling the size of the electorate, and reduced the property qualifications as well as the maximum number of plural votes for the First Chamber. The Social Democrats doubled their seats in the Second Chamber in the first election held under the new laws. In 1918, the third parliamentary reform bill extended the franchise in both chambers to women, and abolished plural voting for the First Chamber. The First Chamber was, nevertheless, to continue to be indirectly elected by Provincial Councils and Electoral Colleges, and the property qualification for members of the First Chamber was dropped only in 1933. When the reform went into force in 1921, the Social Democratic Party tripled its seats in the First Chamber, whereas those of the Conservatives were cut by half.

In the negotiations over these reforms, hoping to preserve some part of their parliamentary strength, Conservatives and Liberals insisted upon provisions in the electoral laws that, ironically, turned out to favor the Social Democrats. The Conservatives insisted upon proportional representation, which in fact helped the Social Democrats win seats from the Liberals in the towns, and encouraged the party to moderate its program in order to attract these voters. (The Social Democrats, on the other hand, debated the merits of single-member constituencies, which they thought would help to create more decisive parliamentary majorities, as in Britain.)

The electoral method chosen for the First Chamber was a Liberal idea. Until 1915, the Liberal program called for abolishing the First Chamber entirely, in order to create what they called "lower-house parliamentarism." However, when the Social Democrats' seats in the Second Chamber surpassed those of the Liberals, direct rule by the Second Chamber looked less attractive; the Liberals did not wish to replace Conservative power with Social Democratic power. A Swedish book analyzing the American political system provided a solution. Noting that the U.S. Senate constituted a brake on the House of Representatives through differences in electoral methods rather than property qualifications, the Liberals shifted to support for bicameralism, with indirect election, longer periods of office, and reelection by stages in place of the financial qualifications for the First Chamber. In the end, however, this effort to place constraints on Social Democratic control of parliament was one of the institutional factors that eventually allowed the Social Democrats to control the executive without interruption for 44 years.[7]

Class-based politics. In sum, the way in which the franchise was extended reconfirmed the class basis of Swedish politics. As political incorporation first of the farmers, then of the workers resulted in electoral gains to class-based parties – and, as we shall see, in the passage of policies aimed at these constituencies – a logic of politics was established, one premised on transparent relationships between class identities, institutional representation, and public policies. These early experiences encouraged the building of organizations based on these class groupings, the development of ties to the political parties, and the use of parliament to enact social reforms, all of which created a system of interest representation that gave privilege to interests that were class-based.

Yet, with the clarification of the relationship between economic groupings, political parties, and representative institutions, which might have produced a situation of irreconcilable class conflicts embodied in the institutions themselves, mechanisms were developed to bridge these conflicts. The committee and *remiss* system, which developed from the opposition between the monarch and parliament, was an intended institutional solution. The establishment and maintenance of an institutional veto point, the First Chamber, and the reliance on proportional representation to slow the decline of the Conservatives, became, unintentionally, institutions for conciliation as well.

From minority rule to majority rule. In 1932, the unexpected Social Democratic electoral victory and alliance with the Farmers' Party effected a sea change in the Swedish system that Olle Nyman has called a shift from minority parliamentarism to majority parliamentarism. The very institutions that were designed to block popular change abruptly switched to favor the Social Democrats. The Royal Committees, introduced to allow the monarchical bureaucracy to avoid parliamentary opposition, now helped to promote Social Democratic legislation. The Upper House of parliament, long a veto point used by conservatives, suddenly ensured continued Social Democratic rule despite electoral fluctuations.[8]

After this electoral realignment, the system worked as though the veto points had disappeared. Once a decision had been taken in the executive arena, parliament was unlikely to change it, as the executive government rested on stable parliamentary majorities. Similarly, with proportional representation and fairly stable electoral results, parliamentary decisions were generally not challenged by reactions from the electorate. In contrast to Switzerland, interest groups or voters could not veto legislation with referenda; this decision was strictly parliamentary, which in the case of stable parliamentary majorities, meant that the party that controlled the executive could control the use of the referendum. In contrast to France, the electorate did not contain pockets of "surge" voters that tempted politicians to defect from the parliamentary coalitions.[9] Only on the very rare occasion of an electoral realignment – or the threat of one – did the electoral arena become significant for specific policy proposals. Consequently, policy making was concentrated in the executive, with interest-group representatives under pressure to compromise as the probability was high that executive proposals would pass unscathed through parliamentary deliberations. The political logic of this system entailed building a majority coalition in the executive arena.

Executive dominance and interest-group influence

The rest of this chapter will examine the ways in which this institutional legacy helped to forge a consensus for Social Democratic policies. Within the framework of Swedish political institutions, interest-group influence was effectively contained within executive proceedings. Without the possibility of parliamentary or electoral vetoes, the only opportunity for affecting political decisions was at this executive stage. For unions and employers, this was an effective route of influence. In fact, executive decision making came to mean, in practice, that if these two groups could agree, a policy was sure to be enacted.

But for doctors, executive decision making was a disadvantage. With political negotiation largely restricted to the committee and *remiss* phases of the policy process, the medical profession was required to present its views in a forum where its opinions were balanced against the demands of the main labor market organizations – the employers (Sveriges Arbetsgivarförening, or SAF), and the unions (Landsorganisationen i Sverige, or LO, and Tjänstemännens Centralorganisation, or TCO). Although, like French and Swiss doctors, Swedish doctors were able to sway members of parliament and gain ample press coverage for their views, this route of political influence was not as effective in the Swedish system. In marked contrast to the French and Swiss medical profession, the Swedish medical profession was unable to veto executive decisions through another political arena. This allowed Social Democratic politicians to introduce a number of health policies without obstruction from the medical profession.

ALTERNATIVE EXPLANATIONS

This interpretation differs from alternative explanations that have been advanced for the development of the Swedish health system. Swedish health care politics have often been interpreted in terms of a long-standing tradition of public provision of health services. According to this view, an early commitment to public health provision accounts for Sweden's current system of "socialized medicine." The early period explains the latter, it is claimed, either because these early developments indicate that Swedish cultural values support community provision of health care or because these initial steps created an enduring institutional structure that shaped future policy developments. Government ownership of hospitals, for example, may be traced to the Reformation, when hospices were appropriated by the state – in the person of Gustav Vasa – along with other church property. Perhaps more important for recent developments, however, were the introduction of a public health officers corps in the seventeenth century and the creation of the County Councils in 1862. The County Councils were given responsibility for hospital care, and importantly, the right to tax citizens to pay for these services. Odin Anderson argues that this "dominant characteristic" of Sweden's health care system resulted in a concentration of resources at these public hospitals that impeded the development of ambulatory care outside of hospitals and explains the "still heavy emphasis on institutional services in Sweden, and the highest bed-to-population ratio in Western countries up to the present time."[10]

At this chapter will demonstrate, however, early state intervention in health care did not prevent development of private medical practice within the public institutions. Nor did it preclude political conflicts over the role of government in health care provision. Health care politics in the twentieth century were far from untroubled and hardly predictable. National health insurance was hotly debated from the 1890s onwards, but could not be enacted until after the Second World War. At that time, plans for a national health service along the lines of the British National Health Service (NHS) were considered, but they were blocked by massive political opposition. Consequently, prospects for private medical practice improved with the enactment of national health insurance. Nearly twenty years later, however, new legislation was added that placed constraints on private practice and converted Sweden's system to a de facto national health service. The persistence of health care institutions – or the nature of Swedish national culture – cannot account for changes in Swedish health policy, when such changes include both policies that helped to encourage the expansion of a private medical market and others that caused this market to contract.

PROFESSIONAL DOMINANCE

Another approach has focused on the preferences of the medical profession. Perhaps in Sweden the preferences of the profession ran to more socialized forms of medical care. As Dr. Bo Hjern, an official of the Swedish Medical Association, put it in 1976, "A Swedish doctor rarely asks himself the question whether he enjoys being a public servant. He is so used to being one that the question is not so emotionally charged as in many other countries."[11] His older colleagues who remember the battles over socialized medicine might not agree, however. Conservative MP Dr. Gunnar Biörck, for example, refers to recent developments in Swedish health care policy as "steps in subjugating a free profession."[12] Many Swedish physicians were opposed to national health insurance and to the restrictions on private medical practice that have since been introduced. In historical terms, Swedish doctors were no more supportive of socialized medicine than were doctors throughout Western Europe.[13]

Professionalization

Garpenby has argued that the Swedish process of professionalization was accomplished through the state, and that therefore Swedish physicians maintained an orientation to the public sector. It is true that Swedish professionalization was aided by the state; this is, in my view, what made it so successful by the standard measures of professionalization. The first Swedish medical faculties were established at the end of the seventeenth century, but both a university route and an apprenticeship route to professional credentials (*fältskärare, kirurg*, the Swedish equivalent of the Swiss *Wundearzt* and the French surgeon) were available. The Royal Academy of Medicine (Collegium Medicum) was established in 1663 by four Stockholm doctors, who then received official royal recognition. In 1685 the barbers upgraded themselves to the Surgical Society (Societas Chirurgica), but the Collegium Medicum refused to relinquish its authority to examine the surgeons. Finally, in 1797, the Surgical Society was incorporated into the Collegium Medicum. In 1813 the Collegium Medicum was replaced by the "Health College" (Sundhetskollegiet), which became the National Board of Health (Medicinalstyrelsen) in 1877.[14]

Thus, university doctors were granted a government agency that they used to control professional licensing. This granting of privilege to the profession was not unlike the situation in Britain, where the Royal College of Physicians was granted a charter to examine physicians by Henry VIII in 1518. However, the Swedish Collegium Medicum was part of the government, whereas the British Royal College (and later, the Royal

College of Surgeons) was an independent body, licensed by the government. Although the Collegium Medicum was incorporated into the government, however, the Swedish academic elite was more successful than physicians in other countries in forcing the surgeons to subsume themselves into the physicians. The divisions between different types of practitioners were overcome, and unlicensed practitioners were outlawed.

The Collegium Medicum was highly successful in limiting the number of licensed physicians, and Sweden still maintains a relatively low physician-to-population ratio.[15] Thus, in terms of establishing a market monopoly and controlling the number of doctors, the Swedish profession was highly successful, but relied on the absolutist state. At the same time, however, this state took an active role in establishing public forms of health care (public health officers and public hospitals). In a reversal of the Swiss situation, Swedish government institutions were used to establish a strictly enforced legal monopoly on medical practice and to limit the numbers of doctors very effectively.[16] Yet these same institutions were to prove to be a disadvantage in political conflicts over the status of private medical practice under national health insurance and extensive public provision of care.

Medical organizations

Alongside the development of the government bureaucracy for control of licensing, the Swedish Medical Society (Svenskaläkarsällskapet) a scientific society for doctors, was founded in 1808. This society still exists, and zealously avoids all involvement with "economic" issues. As measured by government response to its *remiss* statements, the Swedish Medical Society is more successful as a lobbying group than the Swedish Medical Association (Läkarförbundet), although on medical issues, as opposed to economic issues, the Association has also been influential.[17]

The movement for a more economically oriented professional association began at the end of the nineteenth century, with the formation of a national association for public health officers (Svenska Provinsialläkarföreningen) in 1880. Several meetings of physicians were held in the 1880s with the object of building a national medical association, but there was resistance, especially from the Medical Society. In 1893, the first national medical association (Allmänna Svenska Läkarföreningen) was formed, but it lacked financial resources and personnel, and was quickly disbanded. The organizational innovation that produced a permanent association was the development of *local* medical associations in the 1890s that then federated to form a second national medical association (Allmänna Svenska Läkarföreningen) in 1903. This was reorganized in 1919 into the Swedish Medical Association. From the 1920s on the Association has controlled specialty licensing.[18]

Thus, if we compare Swedish professionalization and organizational developments with those in France and Switzerland, the Swedish profession compares quite well. It successfully eliminated competing forms of medical practice, established government control over licensing, and set strict limits on the numbers of doctors. This control was carried out by the state rather than by an independent organization of the profession. But enforcement by the state was essential for medical monopoly throughout Europe.

Rather than discounting this strong, albeit "state-led" professionalization process, this chapter argues that we should recognize the disjuncture between these classical stages in the professionalization process and success at maintaining private medical practice through political means. The Swedish profession was certainly a profession, yet it was less successful as a political lobby group in the twentieth century. This lack of success was not caused by organizational weaknesses, for the Swedish medical profession developed a unified national organization with high levels of membership (See Table 6, page 84). The technical expertise of the profession was certainly respected, as well. There were no proposals for lay medicine or the elimination of medical monopoly, and medical associations were carefully consulted on medical issues. But Swedish political institutions afforded only limited veto points to the Swedish medical profession. When other interest groups and political actors judged the economic conditions of practice to be political rather than professional matters, the medical profession, unlike its counterparts elsewhere, was not in a veto position, despite its organizational strength and professional resources. Thus, as discussed in Chapter 2, the dimensions of technical autonomy and market monopoly are quite separate from political influence concerning issues of economic autonomy.

THE SOCIAL DEMOCRATIC MODEL

Yet another argument focuses on the activities of the Swedish Social Democratic Party and the associated Trade Union Federation.[19] New reforms were introduced following Social Democratic electoral gains, and the content of the reforms roughly parallels other Social Democratic initiatives, rather than appearing as highly specific to the health care area. The Social Democratic model "fits" the Swedish case rather well also in terms of the influence of interest groups on health insurance policy making. Although the medical profession was highly visible during debates over health insurance policies, its role pales in comparison with that of more "class-based" groups, such as the Swedish Employers' Federation (SAF), the Trade Union Federation (LO), and even the Federation of Salaried Employees (TCO). In the context of class-based politics, support for health care reforms was widespread. Swedish employers were willing to consider national health insurance at quite an early date; TCO and LO provided a ready source of constituents who could be courted by political parties willing to promote social policies.

Nevertheless, although there is evidence to support the Social Democratic model, the timing of reforms does not exactly coincide with increased Social Democratic electoral strength or increases in union membership. How can we account, for example, for the fact that national health insurance was not enacted until 1946, although the Social Democratic Party was taking the largest share of the electorate as early as 1917, and held the largest number of parliamentary seats in both chambers of the Swedish Riksdag by 1921? Or, to draw a cross-national comparison, despite much higher levels of unionization and a larger Social Democratic majority in Sweden, at the same time that Britain enacted its National Health Service, such a service was rejected in Sweden. Moreover, the Swedish Social Democrats rarely enacted legislation based on their parliamentary majority, against the wishes of other parties – at least not in the health care area. Most health care policies were supported by the majority, if not all, of the political parties, and by a broad array of interest groups, always including SAF, TCO, and LO. Both factors – the Social Democratic electoral success and the development of these producer organizations – were important to the outcome in the Swedish case. But in order to explain the impact of these factors on policy making, we must turn to the framework of political institutions in which they were embedded.

SWEDISH HEALTH POLITICS: AN OVERVIEW

Political institutions provide the critical link between the electoral success of the Social Democratic Party and the ability of the party to convert these gains into concrete policy results, without which continued electoral success might not have been possible. Similarly, institutions help to explain why policy making tended to mean negotiations between SAF, TCO, and LO. Because minority interests could not veto proposals at other points in the process, policy debates were restricted to the executive arena where they were dominated by these large organizations. This, in turn, reinforced the logic of aggregating interests into these organizations. Through a review of the development of Swedish national health insurance politics in the twentieth century, this chapter presents an alternative interpretation for the Swedish system by focusing on Swedish political institutions. This interpretation relies on some of the same factors discussed in other analyses of Swedish politics: the importance of the executive administration, patterns of "corporatist" or "societal" bargaining, and the electoral success of the Social Democratic party. It argues, however, that the lack of veto points is a critical part of this pattern.

In order to capture the texture and substance of Swedish health policy debates, we must consider the framework established by Swedish political institutions. Consensus for political decisions was made possible not only by the "Social Democratic hegemony," but because the bargains enforced at the executive level could not be overturned in a different political arena. In contrast to the French as Swiss systems, there were few veto points. Once a decision was made in the executive arena, parliament was unlikely to change it, as the executive government rested on stable parliamentary majorities. Moreover, as the parties followed party discipline, interest groups needed to convince the party leaderships in order to have an effect. The coalitions of swing voters that permitted small constituencies to sway votes in the French case were missing in Sweden, and as the parties had rather stable constituencies they were not prone to opportunistic shifts. Similarly, as recourse to the referendum was not an option for interest groups, the electoral arena was not available as a veto mechanism.

The lack of veto opportunities made it impossible for groups opposed to executive decisions to overturn these decisions, and hence the effective point of decision was in the executive. This concentrated policy decisions in the Royal Committees and promoted a pattern of consensual decision making among the large producer organizations. When veto opportunities opened up, however – at times when the First Chamber was still dominated by the Conservatives, and when the possibility of electoral realignment threatened the parliamentary coalition – interest groups switched from cooperation to defection and attempted to use these veto opportunities to block policies.

Thus, through a series of unrelated historical events, the Swedish political system came to work according to a rather straightforward political logic. Voters voted according to their class position and joined interest groups with ties to those same political parties. Employees enrolled in the unions – LO and TCO – and voted for the Social Democratic Party. Farmers joined the farmers' organizations and voted for the Farmers Party. Employers joined the employers' organization and voted for the Conservative Party; small employers and craftsmen were represented in a small business organization as well as the employers' organization and voted for the Liberal Party.[20]

Political decisions were based on agreements worked out in executive procedures between these groups. The commission and *remiss* system constituted a mechanism for reaching consensus within society and between parties that undergirded the Social Democratic approach to power. Further, the emphasis on executive rather than parliamentary or electoral arenas of decision making positioned the County Councils to control the agenda of the reform process to an unprecedented degree; County Council politicians were able to parlay their political resources into ever greater administrative control and direction of health care services. Holding this system together, however, was the lack of veto opportunities that encouraged cooperative strategies.

The next sections of this chapter will show how this political pattern was built up, and how it affected the development of the health system. Before 1932, Swedish parliamentary government was based on unstable minority governments, and the First Chamber still functioned as a veto point. Although this political situation made it difficult to enact policies, under the surface some of the basic elements of the Swedish pattern were established nonetheless. The committee system was responsible for health insurance legislation that although more minimal than that in either France or Switzerland, was organized in such a way as to lay the groundwork for national health insurance. After the Second World War, Social Democratic rule was used to establish the basic elements of the Swedish welfare state. With a strong parliamentary majority, the executive could enact legislation unimpeded by interest group resistance. An electoral shift in 1948, however, threatened Social Democratic control of the executive, thereby creating a strategic opening for interest-group dissent and eliminating a controversial plan for a national health service. Finally, during the 1950s and 1960s, Social Democratic control of the executive was consolidated and a number of far-reaching reforms were introduced.

PARLIAMENTARY INSTABILITY

Early efforts to enact national health insurance in Sweden provide important evidence about the institutional conditions that underpinned the Swedish model. During the first phase of parliamentary rule, Sweden experienced the same unstable coalition governments as did France. But if we follow the reform process closely, we can observe the institutional mechanisms for conciliation that allowed for slow but steady policy formation, despite many changes in government and interest-group conflicts.

Although Swedish electoral laws from 1866 to 1918 resulted in the maintenance of a Conservative majority in the First Chamber that could veto legislation, and despite the lack of stable parliamentary majorities, the committee system protected Swedish policy making from the vagaries of the shifting parliamentary coalitions. Committees appointed by one government prepared legislative proposals, only to submit them several years later to a new government in a completely different political environment. Nevertheless, the parliamentary practice was to continue the work of the committees, despite the change in government. Thus, interest groups could not count on the partisan shifts to disrupt the process, as in France.

Although the political process differed, the policy ideas should now be familiar. Swedish policy proposals and political interests in this first phase of health legislation were remarkably similar to those in France and Switzerland. Reform initiatives came mainly from Liberals, often supported by Social Democrats, but also from Conservatives. Swedish doctors, like their counterparts in France and Switzerland, were not inclined toward government support for health insurance, but their main concern was with the effect of health insurance programs on relations between physicians and sickness funds. Physicians in all three nations were adamant that increased government funding for the ambulatory sector not interfere with private medical practice.

Early sickness fund laws

Efforts to enact national health insurance (or more correctly, "compulsory health insurance," as these programs were called) failed. In its place, a series of laws providing for government subsidies for voluntary health insurance was passed in 1891, 1910, and 1931. Early Swedish legislation is thus comparable to prewar French and Swiss legislation. If anything, however, Swedish government programs for health insurance lagged behind those of other European countries. Switzerland's Sickness and Accident Insurance Law of 1911 provided for the same kind of government subsidies to voluntary health insurance, but with two critical differences: The Swiss subsidies were initially larger and they were paid on behalf of all sickness fund members with no income restrictions. French government subsidies to the sickness funds (*mutuelles*) were originally smaller than in Sweden and Switzerland, but in 1930, France introduced national health insurance for low-income earners.[21]

As we saw, early health insurance legislation in Switzerland and France bore the characteristic impact of political patterns: referendum politics in the first case, and a mixture of executive power and parliamentary concessions to interest groups in the second. In Switzerland, Radical-Democratic politicians had attempted to introduce national health insurance legislation but were blocked by the referendum. In France, parliamentary consensus for national health insurance stemming from questions of nationalism overrode the parliamentary blockages, but the weak parties and parliamentary committees enabled selected interest groups to demand important concessions in features of the legislation. In the Swedish case, we observe yet a third pattern. National health insurance was blocked not by partisan or interest-group conflicts, but for financial reasons. Instead of national health insurance, a series of sickness fund laws was introduced. As in France and Switzerland, doctors, sickness funds, and small businessmen opposed an expanded role of government, and they were to some extent successful in using their parliamentary contacts to oppose reforms. But the logic of the Swedish system was already beginning to point to executive level bargaining that excluded these groups.

Working-class mobilization

Early efforts to enact national health insurance in Sweden did not constitute a purely conservative response to the "social question" nor did they represent the triumph of the Social Democratic rise to power. The Sickness Fund Laws of 1891, 1910, and 1931 were all enacted at times of heightened worker unrest and increasing representation of the left in the Swedish parliament. Yet they were not introduced by Social Democratic representatives against the resistance of the center and right. The 1891 law was enacted at a time when both Liberals and Conservatives were interested in promoting "social peace" in the heated atmosphere of the crisis in Swedish-Norwegian relations, and as a result of large electoral gains for the left in the Stockholm elections to the Second Chamber. The 1910 law came in the wake of the 1909 general strike and as the effects of the 1907 voting rights reform began to be felt. The 1931 law was enacted in the same month that newspaper headlines were dominated by an event that constituted a watershed in the history of the Swedish labor movement: the killing of two strikers and four spectators by the military at Ådalen.[22]

Although stimulated by working-class mobilization, health insurance legislation was not a top priority of union and Social Democratic leaders. In contrast to the German pattern in which the funds served as a crucial organizational tool for unions and the Social Democratic Party,[23] in Sweden the sickness fund movement was more closely linked to the Temperance movement and to the Liberal Party.[24] Consequently, if any party exerted the leading role in health insurance reform it was the Liberals, whereas the Social Democrats and LO focused on workmen's compensation, universal suffrage, the eight-hour day, and unemployment measures.[25] Moreover, these laws were hardly radical; they constituted extremely minimal responses to pressures for social change.

The Sickness Fund Law of 1891, for example, was virtually the only result of the Worker's Insurance Commission of 1884–1889, which had been set up at the instigation of the Liberal Adolf Hedin to consider working conditions, as well as insurance for work accidents and old age. The committee decided to consider national health insurances as well, but dropped it in favor of state subsidies for voluntary health insurance. The only other piece of legislation produced by the commission was the 1901 law on employer liability for industrial accidents, which actually benefited employers by allowing them to insure themselves against liability claims.[26]

The 1910 law was introduced by a conservative government that stressed the role of expanded voluntary health insurance in reducing welfare expenditures (*fattigvården*). Although K.J. Höjer, who was later to serve on the famous Social Services Committee (*Socialvårdskommitté*) of the 1930's, describes this period following the 1907 suffrage reform as one of increased possibilities for improved social policies, he views the sickness fund law as a continuation "of the road started already in the previous century. . . . There was no question at all of re-organizing the sickness fund movement in such a way that it could come to play the role of national health insurance." The more pressing issues, according to Höjer, were old age, invalidity, and accident insurance.[27]

Policy problems

The Sickness Fund Laws provided for government subsidies to local "sickness funds" (*sjukkassor*) that provided mainly cash benefits to cover income lost during periods of illness. In some cases, they provided coverage for medical treatment as well, for which they often attempted to hire physicians on a contract basis to provide treatment to members for low flat fees. Despite the subsidies, however, membership in the Swedish voluntary sickness funds had grown relatively slowly. As late as 1925, only 13.3 percent of the Swedish population was enrolled in sickness funds (or 17.5 percent of the adult population), as compared with 60 percent for Denmark. Moreover, very few of these persons were insured for medical treatment; in 1921, only 12 percent of sickness fund members were covered. In addition, as in other countries, the organization of voluntary insurance was rather haphazard, with funds unevenly distributed throughout Sweden and engaged in highly competitive practices that interfered with adequate provision of social security.[28]

Influenced by international developments, Swedish politicians from a number of parties proposed national health insurance as a remedy. Beginning in 1913, proposals for compulsory health insurance for low-income earners were drawn up by a series of committees appointed by successive Liberal, Conservative, and Social Democratic governments. The most important of these proposals, the 1919 proposal of the Social Insurance Commission, which had been appointed by Conservative Oscar von Sydow, head of the Department of the Interior in a nonpartisan government, called for a combination of compulsory and voluntary insurance that would cover cash benefits, drugs, and medical treatment for an estimated 80 percent of the population. In contrast to earlier proposals, the committee envisioned a system of public sickness funds that would replace the previously established voluntary funds.[29]

Sickness fund opposition

Just as the pressures for national health insurance reforms did not come directly from the Swedish labor movement, opposition to reform did not come from expected quarters. Although the Swedish Medical Association

(*Sveriges Läkarförbund*) had been founded in 1903, the Association did
not play an especially important role in these early debates. Nor did
business groups attempt to oppose reform. Instead, it was the sickness
funds, organized in Sweden's General Sickness Fund Association (*Sveriges
Allmänna Sjukkasseförbund*) and the National Sickness Fund's Central
Organization (*Rikssjukkassornas Centralorganisation*), that fought the
national health insurance proposal. Nevertheless, the proposal was eventually shelved for financial rather than political reasons, by both Conservative and Social Democratic governments in 1919, 1921, and 1922.

    In 1925, Statens Besparingskommité, the State's Budget-Cutting
Committee (appointed by a Conservative government), urged that plans
for national health insurance be abandoned. Instead, a new sickness fund
law should be enacted, but one that would rationalize the voluntary
health insurance system. State subsidies should be allocated to only one
sickness fund per local area, the committee argued. This would allow
better coordination between sickness, pension, and workmen's compensation benefits, which would lower administrative costs and eliminate
eligibility for pension supplements in some cases.

    Gustav Möller, Social Democratic Minister of Social Affairs in 1925,
who has been called the architect of the Swedish welfare state, agreed
with the conservative committee's assessment. National health insurance
was inappropriate. But, he added, it should be kept in mind as a future
goal. Möller retained the budget-cutting committee's suggestion for
rationalization – only one fund per local area would be subsidized – but
the focus was now on smooth transition to national health insurance at a
later date.[30]

    Although the sickness fund movement was interested in increased
government subsidies, the plan for restricting the subsidies to one fund
per local area generated opposition. The Swedish situation was complicated by the fact that the sickness fund movement was split into two
competing movements, each based on a different approach to health
insurance and each represented by a separate association. Founded in
1907, the General Sickness Fund Association represented the smaller
funds that were restricted to a local area. In 1916, a second association,
the National Sickness Funds' Central Organization, was founded to
represent the national funds. The former, the association of local funds,
had a more political orientation than the association of national funds. It
stressed the importance of membership participation in the sickness funds
and its role in political education. Since its founding, this organization
had lobbied for national health insurance. The association of national
funds, on the other hand, was more bureaucratically inclined. The national funds were responsible for extending the sickness fund movement
to the Swedish countryside and were more concerned about pooling risks,
for which large funds were needed, than about the democratic character

of the funds. In contrast to the association of local funds, the association of national funds was opposed to national health insurance. Both associations did have ties to the Temperance movement and to the Liberal Party, but the links between the national funds – the more conservative group – and the Liberal Party were much stronger, not least because G.K. Ekmann, Prime Minister for several years in the 1920s and the head of the Radical-Liberal Party, was a former president of the largest national fund, a Temperance fund.[31]

The fund movement adeptly used its parliamentary contacts to block proposals for the new sickness fund law. The first proposal, in 1926, limited government funds to one sickness fund per local area. After protests from both sickness fund organizations, a compromise was reached. The law would cover two types of funds, central and local. The local funds would cover smaller territorial areas for short-term risks, and the central funds would serve a larger area, equalizing expenditures by picking up the costs of long-term illnesses.

In 1927, the first attempt to enact this system failed, as a result of lobbying by national funds. By 1928, however, pressured by stagnating membership figures and the possibility of vastly increased government subsidies, the two organizations were able to agree on this reorganization of voluntary health insurance. Differences remained, however, for the association of local funds maintained its support for national health insurance, whereas the national funds remained opposed. Once the sickness fund organization agreed to divide their area of operations into local and regional jurisdictions, however, the rift between the two organizations was largely eliminated. This compromise removed one of the main political and administrative impediments to health insurance legislation, and the executive government presented a new sickness fund proposal in 1930.[32]

Medical protests and the Sickness Fund Law of 1930

Now, for the first time, the Swedish medical profession emerged as an important pressure group. The leadership of the Swedish Medical Association was willing to accept a new sickness fund law, but the majority of its members were not. Many doctors perceived the introduction of a new requirement for sickness funds to provide medical benefits as a threat.

As elsewhere, relations between the medical profession and the sickness funds were strained. In 1907, the Swedish Medical Association's committee on sickness funds had warned of the threat to physicians posed by the sickness funds. Pointing to the poor working conditions of German and Danish doctors, who were often hired by sickness funds on a contract basis and paid at low rates, referred to by Swedish doctors as

"piece-rates," the committee argued that Swedish doctors would face
the same problems if the funds became more involved in the provision
of medical benefits. In fact, much of the early activity of the Medical
Association, which had been founded in 1903, was aimed at eliminating
the contract practices of the funds, and one of the problems of the
Association was preventing doctors in need of employment from signing
such contracts. Thus, in Sweden, doctors with a private practice developed the same ideas of "liberal medicine" as private practitioners in
France and Switzerland.

By requiring the sickness funds to provide medical benefits, the 1930
sickness fund law threatened the private medical market.[33] Medical
opponents argued that this was a step toward national health insurance,
after which "the free calling of medicine would become only a pretty
memory."[34] The medical profession's representative on the committee
that prepared the 1930 reform, Dr. Gibson, warned that the committee
members had been chosen for their pro-insurance bias, and were designing
the 1930 law in order to pave the way for national health insurance.
In Gibson's view, medical benefits should be voluntary, cash benefits
limited, and the waiting period longer; as much as possible, mandatory
benefits should thus be restricted and kept from encroaching on the
private medical market.[35]

Although twenty-one out of twenty-eight local medical associations
objected to compulsory medical benefits, the Central Steering Board of
the Swedish Medical Association decided to support the 1930 proposal.[36]
Despite open criticism of this decision in the Association's journal,
Läkartidningen, the leadership held its ground, asserting that

It has been said that the majority of the country's doctors are of a different
opinion concerning the proposals put forth in the health insurance question than
the National Board of Health [Medicinalstyrelsen] and the Swedish Medical
Association's Central Steering Committee [Centralstyrelsen]. This, however,
appears to have its natural explanation in the circumstance that these Boards have
at their disposition a more thorough knowledge of the details of these proposals
than what many of the doctors out in the countryside in general have obtained for
themselves.[37]

The leadership was accused of ignoring the opinions of its local affiliates,
not only by members of the medical profession,[38] but also by a group
known as the "Taxpayers' Association" (*Skattebetalarnas Förening*).
Much of the debate focused on a Swedish Medical Association survey of
local medical associations, with revealed that the majority of local affiliates
opposed compulsory medical benefits. The Taxpayers' Association went
so far as to publish the results of this survey and to distribute it to all
members of the Riksdag. Newspaper coverage of these events highlights
the role of the Taxpayers' Association, but doesn't describe the size or
composition of the group. Clearly, the Taxpayers' Association cooperated

with one or more powerful officials of the Swedish Medical Association, for otherwise it certainly could never have obtained the results of an internal survey, particularly one whose results the leadership of the organization was choosing to ignore.

Given the reactions to health insurance initiatives in other countries, we might expect that employers would constitute a potential source of "tax opposition." It is known that later, in the 1940s and 1950s, the Taxpayers' Association played an important role in influencing public opinion through the journal *Sunt Förnunft* (roughly translated, "Common Sense"). It was an unusual group, for its only activity was to influence public opinion; it never partook in *remiss* activities. At that time, the organization's steering committee was dominated by powerful industrialists like Jakob Wallenberg, who served as president from 1953 to 1969. But whatever ties there might have been between industry and the Taxpayers' Association, and despite the Taxpayers' campaign, the Swedish Employers' Association stated in 1925 that it *supported* national health insurance. Or, to be more exact, the association stated that it opposed plans for rationalization of voluntary health insurance through a new sickness fund law, when only through national health insurance could this rationalization be effectively achieved.[39]

Direct appeal to Members of Parliament

Like their counterparts in France and Switzerland, the opponents of the 1930 sickness fund law circumvented the more moderate associational leadership and appealed directly to members of parliament and to the press. And the strategy worked, briefly. The 1930 Sickness Fund Law passed in the Second Chamber but was blocked by a last-minute push from Conservatives in the First Chamber, for which Swedish private practitioners claimed credit.[40] For those interested in the public image of the profession, it is of note that during the parliamentary debate, Dr. Järte, a Conservative MP and physician, was forced to defend the motives of opponents to the reform, as had been the case in France and Switzerland: "The majority of Sweden's office practitioners criticize the reform for reasons that honor the corps, as one can easily calculate what doctors would come to earn from social insurance. But they say with their foreign colleagues in mind: lead us not into temptation."[41]

Thus, like the French liberals, Swedish doctors with parliamentary connections used their direct access to the parliament to circumvent the more moderate views of the medical association leadership. In France, this strategy worked for another thirty years, and indeed allowed the liberal leaders to form a new medical association. In the long run, however, this was not an effective political strategy in Sweden. For although the doctors and the taxpayers were successful in gaining access to selected conservative MPs, they seemed unable to penetrate the official commission and *remiss* procedings. Neither the Swedish Medical Association nor the Employers' Federation – the groups that we might expect to represent the views of these opponents – responded to these attacks. Indeed, if we examine the official records, we find barely a trace of either the Taxpayers' Association or the local medical associations. Instead, we find that the National Board of Health (*Medicinalstyrelsen*) – to which the Medical Association submitted its positive reply along with some dissenting comments of the locals – strongly supported the reform, as well as the two sickness fund associations, the Employers' Federation, the Pension Board, the Welfare Inspector, the Federation of County Councils, and the Swedish Welfare Association.[42]

Executive policy making

The Swedish policy process was based on executive access, and government officials were the gatekeepers to that access. Swedish medical association leaders were concerned that if they did not cooperate in drafting health insurance legislation, they could be excluded from decision making, as they had in the past. By analogy, in a political system in which good relations with the executive were at a premium, it is not surprising that employers might choose an independent organization such as the Taxpayers' Association, to express discontent, rather than damaging the neutral image of the Employers' Association.

Comparatively speaking, neither stance is unusual. Medical Association leaders in France and Switzerland had also agreed to cooperate during national health insurance preparations in the early twentieth century, and during the debates about controls on doctors' fees in the 1950s. But these decisions were overturned by militant members, such as the Paris practitioners and French-Swiss doctors who had access to alternative routes of political influence.

Employer association leaders, too, had displayed a willingness to cooperate. As will be recalled, the Swiss Employers' Association was willing to support national health insurance, but its members were not; the referendum provided the vehicle for these employers to express their dissent from the leadership. In France, employers were not cohesively organized in the 1920s, so that we do not observe a separate associational (or oligarchical) interest in cooperation. But in France, too, it was the small employers who were most strongly opposed to the 1928 payroll tax, and these employers relied on direct parliamentary appeals. Later, the CNPF was interested in cooperation with the executive, whereas the CGPME vetoed proposals as long as parliamentary blockage proved effective.

In Sweden, the mix of cooperative associational leadership and membership militance was no different, but the institutional circumstances were. The Taxpayers' Association and the private doctors appealed directly to members of parliament. But, according to Nils Elvander, this is not where effective political pressure occurs in the Swedish system. "Group influence [he says] is expressed mainly in the preparatory stages [of policy making] – through representation on investigative commissions and so-called *remiss* comments on commission reports – and at the executive stage in the agencies. The least significant target is parliament."[43]

Passage of the 1931 Sickness Fund Law

Swedish procedures for interest representation were not vulnerable to political opposition outside of the official *remiss* proceedings. Although the parliamentary majorities were not stable, neither were the parties fractionated and cross-cut by electoral competition. The First Chamber could be used as a veto point, but the Conservatives would be risking their chances of gaining Liberal support by vetoing a policy affecting the Liberal sickness funds, and the reliable constituency of the Conservatives, the Employers Association, was not publicly fighting the law. Thus, it is no wonder that, even if the doctors and taxpayers were successful in winning over Conservative MPs to their cause in 1930, the Sickness Fund Law was still approved by the Riksdag in May 1931 by majorities so large that no vote was taken.

The 1931 law shaped the future development of the system, as it transformed the sickness fund movement from a randomly scattered group of voluntary associations to a national network of coordinated insurance funds that was later to serve as the basis for national health insurance. As a result of the law, state subsidies more than doubled within three years, medical benefits were greatly increased, and voluntary membership expanded from 1 million in 1930 to 1.5 million in 1940 and 2.5 million in 1945 – a shift from 20 percent of the adult population (persons over 15 years of age) to 48 percent.[44]

This law was made possible, not by a long-standing tradition of government intervention, nor by any predisposition of the medical profession to health care programs, but by a long process of political negotiation. Furthermore, the law was prepared not by a conflictual process that pitted the Social Democrats against the other parties, but by a multiparty process that, as a result of the committee system, continued uninterrupted through twelve different changes in government. Given this political context, we can understand the position taken in 1930 by the steering committee of the Medical Association. Not always included in health care policy making and surrounded by interest groups and bureaucratic agencies that supported the reform, it made sense for the leadership to cooperate; it is not at all clear what gains were to be made through protest. The First Chamber briefly provided a means for "free market" opponents to veto the law – just as the sickness funds had used their contacts to the Liberal Party to veto the 1926 and 1927 proposals – but the party system was simply not open to minority cleavages when not supported by the associations that took part in the executive negotiations. Thus, although it was not complete, even in this period before the Social Democratic rise to power, we can observe the beginnings of executive-level policy consensus in Sweden.

MAJORITY PARLIAMENTARISM AND THE POSTWAR SETTLEMENT

The agreement between the Social Democrats and the Farmers' Party to exchange farm price supports for employment measures effected a political realignment. From 1932 on, the executive was governed by majority parliamentary coalitions in place of the unstable minority governments of the 1920s and earlier. This shifted the balance of institutional power from parliament to the executive, reversing the previous shift from king to parliament. In contrast to France, executive dominance was not achieved by institutionally circumventing parliament, but by the political strategy of consolidating an effective parliamentary majority, such that executive decisions would with certainty be ratified by parliament.

Once the risk of parliamentary veto was removed, the effective point of decision was more firmly rooted in the executive than ever before. Previously the commissions had protected policy making from the shifting parliamentary majorities; now within the context of Social Democratic majorities they provided an arena for hammering out policy compromises under Social Democratic leadership. This shift in power was buttressed by a reorganization of the political parties and interest groups that was to strengthen the pattern of executive-induced political compromise. The two competing liberal parties regrouped into a single party, representing largely urban, small business interests. Wealthier farmers moved into the Conservative Party, leaving the Farmers' Party to represent farmers proper, rather than large landowners. Interest organizations grew at an unprecedented rate, leading to the coining of the phrase, "Organization Sweden."[44a] Thus, the Swedish model was now consolidated. As Douglas Verney wrote in 1957:

[T]he stability of the Swedish political system in the last twenty years has led some observers to suggest that the liberal period of competing political parties has given way to a settled social order in which Government tends in some ways to adjudicate the claims of various large social groups, none of which can expect to strengthen its position perceptibly. . . . It would be reading too much into this development to regard it as a return to the old order in which social groups, like the Estates, meet together to be administered by a comparatively disinterested government. On the other hand, it may be no accident that in a country which has had so short an experience of liberalism and individualism, these tendencies towards the traditional representation of interests of the realm should be observed and discussed.[45]

The following sections of this chapter argue that this pattern was not ideological, however, but the result of the closing off of traditional veto points by filling these political arenas with sufficient Social Democratic representatives to preclude the overturning of executive decisions by groups disadvantaged by the executive-level consensus.

Introduction of national health insurance

As in France and Switzerland, the end of the Second World War was viewed as the moment to enlarge the scope of social citizenship. In fact, the proposals of the Swedish Social Democratic government were not so different from those in France and Switzerland; the Swedish welfare state was to be based on the standard set of social insurance programs considered throughout Western Europe at that time. What differed, however, were the opportunities for disruption of these plans for reform, and hence the ability of interest groups to demand abandonment or revision in the social programs. In 1946 and 1947 alone, legislation was promulgated on pensions, family allowances, health insurance, and housing subsidies. With a popular mandate to continue the Keynesian policies of the 1930s, the Social Democrats were now able to introduce the main pillars of the Swedish welfare state.[46] Consequently, this period is known as the Social Democratic "Harvest Time."

This partisan element is without a doubt a critical factor in the postwar reforms. The reforms had been outlined in *The Postwar Program of the Workers' Movement (Arbetarrörelsens Efterkrigsprogram)* or *The 27 Points (De 27 Punkterna)* – Sweden's version of Britain's Beveridge Plan, and published jointly by LO and the Social Democratic Party in 1944. The party now had the electoral strength necessary to implement the reforms. At the same time, it was prodded to take action by Communist gains in the 1944 elections.

With regard to national health insurance, however, support for the program was widespread, extending far beyond the Social Democratic Party and its electoral base, LO. Although the Social Democrats held a sufficient electoral majority to be able to enact the reform on their own, this proved to be unnecessary. All of the political parties supported the national health insurance law of 1947, and it passed by a nearly unanimous vote. Not every interest group was completely in favor of national health insurance. But in contrast to the French and Swiss cases, doctors, employers, and white-collar workers did not have recourse to a veto point. Unable to threaten parliamentary or referendum vetoes, each group expressed misgivings but agreed to cooperate.

The Swedish Employers' Federation pointed to the virtues of voluntary insurance and questioned the financial wisdom of immediately introducing national health insurance, but essentially agreed to the reform. The white collar union TCO noted that most of its members would not benefit from the reform, but in the name of solidarity (and possibly out of a wish to establish good working relations with LO and the government) it lent its support:

The introduction of national health insurance will doubtlessly be viewed by large groups of salaried employees as a rather serious intervention in the freedom of the individual citizen, so much more so as this intervention will appear as of little personal benefit to many employees. Nevertheless, . . . TCO wishes to support this proposal in principle, out of consideration for the valuable step that this reform constitutes in the striving for better social conditions in this country.[47]

The Swedish Medical Association stated that it preferred voluntary insurance to compulsory insurance, and urged the government to concentrate on more pressing public health needs. It would, however, go along, particularly as the proposal provided for a reimbursement mechanism for payment and for a free choice of doctor. In this context, the medical profession – or any other interest groups – was not in a veto position. The government had the parliamentary votes necessary to enact the law, and there was no alternate channel of *political* influence – such as the French parliament or the Swiss referendum – where the doctors could make their own point of view prevail over a majority consensus.[47a]

Small businessmen in fact specifically complained about their exclusion from political decision making. Although the Social Democratic Party asserted in electoral campaigns that its crisis measures had helped small businesses out of the Depression, the Association of Swedish Craftsmen's journal, *Hantverk och Industri*, denounced this as an insult: "Seldom have Swedish firms had such reasons to enter a new year so doubtful and hesitant. The economy is regulated, controlled, and directed to a degree without parallel even during the war."[48] This group, however, was not consulted on the matter of national health insurance – at least there is no record of a *remiss* comment from this group. In fact, the group itself complained that small businessmen were underrepresented in the Riksdag, and announced a campaign to improve the political standing of this group. Complaints to the political parties, however, resulted in the addition of only rather insignificant numbers of small businessmen to the party lists, overwhelmingly concentrated in the Liberal Party.

Conservative backlash

Two years later, however, an opportunity presented itself to these opponents of government expansion. The opposition parties were gearing up for the 1948 electoral campaign, and hoped that the 1947 balance of payments crisis would erode Social Democratic electoral support. Although enacted into law, national health insurance was delayed by the pending commune reform, which was to consolidate the most local bodies of government – the primary communes – into bigger units, more suitable for social policy implementation,[49] and by disagreements within the labor movement and the Social Democratic party over the cash benefits portion of the law.[50] During this delay, the release of a government report calling for the creation of a national health service, by placing all hospital and office doctors on a government salary and eliminating all forms of private medical practice, provided a focus for a conservative backlash. This opportunity was seized by political parties and interest groups that saw a chance to revise the Social Democratic status quo.

The 1948 Höjer proposal

The Höjer commission, chaired by J. Axel Höjer, director of the National Board of Health and brother of Karl J. Höjer, the second chairman of the Social Services Committee, had been appointed by the government in 1943 to study the need for reorganization of Swedish ambulatory medical care and to make recommendations that would be used in the final scheme for national health insurance. The report included a thorough and lengthy analysis of ambulatory care, an overview of international developments – with particular emphasis on the British NHS – and recommendations for the total reorganization of Swedish health services. These recommendations ranged from building local health centers to a reform of medical school curricula. Of more immediate concern were the provisions for the consolidation of all forms of outpatient care into one system under the auspices of the County Councils and the eventual transfer of all doctors to full-time salaries. Salary, the report argued, was the only rational and efficient means of physician remuneration and constituted a necessary step in providing affordable medical care to all citizens.[51]

In sum, the Höjer report was a proposal for a national health service, a national health service whose ambitions surpassed those of the NHS. Not only would hospital inpatient care be delivered at virtually no cost, but all forms of outpatient care – whether taking place in doctors' private offices, in the government offices of public doctors, or in the hospital outpatient clinics – were to be integrated into this service. Private patients and private fees – something that all Swedish doctors, both hospital and office-based, private or public, depended on – would be eliminated; all doctors would eventually be paid a government salary.

Medical and business protest. The Swedish Medical Association dropped its usual conciliatory stance to protest the Höjer reform.

It was not the principle of compulsory health insurance that became the chief issue but methods and amount of payment and professional freedom as the profession defined it. . . . a salaried service was beyond tolerance.[52]

The two physicians who sat on the commission, aside from Höjer himself, issued dissenting opinions, criticizing the commission for going far beyond its appointed field of inquiry and disavowing its recommendations for full-time salaries. Immediately upon publication of the report, the Association launched a campaign against the proposed reforms – and against J. Axel Höjer personally – in the medical press, in the newspapers, and by appealing to other interest groups.

The newspapers gave front-page coverage to the Association's comments on the reform, often adding editorial criticisms of their own. The report was depicted as a doctrinaire call for the immediate socialization of medicine and the downgrading of doctors from free professionals to state civil servants. The Conservative *Svenska Dagbladet* editorialized: "Mr. Höjer's goal emerges with frightening clarity: the profession's total socialization and the economic levelling of physicians, decreasing the quality and increasing the costs of health care for citizens." The Liberal *Dagen's Nyheter* was equally critical, noting that a national health service might be appropriate for Britain, but not for Sweden. Only the Social Democratic *Morgontidningen* supported the reform, castigating the other papers for acting as if "not the public health but guild interests should be the guidepost for reform."[53]

The Medical Association's lobbying efforts were successful not only in getting newspaper coverage, but also in convincing other groups to come to their defense. The Conservative Party's Business Group (*Högerns Företagargrupp*) warned of the consequences of socialized medicine, based on its experience of hassles and bureaucracy "that state collectivism brings" and praised the competitive free market for encouraging "individual initiative" among private doctors.[54] In its *remiss* answer to the Höjer report, the Swedish Employers' Association objected to the high costs of the reform and to this "complete socialization of the medical profession," and concluded that the reform was "completely unacceptable." The Employers' Association took the opportunity to criticize the Social Democratic approach more generally:

If the government persists with social policies that are constantly ahead of the economic development of the country and do not build upon a real weighing of the desirability of the reforms and the economic possibilities to bear the costs connected therewith, it appears, namely, out of the question to implement a monetary policy program of stabilization.[55]

Even LO, which fully adhered to the goals of the report, suggested that a fuller cost analysis might be advisable, given the discrepancies between Höjer's estimates and those made by the Medical Association. Like TCO, LO was concerned that a real weighing of goals and resources take place, not only within the health sector, but also between various types of social services.

The County Councils. But interest groups were not the only *remiss* bodies that spoke out against the Höjer reform. The Social Democrats' own bureaucracy and the Federation of County Councils, the local unit of government that owned and administered hospitals, recommended that no legislative action be pursued based on the Höjer report. The Federation of County Councils, headed by loyal Social Democrat Erik Fast, and the vast majority of individual County Councils were particularly concerned with the outpatient clinics (*polikliniks*) at hospitals, which had constituted a source of strife between hospitals and doctors for many years.[56] The original purpose of the Höjer commission had been to investigate the legal right of County Councils to maintain such clinics. The County Councils feared that by eliminating private practice within hospitals and by converting hospital doctors to a salary system, the Höjer reform would drive doctors away from hospital practice and into the private sector. Consequently, hospitals would find it more difficult not only to staff their outpatient clinics – the initial bone of contention – but to staff their inpatient wards as well. The Councils argued that the government should first increase the number of doctors, and only later – when, it was implied, the market position of doctors would be considerably weakened – should it address the question of jurisdiction over hospital outpatient care.

The reform is abandoned. The debate continued throughout 1948. *Svenska Dagbladet's* yearbook notes that no other legislative proposal received as much nor as critical press coverage in 1948 as the Höjer reform. Höjer himself was attacked both in the bourgeois press and in the medical journals. Heidenheimer describes the acrimonious tenor of these debates, in which the Medical Association chairman Dag Knutson referred to Höjer as a "dangerous man who must be removed from his post as soon as possible," while Höjer "felt entitled to label the [Association director as] pro-Nazi."[57] Debate over the Höjer reform became so heated that it was viewed as politically impossible to draft a legislative proposal or to take up the question in the Riksdag – a highly unusual end to a Swedish Royal Committee study. But the pattern was the same for economic and tax policy as well: The nonsocialist parties relied on the press to carry out an electoral campaign that has been singled out as being unusually aggressive and ideological in tone.[58]

The potential breakdown of future prospects for Farmer-Labor coalition governments, as well as electoral losses, placed the Social Democratic Party in a vulnerable position. Although the Social Democratic MPs held sufficient seats to enact any reform, potential electoral losses presented opponents of Social Democratic policies with a veto opportunity. These electoral pressures created a strategic opening for the medical profession. Unlike its grudging acceptance of national health insurance, the profession now declared itself absolutely opposed to the Höjer reform. In the face of these electoral pressures, the Social Democratic government backed down completely, not only on the Höjer reform, but also on a controversial proposal for a new inheritance tax, as well as other elements of its economic program.

The defeat of the Höjer reform has been viewed as a victory for the Swedish Medical Association. And it was. Private medical practice was preserved both within public hospitals and in private offices. No local health centers would compete with private office practice. Doctors would be paid on a fee-for-service basis, and they would be paid by patients and the insurance funds rather than by a salary from the state, as proposed by Höjer. Thus, in place of a national health service, a new national health insurance law was introduced in 1953, and went into effect in 1955. The program covered the entire population for medical and cash benefits, which would be provided through the preexisting sickness funds, and paid for by payroll tax contributions from employers and employees, as well as subsidies from the government.[59]

Whether the failure of the Höjer reform should be credited entirely to the lobbying campaign of the medical profession, however, is debatable. For the complaints of the medical profession reached ears that were very receptive, to say the least. In 1945 and 1946, the Social Democratic Party was perceived as having a mandate to establish a Swedish welfare state; no party dared to voice opposition to these reforms. As in many other countries, however, the climate of public opinion shifted rather quickly after the war. Particularly as the party moved from enacting social policies to introducing new taxes to pay for them – as well as toward a planned economy – the consensus for social democracy began to erode.[60]

Reactions to the Höjer reform fit very neatly into this general backlash against the welfare state. The Swedish Employers' Federation, for example, used its defense of professional freedom as an opportunity to criticize the government, charging that monetary stabilization would be impossible as long as the government continued to introduce expansionary social policies. These exchanges came to a head in the 1948 election campaign, a campaign that has been singled out as being unusually vicious and ideological in tone, with a general attack on socialism led by the nonsocialist parties. Socialized medicine was one of several issues through which these conflicts were played out. The Social Democrats suffered only a small loss in this election, but it is considered a turning point for the Social Democratic Party, nevertheless.

The Social Democrats' share of the popular vote decreased by only 0.6 percent – from 46.7 percent of the popular vote in 1944 to 46.1 percent in 1948, compared with a decline of several percentage points for the Conservatives (from 15.9 percent to 12.3 percent) and the Communists (10.3 percent to 6.3 percent), while the Liberal Party nearly doubled its share of the electorate (from 12.9 percent to 22.8 percent) through a 10 percent increase in voter participation. Yet this was sufficient for the party to lose three seats in the Second Chamber, narrowing the Social Democratic majority there to 112 seats to 110 held by the Conservatives, Farmers, and Liberals. Not only was the margin small, but the continued downward trend from 134 seats in the 1941 elections, despite the large number of social reforms, was worrisome. However, Social Democratic control of the executive was saved by its absolute majority in the First Chamber, where its representation had increased from 75 seats in 1941, to 83 in 1945, 86 in 1947, and 84 in 1949. Thus, the First Chamber had been transformed from a veto point to a guarantor of Social Democratic control of the government. Indeed this led to a discussion of the abolition of the First Chamber in 1953, but the Social Democrats refused.[61] The 1948 election thus exposed the vulnerability of the party to small electoral shifts, but the First Chamber provided a counterbalance. This election marks the definitive end to the postwar "Harvest Time" and the beginning of a period of Social Democratic pragmatism.

In sum, the abandonment of the Höjer reform was related to a general retrenchment on the part of the Social Democratic Party when faced with political opposition to its more controversial policies. This opposition came from interest groups – those directly affected by the reforms, such as the medical profession, but also some that viewed these policies as part of a more general conflict, such as the Employers' Federation – and from the nonsocialist parties. The opposition of the Farmers' Party was of particular concern, for the Social Democrats still looked to the Farmers' Party as a possible coalition partner. The Farmer's Party was specifically opposed to the Höjer reform, and generally played an important role in pushing Social Democrats away from planning and toward welfare expansion.[62] But this retrenchment was also recommended to the Social Democratic leadership by the Federation of County Councils, as well as its own bureaucracy. It was this sign of a possible electoral realignment that created a strategic opening for the medical profession, and indeed for employers as well, to break away from their usual conciliatory behavior and to press harder at all phases of political negotiation.

HARPSUND DEMOCRACY: THE 1950s AND 1960s

The defeat of the Höjer reform preserved a number of forms of private practice that were of significance to the medical profession. It was not long, however, before the economic autonomy of doctors was threatened once again. After the setback of the late 1940s, the Social Democratic government went ahead with a number of health policies, often without consulting the medical association. The overall direction of these policies was to reduce the market power of doctors by increasing their numbers and reducing the scope of private practice. But in health and in other policy areas, the pattern was the same – incremental policy making introduced through executive negotiations, where the emphasis was on technical preparation of reform rather than partisan conflict.

Indeed, in the 1950s and 1960s, so much decision making was removed from the parliamentary arena to tripartite agreements between the Social Democratic party, the Employers' Association, and the Trade Union Confederation that this is the era famed for "Harpsund" democracy, a reference to the retreat where labor and employer leaders met with government officials to decide on policy. The notable institutional feature is the absence rather than the presence of institutional constraints. The Social Democratic majority in the First Chamber stabilized the executive rather than providing a point of veto. The narrowness of the Second Chamber majority and the knowledge that proportional representation would allow for sudden electoral shifts encouraged the Social Democrats to obtain nonsocialist support for policies and to reach out for a broader, white-collar constituency. But party discipline and the stable majority governments, some in coalition with the Farmers' Party, prevented the parliamentary stalemate of the French Fourth Republic. Referenda were used in a few select cases, but they were closely controlled by the governing parties and did not provide the kinds of opportunities for interest-group threats that occurred in Switzerland.[63] At no time was the medical profession able to avail itself of a similar strategic opening like that of 1948.

Private medical practice

As enacted, the National Health Insurance Law allowed for a variety of forms of private medical practice. Within public hospitals, senior doctors could receive private patients both as inpatients in "private beds" or during private ambulatory consultations. Outside the hospitals, a small number of private clinics were in existence; private ambulatory consultations took place in private doctors' offices, as well as at the offices of district and provincial doctors. The district and provincial doctors were subsidized by the government and were paid a part-time salary, in return for which they agreed to treat low-income patients at fixed rates but were free to treat private patients. Swedish national health insurance covered doctors' fees for all of these forms of private practice. As in France, patients paid doctors directly, and were later reimbursed by the insurance agencies. Also as in France – and in Switzerland as well – patients were reimbursed for a percentage of an official fee schedule (75 percent), and doctors were free to extra-bill for all patients coming to their private offices or clinics, even though these patients were insured by the national health insurance program. Even within public hospitals, for patients defined as public patients, hospital doctors were paid for outpatient visits on a fee-for-service basis by patients; but these charges were restricted by the official fee schedule.

In the big cities, where the bulk of Sweden's population is concentrated, the extent of this private medical sector was considerable. Private inpatient care – that is, private beds in public hospitals and private clinics – was never extensive.[64] But private outpatient care, on the other hand, was widespread in Stockholm, Göteborg, and Malmö. In Stockholm, as much as 70 percent of outpatient consultations in September 1968 took place in the private sector, 62 percent at the offices of private practitioners. In the rest of the country, private practitioners were responsible for 22 percent of outpatient consultations in the same month.[65] In addition, all visits to hospital outpatient departments were covered by the same reimbursement system, except that doctors in the outpatient clinics were required to stick to the reimbursement fee schedule.

Increasing the number of doctors. Step by step, Social Democratic governments reorganized the health system and eliminated opportunities for private medical practice. As in France, the executive aimed to increase government planning and to achieve a better distribution of hospital resources through the regionalization policies of the 1950s. At the same time, governments took steps to reduce the market power of doctors by increasing their numbers and reducing the scope of private practice – that is, the exit opportunities for doctors. Each of these reforms was prepared in the executive and easily ratified in parliament; but the calmness of the process should not lead us to overlook the invasiveness of the reforms.

Over the opposition of the Medical Association, the government expanded the number of physicians through the building of three new medical schools and an increase in class size. As a result, the number of doctors licensed each year increased by a factor of seven between 1947 and 1972. These increases began in the early 1950s. The first step was in fact the importation of 100 Austrian doctors, which had been suggested by Höjer in the early 1940s and repeated in the Höjer report of 1948. The fact that the government could oppose the Swedish Medical Association so soon after the defeat of the Höjer reform lends further support to the thesis that the profession triumphed in 1948 because political opportunities for opposition to government policies presented themselves, rather than because the profession could, by itself, threaten to sabotage the health care system. The profession's control over the number of doctors was further eroded when the government took over specialty accreditation from the Swedish Medical Association in 1960.[66]

The 1959 Hospital Law. In 1959, the state began to take direct steps to restrict private medical practice. The 1959 Hospital Law eliminated private hospital beds and private fees for hospital inpatient care. The law also required hospitals to provide hospital outpatient care, thereby competing with the private office hours of the hospital doctors and with the private office-based practitioners. Consequently, hospital outpatient visits increased from 7.4 million in 1952 to 18.4 million in 1963, or more than 40 percent of medical consultations.[67] In response to the law, some doctors tried to revive the private clinics – if the government would attempt to draw patients away from private offices to public outpatient departments, the medical profession would counter by starting new private clinics. But this movement suffered a failure of nerve when the National Board of Health and Welfare announced plans to build local health centers in the mid-1960s.[68]

ABSOLUTE MAJORITY: THE 1969 SEVEN CROWNS
REFORM

The most dramatic threat to the private sector came in 1969, with the introduction of the "Seven Crowns" reform. This reform eliminated private practice from public hospitals entirely and replaced fee-for-service payments to hospital doctors with full-time salaries.

Like the French Debré reform and the Decrees of 12 May 1960, the Seven Crowns reform was motivated by political as well as health policy factors. The reform was part of a package of policies – in the areas of health care, taxation, and economic policy – that aimed to solidify the party's electoral standing at a time when it was at the peak of its power, but when its future control of the government was in jeopardy. The Social Democrats had finally agreed to abandon the First Chamber, and in 1970 new elections would be held for the shift from a bicameral to a unicameral parliament. This constitutional change would make the Social Democratic Party more vulnerable to electoral swings and reduce the political influence of the County Councils.[69] Although the future looked uncertain, the Social Democrats had won a landslide victory in the 1968 elections, winning an absolute majority for the first time since 1940. With such a margin, they could undertake fairly bold policy initiatives, and they were under pressure to do so quickly, before the 1970 elections.

Moreover, they viewed social policy expansion as the route to electoral success. The struggles over superannuated pensions had shown that the public was ready for increased social reform. When the Liberal Party lost nearly one-half of its voters as a result of its negative stance on the pensions, the parties began to outbid one another in the social policy area: "The opposition understood that they had burned their fingers in the ATP conflict [superannuated pensions conflict]"[70] The 1968 electoral success seemed to be a result of Social Democratic training and employment programs (the "Active Manpower Policy"). At the same time, the party was under fire because the recently released Low-Income Commission Study showed that twenty years of Social Democratic rule had failed to eradicate poverty in Sweden.[71]

Thus, as in France, questions of executive power provided the political motivations for a massive reorganization of the health system. But in contrast to France, the ability of the executive government to impose reform rested on its parliamentary majority and bargaining practices developed over decades.

Provisions of the Seven Crowns reform

The Seven Crowns reform was prepared and introduced in three steps. First, in executive proceedings, the government prepared the proposal, minimizing interest-group comment as much as possible. Second, the proposal was debated in parliament, where it was enacted into law by the Social Democrats' absolute majority – but Center and Liberal MPs also voted for the law. Third, after passage of the law, negotiations between the Federation of County Councils and the Swedish Medical Association completed the reform. Thus, the name "Seven Crowns" refers to a series of measures introduced both through a legislative proposal and later, in conjunction with the new law, through collective bargaining between the County Councils and the Medical Association.

The legislative portion of the reform transformed the payment mechanism for hospital outpatient care. Patients would no longer pay doctors directly, and then wait for reimbursement from national health insurance. Instead, they would pay the hospital a uniform flat-fee of 7 crowns (hence the name of the reform), which was worth about $1.40 at the time. National health insurance would pay 31 crowns for each visit directly to the County Councils. At the same time, the private office hours of senior physicians were eliminated; no private practice was to be carried out within the walls of public hospitals.

Once the reform had been approved by the Riksdag, the Swedish Medical Association and the Federation of County Councils held negotiations to decide how to pay doctors for hospital outpatient work, now that they would no longer be paid on a fee-for-service basis by patients. In these negotiations, it was decided to pay all hospital doctors a salary that would cover both outpatient and inpatient duties at the public hospitals. Initially, it had been intended to extend the flat-rate "Seven Crowns" system to public district doctors and private office-based practitioners. Negotiations over the exact details of the plan for the private practitioners broke down, however. Nevertheless, this failure aided the government.

Because the private practitioners were left out of the reform, patients would have an economic incentive to seek care at hospital outpatient clinics where they would pay 7 crowns, rather than at private offices, where they would pay full fees, later receiving only a partial reimbursement if the doctors extra-billed. This would hurt the office-based practitioners, and at the same time, close off an "exit" option for hospital doctors dissatisfied with the reform. Senior doctors would not easily be able to transfer their private hours to private offices outside the hospitals, and complete exit into full-time practice would also be made more difficult by the new incentive structure.[72]

Together, the Seven Crowns reform and the related negotiations introduced several of the more controversial points of the Höjer reform. The County Councils would have sole jurisdiction over outpatient care within public hospitals, and service within the outpatient clinics (*polikliniks*) would become a mandatory part of hospital duties. Furthermore, hospital doctors would in future be paid a full-time salary. Had the Federation of County Councils and the Swedish Medical Association been able to agree on extending the reform to private practitioners, Höjer's program would have been complete: All private office-based practitioners would have been placed under the jurisdiction of the County Councils, thereby establishing a fully integrated national health service for ambulatory care, completely under the control of one government body, the County Councils.

Like the French Debré reform, the Seven Crowns reform was intended as a rationalizing measure. In eliminating the reimbursement system for hospital outpatient care, the direct costs to patients of each visit would be comparable to the costs for hospital inpatient care, which had been set at a flat rate since 1955. It was hoped that the reform would remove the economic incentives to choose the more costly inpatient care.[73] The reform was intended to rationalize the behavior of physicians as well as patients. If private medical practice was removed from public hospitals, senior physicians would no longer prefer to spend time in their private office hours, leaving the *polikliniks* to be staffed by the junior physicians. Removing the lucrative private practice available to senior hospital doctors in the cities would, in addition, reduce one of the differences between city and rural hospital practice, which might encourage more doctors to move into rural areas. It would also make doctors' incomes more subject to tax scrutiny, a topic of concern since a recent tax investigation had revealed substantial unreported income among doctors.

Finally, it was thought that the transfer from fee-for-service to salary payment for hospital outpatient care would solve some irrationalities stemming from the reimbursement fee-schedule. Because the fee schedule had not been revised in accordance with technological changes, specialists in some areas were earning disproportionately high incomes. X-rays, for example, took much less time to carry out than in 1955, yet fees were fairly stable in relative terms. Consequently, it was felt that radiologists were earning windfall profits – particularly when compared with less technologically oriented specialties such as psychiatry and pediatrics. In addition, fees charged by doctors were continually increased. Despite recent increases in the schedule, reimbursement failed to keep up with doctors' fees. Insurance authorities were faced with a choice between patient disatisfaction at being reimbursed at less than the promised rate of 75 percent, or the prospect of maintaining the 75 percent rate by continually raising the reimbursement schedule to match doctors' fees. The Seven Crowns reform would stop this cycle by eliminating the reimbursement mechanism altogether and replacing it with a salary system. Salary, moreover, would result in more equal incomes for doctors.[74]

Professional politics

Given the tremendous public reaction to the Höjer reform, we might well wonder why this reform was rejected out of hand in 1948 but passed into law in 1969. The passage of the Seven Crowns reform has been interpreted in terms of the "deprofessionalization" of the swedish medical profession. The deprofessionalization thesis focuses on the changes in the relative power of the medical profession vis-à-vis the County Councils and on the role played by the leadership of the Swedish Medical Association. Although the Association criticized the Seven Crowns reform – in particular the elimination of private practice from public hospitals and the neglect of the private practitioners – the Association eventually accepted the reform when it was enacted by the Riksdag, and pursued a moderate course in subsequent salary negotiations with the Federation of County Councils. Carder and Klingeberg assert that the Medical Association leadership withheld information from its members and purposely kept a low profile, in order to be able to "concede" to government demands without being held accountable for this by its membership.[75]

There were advantages for the leadership in accepting a salary form of payment. With an increased number of physicians, which not only weakened the market position of doctors but also brought in a large cohort of younger doctors, the leadership could improve the situation of its members more effectively by pursuing a hard line in salary negotiations than by clinging to private practice privileges. In addition, inequalities caused by the reimbursement system as well as differences in access to private patients were creating friction among the Association's membership that would be mitigated through the more rational distribution of a salary system. At the same time, as Heidenheimer points out, the position of the County Councils, and especially their Federation, had been strengthened by an increased reliance on centralized planning through the regionalization of the health system, the delegation of several new responsibilities to the Councils, and because negotiations with the medical profession now took place on a national level, between the Federation of County Councils and the Swedish Medical Association.[76]

The political framework

As in other cases of health insurance reform, however, the decision of the Medical Association to cooperate must be viewed within a broader strategic and political context. With the absolute Social Democratic majority in the parliament, passage of the Seven Crowns law was a fait accompli. This explains the conciliatory stance of the Swedish Medical Association leadership both during the preparatory stage preceding the parliamentary debate and in the negotiation stage that followed the passage of the law by parliament. The constraints imposed on the leadership by this political context, and not professional interest, led the leadership to cooperate rather than protest.

The remiss process. During the *remiss* proceedings, the Swedish Medical Association did in fact object to points in the Seven Crowns proposal that hurt two groups within its membership: senior hospital doctors and private office practitioners. The senior hospital physicians protested the removal of private practice from public hospitals, whereas the private office practitioners were concerned about the discrepancy between the 7 crowns that would be charged in the hospital outpatient departments and the full fees charged in private offices. As Conservative MP Dr. Gunnar Biörck accused, the Seven Crowns reform entailed "the total socialization of Swedish health care overnight, through changed employment conditions for hospital doctors and the economic freezing-out of private practitioners." These market disadvantages were to be used, he argued, to make the private practitioners "sufficiently soft . . . to fall into the hands (or arms) of the County Councils."[77]

Younger hospital doctors and rural practitioners were not affected by the removal of private practice from the hospitals or the competitive pressures against private office practice and extra-billing. The younger doctors would benefit from the more even distribution of hospital work; rural practitioners would be hurt by the competition from the hospital outpatient clinics, but this private practice was less widespread than in the cities, and these doctors did not tend to override the fee schedule to the same extent as the urban practitioners. Thus, professional interests were divided. As in France and Switzerland, restrictions on private practice were of concern to senior hospital physicians and urban private practitioners, but not to younger doctors and rural practitioners. Yet the Swedish Medical Association, like the French and Swiss Medical Associations, chose to defend the private sector. Drawing on the language of Swedish industrial relations (almost with the same phrases as the French CSMF in 1960), the Swedish Medical Association charged that "It is unreasonable that this free sector be abolished through a legislative decision. The reform ought to be limited to the outpatient care that is under the jurisdiction of the public authorities while the right to the private sector, on the contrary, should be regulated through contracts between the labor market partners." The neglect of the private office-based practitioners was a second, serious flaw in the reform that would impede coordination between outpatient and inpatient care. The Association concluded that the draft proposal could not be used as a basis for reform. It lacked documentation, and passage of the reform would result in an influx of patients to hospital outpatient clinics, producing long lines at the *polikliniks* and inadequate treatment. In order to assure passage of the reform's positive aspects, particularly for patients, the Association was, however, willing to cooperate "to draft and implement a new, thoroughly worked-out proposal."[78]

Although moderate in its presentation, the Swedish Medical Association did indeed voice objections to the Seven Crowns Reform; it did not simply accept the government's plan for reform. When the Association's lobbying efforts at the executive stage failed, however, cooperation made sense, even though the leadership was faced with membership protests. For although the Association had the organizational resources to mount a strike or other protest activity, collective action was not effective against a united executive government. Thus, the weak position of the Swedish medical profession was fundamentally of a political rather than an economic or organizational nature. Even though the increases in medical school admissions would be expected to weaken the market position, the number of inhabitants per doctor remained lower in Sweden than in other countries where the medical profession was more successful in defending its access to a private market.[79] Furthermore, the Medical Association had successfully carried out several economic actions – such as a strike in 1957 in which doctors organized an alternative private health service, the building of private clinics in the early 1960s, and a strike threat in 1965 that resulted in substantial increases in the reimbursement schedule. Each time, however, the government had reacted by taking a *political* step that constrained the private market. The defeat of the Höjer reform was met with the increases in medical school admissions in the 1950s; the 1957 strike was followed by the 1959 Hospital Law; the private clinics were combated by announcements that the government planned to build local health centers in the mid-1960s; the increases in the fee reimbursement schedule in the late 1960s resulted in the Seven Crowns reform.

The Swedish medical profession lost in the political arena not in the market arena, and as the preceding analysis has shown, Swedish physicians were politically disadvantaged. In 1969, as with the 1931 Sickness Fund Law and with the 1947 National Health Insurance Law, the Medical Association was faced with unified support for an expanded government role in health care. The Employers' Federation, in sharp contrast to its opposition to the Höjer reform, now supported restrictions on private practice and the elimination of the reimbursement mechanism as a means of controlling health care costs. The reform would lead to a more rational organization of health care, SAF stated in its *remiss* paper, and doctors would be able to devote themselves more fully to the care of patients if they were removed from financial matters. LO and TCO were strongly in favor of the reform, as was the Federation of County Councils. The Councils were especially concerned with rising hospital costs. The increased inpatient fees provided for under the law would discourage hospitalization and increase revenues, reducing the need to raise local taxes.[80]

Accelerated policy making. Not only was there widespread support for the reform from a number of central political actors, but use of the executive arena allowed the Social Democratic government to accelerate the reform process and to discourage lengthy discussions over the reform's more controversial points. From a procedural point of view, the Seven Crowns reform was highly unusual, as it was essentially worked out between the Federation of County Councils, the Social Department, and the National Health Insurance Office, without the presence of representatives of the Swedish Medical Association. The restriction of the preparatory stages to high levels of the bureaucracy was of strategic importance, for it helped to assure the passage of the reform within a year. There was less time for opposition to the reform to develop within the medical profession, or for the profession to launch an opposition campaign among potential allies.[81]

This pressing time frame for the reform and the attempts to minimize interest group input, however, were related to the overall electoral strategy of the Social Democratic Party. Indeed, that strategy was not limited to the health area. A 1970 tax reform was passed through the same kind of process: Preparation was not carried out through a Royal Committee, the Social Democrats were accused of precluding public discussion of the reform, and the reform process was controlled completely from within the government with little input from the political parties.[82] For the officials of the Social Department and the Social Minister Sven Aspling, the absolute parliamentary majority won by the Social Democrats in the 1968 election provided an opportunity to introduce reforms that had been in the works for a number of years, and to push things through more quickly than usual.

Sources of conciliation. In spite of this rather extraordinary position, the party did not impose reforms based on its electoral majority; it relied on consensus among certain key parties and interest groups, but a consensus that was aided by the structure of Swedish interest representation. Here the role of the County Councils was crucial. During the postwar period, nearly 50 percent of MPs held posts on County Councils; within the Center Party, the proportion ranged from 67 percent to 85 percent.[83] As an informal political coalition, known as the "County Council Party," or *Landstingspartiet*, members of the County Councils were essential in convincing their fellow party members to vote for health reforms. Thus, a certain multipartisan aspect lay beneath the surface of the Social Democratic initiatives, causing some doctors to complain bitterly that the socialization of the medical profession was accomplished with the help of nonsocialist politicians.[84]

A second source of conciliation was provided by the continuing negotiations between the main labor market organizations. Brought into nearly constant contact with one another and with the government, neither SAF, LO, nor TCO had a strong interest in disrupting collective bargaining agreements by turning national health insurance policies into symbolic ideological issues. SAF was willing to accept national health insurance and restrictions on private practice. LO was willing to discuss cost containment and to weigh benefit increases against their financial implications. TCO was willing to give up special fringe benefit schemes in the name of solidarity with all wage earners.

The same procedures that brought together a limited number of central political actors and encouraged cooperative bargaining shut out potential sources of particularistic vetoes of government policies. Groups such as the medical profession – or earlier, the Taxpayers' Association – were not privileged with the same kind of access to political decision making as were the County Councils or the labor market organizations. In the context of Royal Committees and bureaucratic politics, the medical profession was only one of several interest groups that had to be polled. Moreover, if the labor market organizations agreed, it was not necessary to represent the profession in a Royal Committee or even to set up a committee.

Parliament. In parliament, hardliners within the profession were able to recruit a number of Conservative politicians to vote against the Seven Crowns reform, as they had in the past. But this opposition was insufficient to override the nearly unanimous votes of the Social Democratic,

Liberal, and Center parties. As Conservative MP and physician Kaijser protested, "the Parliamentary decision is a mere formality . . . the real decision has taken place over the heads of the MPs."[85]

Dissident views were expressed in the press, as well. One economically liberal newspaper stated:

It is not too much to demand that Parliament and the Swedish people be given the opportunity to discuss and examine thoroughly a reform proposal which can be said to entail the "socialization" of the majority of the medical profession.[86]

Another liberal paper ran the headline, "Health Care Reform Resembles Coup," and later in the month warned that "this secret socialization will surely cause a rapid emigration of doctors from Sweden to countries with freer working conditions."[87] But with the support of the Liberal and Center parties, the Social Democratic majority held firm. The Seven Crowns reform became law on 3 December 1969.

Negotiation. After passage of the law, the conflict passed to the collective bargaining arena, where the Swedish Medical Association agreed – despite strong criticisms from some of its members – to a salary system of payment. The leadership was attacked for not informing the membership about the full implications of the reform and for not pursuing a hard line in the negotiations with the Federation of County Councils. There were even demands that the membership be polled for its views. The leadership defended itself on the grounds that it was "stuck" in a situation where it was hard to bargain with resolution and strength.[88] Once again, when politically isolated, the Association pursued a moderate course of action, despite membership criticisms.

Results of the Seven Crowns reform

With the enactment of the Seven Crowns reform, the Swedish health system moved a decisive step toward becoming a national health service. The vast majority of doctors worked as salaried employees of the government. Patients paid only a small sum at the time of treatment, with the rest of costs being paid for through national health insurance and local taxes. At private office-based practitioners, on the other hand, patients continued to pay full fees with subsequent reimbursement from the insurance funds. Consequently, the percentage of full-time practitioners dropped from 15 percent in 1964 to 6 percent in 1979, and the average age of private practitioners rose to 57 years, compared with an average of 39 years for the profession as a whole.[89]

In 1975, however, the private practitioners were given the option of registering with the insurance funds in return for adhering to a fee schedule. Thus, virtually all forms of private practice were incorporated into the government scheme. From this time on, visits to unregistered doctors would not be covered by national health insurance. As the private practitioners had

found it hard to compete with the public sector . . . the reform in 1975 and the new system of reimbursement was an improvement for the private practitioners. It was clear, however, that the social democratic government was aiming at limiting private practice. Therefore, some of the hospital doctors who used to have private practices in their spare-time were excluded from the possibility of reimbursement under the health insurance scheme.[90]

Hospital doctors were required to have the permission of the County Council for which they worked before opening up a part-time practice. The hospital's need for overtime was required to be fulfilled before doctors could go into overtime private practice.[91]

Post-1976 changes

When the nonsocialist government came to power in 1976, the restrictions on spare-time private practice for hospital doctors were lifted and, at the initiative of the Conservative Party, a study was made of the need for private practitioners. At the same time, however, plans for putting all private practitioners under the jurisdiction of the County Councils for planning purposes only, resulted in protests by private practitioners in 1979.[92]

In 1982, the Social Democrats were returned to power and reintroduced restrictions on private practice. Previous limits on private practice had reduced the number of full-time private practitioners, and the numbers had continued to decrease under the non-socialist government. In 1975, there were 800 full-time practitioners; in 1984, only 600. But during the early 1980s the number of spare-time private practitioners increased dramatically – from 233,000 patient visits to spare-time practitioners in 1981, to 346,000 in 1982, the number in 1983 jumped to more than 600,000. The number of spare-time private practitioners may have increased as a result of a hospital doctors' strike in January 1982 – developing a spare-time private practice protected the exit opportunities of doctors in public hospitals. In addition, many doctors signed up when the Social Democrats returned to power in the fall of 1982, anticipating that the Social Democrats might move to curtail spare-time private practice in the future.[93]

Repeating the pattern of the past, the Social Democratic government countered doctors' efforts to exit from the public sector by imposing new restrictions on private practice. The controversial Dagmar reform of 1986, like the Seven Crowns reform, was worked out largely between the Social Department and the Federation of County Councils. Under this reform, government subsidies to hospitals would no longer be paid for each patient visit, but would be distributed according to the number of inhabitants. This change was meant to assure that funding for health care would be evenly distributed, and not reward overuse of the system, which generally occurred in the better-funded areas, such as the cities. In addition, the law changed the possibilities for doctors to sign up for private practice. Doctors who had previously signed up could continue their private practice, but hospital doctors would no longer be required to sign contracts with County Councils. Full-time private practitioners, as well, would be required to sign contracts with the County Councils for their patients to be covered by national health insurance. At the same time that Social Democratic policies increased the control of the County Councils over the private sector, more authority was delegated to the individual County Councils, and the oversight powers of the National Board of Health and Welfare were lessened. Thus, Social Democratic health policy of the 1980s continued to restrict private practice, but private medical practice increased at the margins, and the health system became more decentralized.

An End to the Social Democratic Model?

The enactment of the Seven Crowns reform was both the culmination of a long period of Social Democratic rule and the start of a new era. The elimination of the First Chamber has destabilized the Swedish system, allowing for more frequent shifts in government during the 1970s and 1980s, and undermining the certainty of continuous Social Democratic rule that provided the political framework for the period of Harpsund democracy. With this destabilization, more conflicts within Swedish society have become apparent. The old, class-based politics have not captured the young or professional groups; the strategy of national economic management with generous social policies is not adapted to the global environment. Indeed, the shifts between Conservative governments trying to expand the private sector and Social Democratic governments trying to cut it back, are representative of more general changes in the Swedish model since 1976. Not only has the emphasis on a nationally planned public health system come to be questioned, but key features of the Swedish post-Second World War settlement – such as centralized collective bargaining and wage agreements, the class-based party system, and the ability of SAF, TCO, and LO to represent divergent interests – are now under debate.

As this analysis of the piecing together of the Social Democratic model shows, however, these conflicts are not new; they were always part of Swedish society. The difference is the ability of the system of political representation to make some conflicts less politically relevant and to find ways of adjudicating among the others. Whereas previously the Social Democrats could weather a storm such as the 1948 election, slowing down their policy agenda but maintaining their position as the governing party, the increased instability of a unicameral system based on proportional representation is reversing the Swedish pattern of radical policies achieved through institutions meant to impede change.

EXECUTIVE-INDUCED COOPERATION AND HEALTH POLITICS

The Swedish state was able to take steps to control the medical market because its actions could not be vetoed in alternative arenas. This was not simply a matter of Social Democratic electoral victories. Similar expansions of public health insurance, controls on doctors' fees, and salaried payment had been supported by the French Gaullists and by nearly unanimous votes from the full spectrum of Swiss political parties. The Swedish executive was able to go further than these governments because the initial policy changes were not blocked; rather, they led to further interventions.

Nor were these policy changes a result of peculiar preferences on the part of the medical profession or a result of any inherent economic or organizational weaknessess. Like French and Swiss doctors, the Swedish private practitioners viewed market autonomy as the key to professional freedom. These doctors promoted a liberal model of medicine, protesting mandatory medical benefits under the 1930 Sickness Fund Law, begrudgingly accepting national health insurance but insisting on the same reimbursement payment as in France, blocking the Höjer plan for a national health service and attacking the medical association leadership for not protesting more forcefully the Seven Crowns reform. Thus, Swedish medical opinion did not differ radically from that in other countries, nor did the medical association seem incapable of collective action.

The striking difference between the Swedish medical profession and the others lay in its strategic political position. Although strikes had indeed been effective in the past – for example, in increasing doctors' fees – these victories were short-lived. After each successful strike, the government took a *political* step to constrain the private market, such as removing private beds from public hospitals or eliminating the fee system entirely, as under the Seven Crowns reform. Not only did the Social Democratic government hold the parliamentary votes that would ensure passage of the legislation, but like the de Gaulle government, it buttressed its reform by changing market incentives to both doctors and patients. In France, the individual contract had assured the widespread acceptance of the negotiated fee schedules by making it much cheaper for patients to go to the doctors who agreed to lower their fees, thereby breaking the French doctors' strike. In Sweden, the Seven Crowns reform made private office practice less attractive to patients, because hospital outpatient care was now virtually free, whereas in private offices, patients were required to pay the full fee and were later reimbursed for a portion of the fee. This would make it difficult for doctors wishing to protest the Seven Crowns reform to flee to the private sector.

Thus, the idea that doctors can block any reform by going on strike appears to be a myth. In economic conflicts, the government can use political means to change the terms of the conflict. And we might note that the profession that received the greatest concessions from the government – the Swiss doctors – never went on strike, and seems to have profited both from the electoral reactions to health insurance referenda and the fears of policy makers that it might launch a referendum. In Sweden, the Social Democratic government was able to convert its electoral gains into concrete policy decisions because political bargains worked out within Royal Committees were enforced by stable parliamentary majorities that closed off veto opportunities for dissident groups. Only when electoral realignments provided a strategic opportunity for veto did interest groups defect from this game of cooperative bargaining.

The Swedish pattern of executive-induced compromise was built up in a series of steps through a combination of constitutional rules, electoral results, and historical accident. Policies were made by consensus, but in a process that increased the probability of agreement by concentrating decisions at a single point with a group of actors that repeatedly met. The forging of consensus does not mean that conflicts or disagreements were nonexistent, but the conditions for conciliating conflict were helped by the lack of decision points where single actors could unilaterally overturn the executive-level consensus. The framework for this process was a double framework: the long period of political control by the Social Democrats of the executive, and the committee and *remiss* procedures that moved decision making to a protected arena, even when the First Chamber and parliament could be used as veto points.

These institutional features did not determine that Social Democrats would be so successful in getting out the popular vote or that union organizers would be able to consolidate such a large variety of workers' interests into a single confederation. But what the institutions did accomplish was to eliminate sources of political blockage and interest-group veto that in other countries put a stop to the very policies that helped to encourage the Social Democratic vision of politics and policies. Had the Swedish population in 1946 been presented with a referendum against the National Health Insurance Law, it is not clear that the majority of the population that was already voluntarily insured would have reacted any differently than the Swiss. Indeed the TCO stated that the reform would not benefit its membership. Had parliament been more effective as a veto point, the access of Swedish liberal doctors to parliament might have impeded the socialization of medicine. Instead, the majoritarian politics of the executive area were protected from the diversity of interests that countered executive decisions elsewhere. The Swedish case is an example of what can happen when the executive can enact its legislation program without risk of legislative or electoral vetoes.

6

The limits of institutions

In an age when distrust of politics is rife, welfare state programs stand as testimony to the potential of positive government. When these programs work, they provoke enthusiasm for government intervention; when they do not, the discouragement extends from the policies to the entire process of politics. This book takes neither an optimistic nor a pessimistic view of public policy. Nor does it end with a call for a specific program of action. Instead, it will close by presenting the limits of institutionalist analysis. For only by making these limits explicit can we put institutions to use making better public policies.

The political decisions examined in the preceding chapters all involved a central conflict between doctors and executive governments. Governments in the three nations attempted to regulate medical markets, whereas doctors fought to maintain a free market. Each victory by government reduced the market freedom of doctors, whereas each success of the medical profession protected its market position within the framework of a given health insurance system. In Sweden, national health insurance was extended to the entire population, the government regulated doctors' fees, fees were replaced by salaries, and the rights of doctors to practice privately were restricted. Swedish executive governments were able to introduce these policy changes because political bargains worked out within Royal Commissions were enforced by stable parliamentary majorities. In France, as well, executive governments introduced nearly universal social security coverage, and later utilized this financing mechanism to regulate doctors' fees and to introduce full-time salaried hospital practice. Executive action in France, however, was countered by parliamentary vetoes. Interest groups were able to use the parliamentary veto point to oppose the development of a centralized social security system and to delay fee regulation and restrictions on private practice. Major increases in governmental control of the health insurance system were possible only at times when the executive government could cir-

:umvent the parliamentary veto point. In Switzerland, referendum politics blocked the introduction of national health insurance and hampered subsequent efforts to regulate medical fees. With these early steps effectively precluded, discussion of restrictions on private practice became a non-issue.

In all of the cases presented here, we see the effects of legislation, and despite the difficulties of rational decision making, many of these laws did indeed accomplish what their legislators intended. But policy making is difficult. Enacting laws depends on the cooperation of a number of actors during "windows of opportunity" that may open up only rarely. The contribution of this book is to point to systematic differences in the likelihood that legislators can enact their programs. Although recognizing the role that a variety of contingent and unpredictable factors play in specific political decisions, it underscores the predictable effects of formal political institutions in accounting for the number of these windows and their frequency within a given political system. What is a window of opportunity for a legislator wishing to promote change, however, is, conversely, a blocked opportunity for interest groups hoping to prevent a move away from the status quo. For the ability of interest groups to influence these political decisions, it has been argued, depends precisely on the number of veto points within these political systems. Therefore, it is the closing-off of these veto points that creates the opportunity for legislators to push their program unscathed through the political process.

The critical difference between the three cases lies in the design of national political institutions and in the political practices that have developed around these institutions. Each of the health insurance histories is marked by patterns of political activity that are nationally distinct and account for the divergent policy outcomes. Yet the dissimilar political behaviors can be understood by applying a common framework.

This book has focused on the contraints placed on executive governments by the need for assenting votes to ratify executive proposals. The key variable is thus the way in which political institutions partition votes into separate political arenas or jurisdictions. This partitioning, which depends on formal constitutional rules and on electoral results, determines whether electoral victors can enact new legislation or whether a block of opposing votes will consistently overturn progressive proposals. Such a block of votes has been termed a "core" in the institutional literature. Cores are viewed as the source of stability – that is, lack of change in the status quo, in systems of majority rule.[1] Here, these partitioned votes will be called veto points.

Thus, once executive governments decide to propose legislation, a critical question is whether politicians or voters in other parts of the system can veto the executive decision. If so, interest groups with access to these votes will be able to demand changes in the legislation or to block it entirely. The existence of veto points, in sum, depends upon the formal constitutional provisions that set forth the relationship between the executive and legislative branches of government, and on the rules of the electoral system, which affect the types of electoral majorities that are produced and the mechanical translation of those majorities into legislative seats. At the same time, de facto characteristics – features of political systems that may not be deducible from the formal constitutional rules such as the extent to which the party system is fragmented, the practice of party discipline, and traditional electoral patterns – will affect the chances that the political party in the executive can indeed enact its legislative program.

In Sweden, the greatest degree of change was possible. Members of the political party that controlled the executive could make decisions unimpeded by vetoes from either parliament or the electorate because executive governments rested on stable parliamentary majorities and these in turn were based on stable voting patterns. Further, as we saw, the upper house of parliament, in most political systems thought of as a veto point, worked to stabilize Social Democratic control of the executive, despite electoral shifts; the votes of the upper house supported rather than blocked the executive. Thus, the proportion of votes in each of these decision-making arenas – the political jurisdictions – were exact transformations of one another. The independent action of the Swedish executive was possible, not because the executive was cut off from the other arenas, but rather because executive action was buttressed by supporting votes in the other arenas. Consequently, the Swedish executive could enact legislation without fearing vetoes from the parliamentary and electoral arenas.

The situations in France and Switzerland were very different. In France, the executive government of the Third and Fourth Republics was dependent upon parliamentary support, both de jure and de facto; executive proposals were vetoed by the withdrawal of supporting votes from the parliamentary coalitions. The disjuncture between the parliamentary coalition and the electoral majorities that supported them further destabilized the parliamentary majorities, as we saw, by creating incentives for opportunistic action by the parliamentary parties and the entry of surge parties. Only when the executive bypassed the parliamentary veto point entirely, through the constitutional provisions of the Fifth Republic and the special regime of the Provisional Government of the Liberation, could the executive enact laws without parliamentary veto. It was at these points that major health legislation was passed.

In Switzerland, the referendum was the most important veto point. Swiss political arenas did not allow one political party singly or in coalition to control the executive to introduce policy initiatives. The collegial executive imperfectly mirrored the distribution of votes in parliament, which dampened the effects of electoral victories as the executive government remained unchanged despite electoral shifts; no executive party could claim exclusive credit for new proposals. Nevertheless, as in Sweden, there was a clear relationship between the proportion of votes for each party in the executive and the proportion of votes in the legislature. The Swiss executive, like the Swedish executive, was thus able to marshall the parliamentary votes needed to pass its legislative initiatives into law; the parliament was not the veto point.

Instead, the policy blockage in the Swiss system came from the electoral arena. But it was not elections that blocked policies, it was the referendum. Like the Swedish system and unlike the French, parliamentary seats did reflect electoral majorities. Even with the disproportionate number of rural seats in the Ständerat, this arena did not constitute the veto point for health policy. The history of national health insurance politics in Switzerland shows that the vetoes came about through referendum votes that diverged sharply from election results. The veto point was formed by a discrepancy in votes that were partitioned into a separate political jurisdiction; an electoral core could be found that preferred the status quo to new proposals. Thus in Sweden, the lack of veto points restricted decision making to the executive arena. In France, unstable parliamentary majorities shifted decision making to the parliamentary arena. In Switzerland, decision making was moved to the electoral arena.

The system of political arenas and their veto points is the political framework within which specific policy struggles take place (Table 8). The distribution of votes into these different jurisdictions gives a prediction of how likely legislation is to pass, and where the expected bottlenecks are to be found. The impact of this probability of passage is not simply that we know from the outset whether or not legislation is likely to go through; more importantly, all of the interest groups and politicians that participate in drafting the legislation and bargaining over specific provisions make the same probability estimates and use these to determine their strategies and lobby efforts.

Interest-group behavior is therefore not an independent variable; this behavior always refers to a distinct political system with predictable veto points. Depending upon the political institutions, different political strategies make sense; the benefits of cooperative stances versus conflictual stances, the types of exchanges that can be made, and the specific politicians that need to be persuaded to change their vote – all depend upon the organization of the political system. In sum, the institutions affect the chances of each group to impose its wishes on the others. Therefore, the institutions alter the constellation of groups that are per-

Table 8. *Political arenas and veto points*

Country	Political arenas		Veto points
	De jure rules	**De facto results**	
Sweden	Prime minister invested by parliament First Chamber designed as a veto point Proportional representation	Stable parliamentary majorities First Chamber supports executive government Stable voting	No veto points
France Third and Fourth Republics	President invested by parliament Proportional representation	Unstable parliamentary majorities Sudden electoral shifts	Parliamentary veto point
France Fifth Republic	Direct election of president Direct executive legislation	Executive circumvents parliamentary veto point	No veto points
Switzerland	Collegial executive Proportional representation Referendum	Proporz system Stable voting Negative voting	Referendum veto point

tinent to a given policy decision, as well as the relative importance of these groups. Institutions change the array of relevant actors and redefine the political alternatives.

A limited theory of institutions

A number of studies of public policy have expanded our concept of the political by pointing to the critical role of the social definition of issues and the subtleties of agenda setting. From this perspective, the politics and sociology of knowledge frame the construction of public policies. Other investigations have emphasized policy implementation and the ways in which policies are significantly revised once they enter bureaucratic and local arenas, where interest group–agency negotiations continue. By contrast, this book has reasserted the significance of politics more conventionally understood. This is not to say that preparliamentary and postparliamentary politics are unimportant, but simply, that in this particular case, we have something to gain by focusing in on the standard legislative process.

Differences in procedural rules can indeed make a substantive difference to policy outcomes. Thus, we do not have democracy for the welfare state or democracy against the welfare state, but different democracies whose specific institutional designs have affected the rules of the game for specific political contests. At the broadest level of generality, the opportunities and constraints established by political institutions influenced the formation and aggregation of interests, the lines of political cleavage, the rules of political strategy, and the practical meaning of political power.

Within these institutional constraints, however, many different courses of action were possible. The institutions did not exert their effects by limiting the range of policies considered or the perceptions or even the actions of interest groups. The actors assessed their goals, interests, and desires independently of the institutions; the institutions affected only the strategic opportunities for achieving these objectives. Moreover, these actors were free to make mistakes. This argument thus does not depend on actors socialized to limit themselves to the terrain marked out by institutions. Nor does it require levels of rational calculation that surpass what seems intuitively credible. In each case, the institutional effects were obvious, and explicitly discussed by politicians and interest groups. The actors did not always follow the rules of the game – they sometimes tried to break them or to change them. Some of these institutional changes worked in the ways that their framers hoped; others had quite unintended consequences.

The model presented here is therefore limited. I do not claim either a general theory of institutions or a general model of health policy. There is not an invariant correlation between a given set of political institutions and a specific set of health policies. Rather, by spelling out the effects of constitutional rules and electoral results at a high level of specificity, we can understand some of the recurring patterns of politics and policy making in individual polities. Some aspects of these institutions and their effects match the predictions of more general theories of institutions. But, as we saw, these institutional configurations were hybrids; pieces were borrowed from different political philosophers and from different existing political systems. (The United States was a favorite source of institutional inspiration, even though American institutions often had different effects when inserted into a corner of another political system.)

The ways that these institutions worked in practice depended upon the exact combination of institutional features, historical accident, as well as conventions and interpretations that developed around these institutions. For example, not every Swiss referendum overturned legislative decisions. But enough did so that policy makers began to bend to interest-group demands in order to avoid the risk of referendum challenge. In practice, the limits of the institutions were identified by testing these limits; the extent of executive power, for example, was established by trying to introduce new legislation, and seeing how much withstood legal or other challenges. Nevertheless, although history, interpretation, and convention may have affected the establishment of the institutions, these institutional practices, once established, exerted their effects without a need for much learning of the rules. Interest groups entered these systems and aimed their efforts wherever they could. But it was only at the points in the system where the decision-making process was vulnerable (because a core of decision makers could veto proposals) that these lobbying efforts met with success.

PARTISANSHIP

The importance of these formal institutions and their veto points is an essential difference between the analysis presented here and the argument that partisanship, and particularly that of leftist parties, has been essential for enacting social programs such as national health insurance. Pressure from the left is indeed an important impetus for national health insurance. But it is not the only impetus. And there are indeed differences in the number of votes going to the left in Sweden, France, and Switzerland. But a lack of left votes was never the stumbling block for reformers. Instead, the problem was how to use electoral gains to generate policy results.

The Swedish Social Democrats succeeded in convincing both politicians from other parties and major interest groups to agree to national health insurance reforms, despite the sacrifices that these reforms required, because negotiations were contained within the executive without recourse to other arenas. In France, too, many parties – Socialists, Communists, Gaullists, and Catholic Socialists – participated in national health insurance legislative efforts. It was not the weakness of the left but the lack of stable parliamentary majorities that blocked reforms, and the reforms that were enacted were imposed by a conservative executive. In Switzerland, not only the Social Democratic Party, the largest political party in Switzerland, but all three leading parties (the Social Democrats, the Radical-Democrats, and the Catholic-Conservatives) approved reforms only to see these reforms vetoed by referenda. Indeed, had the Swiss Social Democrats' electoral victories been more easily translated into policy results, these electoral victories might have snowballed into larger electoral gains, as in the Swedish case.[2]

PROFESSIONS

Despite the abundant evidence of professional power in each of the three national cases, the political framework in which the medical associations and their members were located very much influenced professional preferences, strategies, and organizations. The public impact of these professions was thus mediated by representative institutions. In Sweden, where professional representation was channeled through participation on expert commissions and written responses to government proposals, medical association leaders pursued a cooperative course as long as strategic opportunities for veto remained closed. When a strategic opportunity for veto opened up, however, the association immediately dropped its conciliatory stance. The public position taken by medical association leaders, as we saw, was not always based on a majority vote by the doctors they represented. Under conditions of restricted access to political decision making, a cooperative strategy appealed to the medical association's leadership. Because it was highly improbable that dissatisfied doctors could start a competing professional association with the same official ties to the executive, the Swedish Medical Association leadership was able to carry out decisions that were unpopular with significant portions of the membership. Swedish cooperative behavior was induced by Swedish procedures for representation.

In France, the opportunities available to the medical profession were very different. Because parties, other than the left, were based on professional rather than economic groupings, the medical profession was able to become an important component of the leadership of the radical, republican left and Gaullist parties. In parliament, doctors were able to mobilize other deputies to fight government initiatives, working both through parties and as representatives on parliamentary commissions. Because these doctors were active as politicians and as local notables, but not as official representatives of a medical association, the opinions of the

French medical elite prevailed over the sometimes more moderate views of the medical unions, or the majority of their members. Thus, the noncooperative stance of French doctors may be explained by the veto opportunities proffered by the political system. Once steps were taken to decouple the executive from the parliament, however, the parliamentary veto point was closed. At that point, policies were enforced despite medical protests.

In Switzerland, several features of the political system worked to the advantage of the medical profession. Direct legislative veto by the electorate through the referendum overrode legislative decisions, even after agreements had been reached by the executive, the parties, and the legislature. Because interest groups could call for referenda, they were in a strategically critical position. Consequently, rather than producing the politics of compromise typical of the Swedish system, regular consultation of interest groups by the Swiss executive bureaucracy produced the opposite effect. Even relatively small groups were endowed with a powerful voice in policy making, with minority interests effectively able to override the majority point of view. The repercussions of the referendum explain why so many commentators have pointed to the dominant role of interest groups in Swiss politics.

CLASS

By analogy, this institutional approach might be taken into account when comparing differences among employer, small business, and union organizations, as well as the relative political weights of these groups. Certain aspects of a class model fit all three cases, especially the Swedish case, where employers, faced with a highly unionized and politicized labor movement, readily agreed to many health care reforms. Nevertheless, the differences in the cases may have more to with differences in interest representation than with differences in the class structure.

Three aspects of a "class analysis" help to explain the health care policies pursued in the three nations. First, the opinions of employers – and changes in these opinions – were crucial in explaining the actual actions taken by these governments in specific instances of policy making. Second, the medical profession appears particularly successful at times when small businessmen and farmers (the petite bourgeoisie) were politically active, mounting campaigns against the growth of government and increased taxation – in 1948 in Sweden, in the mid-fifties in France during the rise of Poujadism, or in Switzerland just after the Second World War. Third, the political and organizational power of the working class accounts for the pressures for reform on both policy makers and employer associations.

Business associations

In each country, employers provided crucial support for the medical profession. In fact, each time the medical profession achieved a major victory – blocking the Höjer reform in Sweden, modifying the French social security system in 1928 and 1945, and stopping national health insurance in Switzerland in 1949 and 1954 – employers were also opposed to these legislative proposals. In all three nations, the most consistent support for the medical profession came from small businessmen who identified with the position of doctors as entrepreneurs and who objected to paying health insurance contributions. Large employers, on the other hand, tended to be less opposed to such social charges, often providing them on a voluntary basis, but were eager to control costs – even if this meant restricting the medical profession.

In each country, separate organizations existed for industrialists, employers (which tended to be dominated by the owners of large firms), and small businessmen (often shopkeepers or craftsmen). Because the political systems were organized in different ways, however, the political impact of these organizations varied. Swedish executive policy making depended on the cooperation of the Swedish Employers' Association (SAF), whereas the small employers complained, as we saw, that their views were ignored. Like Swedish doctors, Swedish small businessmen did not have recourse to an alternative veto point that could override executive-level consensus. Consequently, we are hardly aware of the small businessmen in the Swedish case; they were drowned out by the much louder voice of the large industrialists who tended to make the policy of the Swedish Employers' Association. In France, on the other hand, the small business organization and its members were influential as long as parliament was the relevant decision point. Small businessmen were critical to the revoking of the 1928 Social Insurance Law and to the MRP about-face on the extension of social security to the self-employed in 1947. By 1960, however, the situation had changed. The large employers of the CNPF were willing to support social security reforms, whereas the small employers of the CGPME were opposed.

Because the balance of power abruptly shifted from parliament to the executive, however, the small businessmen who relied on parliamentary influence lost out to the large employers who had direct ties to the executive. Indeed, the difference in opportunities for influence available to the two groups may explain the hostile relationship between the CGPME and the CNPF. The CGPME used parliamentary recourse to block plans for economic modernization that the CNPF supported. Abrupt circumvention of the small employers did not improve the relationship between the two, and, suddenly excluded from the political process, small employers sometimes turned to extra-political means to protest the actions of the state.

In Switzerland, we observe yet a third configuration. The referendum kept the power of the smaller groups alive. Consequently, employers, industrialists, farmers, and small businessmen each had at their disposal a powerful interest organization. Swiss small businessmen benefited from their control of an autonomous interest organization, whose political relevance was maintained by the organization's recourse to the referendum – most recently, as we saw, in 1987. Thus, although small businessmen served as extremely useful allies for the medical profession in all three nations, their role was mediated by the same institutional features that affected the political power of doctors. Jean Meynaud specifically contrasts the role of small business organizations in France and Switzerland, pointing out that Swiss small employers are not systematically excluded, as they are in France:

The Swiss employers, despite several notorious divergences of interest, are more united and better armed for coordinated action than those in other countries. In France, the small and medium enterprises openly criticize the "technocratic" tendency of the "grand patronat," the process sometimes degenerating into demagogic attacks (Poujadism): Entrepreneurs of a modest dimension often took recourse, under the Third and Fourth Republics, to procedures of open agitation, their contacts with the administrative services being rare. One does not observe such a cleavage between the Swiss Employers' Association and the Association of Small Businesses.[3]

The role of farmers' organizations appears to differ as well. One cannot, therefore, read a nation's class structure from its system of organized interest groups. There is an important distinction between class structure and its political representation, with the institutions of interest representation playing a critical role in the translation between social structure and political power. Moreover, this translation entails not only the organization of members of a specific socioeconomic category into an interest association, but also the ability of this organization to achieve effective political gains.

Unions

Turning to the role of working-class organizations, we observe that the same institutional features affect a similar problem of translation. Certainly, no one would disagree with the observation that the Swedish labor movement has had a significant impact on health care politics. With the large majority of workers organized into a single trade union confederation that conducts wage negotiations on a national basis and maintains strong ties to the Social Democratic Party, we can understand why Swedish employers seemed ready to acquiesce to national health insurance. But it is far more difficult to understand why the Swiss labor movement has been so ineffectual. With 35–45 percent of industrial workers enrolled in unions, the Swiss labor force is certainly more unionized than the French, with about 20–25 percent.[4] We can add infinite complications to the model, pointing to the importance of religious and ethnic differences, centralized versus decentralized wage negotiations, craft versus industrial unions, political radicalism versus labor quiescence. But the result is always that the organizational and electoral gains of the Swiss labor movement are not translated into concrete policy gains. Thus, the problem for the movement is not a lack of membership recruitment and political mobilization, but rather the lack of results from the significant gains that have already been made.

In the French case, by contrast, some regime changes have placed the labor movement in an unusual position of power, whereas others have nearly disenfranchised it. The enactment of the Social Security Ordinances during the Liberation period is an example of the first case; the unilateral reduction in power of the elected administrative boards of the social security funds at the outset of the Fifth Republic – and the eventual elimination of these elections – is an example of the second.

THE STATE

Similarly, in each case there is some evidence in support of a state-centered approach, with the constitutional changes in France perhaps the most dramatic proof for this type of argument. In each country, there were indications that the state pursued reforms for motivations not directly related to pressure from social groups. Lending support to the bureaucratic theories of politics previously discussed, this pressure came from local administrators who demanded aid from the central government in managing health care programs and from decisions made within the executive to increase the scope of state power.

There is, in fact, no evidence of great public pressure for health insurance programs just after the Second World War. (There were no mass demonstrations or petitions to these governments. The interesting exception is the Swiss case, where women's and family groups successfully petitioned for a constitutional initiative for maternity insurance, and maintained a steady pressure for its enactment. These efforts were successful in placing the issue on the political agenda – proposals for maternity insurance were actually produced – but no legislation was ever passed.) Instead, the executive governments of Sweden, France, and Switzerland anticipated this demand – long included in socialist party platforms and union programs – and enacted social reforms with the full support of parties across the political spectrum.

health insurance was regarded as a natural component of this new era. Similarly, the modifications of these programs concerning the relationship of health insurance to the role of doctors, their freedom to set their own fees, and their right to a private practice were introduced in response to the problems of managing the health care system and to the political imperatives of the executive. In Sweden, the Seven Crowns reform was enacted at the instigation of the Federation of County Councils and as part of the Social Democratic Party's efforts to consolidate its power in the face of a new parliamentary system. In France, the social security funds had lobbied for controls on doctors' fees for thirty years, with few results. The decrees of 12 May 1960 were enacted as part of the executive's efforts to take over the administration of social security – a demand voiced by regional social security directors, and to legitimate the new political order of the Fifth Republic – as was the Debré reform. In Switzerland, the 1964 health insurance revision was passed over the opposition of doctors and employers, at the behest of the cantons, who wanted improved national funding for health insurance in order to ease the burden of hospital costs. Thus, the interest of the political executive in increasing its control over medical markets is present in all three nations, regardless of the party composition of these governments.

Indeed, health insurance in the three countries has come a long way from the voluntary sickness fund movements of the nineteenth century. As de Swaan notes, "Today, only a century later, not much more remains of this vast archipelago of working men's associations than some faded banners, yellowed papers and here and there a union or an insurance company that can trace back its pedigree to some friendly society long since defunct."[5] In each country, the pressures of actuarial consolidation and government policies rationalized the mutualist movements such that they lost their political character. In Switzerland, they were commercialized; in Sweden, they were slowly incorporated into the bureaucracy; and in France, they were taken over by the state through political controls on self-representation, management by the Minister of Labor, and fiscal pressure from the Minister of Finance.

We can view the rapid increase in new social programs after the Second World War as part of a continuing struggle over the role of the central state. The welfare state constituted a direct appeal to citizens that by-passed established institutions of interest intermediation. Such programs aided a general political transformation of parliamentary democracy. This "second wave" of nation-building entailed the weakening of political parties, a shift in power from parliaments to bureaucracies, the rise of corporatist bargaining patterns, and a revision of the relationship between central and local governments.

Many of these changes occurred before the Second World War. But the last change – the shifting national-local relationship – took place between 1945 and 1960. Localities lost a great deal of their political power but were at the same time given more administrative functions. This modification of the political-administrative structure of the state helps to explain why governments were able to expand their role in health care and why they were motivated to do so. National governments became more powerful by managing the responsibilities of the localities, whereas the localities were willing to subordinate themselves to the central state because they no longer had the fiscal and regulatory capacities to meet their health care obligations.[6]

The role of local governments in championing welfare state expansion – and more broadly the role of intergovernmental relations in the welfare state – is a topic worth further investigation. The matter can rest here, however, with the observation that even the role of local government was channeled by the points of access of the political system. In Sweden, the county council politicians were organized into the same type of centralized, national interest group – the Federation of County Councils – as unions, employers and doctors; they were also spread throughout the political parties and held parliamentary seats. In France, mayors penetrated the parliament and the executive ministries through the *cumul des mandats*, the holding of several simultaneous political posts that pushed local interests to the center of national politics. In Switzerland, the cantons were officially consulted as an interest group, and cantonal politicians exerted influence as well through the autonomous local political parties and by the federalist relegation of much policy, such as hospital planning, to the cantonal level.

Thus, political institutions mediate the impact of other causal factors on the development of welfare state policies. These factors are important, but political institutions determine how great the impact of a particular variable will be. Political institutions do not predetermine any specific policy outcome; rather, they construct a strategic context in which political actors make their choices. If these institutions remain fairly stable over time, the choices follow characteristic patterns. The logic of each political system accounts for consistencies in the ways in which individual, extraordinary decisions are made within a given political framework. Further, these political frameworks produce different patterns of political behavior that might be thought of as the characteristic "policy style" of a given country.[7] However, rather than thinking of these behavioral patterns as stemming from implicitly accepted norms, this analysis has shown how institutions and their logics affect even the micro-politics of reform, simply by making some courses of action more difficult and facilitating others.

OTHER NATIONS, OTHER POLICIES

The analysis of political veto points could be carried out with other nations and for other policy areas. The results of other studies of health care politics fit into this general framework. The work of Eckstein and Klein has shown that for the British case, parliamentary majorities allowed both the National Insurance Act of 1911 and the National Health Service Act of 1946 to be enacted despite interest-group opposition, as in the Swedish case. In Italy, on the other hand, the situation resembled the French case. Unstable parliamentary majorities with fractionated political parties provided ample scope for interest-group influence and blocked health insurance legislation throughout most of the postwar period. Only when the Italian Communist Party and the Christian Democratic Party decided to cooperate at the executive level could the Italian national health service be introduced. This government coalition allowed the executive to withstand parliamentary bargaining as well as medical and sickness fund opposition.[8]

Political institutions affect not only the logic of interest group influence during the legislative process, but the likelihood of government intervention can influence the climate of negotiation even for nonlegislative parts of the policy process. In the health area, negotiations between doctors and sickness funds were affected by legislative provisions that established the basic conditions for negotiations, and the threat of government intervention was a key factor in inducing the parties to reach agreement. In the German case, we can observe both the impact of political institutions on the legislative process and the ramifications of government intervention for extra-political negotiations. Two institutional features – one de jure, one de facto – have shaped the routes of influence for medical interests. The Second Chamber, or Bundesrat, is a formal veto point, where the presidents of the provincial governments must ratify proposals; as these politicians are responsible for hospitals, this arena has proved to be critical for vetoing legislative proposals viewed as disadvantageous for hospitals. Because postwar governments of the Federal Republic have rested on coalitions that have nearly always included the Liberal FDP – whose constituency is small business interests, doctors, pharmacists, and similar self-employed groups – German doctors have been able to receive extraordinary concessions during the legislative process. Despite these veto opportunities, however, the threat of government intervention has created the conditions that have allowed voluntary agreements between the Associations of Sickness Funds and the Associations of Insurance Doctors to set limits on doctors' fees.[9]

Placing policy conflicts and interest-group bargaining within the framework of national political institutions is equally applicable to other policy domains. No matter what the area, the relationship between different political arenas and the representatives that occupy them influences the legislation that sets specific policies in motion, and the activities taken to ensure that this legislation is enforced. The same general principles will apply. The greater the number of veto points, the more resistant the political system will be to policy change, and thus to give advantage to interests that wish to preserve the status quo. But the specific constellation of interests and the strategies they may choose to employ can vary with the specific policy.

IMPLICATIONS FOR THE UNITED STATES

The United States is often used as an example of blocked national health insurance policy making. Proposals for national health insurance have been discussed in the 1910s, the 1940s, the 1960s, and the 1970s, and are currently being debated. From the vantage point of the average American citizen, health politics have often seemed rather inevitable and the barriers to change insurmountable. Medicine is a highly technical and costly area that seems to have developed according to its own dynamic. In the United States the organized medical profession, the American Medical Association (AMA), appears to have been sufficiently powerful to veto any reform that does not meet with its approval. The political left has held that big business can block any move toward socialized medicine. Those of a more formal political bent have judged American political parties incapable of promoting social reforms, or have found the federal structure of government incompatible with such large-scale national endeavors.

The history of national health insurance reforms in France, Switzerland, and Sweden leads one to question some of these assumptions, however. Many of the factors that have been charged with blocking health insurance in the United States were also present in Europe, but legislation was enacted, nevertheless. The European examples are not polar opposites of the United States; in fact, the similarities stand out more than the differences. Neither interest group politics, partisanship, nor federalism comprised insurmountable obstacles to European national health insurance policy making. Different forms of governance over the health sector emerged as a result of many separate political decisions. These decisions were not based on unified public opinion for a particular program. Opinions within these countries were diverse. Important segments of the medical profession opposed the reforms, employers and farmers objected to the costs of the programs, support from unions was not always unequivocal, and the role of the general public remained obscure.

These conflicts among interest groups do not seem so very different from those that have occurred in the United States. The protests of the voluntary sickness funds against early European programs are analogous to those of American insurance companies against national health insurance from 1915 to 1920. The protests of small businessmen against French social security in 1946, or those of Swedish businessmen against the 1948 Höjer reform, do not appear strikingly different from the objections of American business to "socialized medicine" in the late 1940s. French farmers disliked compulsory health insurance. Arthur Altmeyer, who participated in the drafting of the Social Security Act of 1935, notes that American farmers were a consistent source of opposition to national health insurance.[10] The pressures from Swedish County Council politicians, French regional social security directors, and Swiss cantonal politicians for increased national funding and regulation of the health sector in the 1960s has an American parallel in the support for expansion of federal health and social policies from the Association of Governors in the late 1960s. Thus, if we compare European interest-group demands with those in the United States, there is nothing that leads us to believe that American interest groups constitute an insurmountable political obstacle to health insurance policy making. Nor does the presence or absence of socialist parties seem to be the key. The European policy debates were not simply a matter of left-wing parties pushing for reform against the resistance of the right; the political patterns were more complex, and successful reforms were supported by political parties across the political spectrum. Nor does federalism appear to rule out national health insurance programs. In the Swiss case, it was not federalism that blocked national health insurance, but rather the dynamics of referendum politics.

National health insurance politics in Europe were influenced by the strategic contexts of political veto points. Similarly, the political feasibility of reform in the United States will depend upon the political process and the system of veto points. It is not interest group opinion alone, nor the institutions alone, that set the limits to what is politically feasible. What matters is the strategic scenario that develops as interest groups, politicians, and members of the executive government struggle to utilize political institutions with their veto points to enact, amend, or block policies. This is what constructs the boundaries (but also the possibilities) of politics.

THE LIMITS OF INSTITUTIONS

This book has argued that political institutions shape political activity in important ways. Political institutions do not predetermine policies. Instead, they are an integral part of the strategic context in which political conflicts take place. Political institutions set boundaries within which strategic actors make their choices. The implication of this book is that political analysts must begin with an analysis of institutions if they are to understand the patterns of political behavior. These patterns do not develop independently; they develop within specific national political frameworks. Political institutions can be thought of as the outermost framework for political conflicts. The institutions do not produce or direct political conflicts but they do define the terms for these conflicts. The institutions explain many aspects of the life within them – the types of interest organizations that will be successful, the pressures to consolidate interest, the usefulness of membership mobilization, and the degree to which cooperation versus defection is likely to be a fruitful strategy. But the interests, strategies, and resources of political actors cannot explain the institutions, so I prefer to start thinking about politics with the institutions. But no view of politics can rely exclusively on either institutions, or interests and actors. Both components are necessary to our understanding of the past, and to our role as the subjects of the future.

Like many other institutionalist analyses, this book supports the view that there is no straight line between interests and politics. In contrast to approaches that seek the roots of political activity in social forces, the cases discussed here have shown that politics can be independent of social power. Similarly, although social scientists have viewed the welfare state through a number of conceptual lenses, this book has argued that systems of political representation constitute lenses themselves. Much of our information about political pressures, and even about the social structure, comes to us through the process of representation. But because political systems are sensitive to different pressures at different points, the procedures for representing interests project different pictures of society and social demands.[11]

From this perspective, welfare states result from a discrete series of political decisions. Although there may be some continuity over time in the decisions made in a particular country, there is no underlying social truth that explains these political differences. Nor is there a predetermined destination to the welfare state. The future of the welfare state is open; it will depend on concrete political decisions made by actors in strategic contexts. Struggles between interest groups and governments will continue to set the limits to government intervention, just as they will continue to shape the instruments of policy making themselves. Political systems, then, are best viewed not solely in terms of formal institutional features, such as "the state," "parties," or "bureaucracies," but in terms of complex sets of relationships among social and political actors engaged in a struggle for power. For limited periods of time, these systems may achieve a certain stability, enabling us to characterize them according to the different political logics by which they work. Nevertheless, these arrangements are always subject to change, because of new issues that emerge, new groups that may form, attempts to utilize different organizational strategies or resources, changing alliances, or new political programs. In these ways, the system of interest representation as it works in practice provides a framework for understanding politics. But it is only that, a framework, not a guide to predicting the future. Instead, we might expect continuing struggles over the role of the state, with the autonomy of the state continually bounded by the procedures through which its legitimacy is maintained.

Notes

Chapter 1

1 Martha Derthick, *Policy-Making for Social Security* (Washington, DC: The Brookings Institution, 1979), p. 337.

2 T.H. Marshall, "Citizenship and Social Class," in T.H. Marshall, *Class, Citizenship and Social Development* (Chicago: University of Chicago Press, 1964), pp. 71–134; Richard M. Titmuss, *Commitment to Welfare* (London: George Allen and Unwin, 1967). For more current discussions of the relationship between democracy and the welfare state, see Morris Janowitz, *The Social Control of the Welfare State* (NY: Elsevier, 1976); Amy Gutman, ed., *Democracy and the Welfare State* (Princeton: Princeton University Press, 1988); Sheldon S. Wolin, "Theorizing the Welfare State. I. Democracy and the Welfare State. The Political and Theoretical Connections Between Staatsräson and Wohlfahrtsstaatsräson," *Political Theory*, Vol. *15*, no. 4 (1987), pp. 467–500; Claus Offe, "II. Democracy Against the Welfare State? Structural Foundations of Neoconservative Political Opportunities," *Political Theory*, *15*, No. 4 (1987), pp. 501–537.

3 There are a number of competing institutional approaches for the analysis of policy making. These will be discussed in a later section of this chapter. Some of the most important for comparative public policy are Douglas E. Ashford, *Comparing Public Policies: New Concepts and Methods* (Beverly Hills, CA: Sage Publications, 1978); Arnold J. Heidenheimer, "Comparative Public Policy at the Crossroads," *Journal of Public Policy 5*, no. 4 (1985): 441–465; Fritz W. Scharpf, "Policy Failure and Institutional Reform: Why Should Form Follow Function?" *International Social Science Journal*, *38*, no. 2, Special Issue 108, "The Study of Public Policy," (June 1986): 179–189.

4 On political logics, see Douglas E. Ashford, "The British and French Social Security Systems: Welfare State by Intent and by Default," in Ashford and E.W. Kelley, eds., *Nationalizing Social Security* (Greenwich, CT: JAI Press, 1986), pp. 96–122. On rules, see Fritz W. Scharpf "Decision Rules, Decision Styles, and Policy Choices," *Journal of Theoretical Politics* 1 (1989): 149–76.

5 Theodore J. Lowi, *The End of Liberalism*. 2nd ed. (New York: W.W. Norton & Co, 1979); Charles S. Maier, *Recasting Bourgeois Europe* (Princeton: Princeton University Press, 1975); E.E. Schattschneider, *The Semi-Sovereign People* (New York: Holt, Rinehart & Winston, 1960); Philippe C. Schmitter, "Still the Century of Corporatism?" and "Modes of Interest Intermediation and Models of Societal Change in Western Europe," in Schmitter and Gerhard Lembruch, eds., *Trends Towards Corporatist Intermediation* (London and Beverly Hills: Sage Publications, 1979), pp. 7–52, 63–94.

6 The figures were originally cited as inhabitants per doctor – 1120 in Sweden,

940 in France, and 710 in Switzerland, in James Hogarth, *The Payment of the Physician. Some European Comparisons* (NY: Macmillan Co. (Pergamon Press), 1963), pp. 60, 139, 281. For more recent figures, see Table 5 in Chapter 3.

7 Harold Wilensky and Charles Lebeaux, *Industrial Society and Social Welfare: The Impact of Industrialization on the Supply and Organization of Social Welfare Services in the U.S.* (New York: Russell Sage Foundation, 1958); Wilensky, *The Welfare State and Equality* (Berkeley, CA: University of California Press, 1975); F. Pryor *Public Expenditure in Communist and Capitalist Nations* (Homewood IL: Irwin, 1968).

8 Brian Abel-Smith, "The Major Pattern of Medical Financing and the Organization of Medical Services that Have Emerged in Other Countries," *Medical Care*, Vol. 3, No. 1 (January–March 1965): 33–40; Milton Roemer, *Comparative National Policies on Health Care* (New York: Marcel Dekker, 1977); this is the logic followed by Karl Polanyi, *The Great Transformation* (Boston: Beacon Press, 1944).

9 Phillips Cutright, "Political Structure, Economic Development and National Social Security Programs," *American Journal of Sociology 70*, No. 3 (March 1965): 537–50; Christopher Hewitt, "The Effect of Political Democracy and Social Democracy on Equality in Industrialized Societies: A Cross-National Comparison," *American Sociological Review 42*, (June 1977): 450–464; Douglas A. Hibbs, "Political Parties and Macroeconomic Policy," *American Political Science Review 71* (December 1977): 1467–87; Roemer, *Comparative National Policies*; Harold Wilensky, *The "New Corporatism," Centralization and the Welfare State* (Beverly Hills, CA: Sage, 1976); Wilensky, "Leftism, Catholicism, and Democratic Corporatism: The Role of Political Parties in Recent Welfare State Development," in Peter Flora and Arnold J. Heidenheimer, *The Development of Welfare States in Europe and America* (New Brunswick, NJ: Transaction Press, 1981), pp. 345–382.

10 Murray Edelman, *The Symbolic Uses of Politics* (Urbana: University of Illinois Press, 1964); Michael Lipsky, "Protest as a Political Resource." *American Political Science Review 62*, no. 4, (December 1968): 1144–1158; Roger Cobb and Charles Elder, *Participation in American Politics: The Dynamics of Agenda Building* (Boston: Allyn and Bacon, 1972); Joseph Gusfield, *The Culture of Public Problems* (Chicago: Chicago University Press, 1981); Barbara Nelson, *Making an Issue of Child Abuse: Political Agenda-Setting for Social Problems* (Chicago: University of Chicago Press, 1984); Deborah A. Stone, *Policy Paradox and Political Reason* (Glenview, IL: Scott Foresman, 1989).

11 Roy Lubove, *The Struggle for Social Security* (Cambridge, MA: Harvard University Press, 1967); Gaston V. Rimlinger, *Welfare Policy and Industrialization in Europe, America and Russia* (NY: John Wiley, 1971); Odin W. Anderson, *Health Care: Can There Be Equity? The United States, Sweden and England* (New York: John Wiley, 1972).

12 Douglas A. Ashford, *The Emergence of the Welfare States* (Oxford and New York: Basil Blackwell, 1986) is particularly sensitive to such political motivations as well as to the interrelationship between political doctrines and political movements.

13 See Derthick's account of the objections raised by Wilbur Mills, *Policymaking for Social Security*, p. 327.

14 For classic pluralist views, see David Truman, *The Governmental Process, 2nd Edition* (1971); Robert Dahl, *Who Governs?* (New Haven: Yale University Press, 1961). For criticisms that apply particularly to the area of public policy, see Lowi's *End of Liberalism* and his article, "Four Systems of Policy, Politics

and Choice," *Public Administration Review 32*, no. 4 (July–August 1972): 298–310.

A number of studies examine the political role of the medical profession in one country. For the United States, see, Oliver Garceau, *The Political Life of the American Medical Association* (Cambridge: Harvard University Press, 1941); Odin Anderson, *Uneasy Equilibrium* (New Haven: Yale University Press, 1968); Joseph Kett, *The Formation of the American Medical Profession: the Role of Institutions, 1780–1860* (New Haven: Yale University Press, 1968); Theodore Marmor, *The Politics of Medicare* (Chicago: Aldine Publishing, 1973); Ronald L. Numbers, *Almost Persuaded: American Physicians and Compulsory Health Insurance* (Baltimore: Johns Hopkins, 1978); Paul Starr, *The Social Transformation of American Medicine* (NY: Basic Books, 1982). On Canada, see C. David Naylor *Private Practice, Public Payment. Canadian Medicine and the Politics of Health Insurance, 1911–1966* (Kingston: McGill-Queen's University Press, 1986); on Germany, Frieder Naschold, *Kassenärzte und Krankenversicherungsreform. Zu einer Theorie der Statuspolitik* (Freiburg im Breisgau: Verlag Rombach, 1967), William Safran, *Veto Group Politics: The Case of Health Insurance Reform in West Germany* (San Francisco: Chandler, 1967), and Christa Rauskolb, *Lobby in Weiß* (Frankfurt: Europäische Verlagsanstalt, 1976); On France, Hatzfeld, *Le Grand Tournant de la Médecine Libérale* (Paris: Les Editions Ouvrières, 1963); on Switzerland, Gerhard Kocher, *Verbandseinfluß auf die Gesetzgebung. Ärzteverbindung, Krankenkassenverbände und die Teilrevision 1964 des Kranken- und Unfallversicherungsgesetzes.* 2nd Ed. (Bern: Francke Verlag, 1972); Erich Wyss, *Heilen und Herrschen: Medikalisierung, Krankenversicherung und ärztliche Professionalisierung 1870–1911*, unpublished Lizentiatsarbeit, University of Zürich, 1982.

15 Talcott Parsons, *The Social System* (Glencoe, Illinois: Free Press, 1951), pp. 428–79.

16 William A. Glaser discusses inclusion of economy autonomy in the World Medical Association's code of ethics in *Paying the Doctor: Systems of Remuneration and Their Effects* (Baltimore: Johns Hopkins, 1970), pp. 90–100; Odin Anderson discusses the medical profession's seemingly universal preference for fee-for-service payment, in opposition to planners that prefer salary in *Health Care*, p. 196; On French doctors, see Henri Hatzfeld, *Le Grand Tournant de la Médecine Libérale*.

17 Eliot Freidson, *Profession of Medicine: A Study of the Sociology of Applied Knowledge* (New York: Dodd, Mead & Company, 1970); cf. J. Ben David, "Professions in the Class System of Present Day Societies," *Current Sociology 12* (1963–4): 247–98; Everett C. Hughes, "Professions," *Daedalus 92* (1963): 655–68; Harold Wilensky, "The Professionalization of Everyone?" *American Journal of Sociology 70*, no. 2 (September 1964): 137–158.

18 Jeffrey Berlant, *Profession and Monopoly* (Berkeley: University of California Press, 1975); Magali Sarfatti Larson, *The Rise of Professionalism. A Sociological Analysis*, Berkeley: University of California Press, 1977); cf. Terence J. Johnson *Professions and Power* (London: Macmillan, 1972); on Adam Smith and the British medical profession, see A.P. Carr-Saunders and P.A. Wilson, *The Professions* (Oxford: Oxford University Press, 1933); on licensing as a barrier to competition, Milton Friedman, *Capitalism and Freedom* (Chicago: Chicago University Press, 1962), pp. 149–60.

19 Paul Starr, *The Social Transformation of American Medicine* (NY: Basic Books, 1982).

20 Theodore R. Marmor and David Thomas, "Doctors, Politics and Pay Disputes: Pressure Group Politics' Revisited," *British Journal of Political Science 2* (October 1972): 436–437.

21 Harry Eckstein, *Pressure Group Politics: The Case of the British Medical Association* (London: Allen & Unwin, 1960) p. 16; Rudolf Klein, "Ideology, Class and the National Health Service," *J. of Health Politics, Policy and Law 4* (Fall 1979): 484, and *The Politics of the National Health Service* (London: Longman, 1983); Theodore R. Marmor, *Politics of Medicare*, p. 114; Deborah A. Stone, *The Limits of Professional Power* (Chicago: University of Chicago Press, 1980); William A. Glaser, *Paying the Doctor, Paying the Doctor Under National Health Insurance: Foreign Lessons for the United States, 2nd ed* (Springfield, VA: National Technical Information Service, US Dept. of Commerce, 1976), and *Health Insurance Bargaining: Foreign Lessons for Americans* (NY: Gardner Press, 1978); Arnold J. Heidenheimer, "Conflict and Compromise Between Professional and Bureaucratic Health Interests. 1947–1972," in Heidenheimer & Nils Elvander, eds., *The Shaping of the Swedish Health System* (London: Croom Helm, 1980) pp. 119–42. See also: Christa Altenstetter, "The Impact of Organizational Arrangements," in C. Altenstetter, ed., *Changing National-Subnational Relations in Health* (Washington, DC: Fogerty International Center and Department of Health, Education and Welfare, 1976), pp. 3–33; Giorgio Freddi and James Warner Björkman, *Controlling Medical Professionals. The Comparative Politics of Health Governance* (London: Sage Publications, 1989); Paul J. Godt, "Confrontation, Consent, and Corporatism: State Strategies and the Medical Profession in France, Great Britain, and West Germany," *Journal of Health Politics, Policy and Law 12*, no. 3 (Fall 1987): 459–481; Howard M. Leichter, *A Comparative Approach to Policy Analysis: Health Care Policy in Four Nations* (Cambridge: Cambridge University Press, 1979); Victor G. Rodwin, *The Health Planning Predicament: France, Québec, England and the United States* (Berkeley: University of California Press, 1984); David Wilsford, "The Cohesion and Fragmentation of Organized Medicine in France and the United States," *Journal of Health Politics, Policy and Law, 12*, no. 3 (Fall 1987): 481–503.

For studies that place the activities of the medical profession in the context of the pressures exerted by other interest groups, and that place greater theoretical emphasis on theories of political sociology and political economy, but perhaps less on political institutions, see: Robert R. Alford, *Health Care Politics: Ideological and Interest Group Barriers to Reform* (Chicago: University of Chicago Press, 1975); J. Rogers Hollingsworth, *A Political Economy of Medicine: Great Britain and the United States* (Baltimore: Johns Hopkins, 1986); William Safran, *Veto Group Politics*; Rosemary C.R. Taylor, "State Intervention in Postwar Western European Health Care: The Case of Prevention in Britain and Italy," in S. Bornstein, D. Held and J. Krieger, eds., *The State in Capitalist Europe* (London: George, Allen & Unwin, 1984), pp. 91–111.

22 On Marxist theories of the welfare state, see James O'Connor, *The Fiscal Crisis of the State* (NY: St. Martin's Press, 1973); Ian Gough, *The Political Economy of the Welfare State* (London: Macmillan, 1979); Theda Skocpol, "Political Response to Capitalist Crisis: Neo-Marxist Theories of the State and the New Deal," *Politics and Society, 10* (1980): 155–201; Skocpol and Edwin Amenta, "States and Social Policies," *Annual Review of Sociology, 12* (1986): 131–157; Claus Offe, *Contradictions of the Welfare State* (Cambridge: MIT

Press, 1984); John Myles, *Old-Age in the Welfare State: The Political Economy of Public Pensions*, (Boston: Little Brown, 1984); Jill Quadagno, "Theories of the Welfare State," *Annual Review of Sociology*, *13* (1987): 109–28. On business liberalism, see Quadagno, "Welfare Capitalism and the Social Security Act of 1935," *American Sociological Review 49* (1984): 632–47; Skocpol and Amenta, "Did Capitalists Shape Social Security?" *American Sociological Review*, *50*, no. 4 (1985): 572–4, and Quadagno reply, pp. 575–7; G. William Domhoff, "Corporate Liberal Theory and the Social Security Act," *Politics and Society 15*, (1986–7): 297–330. On social democratic power model, see Gösta Esping-Andersen and Walter Korpi, "Social Policy as Class Politics in Post-War Capitalism," in Goldthorpe, ed., *Crisis and Order in Contemporary Capitalism* (Oxford: Clarendon Press, Oxford University Press, 1984), pp. 179–208; Esping-Andersen, *Politics Against Markets: The Social Democratic Road to Power* (Princeton: Princeton University Press, 1985) and *The Three Worlds of Welfare Capitalism* (Princeton: Princeton University Press, 1990); Korpi, *The Democratic Class Struggle* (London: Routledge and Kegan Paul, 1983); John D. Stephens, *The Transition from Capitalism to Socialism* (London: Macmillan, 1979).

23 Peter Baldwin, *The Politics of Social Solidarity and the Bourgeois Origins of the European Welfare State, 1875–1975* (Cambridge: Cambridge University Press, 1988), discusses the role of the middle classes and the inadequacy of the social interpretation of the welfare state; farmers' parties in the Finnish case are stressed by Olli Kangas, "The Politics of Universalism: the Case of Finnish Sickness Insurance," *J. of Social Policy*, *21* (January 1992); Bo Rothstein, *The Social Democratic State* (Cambridge: Cambridge University Press, forthcoming) reinterprets the origins and implementation of the Swedish welfare state.

24 On age in American politics, see Quadagno, "Welfare Capitalism." On gender and the welfare state, see Jane Jenson, "Gender and Reproduction: Or, Babies and the State," *Studies in Political Economy 20* (1986), pp. 9–43; Barbara Nelson, "The Gender, Race, and Class Origins of Early Welfare Policy and the Welfare State: A Comparison of Workmen's Compensation and Mothers' Aid," in Louise A. Tilly and Patricia Gurin, eds., *Women, Politics, and Change* (NY: Russell Sage), 1990, pp. 413–35; On the variability of political cleavages across nations, Seymour Martin Lipset and Stein Rokkan, "Cleavage Structures, Party Systems, and Voter Alignments: An Introduction," in Lipset and Rokkan, eds., *Party Systems and Voter Alignments: Cross-National Perpsectives* (NY: Free Press, 1967).

25 Pluralist theorists have never claimed, of course, that the world is free from large inequalities of power. Rather, the pluralist claim is that multiple sources of power prevent the development of a ruling elite, and that, overall, the political system is responsive to a variety of groups, even those that at first sight may appear disadvantaged. Furthermore, the fact that in any one policy area political participation may be limited to the interest groups most directly affected by the problems that require government intervention is viewed as a good thing. These interest groups are thought to know more about the problem at hand than government officials. Their participation in bringing social problems to the attention of governments and in drafting solutions therefore provides a mechanism by which governments can respond effectively to the emerging problems of modern societies. Nevertheless, a consistent bias in favor of some social actors at the expense of others does indeed damage the pluralist claim that plural and balanced social pressures are the source of political decisions.

26 James March and Johan P. Olsen, *Rediscovering Institutions. The Organizational Basis of Politics* (New York: The Free Press, 1989). For other reviews
and comments, see Robert H. Bates, "Contra Contractarianism: Some Reflections on the New Institutionalism," *Politics & Society 16* no. 2–3
(June–Sept. 1988): 387–401; G. John Ikenberry, "Conclusion: an institutional
approach to American foreign economic policy," *International Organization
42* no. 1 (Winter 1988): 219–243; W. Richard Scott, "The Adolescence of
Institutional Theory," *Administrative Science Quarterly 32* (December 1987):
493–511.

27 Suzanne Berger, *Peasants Against Politics: Rural Organization in Brittany,
1911–1967* (Harvard University Press, 1972) and her "Introduction" in S.
Berger, ed., *Organizing Interests in Western Europe: Pluralism, Corporatism
and the Transformation of Politics* (Cambridge: Cambridge University Press,
1981), pp. 1–23; other examples include, Douglas Ashford, *Emergence of
the Welfare States*; Peter A. Hall, *Governing the Economy: the Politics of
State Intervention in Britain and France* (Cambridge: Polity Press, 1986); Ira
Katznelson, *City Trenches: Urban Politics and the Patterning of Class in the
United States* (NY: Pantheon, 1981); S. Steinmo, K. Thelan, and F. Longstreth,
Structuring Politics (Cambridge: Cambridge University Press, 1992); Victoria
C. Hattam, *Changing Conceptions of Class and American Political Develop-
ment, 1806–1896* (Princeton: Princeton University Press, 1992); Margaret
Weir, *Politics and Jobs: The Boundaries of Employment Policy in the United
States* (Princeton: Princeton University Press, 1992).

28 For articles that are particularly good at explaining the advantages of the
rational choice approach in comparison to competing approaches, see Samuel
Popkin, "The Political Economy of Peasant Society," in Jon Elster, ed.,
Rational Choice (NY: New York University Press, 1986), pp. 197–247; Terry
M. Moe, "Interests, Institutions, and Positive Theory: The Politics of the
NLRB," *Studies in American Political Development, 2* (1987): 236–299. For
overviews and examples relevant to the approach taken here see Kenneth A.
Shepsle, "Institutional Equilibrium and Equilibrium Institutions," in Herbert
F. Weisberg (ed.). *Political Science: The Science of Politics* (New York:
Agathon Press, 1986); Shepsle and Barry R. Weingast, "The Institutional
Foundations of Committee Power," *American Political Science Review 81*
(1987): 85–103; John E. Chubb, *Interest Groups and the Bureaucracy. The
Politics of Energy* (Stanford: Stanford University Press, 1983); Thomas H.
Hammond and Gary J. Miller, "The Core of the Constitution," *American
Political Science Review 81* (1987), 1155–1173; John A. Ferejohn, "The Struc-
ture of Agency Decision Processes," in Matthew D. McCubbins and Terry
Sullivan, eds., *Congress: Structure and Policy* (Cambridge: Cambridge University Press, 1988), pp. 441–461; Terry M. Moe. "The Politics of Bureaucratic
Structure," in John E. Chubb and Paul E. Peterson, eds., *Can the Government Govern?* (Washington, DC: The Brookings Institution, 1989), pp.
267–329; George Tsebelis, "Elite Interaction and Constitution Building in
Consociational Democracies," *Journal of Theoretical Politics 2*, no. 1 (1990):
5–29.

29 Among the classic works are Herbert A. Simon, *Administrative Behavior* (NY:
Macmillan, 1957); James G. March and Herbert A. Simon, *Organizations*
(NY: John Wiley, 1958); Richard M. Cyert and James G. March, *A Behavioral
Theory of the Firm* (Englewood Cliffs, NJ: Prentice Hall, 1963). For a review,
see Charles Perrow, *Complex Organizations: A Critical Essay, 3rd Ed.* (NY:
Random House, 1986). For public policy, see March and Olsen, "Organizing
Political Life: What Administrative Reorganization Tells Us About Govern-

ment," *The American Political Science Review* 77 no. 2 (1983): 281–296, and the case studies in *Rediscovering Institutions*.

30 On corporatism, Lehmbruch and Schmitter, *Trends Towards Corporatist Intermediation*; John Goldthorpe, ed., *Order and Conflict in Contemporary Capitalism* (Oxford: Clarendon Press, New York: Oxford University Press, 1984); Schmitter and Wolfgang Streeck, *Private Interest Government: Beyond Market and State* (London, Beverly Hills: Sage Publications, 1985); Peter J. Katzenstein, *Small States in World Markets: Industrial Policy in Europe* (Ithaca & London: Cornell University Press, 1985). It should be noted that a concern with building organizations and the problems of relationships between the leaders and members of these organizations is critical for many studies of class politics, particularly those that combine a theoretical interest in class with an emphasis on "resource mobilization." On the resource mobilization, see Charles Tilly, *From Mobilization to Revolution* (Reading, MA: Addison-Wesley, 1978); see Walter Korpi, "Power, Politics, and State Autonomy in the Development of Social Citizenship: Social Rights During Sickness in Eighteen OECD Countries Since 1930," *American Sociological Review*, 54 (1989): 309–328, for a discussion of class politics approaches to the welfare state and the resource mobilization perspective. On the role of corporatism in the German health system, see Stone, *Limits of Professional Power*, Jens Alber, "Die Gesundheitssysteme der OECD-Länder im Vergleich," *Staatstätigkeit, Politische Vierteljahresschrift*, Special Issue 19, (1988): 116–150.

31 Fritz W. Scharpf, "A Game-Theoretical Interpretation of Inflation and Unemployment in Western Europe, *Journal of Public Policy* 7 (1987): 227–257.

32 Theda Skocpol, "Bringing the State Back In: Strategies of Analysis in Current Research," in Peter B. Evans, Dietrich Rueschemeyer, and Theda Skocpol, eds., *Bringing the State Back In* (Cambridge: Cambridge University Press, 1985), pp. 3–37; see also Margaret Weir and Skocpol, "State Structures and the Possibilities for 'Keynesian' Responses to the Great Depression in Sweden, Britain and the United States," in *Bringing the State Back In*, pp. 107–163; Ann Shola Orloff and Skocpol, "Why Not Equal Protection? Explaining the Politics of Public Social Spending in Britain, 1900–1911, and the United States, 1880s–1920," *American Sociological Review* 49 (1984): 726–750.

33 On wars, see Fred Block, "The Ruling Class Does Not Rule." *Socialist Revolution* 7, no. 33 (1977): 6–28; Larry J. Griffin, Joel Devine, and Michael Wallace, "Monopoly Capital, Organized Labor, and Military Expenditures in the United States, 1946–1976," *American Journal of Sociology* 88 (1982): 113–153; Maier, *Recasting Bourgeois Europe*; Marshall, "Citizenship and Social Class;" O'Connor, *Fiscal Crisis of the State*; Titmuss, *Commitment to Welfare*; Wolin, "Theorizing the Welfare State. I. Democracy and the Welfare State." On the international economy, David Cameron, "The Expansion of the Public Economy: A Comparative Analysis," *American Political Science Review* 72 (1978): 1243–61; Katzenstein, *Small States in World Markets*.

34 The literature on bureaucracy, organization theory, and public policy is too vast to cover in a footnote. Some outstanding examples are Graham T. Allison, *Essence of Decision: Explaining the Cuban Missile Crisis* (Boston: Little Brown, 1971); Hugh Heclo, *Modern Social Politics in Britain and Sweden* (New Haven and London: Yale University Press, 1974); Michael Lipsky, *Street-Level Bureaucracy: Dilemmas of the Individuals in the Public Services* (NY: Russell Sage, 1983); Robert D. Putnam, *The Comparative Study of Political Elites* (Englewood-Cliffs, NJ: Prentice Hall, 1976); Harvey Sapolsky, *The Polaris System Development: Bureaucratic and Programmatic Success in Government* (Cambridge, MA: Harvard University Press, 1972); James Q.

Wilson, *Political Organizations* (NY: Basic Books, 1973); John Zysman, *Governments, Markets, and Growth* (Ithaca and London: Cornell University Press, 1983).

35 Peter Flora and Jens Alber, "Modernization, Democratization, and the Development of Welfare States in Western Europe," in Flora and Heidenheimer, eds., *The Development of Welfare States in Europe and America* (New Brunswick, NJ: Transaction Books, 1981), pp. 37–80. Douglas Ashford stresses such political motivations in his work *The Emergence of the Welfare States*.

36 See the discussion in Arend Liphardt, "The Political Consequences of Electoral Laws," *American Political Science Review 84* (1990): 481–496.

37 I am grateful to a reviewer for this formulation.

38 Indeed it would be absurd to argue that institutions themselves produce political action, for the institutions are just a set of rules; institutions themselves cannot act. Rather, by selecting a case in which interest groups seem to demand the same things, and in which many of these groups are organized in similar ways, this study allows one to hold the interests constant and to observe the effects of the institutions on the policy process.

Chapter 2

1 The definition of "liberal" used here is the standard European economic liberal tradition, as defined by writers like Adam Smith. In the United States, however, this tradition is generally labeled "conservative." Despite the stress on economics, these writers considered *economic* freedom to be the precondition for *political* freedom, as do contemporary economic liberals – for example, Milton Friedman. Similarly, medical associations that promoted the "liberal" model of medicine considered economic autonomy for doctors to be essential for achieving noneconomic ends: therapeutic freedom, trust of the patient, freedom from bureaucracy, maintaining medicine as an interpretative art where treatment must follow the individual needs of the patient and not government directives, and doctors' freedom over their own time. These issues have been touched on in Chapter 1 and will be returned to in more detail in subsequent chapters. See Chapter 1, note 16.

2 Hirschman's terms "exit," "voice," and "loyalty" have been used to analyze the behavior of consumers via-à-vis public health systems, particularly in the work of Rudolf Klein. In this book, rather than focusing on the ability of *patients* to exit from the public system, the focus is on the ability of *doctors* to exit. Furthermore, in contrast to the fear of "brain drain," which emphasizes the ability of doctors or other highly skilled professionals to exit from a particular country, exit to the private sector, or partial exit – which takes place, for example, when a publicly employed physician treats a private patient in a public hospital or, more abstractly, when a publicly insured patient must pay a partial private fee directly to the doctor – is much more convenient for the doctor. See discussion in Albert O. Hirschman, *Essays in Trespassing: Economics to Politics and Beyond* (Cambridge: Cambridge University Press, 1981), p. 235; and Rudolf Klein, *The Politics of the NHS. 2nd Ed.* (London: Longman, 1989), pp. 105–144.

3 The possibility of pockets of private practice within public systems is actually caused by the economics of government health programs. By subsidizing the health sector, these governments increased the demand for health services. Yet by attempting to push prices below their equilibrium point, they created

market pressures for increased supply of services. This provided an opportunity for the private sector.

4 Starr, *Social Transformation*. On professionalism in Europe, see Matthew Ramsey, "The Politics of Professional Monopoly in Nineteenth-Century Medicine: The French Model and its Rivals," in Gerald Geison, ed., *Professions and the French State, 1700–1900* (Philadelphia: University of Philadelphia Press, 1984), pp. 225–305.

5 Freidson, *Profession of Medicine*, p. 25. Technical autonomy goes beyond the legal requirement of the license to everyday acceptance that an individual doctor has the autonomy to make medical decisions free from the supervision of other occupations in the division of labor. In his extremely interesting book, *The System of the Professions* (Chicago: Chicago University Press, 1988), Andrew Abbott extends this concept by looking at how competing professions – such as doctors, psychologists and social workers – continue to fight jurisdictional battles over territory.

6 A second new dimension to professional politics concerned the development of specialty licensing in the early twentieth century. As Rosemary Stevens has commented, "Whereas the theme of medical history of the nineteenth century was the integration of diverse skills into one medical profession, the theme of twentieth-century medical practice is a fragmentation within the profession," *Medical Practice in Modern England: The Impact of Specialization and State Medicine* (New Haven, CT: Yale University Press, 1966) p. 3. Fragmentation according to market position is one line of cleavage; stratification according to functional specialty is a second and distinct cleavage that affected the internal structure of the profession.

7 See Alexander Morris Carr-Saunders and Paul Alexander Wilson, *The Professions* (Oxford: Oxford University Press, 1933), pp. 65–106; Stone, *Limits of Professional Power*; Monika Steffen, "The Medical Profession and the State in France," *Journal of Public Policy*, 7, 2, (1987): 189–208; Rudolf Braun, "Zur Professionalisierung des Ärztestandes in der Schweiz," in Jürgen Kocka, ed., *Bildungsbürgertum im 19. Jahrhundert* (Stuttgart: Klett-Cotta, 1985), pp. 332–357; Hans Berglind and Ulla Petersson, *Omsorg som yrke eller omsorg on yrket* (Stockholm: Sekretariatet för framtidsstudier, Trosa Tryckeri, 1980); *Läkartidningen* (Journal of the Swedish Medical Association), 75, no. 2 (1986): 1986–2000.

8 General practitioners lobbied for uniform licensing requirements and penalties against unlicensed practitioners, whereas many liberals opposed medical monopoly, and were later to oppose government sanctions against quackery. The Act provided for a General Medical Register that listed licensed practitioners. The Register was supervised by a board that included the old licensing bodies, the Royal Colleges, which remained responsible for granting licensing. No license was required for medical practice; anyone could practice medicine. But only doctors licensed and listed in the General Medical Register could hold government positions. See Carr Saunders and Wilson, *Professions*, pp. 79–83; Ramsey, "Politics of Professional Monopoly."

9 See essays in Freddi and Björkman, *Controlling Medical Professionals*, particularly that of Marian Döhler, "Physicians, Professional Autonomy in the Welfare State: Endangered or Preserved?" pp. 178–197.

10 For a description of the attempt to block the first Canadian compulsory hospital insurance law through a doctors' strike and its failure, see C. David Naylor, *Private Practice, Public Payment. Canadian Medicine and the Politics of Health Insurance, 1911–1966* (Kingston: McGill-Queen's University Press,

1986). There is no example of a strike being used to block legislation by a secure government that introduces national health insurance, or other new programs, or controls on doctors' fees, salaried practice, or restrictions on private medical practice. There are only two counterexamples to my knowledge, and in each case there is a political factor that explains the weakness of the governments in imposing reforms on the medical profession. William Glaser, *Paying the Doctor*, pp. 134–6, discusses the success of the Belgian Medical Association in launching a strike against a government reform in the 1960s, but notes that the government coalition was falling apart; thus there was a political factor that allowed the strike to make an impact. Similarly, in the 1920s in Germany, a doctors' strike was successful in getting the government to address doctors' grievances against the sickness funds, but again only for political reasons. The sickness funds were a Social Democratic domain, and politicians of the right and center wished to undermine this source of Social Democratic organizational power. See discussion in Bernd Rosewitz and Douglas Webber, *Reformversuche und Reformblockaden im deutschen Gesundheitswesen* (Frankfurt: Campus, 1990).

11 Odin W. Anderson, *Health Care: Can There Be Equity? The United States, Sweden and England* (New York: John Wiley and Sons, 1972); Glaser, *Paying the Doctor*; Mark G. Field, *Success and Crisis in National Health Systems: A Comparative Approach* (New York: Routledge, 1989).

12 References specific to each country will be provided in the following, historical section of this chapter. On health insurance and sickness funds, see especially Peter Flora, ed., *Growth to Limits. The Western European Welfare States Since World War II. Vol. 1. Sweden, Norway, Finland, Denmark. Vol. 2. Germany, United Kingdom, Ireland, Italy*, European University Institute, Series C. Political and Social Science, 6.1 (Berlin, New York: Walter de Gruyter, 1986). In addition to the sources cited in note 11, works on comparative health policy particularly concerned with institutions, politics, and history are: Jan Blanpain, with Luc Delesie and Herman Nys, *National Health Insurance and Health Resources: The European Experience* (Cambridge: Harvard University Press, 1978); Freddi and Björkman, *Controlling Medical Professionals*; James Hogarth, *The Payment of the Physician*; Alan Maynard and Gordon McLachlan, eds., *The Public/Private Mix for Health* (London: The Nuffield Provincial Hospitals Trust, 1982).

13 The best source on doctors' fees in Glaser, *Paying the Doctor*. On extra-billing in Canada, see Naylor, *Private Practice, Public Payment*.

14 Simone Sandier, "Health Services Utilization and Physician Income Trends," in Organisation for Economic Cooperation and Development, *Health Care Systems in Transition. The Search for Efficiency*, OECD Social Policy Studies No. 7 (Paris, OECD: 1990), p. 43. Nevertheless, the relationship between mode of payment, physicians' incomes, and patient utilization does not appear to be clear cut, as the mode of payment affects incentives to both doctor and patient, making the two effects difficult to disentangle. Studies also differ with regard to the linkage between fee-for-service payment and rates of prescriptions. In addition to Sandier, see Brian Abel-Smith, *Cost Containment in Health Care. A Study of 12 European Countries* (London: National Council for Voluntary Organisations/Bedford Press, 1984), p. 12.

15 Jens Albert, "Die Gesundheitssysteme der OECD-Länder im Vergleich," *Staatstätigkeit, Politische Vierteljahresschrift*, Special Issue 19, (1988): 116–150; Stone, *Limits of Professional Power*. Ironically, however, doctors' incomes appear to be higher in Germany than in France, according to Sandier, "Health Services Utilization and Physician Income Trends."

16 Mark G. Field, *Doctor and Patient in Soviet Russia* (Cambridge, MA: Harvard University Press, 1958); Milton Roemer, *Comparative National Policies on Health Care* (New York: Marcel Dekker, 1977).

17 On the British National Health Service, see Klein, *Politics of the NHS.*

18 On the preferences of doctors vis-à-vis health services, and their seemingly universal aversion to working for local government authorities or as salaried employees of local health centers, see Blanpain, *National Health Insurance and Health Resources*; Maurizio Ferrera, "The Politics of Health Reform: Origins and Performance of the Italian Health Service in Comparative Perspective," in Freddi and Björkman, *Controlling Medical Professionals*, pp. 116–129; Jan-Erik Lane and Sven Arvidson, "Health Professionals in the Swedish System," also in Freddi and Björkman, pp. 74–98; Monika Steffen, *Régulation Politique et Stratégies Professionnelles: Médecine Libérale et Emergence des Centres de Santé*, Thèse d'Etat, Institute d'Etudes Politiques, Université des Sciences Sociales de Grenoble II, Grenoble, 1983.

19 Victor G. Rodwin stresses particularly the importance of administrative coordination between financing and planning, in *The Health Planning Predicament: France, Québec, England and the United States* (Berkeley: University of California Press, 1984). Refer to Chapter 3 on the French case for further references.

20 Abel-Smith, *Cost-Containment in Health Care*; Robert G. Evans, "Finding the Levels, Finding the Courage: Lessons from Cost Containment in North America," *Journal of Health Politics, Policy, and Law 11* (1986): 585–615.

21 As J. Rogers Hollingsworth, Jerald Hage and Robert A. Hanneman, *State Intervention in Medical Care: Consequences for Britain, France, Sweden and the United States, 1890–1970* (Ithaca: Cornell University Press, 1990), have pointed out, the results of public ownership of the health care sector are quite distinct from the results of government regulation of prices and personnel. If one is interested in the "social efficiency" of health care programs, as they call it – that is, the delivery of the greatest improvement in mortality to the largest number at the lowest cost – they argue that one should focus on the regulatory aspects of government rather than the expansion of public ownership and provision of services.

22 Federal Councillor Tschudi in 1962, cited in Gerhard Kocher, *Verbandseinfluss auf die Gesetzgebung. Ärtzeverbindung, Krankenkassenverbände und die Teilrevision 1964 des Kranken- und Unfallversicherungsgesetzes*, 2nd ed. (Bern: Francke Verlag, 1972), p. 17.

23 The work of Stein Rokkan has outlined the effect of a series of standard political conflicts – church-state, center-periphery, urban-rural, capital-labor – on European party systems. The same conflicts had an impact on health systems, however; interest groups as well as public and private agencies for the delivery of services were as affected as the political parties. The transition to democracy thus molded not just the party system, but also the overall structure of interest groups, specific policy agencies, and the broader set of political institutions. This early period established the political actors relevant for health politics: sickness funds, unions, employers' associations, medical associations, other interest groups (including the private insurance industry), and of course the political parties. It established a basic set of policy agencies, the sickness funds, patterns of hospital ownership, and government bureaucracies to oversee these agencies. In terms of political institutions, the constitutional links between the parliamentary and executive branches of government, as well as between national and subnational political and administrative bodies, set the rules of the game for future policy making. The Rokkan model is used

in this historical section as a convenient map for describing these developments, without necessarily adhering to the causal model he proposes. See Stein Rokkan, "Dimensions of State Formation and Nation-Building," in Charles Tilly, ed., *The Formation of National States in Western Europe* (Princeton: Princeton University Press, 1974), pp. 562–600.

24 William A. Glaser, *Social Systems and Medical Organization* (NY: Lieber-Atherton, 1970) p. 35, cf. 32–5, 80.

25 P.H.J.H. Gosden, *The Friendly Societies in England 1815–1875* (Manchester: Manchester University Press, 1961), p. 1. Cf. Gösta Lindeberg, *Den Svenska Sjukkasserörelsens Historia* (Lund: Svenska Sjukkasseförbundet/Carl Bloms Boktryckeri, 1949). Although many persons, both historians and members of the sickness fund movement, have seen a relationship between guilds, unions, and voluntary mutual associations, attempts to trace the origins of the funds and of the unions to guilds have not turned up sufficient information to prove continuity.

26 J. Tempke, "Bismarck's Social Legislation: A Genuine Breakthrough?" in W.J. Mommsen, ed., *The Emergence of the Welfare State in Britain and Germany 1850–1950* (London: Croom Helm, 1981), pp. 71–83.

27 This coincides with the statistical findings of Peter Flora and Jens Alber, "Modernization, Democratization, and the Development of Welfare States in Western Europe," in Flora and Heidenheimer, eds., *The Development of Welfare States in Europe and America* (New Brunswick, NJ: Transaction Books, 1981) pp. 37–80. Social insurance is established earlier and expands more quickly in nations with conservative monarchies than under those with parliamentary democracies – a legitimacy tradeoff.

28 Flora and Alber, "Modernization, Democratization, and the Development of Welfare States," p. 59; Flora, *Growth to Limits. Vol. 4. Appendix (Synopses, Bibliographies, Tables)* European University Institute, Series C, Political and Social Science, 6.4 (Berlin, New York: Walter de Gruyter, 1987), p. 787. Sources on Sweden, France, Switzerland are provided in Chapters 3, 4, and 5. Different sources sometimes give contradictory dates, because the content of the laws varies, and in many countries a series of sickness fund laws were passed. Some of the earliest laws provide only provisions for government registration of funds but no subsidies.

29 J.M. Baernreither, *English Associations of Working Men* (London: Swann Sonnenschein & Co., 1889, republished by Gale Research Company, Detroit, 1966), p. 300; Gosden, *Friendly Societies in England*, particularly, pp. 9, 156, 177–8; J. Reulecke, "English Social Policy around the Middle of the Nineteenth Century as seen by German Social Reformers," in W.J. Mommsen, ed., *The Emergence of the Welfare State in Britain and Germany 1850–1950* (London: Croom Helm, 1981), pp. 32–49; Sidney and Beatrice Webb, *The History of Trade Unionism* (NY: Augustus M. Kelley, 1965 [1894]), pp. 261 ff. especially, also 19–25; Henry Pelling, *A History of British Trade Unionism, Fourth Ed* (London: Macmillan, 1987), p. 11, p. 62 ff.; Bentley B. Gilbert, *The Evolution of National Insurance in Great Britain. The Origins of the Welfare State* (London: Michael Joseph, 1966).

30 The fact that the socialist government of François Mitterrand took the immediate step of restoring free elections in the social security funds seems to be a continuation of this historic pattern, analogous to the legalization of the mutuals in 1848.

31 Detlev Zöllner, "Germany," in Peter A. Köhler and Hans F. Zacher, eds., *The Evolution of Social Insurance. 1881–1981. Studies of Germany, France, Great Britain, Austria and Switzerland* (London: Frances Pinter, NY: St.

Martin's Press, 1981), pp. 15–17; Gaston V. Rimlinger, *Welfare Policy and Industrialization in Europe, America and Russia* (NY: John Wiley, 1971), pp. 102–122; Arnold J. Heidenheimer, "Unions and Welfare State Development in Britain and Germany: An Interpretation of Metamorphoses in the Period 1910–1950," *International Institute for Comparative Social Research Discussion Paper*, no. IIVG/dp/80-209 (Berlin: IIVG, SP-II, Wissenschaftszentrum Berlin, 1980).

32 B. Guy Peters, "The United Kingdom," in Dan N. Jacobs et al., eds., *Comparative Politics* (Chatham, NJ: Chatham House Publishers, 1983), p. 30.

33 See Flora, *Growth to Limits*, and Stein Kuhnle, "The Growth of Social Insurance Programs in Scandinavia: Outside Influences and Internal Forces," in Flora and Heidenheimer, *The Development of Welfare States in Europe and America*, pp. 125–150.

34 Abram De Swaan, *In Care of the State. Health Care, Education and Welfare in Europe and the USA in the Modern Era* (Oxford: Polity Press/Basil Blackwell, 1988), regrets the lack of scholarly work on the early history of Dutch social insurance and the mutualist movement. His account recaps events only from 1913 on. On Belgium, see William A. Glaser, *Health Insurance Bargaining: Foreign Lessons for Americans* (NY: Gardener Press, 1978), pp. 57–8; On the Netherlands, see Glaser, p. 81, and de Swaan, pp. 210–214; on the Dutch system of representation, the classic work is Arend Lijphart, *The Politics of Accommodation: Pluralism and Democracy in the Netherlands* (New Haven: Yale University Press, 1968). On current health policy in the Netherlands, see Nico Baakman et al., "Controlling Dutch Health Care," in Freddi and Björkman, *Controlling Medical Professionals*, pp. 99–115.

35 On Italy, see Maurizio Ferrera, "Italy," in Flora, *Growth to Limits*, Vol. 2, pp. 385–482, and his "Politics of Health Reform: Origins and Performance of the Italian Health Service in Comparative Perspective." On Spain, see Josep A. Rodríguez and Jesús de Miguel, "Del Poder de la Corporación: El Caso de la Profesión Médica Española," in Manuel Pérez Yruela and Salvador Giner, *La Sociedad Corporativa* (Barcelona: Ariel, 1988), pp. 229–271; and de Miguel and Mauro F. Guillén, "The Health System in Spain," in Field, *Crisis and Success in National Health Systems*, pp. 128–164.

36 On the history of American health care, see Starr, *Social Transformation of American Medicine*, on fraternal orders, specifically pp. 206–9; see also Beth Andrea Stevens, *In the Shadow of the Welfare State: Corporate and Union Development of Employee Benefits*, unpublished dissertation, Department of Sociology, Harvard University, Cambridge, MA, 1984, and "Blurring the Boundaries: How the Federal Government has Influenced Welfare Benefits in the Private Sector," in Margaret Weir, Ann Shola Orloff, Theda Skocpol, *The Politics of Social Policy in the United States* (Princeton: Princeton University Press, 1988), pp. 123–148.

36a Naylor, *Public Practice, Private Payment.*

37 It is difficult to find even reasonably comparable statistics on health care expenditures divided according to public versus private consumption, and it is even more difficult to move from these general financing flows to the distributional consequences of health care financing. Robert J. Maxwell, *Health and Wealth. An International Study of Health Care Spending* (Lexington, MA: Lexington Books, D.C. Heath and Company for Sandoz Institute for Health and Socio-Economic Studies, 1981) discusses these issues at length, and has produced figures that have been collected according to a uniform definition. His sectoral divisions of costs is consistent with Swedish and French national accounts tables, *Appendix 1 till Nationalräkenskaper Årsrapport 1970–1983.*

Konsumtion 1970-1983 Sveriges officiella statistik, SM N 1984: 5.5 (Stockholm: Statistiska Centralbyrån, 1984); *Comptes Nationaux de Santé. Resultats 1950-1977* (Paris: INSEE, Ministère de la Santé, CREDOC, 1979). There are no special national accounts for health care consumption in Switzerland, and Maxwell states that his Swiss figures are underestimated by 5-10 percent, (p. 153), owing to a narrow definition of health and the pluralistic nature of the health system. The main problem, of course, is that statistics on health care consumption are generally collected by the bodies that finance these costs. The larger the proportion of these costs that are paid for by public agencies or social security, the better the accounting system will be – although it will bear the imprint of the specific public program. Conversely, the larger the proportion of the costs that are borne through private insurers or individuals, the less likely that these outlays will find their way into national accounts. In either kind of system, direct payments from patients to doctors may not be fully accounted for.

38 *Statistik über die vom Bunde anerkannten Versicherungsträger der Krankenversicherung,* (Bern: Bundesamt für Sozialversicherung, 1984), Table 29. In 1964, the Swiss Employers' Association estimated that employer contributions for health insurance constituted 5 percent of sickness fund receipts. Because group policies were given a clearer legal status under the 1964 revision of the Sickness and Accident Insurance Law, the percentage has increased since that time, although it should be noted that the trend is for employers to provide sickness cash benefits rather than health insurance covering medical treatments. *Schweizerische Arbeitgeberzeitung* (Journal of the Swiss Employers' Association), 30 January 1964, p. 74.

39 If we recalculate financing according to payor, putting the government subsidies to the sickness funds in the government total and the patient cost-sharing portion in the patient total, the figures do not change substantially. In 1986, the government paid for 35.4 percent of costs (cantonal payments to hospitals and federal government subsidies to sickness funds), the sickness funds paid for 27.2 percent (patient and employer premiums), and patients paid for 34.7 percent (cost-sharing, 3.9 percent, supplemental insurance, 13.5 percent, and expenses not covered by insurance, 23.2 percent). See Pierre Gygi and Andreas Frei, *Das Schweizerische Gesundheitswesen* (Basel: Verlag Krebs, 1988), p. 69; Pierre Gilliand, "Révision de l'Assurance-Maladie Sociale," unpublished report prepared for the Swiss Department of Social Insurance, Lausanne, September 1988, p. 9; Markus Schneider, Jürg H. Sommer, Aynur Keçeci, Léa Scholtes, Arno Welzel, *Gesundheitsysteme im internationalen Vergleich 2d Ed.,* Bundesministerium für Arbeit Forschungsbericht No. 160 (Bonn: Bundesministerium für Arbeit, 1989), p. 7.

40 The number of sickness funds has been reduced over the years as a result of market pressures, from 1,160 funds in 1935 to 729 in 1970 to 346 in 1986, *Konkordat der Schweizerischen Krankenkassen (KSK) Tätigkeitsbericht, 1986-7* (yearly report of the Association of Sickness Funds) (Solothurn, 1987), p. 13.

41 On the Swiss health system, see Albert J. Gebert, "Cooperative Federalism or Muddling through: the Swiss Case," in Altenstetter, ed., *Changing National-Subnational Relations in Health,* pp. 95-139; Pierre Gilliand, *L'hospitalisation en Suisse. Statistiques 1936-1978. Quel Avenir?,* Cahiers d'études de l'Institut Suisse des Hôpitaux, No. 15 (Aarau: ISH, 1980); Glaser, *Paying the Doctor* and *Paying the Doctor Under National Health Insurance*; Pierre Gygi & Peter Tschopp, *Sozial-medizinische Sicherung* (Bern & Stuttgart: Verlag Hans Huber, 1968); Hogarth, *Payment of the Physician*; A. Saxer, *Die soziale Sicherheit in der Schweiz,* 4th ed. (Bern: Verlag Paul Haupt, 1977).

42 On doctors in private practice, see *Schweizerische Ärztezeitung* (Journal of the Swiss Medical Association), *62*, (1981), p. 2738. Figures on specialization from Gygi and Frei, *Schweizerische Gesundheitswesen*, p. 37. Although the provision for unlimited extra-billing for those in "good economic circumstances" was a central political conflict during the postwar period, as I discuss in Chapter 4, this provision is no longer in use, because of difficulties in checking patients' incomes. The significant form of extra-billing is that charged for private patients in hospitals – whether public or private; these are the bulk of charges in the one-third of costs borne directly by patients either through direct payment or supplemental private insurance. In the late 1970s, the incomes of hospital chief physicians became a topic of heated public debate; some hospitals attempted to introduce cellings on the private practice earnings of these doctors.

43 The cantons paid for an average of 38.1 percent of hospital costs in 1986, Gygi and Frei, *Schweizerische Gesundheitswesen*, graph following p. 74; the rate varies from 30 to 70 percent in individual cantons. The confederation, cantons, and local communities own 40.4 percent of the acute care hospitals, but 60 percent of the beds; private nonprofit foundations and associations 44.1 percent of hospitals, 33.1 percent of beds; private-for-profit companies 15.4 percent of hospitals, 6.9 percent of beds, Philippe Lehman, Felix Gutzwiller, and Jean F. Martin, "The Swiss health system: The paradox of ungovernability and efficacy," in Field, *Crisis and Success in National Health Systems*, p. 30. In 1984, it was estimated that 13.4 percent of hospital beds were found in private clinics, but that these clinics treated 15.5 percent of hospitalized patients and 17 percent of maternity cases, Hans Schoch, "Das Privatspital im sozial-politischen Umfeld," *Schweizerische Ärztezeitung*, *65* (1984), pp. 1528–1531. In Switzerland, however, these clinics are thought to play a "subordinate role," Gebert, "Cooperative Federalism or Muddling Through," p. 115.

44 Coordinated planning is difficult because cantonal officials, who meet under the auspices of the Swiss Conference of State Ministers responsible for Health Affairs (*Schweizerische Sanitätsdirektorenkonferenz*, or SDK), strive to improve hospital facilities in their own particular canton, regardless of what is available nearby. Further, hospital charges are higher for out-of-canton patients, so economic as well as political incentives exist for the duplication of services and equipment. On planning, see Gebert, "Cooperative Federalism or Muddling Through;" Leonhard Neidhart, *Föderalismus in der Schweiz. Zusammenfassender Bericht über die Föderalismus-Hearings der Stiftung für eidgenössische Zusammenarbeit in Solothurn* (Zürich & Köln: Benziger Verlag, 1975), pp. 89–94.

45 G. Dorion and A. Guionnet, *La Sécurité Sociale, Que Sais-Je?* No. 294 (Paris: Presses Universitaires de France, 1983), p. 80. The portion of self-payment and the contribution rates have increased recently as a result of cost-cutting measures; see Paul Godt, "Health Care: the Political Economy of Social Policy," in Godt, ed., *Policy-Making in France* (London and NY: Pinter Publishers, 1989), pp. 191–207.

46 A more recent estimate shows that as the patients' portion of costs has risen, private supplementary policies have increased, paying for 6.9 percent of costs in 1985, whereas direct payments comprised 15.3 percent. The total private share, however, remained almost constant at about 23 percent. Schneider et al., *Gesundheitssysteme im internationalen Vergleich*, p. 7.

47 Victor G. Rodwin, "Management Without Objectives: The French health policy gamble," in A. Maynard and G. McLachlan, eds., *The Public/Private Mix for Health* (London: The Nuffield Provincial Hospitals Trust, 1982),

pp. 293–4. On the French system, see also Rodwin, *The Health Planning Predicament*; J.F. Lacronique, "The French Health Care System," in Maynard and McLachlan, pp. 265–288; Paul J. Godt, "Confrontation, Consent, and Corporatism: State Strategies and the Medical Profession in France, Great Britain, and West Germany," *Journal of Health Politics, Policy and Law, 12,* (1987): 459–481; Godt, "Health Care: the Political Economy of Social Policy."

48 Figures on private practice from the French Ministry of Health, obtained directly from CREDOC. Specialization from Schneider et al., *Gesundheitsysteme im internationalen Vergleich,* p. 175.

49 Jean-Jacques Dupeyroux, *Droit de la Sécurité Sociale. 11th Ed.* (Paris: Dalloz, 1988), p. 391. 72.47 percent bound by convention, 6.63 percent have the right to extra-bill (*droit permanent de depassement*) but receive no special benefits; 20.3 percent in Sector II, pay for their own benefits, and patients reimbursed only to fee schedule; 0.59 percent completely out of system.

50 The private clinics accounted for 34.4 percent of total bed capacity in 1978, Jean de Kervasdoué, "La Politique de l'Etat en Matière d'Hospitalisation Privée, 1962–1978," *Annales Economiques 16* (1980): 23–57.

51 Åke Elmér, *Svensk Social Politik. 15th Ed* (Malmö: Liber Förlag, 1983: 112). In 1955, when the national health insurance law went into effect, patients contributed 52.8 percent of health insurance receipts (contributions plus cost-sharing), employers contributed 20 percent, and the state 25.8 percent. By 1967, the patients' portion had been reduced to 38.6 percent, the state's to 13 percent, and the employers' to 47.4 percent, *Allmänn Försäkring* (Stockholm: Riksförsäkringsverket, 1969) The increase in the employer contribution to 85 percent came about as part of the Haga agreement of the mid-1970s, and entailed a reduction in other taxes to compensate for the increase in health insurance contribution. On the Swedish health system, see Anderson, *Health Care: Can there be Equity?*; Arnold J. Heidenheimer and Nils Elvander, eds., *The Shaping of the Swedish Health System* (London: Croom Helm, 1980).

52 Maxwell, *Health and Wealth,* pp. 130–1, 148–9, 151–2.

53 "Promemoria om nyrekrytering av privatpraktiserande läkare," Socialdepartementet Ds S 1982: 9 (Stockholm, 1982), p. 9 and *Socialstyrelsens läkarregister.*

54 Anderson, *Health Care: Can there be Equity?,* p. 125.

55 Organisation for Economic Cooperation and Development (OECD), *Financing and Delivering Health Care: A Comparative Analysis of OECD Countries* OECD Policy Studies No. 4 (Paris, 1987); OECD, *Health Care Systems in Transition: the Search for Efficiency* OECD Social Policy Studies No. 7 (Paris, 1990).

56 Swiss health care expenditures are said to be significantly underreported. The definition of health is narrow, administrative costs are not included, and there is a large amount of private payment, as well as decentralization. Maxwell estimates that his figures for Switzerland are too low by 5–10 percent, *Health and Wealth,* p. 153. Gilliand estimates that spending *including* administrative costs totals between 8.5 and 9 percent of GNP, "Révision de l'Assurance-Maladie Sociale," p. 8.

57 Theodore J. Lowi, "American Business, Public Policy, Case Studies, and Political Theory," *World Politics 16* (1964): 677–715; Peter Bachrach and Morton S. Baretz, "The Two Faces of Power," *American Political Science Review 56* (1962): 947–52; Isaac D. Balbus, "The Concept of Interest in Pluralist and Marxian Analysis," *Politics and Society 1* (1971): 151–77; Robert R. Alford and Roger Friedland, "Political Participation and Public Policy," *Annual Review of Sociology 1* (1975): 429–79.

Chapter 3

1 In the Third Repubic, the political executive consisted of the President of the Republic and a cabinet. The president was elected by the two chambers of the parliament for a term of seven years. The president chose a President of the Council who, in turn, chose the ministers for the cabinet. The cabinet was then approved by parliament. The executive government was empowered to dissolve the Chamber of Deputies, with the assent of the Senate. Conversely, the Chamber could question and dismiss the ministers of the executive. In contrast to a country like Britain, where the head of the majority party is automatically the head of the executive and can pick a partisan cabinet, the multipartyism and the internal fragmentation of the French party system allowed the President of the Republic a wide choice for the President of the Council that could be used to play the parties off against one another. Both Maurice Duverger, *Institutions politiques et droit constitutionnel. Vol. 2. Le système politique français* (Paris: Presses Universitaires de France, 1976), pp. 73–87, and Duncan MacRae, *Parliament, Parties and Society in France, 1946–1958* (NY: St. Martin's Press, 1967), pp. 4–12, 324, upon whose work this description relies, attribute some of the problems of the Third and Fourth Republics to the fact that the executive's ability to dissolve the Chamber of Deputies/National Assembly was not used. Parliamentary majorities and cabinets fell without the electoral iterations that might have brought parliamentary representation more in line with electoral results. Duverger also makes a central point of the distinction between electoral alliances and parliamentary majorities – the first "bipolar," the second "centrist."

2 Duverger, *Institutions politiques et droit constitutionnel*, p. 74, on the "crushing" majority of the rural representatives; on the Conseil de la République of the Fourth Republic, p. 97. The role of the parliamentary commissions in the Fourth Republic is discussed on pp. 113–114; the similarities to the analysis of American congressional committees by Shepsle and Weingast, "The Institutional Foundations of Committee Power," is striking.

3 The informal power of the French local *notable* is legendary. For an introduction to power in the French periphery as well as its role even in the supposedly centralized national politics and administration, see Jean-Pierre Worms, "Le préfet et ses notables," *Sociologie du Travail*, 8, no. 3 (July–Sept 1966): 249–275; Pierre Grémion, *Le pouvoir périphérique* (Paris: Le Seuil, 1976); A. Machin, "Traditional Patterns of French Local Government," in Jacques Lagroye & Vincent Wright, eds., *Local Government in Britain and France. Problems & Aspects* (London: George, Allen & Unwin, 1979), pp. 28–41; Douglas E. Ashford, *British Dogmatism and French Pragmatism: Central-Local Policy-making in the Welfare State* (London: Allen & Unwin, 1981); Jean-Claude Thoenig, "La relation entre le centre et la périphérie," *Bulletin de l'Institut International d'Administration Publique*, no. 36 (Oct–Dec 1975): 77–123, and "Local Government Institutions and the Contemporary Evolution of French Society," in Lagroye & Wright, pp. 74–104; Sidney Tarrow, *Between Center and Periphery: Grassroots Politicians in Italy and France* (New Haven & London: Yale University Press, 1977). Tarrow provides some figures on the occupational status of French and Italian mayors, but doctors are not listed as a separate category. Together, the two catgories to which doctors could belong comprise 49 percent of French mayors (23 percent are teachers and professionals, 26 percent are retired), p. 114.

4 Physicians were archetypal members of the local bourgeoisie known as the

"notables." See Theodore Zeldin, *France. 1848–1945. Vol. 1, Ambition, Love, and Politics* (Oxford: Clarendon Press, Oxford University Press, 1973), pp. 23–42. Henry K. Kerr provides physician representation in parliament for 1973 in *Parlement et Société en Suisse* (St Saphorin: Editions Georgi, 1981), p. 280. For earlier figures, see Pierre Birnbaum, *Les Sommets de l'Etat* (Paris: Editions du Seuil, 1977), pp. 42, 71. For the percentage of physicians within individual parties, see pp. 39, 50.

5 An interesting pattern is the repeated division between the medical faculties and provincial doctors who were given royal support, represented in the seventeenth century by the Chambre Royale and in the eighteenth by the Société Royale de Médecine (constituted around Viq d'Azyr, personal physician of the queen), which had a more public health orientation. For the history of professionalization in France, see Ramsey, "Politics of Professional Monopoly in Nineteenth-Century Medicine: the French Model and its Rivals;" Claudine Herzlich, "The Evolution of Relations between French Physicians and the State from 1880 to 1980," *Sociology of Health and Illness*, 4, (1982): 241–252; Monika Steffen, *Régulation Politique et Stratégies Professionnelles: Médecine Libérale et Emergence des Centres de Santé*, Thèse d'Etat, Institute d'Etudes Politiques, Université des Sciences Sociales de Grenoble II, Grenoble, 1983, and "Medical Profession and the State in France."

6 Steffen, *Régulation Politique et Stratégies Professionnelles*, pp. 230–1.

7 Steffen, ibid, p. 253.

8 Jean Meynaud, *Les Groupes de Pression en France*, Cahiers de la Fondation Nationale des Sciences Politiques No. 95 (Paris: Librairie Armand Colin, 1958), p. 66.

9 On the liberal model of medicine, see Henri Hatzfeld, *Le Grand Tournant de la Médecine Libérale* (Paris: Les Editions Ouvrières, 1963).

10 Glaser, *Paying the Doctor*, p. 124, cf. 127.

11 The practices taken to control the political activities of the French mutual aid societies, such as requiring honorary members (wealthy benefactors who paid contributions and received disproportionate votes on the societies' boards), were described in Chapter 2. In 1870, the funds counted 113,947 honorary members to 731,892 active members, or 13.5 percent of the total membership, Roman Lavielle, *Histoire de la Mutualité. Sa place dans le régime français de la Sécurité Sociale* (Paris: Librairie Hachette, 1964), p. 53. See also pp. 44–57. The prevalent French interpretation of these changes in the laws is linked to the changes in constitutional regime, so that Yves Saint-Jours, for example, states, "The Second Empire began, as the Second Republic had ended, by the taking of action against the workers' societies, which had gone underground, by instituting, in a law of 22 June 1854, a general requirement that workers carry a police identity card and by exercising political control over friendly societies," "France," in Peter A. Köhler and Hans F. Zacher, eds., *The Evolution of Social Insurance. 1881–1981. Studies of Germany, France, Great Britain, Austria and Switzerland* (London: Frances Pinter, NY: St. Martin's Press, 1982), pp. 102, 101–105.

12 On work accidents, Saint-Jours, "France," p. 112–4; on pensions, p. 118; on the late development of social insurance in France, see especially Henri Hatzfeld, *Du Paupérisme à la Sécurité Sociale. Essai sur les Origines de la Sécurité Sociale en France. 1850–1940* (Paris: Librairie Armand Colin, 1971); Jean-Jacques Dupeyroux, *Droit de la Sécurité Sociale* (Paris: Dalloz, 1984), pp. 30–1.

13 Saint-Jours, "France," p. 119; Hatzfeld, *Du Paupérisme à la Sécurité Sociale*.

14 Georges Lefranc, *Les Expériences Syndicales en France de 1939 à 1950* (Paris: Aubier, Editions Montaigne, 1950), p. 310; Hatzfeld, *Grand Tournant de la Médecine Libérale*, p. 40.

15 Lavielle points out that the enactment of French social insurance laws was very closely tied to the electoral cycle, *Histoire de la Mutualité*, p. 92.

16 According to Hatzfeld, this process was markedly different than that leading up to the 1910 pension law. Whereas before, the discussions had centered around the ideological viewpoints of the individual members of parliament, now the locus of decision making became the parliamentary commissions where interest groups held sway. "The relations between public opinion and the parliament seem to have been assured by another couple: interest groups and the parliamentary committees. Public opinion appeared only mediocrely concerned and, in addition, the discussions in the assemblies lost their interest. They became brief, conventional: everything was played out elsewhere," *Du Paupérisme a la Sécurité Sociale*, pp. 153–4, cf. 145. On the 1928 and 1930 laws, see also Hatzfeld, *Grand Tournant de la Médecine Libérale*; Lavielle, *Histoire de la Mutualité*; Lefranc, *Expériences Syndicales en France*, pp. 310 ff.; Dupeyroux, *Droit de la Sécurité Sociale*, pp. 52–3; Saint-Jours, "France;" "Assurances sociales," Ass. S., Cartons 1–7, Ministère du Travail, Archives Nationales, henceforth shortened to "Archives, 1930."

17 "Rapport fait au nom de la commission d'assurance et de prévoyance sociale chargée d'examiner le projet de loi sur les assurances sociales," par M. Edouard Grinda, député, annexe No. 5505, Doc. Parl-Chambre 1923, Carton 5, and "Note relative au projet de loi d'assurance sociale 18 février 1922," Carton 2, Archives, 1930.

18 Before the Chamber of Deputies, Dr. Grinda agreed with the position of the mutual aid societies and argued with the same biological metaphors. Calling the mutuals the "vital cells of the law," Grinda criticized the first project: "'Impregnated with *étatisme*, social insurance is to be consecrated with a purely mechanical automatism, although it can develop only by provoking spontaneity, in calling forth energies, in remaining animated by a vitality that is essentially physiological. To make the organisms of social insurance organisms of the state, to apply administrative and bureaucratic methods, to banish all hope of interest and emulation, that would be to introduce a germ of death," Union Départementale des Sociétés de Secours Mutuels de Nord-Congrès du Fourmies, 26 July 1925, Rapport de M. Maurice Vanlaer, Président de la Commission du legislation sociales sur les assurances sociales, Carton 6, Archives 1930.

19 The French Farmers' Association (Société des Agriculteurs de France) had traditionally taken a strong stand against social insurance. The 1898 law on work accidents was not applied to agricultural employees until 1922. Pressures from the same society severely weakened the 1910 law on pensions; it had voiced opposition to the Eight Hours Law of 1919 even though it did not apply to agriculture, fearing that it would result in a loss of laborers to industry until agricultural salaries were increased. One of the most striking incidents was the alliance of the Society with the *Comité des Forges* (the employers' association of the metallurgical industries) to pressure the French delegate to the 1921 ILO Conference to block all resolutions pertaining to agriculture. When this tactic failed, these societies appealed to the International Court at the Hague, but the Court condemned the French complaint. See J. Malissol, "Quelques pas a travers l'histoire de la protection sociale des agriculteurs" (and editors' introduction), *Revue Paysans, 4*, no. 2 (Aug–Sept

1959), p. 8. This is, of course, a biased source, coming from the journal of a reformist peasant association that wished, among other things, to promote social insurance for agricultural workers.

20 In *Régulation Politique et Stratégies Professionnelles*, Steffen scrutinizes the earlier history of the Union to show that the liberal model of medicine as set out by the 1927 *Charte Médicale* was a relatively new development. When the 1893 Law on Free Medical Assistance to the Poor was enacted, the Union fought for payment by the "visit" and for the right of doctors to determine which patients would qualify. The Union was also engaged in conflicts with the mutuelles, because the Union wanted only low-income persons to be eligible for mutual fund benefits. Payment by the visit, the forerunner of fee-for-service, was a solution to the collection problems experienced by physicians and provided a means to check the income of patients by entering into their homes. Nevertheless, many country doctors preferred capitation payments. By the early twentieth century there was a strong current within the profession that supported more "social medicine," which created an organizational crisis in 1911. The USMF, founded in 1884, disbanded in 1911 over the issue of social medicine. Reconstituted in 1913, the Union developed a pro-social insurance stance, and promoted a national policy of public health.

21 *Concours Médical*, 30 April 1922, p. 1428, cf. 9 Oct 1921, found as clippings in Ass. S. 1, Archives 1930.

22 The Grinda report noted that there was some opposition to the reform among doctors, but concluded that the profession would cooperate and would submit to collective agreements, as long as payments were made on a fee-for-service basis and if doctors would themselves organize the system of controls. An internal document makes it clear that farmers, not doctors, were the most important opponents to the law – but the doctors would in any case be placated by the appointment of a physician as parliamentary rapporteur. See "Note relative . . ." Carton 2; "Rapport Grinda . . ." Carton 5, Archives 1930.

23 Under the Chamber plan, patients would pay the sickness funds for a coupon (*ticket modérateur*, or deductible) that would be used to pay their doctors. The funds would then pay the doctors by dividing a global sum according to the services performed by each doctor, as under the German system. The *ticket modérateur* was to be no more than one-third of daily wages. Under the Senate version, patients would pay doctors directly and would later be reimbursed by the funds for 85–90 percent of the costs. The portion paid by the patient would now be independent of salary. The Senate law also specified that local contracts between medical unions and funds could establish alternate payment systems, including direct third party payment. Both the Chamber and the Senate versions provided for closed panels of doctors (lists of doctors with exclusive rights to insurance practice). Under the Chamber version, the lists would be established by the funds and the funds would only finance treatment by those authorized doctors. Under the Senate version, the lists would be established jointly by the funds and medical unions belonging to the national unions. Ass. S. 6, Archives, 1930.

24 *Revue de la Prévoyance et de la Mutalité, 38*, no. 2, April/May/June 1927, p. 85, in Ass. S. 6, Archives, 1930.

25 Steffen, "The Medical Profession and the State in France," p. 197, citing Raoux 1979: 107.

26 *Concours Médical*, 10 August 1924.

27 Steffen, *Régulation Politique et Stratégies Professionnelles*, chapters 3 & 4; Stephan, *Economie et Pouvoir Médical.*
28 Steffen, "The Medical Profession and the State in France," p. 198.
29 *Médecin Syndicaliste* (journal of the USMF), 1926, pp. 334–336; 1928, pp. 726–748, especially p. 727.
30 The Grinda report and the "Note relative . . ." state that employers in agriculture, commerce and industry argued that the moment was not ripe for social insurance; it would hurt exports and disproportionately hurt small, labor-intensive firms. Employers specifically complained that the contributions were too high, they opposed the payroll tax, and thought that the income limit was too high. Interestingly, they argued against the unification of risks, an argument that was still current in the 1960s. The Comité des Industries Métallurgiques and the Fédération des Industries Chimiques, various provincial Chambers of Commerce (e.g., Chambre de Commerce de Tour et de l'Inere, 15 Nov. 1923), and the Syndicat Général de Commerce et de l'Industrie were reported as being opposed to the law, whereas the Fédération du Bâtiment and the *"patronat Catholique"* would support the law with some reservations. Cartons 2, 5, Archives, 1930.
31 On French business organizations, see Jean Meynaud, *Les Groupes de Pression en France*, Cahiers de la Fondation Nationale des Sciences Politiques No. 95 (Paris: Librairie Armand Colin, 1958); Henry W. Ehrmann, *Organized Business in France* (Princeton: Princeton University Press, 1957).
32 François Goguel, *La Politique des Partis sous la IIIe République, 3e Edition* (Paris: Editions du Seuil, 1958), p. 271; Gérard Massin, "Le Patronat Français et le système de Santé," Mémoire de fin d'assistanat, Ecole Nationale de la Santé Publique, Rennes, 1978.
33 Hatzfeld, *Du Paupérisme à la Sécurité Sociale*, pp. 137, 139, 140; see also Massin, "Le Patronat Français et le système de Santé."
34 On the 1910 law and the workers' identity card, see Hatzfeld, *Du Paupérisme à la Sécurité Sociale*, pp. 241–2. For worker objections to pluralistic funds, see statement of Antonelli, SFIO representative, Commission Chauveau, 26 Oct 1925, Ass. S. 6, Archives, 1930. On the class struggle, Rapport Grinda, p. 55, Ass. S. 5, Archives, 1930. On union complaints about social insurance administration, see *Le Peuple*, 15 Nov. 1923, 6 Nov 1923, 31 Oct 1923, 25 July 1923, also *l'Atelier* 1 Sept 1923, 29 Sept 1923, and other union papers, Ass. S. 6, Archives, 1930.
35 CGTU, "Les Assurances sociales et la classe ouvrière," cited in Lefranc *Les Expériences Syndicales en France*, p. 312.
36 Goguel notes that it was really the employer rather than the communist opposition that was crucial to felling the law, *Politique des Partis sous la IIIe République*, p. 272). Union membership plummeted from a high of 2.4 million in 1919 to 600,000 in 1920, due to violent repression of strikes. By 1926, the figures had increased to 1 million, but the labor movement was split, and would not regain its strength of 1919 until the mid-1930s, p. 208. The argument here, however, is that the impact of the unions on the reform depended on the logic of the parliament not on the membership figures.
37 Dumont cited in Douglas E. Ashford, *Policy and Politics in France: Living with Uncertainty* (Philadelphia: Temple University Press, 1982), p. 228.
38 Under the law, the funds were allowed to provide in-kind benefits and to own hospital establishments, but in order to encourage the CSMF to approve conventions, the funds agreed to waive this right, unless a local health center was approved by the local medical union.

39	Unfortunately, no standard source on social insurance gives the percentage of state financing. In 1919, under the system of state subsidies to the mutuals, the state contribution was 4.45 million francs, or 4.6 percent of receipts and 6.7 percent of expenditures – a much lower rate than in Sweden or Switzerland. Hatzfeld states that the effective total contribution rate was 6.5 percent as opposed to 8 percent (4 percent + 4 percent), as a result of income classes. He points to this dramatic decrease (from 10 percent to 6.5 percent contributions) as well as the tax benefits to industry granted by the Tardieu-Raynaud-Laval government in order to explain why employers were willing to concede to the 1930 law. See *Du Paupérisme à la Sécurité Sociale*, pp. 151, 153–4.

40	Lavielle, *Histoire de la Mutualité*, pp. 78, 112.

41	On the 1915–1920 campaign against national health insurance in the United States, Roy Lubove writes, "The medical profession emerged from the struggle with an awareness of its political power and a determination to use it to protect its corporate self-interest. This was equated with resistance to proposals for change in the financing and organization of medical services," *The Struggle for Social Security* (Cambridge, MA: Harvard University Press, 1968), p. 89.

42	Pierre Laroque, Director General of Social Security in 1945, "La Sécurité Sociale de 1944 à 1951," *Revue Française des Affaires Sociales*, 25, no. 2 (April–June 1971), p. 11.

43	Ehrmann, *Organized Business*, p. 117, cf. chapters 2 and 3.

44	See Steffen, *Régulation Politique et Stratégies Professionnelles*; Hatzfeld, *Grand Tournant de la Médecine Libérale*; Paul Cibrie (President of the CSMF), *Syndicalisme Médical* (Paris: Confédération des Syndicats Médicaux Français (CSMF), 1954), pp. 22–5.

45	The main sources on the politics of the Social Security Ordinances are Henry C. Galant, *Histoire Politique de la Sécurité Sociale Française. 1945–1952*, Cahiers de la Fondation Nationale des Sciences Politiques No. 76 (Paris: Librairie Armand Colin, 1955) and Laroque, "La Sécurité Sociale de 1944 a 1951," as well as the press archives of the Fondation Nationale des Sciences Politiques, hereafter abbreviated as *Dossiers de Presse*, DdP. The government archives pertaining to the Ordinances, including the materials from the commissions of interest-group and governmental representatives that met in the summer of 1945, are now missing. To compensate for this gap, interviews were conducted with M. Pierre Laroque, former Director of Social Security, 18 May 1984, and M. Clément Michel, former Director of the Federation of Social Security Organizations (FNOSS), 7 June 1984 and 18 October 1985.

46	Under the Social Insurance Law of 1930, the funds were to be administered temporarily by a Conseil de Direction whose members and president were designated by the Minister of Labor after being presented by mutual societies and the unions. Eventually, the administration was to be taken over by elected administrative boards (Conseils d'Administration), but such elections were never organized. Antoinette Catrice-Lorey, *Dynamique Interne de la Sécurité Sociale. 2nd Ed.* (Paris: Centre des Recherches en Sciences Sociales, 1982).

47	By 1946, 53 percent of the population was covered by social security, Dorion & Guionnet, "La Sécurité Sociale," p. 12. Gradual extensions of the scheme have brought coverage to approximately 99 percent of the population by 1980, Victor G. Rodwin, "Management without objectives: the French health policy gamble," in A. Maynard and G. McLachlan, eds., *The Public/ Private Mix for Health* (London: The Nuffield Provincial Hospitals Trust,

1982), pp. 293–4. The vast majority of the insured belong to the general scheme, but the system is noted for its many separate schemes and special provisions for certain occupational groups, beginning with agricultural workers, who were allowed to keep the scheme established in 1928 rather than being incorporated into the general system. Sickness and maternity coverage was added for civil servants (who continued to benefit from a special retirement scheme) and government workers in 1947; to students in 1949; to "invalids, widows and orphans of war" in 1950; to "permanent employees of local government" in 1951; to "performing artists" in 1961; to "journalists paid by the line" in 1963; to "artists of plastic and graphic arts" in 1964; and to artists more generally in 1975. Political conflicts caused separate retirement schemes for the self-employed to be introduced in 1948, although the scheme for agricultural employers was not introduced until 1952. In 1961, sickness and maternity insurance was added for the self-employed in agriculture; in 1966, sickness and maternity schemes for artisans, for merchants and industrialists, and for the liberal professions were added.

48 Under previous legislation, work accidents had been covered by the private companies, and employers paid premiums according to the risks of their firm. This portion of the law entailed the greatest change.

49 PV 9 July, 1945 cited in Galant, *Histoire Politique de la Sécurité Sociale Française*, pp. 58–59.

50 Lefranc, *Expériences Syndicales en France*, p. 321; cf. Lavielle, *Histoire de la Mutualité*, p. 139–140. Gaston Tessier, president of the CFTC and the Union of Family Allowances Funds (UCAF), was particularly vocal in his criticisms of the *caisse unique*. "The system in force, based on groupment by affinities, has known how to keep its human aspect, to fulfill a social service. The contacts between the directors of the funds, on the one hand, the insured and their families, on the other, constitutes something irreplaceable, presenting at once educational possibilities and effective control," cited in Lefranc, p. 320.

51 Duverger, *Institutions politiques et droit constitutionnel. Vol. 2. Le système politique français*, pp. 91–110.

52 According to Pierre Laroque, it was impossible for other left parties to appear undemocratic by refusing to hold elections, although it was feared that elections could be used as a pretext by the right for delaying the entire scheme (Interview, 18 May 1984). See also Galant, *Histoire Politique de la Sécurité Sociale Française*. The introduction of elections did not change the composition of the boards with respect to functional representation. The composition of boards of the social security funds would be: 2/3 representatives of employees, 1/9 of employers, 1/9 family associations, 1/9 persons "qualified" in social security. For the family allowances funds, the representation would be: 1/2 employees, 1/4 employers, 1/4 self-employed.

53 It was not intended at this point to include sickness insurance for the self-employed. However, because sickness insurance would be added to the pension scheme at a later point, by blocking the extension of the general scheme to the self-employed, this incident also prevented the emergence of a universal national health insurance scheme.

54 In *Le système politique français*, Duverger notes that this move to the right also brought down the MRP in the end. Leftist Catholics abandoned the party as it moved to the right; but the old right voters went to the new right parties, including the Poujadists.

55 Cited in Jean Meynaud, *Les Groupes de Pression en France*, Cahiers de la Fondation Nationale des Sciences Politiques No. 95 (Paris: Librairie Armand Colin, 1958), p. 92, cf. 91–3; see also Centre d'étude des Relations sociales

(C.E.R.S.) *Sécurité sociale et conflits de classes*, Economie et Humanisme (Paris: Les Editions Ouvrières, 1962).

56 The special scheme for farmers was not introduced, however, until 1952. Galant, *Histoire Politique de la Sécurité Sociale Française*, pp. 107–112; Laroque, "La Sécurité Sociale de 1944 a 1951;" Hatzfeld, *Grand Tournant de la Médecine Libérale* and *Du Paupérisme à la Sécurité Sociale*.

57 Cibrie, *Syndicalisme Médical*, p. 75.

58 The fee schedule would be based on a system of relative fees, called a "nomenclature" that would be set by ministerial decree. The nomenclature contained multipliers and coefficients for each procedure, whereby the multipliers would establish the relative value of the procedure, but the coefficient (or *lettre clé*) would be necessary to translate the relative value into a monetary value. For example, in 1966, an appendectomy was valued at 50K, where K is the coefficient for a surgical procedure, whereas more complicated surgical procedures may be valued as high as 300K. The conventions would give the absolute value for the fees in a given local area, by setting a monetary value for each of the coefficients. In 1966, K was valued at 4.25 francs throughout France. Consultations, on the other hand, under the coefficient C were valued at 13 francs in Paris, 12 in Marseilles, Lyon, and Aix, and 11 in the rest of France. An unusual feature of the French fee schedule is that some fees depend upon whether the physician is a GP or a specialist, and some procedures may be performed only by specialists; this both reflects and exacerbates the antagonisms between French GPs and specialists, which are reputed to be more severe than in other Western European nations. Glaser, *Paying the Doctor*, p. 43.

59 Galant, *Histoire Politique de la Sécurité Sociale Française*, p. 17.

60 There is some controversy about the decision to regulate doctors' fees through negotiations. An ordinance of 3 March 1945 envisioned that tariffs would be approved by the Ministers of Labor, Public Health, and Finances: if conventions were not passed, these ministers would set applicable tariffs directly. The government view is that such an ordinance was "normal" in the context of the generalized price regulations of the war, but that it could not be simply extended into the peacetime period with no renegotiation. Instead, the administration allowed the social security funds to negotiate a solution with the CSMF in the presence of the Conseil Supérieur des Assurances Sociales, as part of the preparation of the Social Security Ordinances. As stated in the introduction to the Ordinance of 19 October: "In the presence of this accord, it has appeared preferable to abandon the formula of 3 March 1945 for one that gave satisfaction to the ensemble of interested parties. It is hoped that this modification will permit a loyal and fruitful collaboration between the medical profession and the social security organisms," *Journal Officiel* (JO) 20 Oct 1945: 6722. But the view of the funds was that the government bowed to pressure from the CSMF in order to assure swift passage of the law (Interview, 7 June 1984, Clément Michel, former Director of the FNOSS). Dr. Paul Cibrie wrote that his lobbying efforts were aided by his personal acquaintance with the Minister of Labor (Parodi), through the Secretary General of the *Conseil National Economique*, Cibrie, *Syndicalisme Médical*, p. 75.

61 *Le Monde*, 8 December 1945; *L'Epoque*, 30 March 1946; *Combat* 8 July 1946. M. Ambroise Croizat, PCF Minister of Labor, describes this campaign in a press conference (29 December 1945, Ministère d'Information, Hors Série No. 76 DdP, 421/01). Some of the attention to these criticisms, it

should be pointed out, may have been connected to fears that the social security administration would become a power base for the CGT.

62 "Médecine, santé publique, population," described in Haroun Jamous, *Sociologie de la Décision: la réforme des études médicales et des structures hospitalières* (Paris: Editions du Centre Nationale de la Recherche Scientifique, 1969), p. 53.

63 *Le Monde*, 2 April 1946. Debré's statement was accompanied by a declaration by *Le Monde*'s medical editor, Dr. F. Bonnet-Roy, to the effect that the paper had felt obligated to publish this view in the interests of impartiality.

64 Galant, *Histoire Politique de la Sécurité Sociale Française*, pp. 59–60.

65 Hatzfeld, *Grand Tournant de la Médecine Libérale*, pp. 78–103.

66 Hogarth, *Payment of the Physician*, p. 157

67 In 1948 and 1950, the CSMF actually withdrew its signature some eleven days after signing an agreement. Hatzfeld, *Grand Tournant de la Médecine Libérale*; *Réforme* 11 Feb 1950; *Action Familiale et Sociale*, No. 2, Nov. 1956.

68 "Les Médecins parlent de la médecine," *Esprit*, *25*, special issue no. 247 (February 1957), p. 204.

69 See Gérard Adam, *Atlas des élections sociales en France*, Cahiers de la Fondation Nationale des Sciences Politiques, Partis et Elections (Paris: Librairie Armand Colin, 1964); Steffen, *Régulation Politique et Stratégies Professionnelles*; *Dossiers de Presse*, 421/04 (1949–1965), e.g., *Combat* 17 Jan 1950, *Réforme* 11 Feb 1950.

70 *Revue de la Sécurité Sociale*, March 1957, p. 12, cf. 9–12; Interview, 7 June 1984, with Clément Michel, ex-director of the FNOSS. These events are described in Hatzfeld, *Grand Tournant de la Médecine Libérale*.

71 Note on tariffs 23 October 1959, and letter from Minister of Labor to Prime Minister, 13 October 1959, SAN 7515, in "Travaux préparatoire à la réforme de la Sécurité Sociale de 1960," (SAN 7514–7519), "Sécurité Sociale-Réformes," (SS 2711–2), "Honoraires," (SS 7082–4, SAN 7557), Direction de la Sécurité Sociale, Ministère des Affaires Sociales et de la Santé, Archives Nationales, referred to as "Archives, 1960."

72 Steffen *Régulation Politique et Stratégies Professionnelles*; *Action Familiale et Social*, No. 2, November 1956.

73 Hogarth, *Payment of the Physician*, p. 158.

74 Jean-Jacques Dupeyroux, "Nouvelles Remarques sur la réforme du 12 mai 1960," *Droit Social*, *23*, no. 11 (Nov 1960), pp. 567–572; *L'Année Politique* (Paris: Presses Universitaires de France, 1957), pp. 180 ff.

75 The old conditions of "fortune" of the patient and "fame" of the doctor were maintained, but now the criteria for these exemptions were to be set forth in decrees. That is, the decision regarding "fortune" would depend on whether the patient had achieved a certain occupational grade, such as general director of an enterprise, while the "fame" of the doctor would depend on his or her titles and degrees.

76 Hatzfeld, *Grand Tournant de la Médecine Libérale*, p. 158. As one doctor said, "'Sirs, you are in the process of creating a divorce between Paris and the provinces,'" Dr. Chaumeil, cited in Hatzfeld, p. 161.

77 *Paris-Presse-Intransigent*, 3/4 Feb, p. 1, DdP, 421–04; 2 Feb 1957. There were also more nuanced articles and some in support of the scheme, but all stressed the opposition of the medical profession, (e.g., *Le Monde*, 1 Feb 1957, 15 Feb 1957, 23 Feb 1957; *La Vie Française*, 7 Dec 1956; *Le Figaro*, 13 Dec 1956; *France Observateur*, 20 Dec 1956; *La Croix*, 16 Dec 1956).

78 On CSMF, *Médecin de France*, March 1957, p. 10706, cited in Hatzfeld,

Grand Tournant de la Médecine Libérale, p. 166. *Le Monde*, 13/14 January 1957, 31 January 1957 on the *Ordre* and the Academy. The *Ordre des Médecins* was particularly concerned that it had not been consulted by the government, arguing that controls on doctors' fees interfered with patient's free choice of doctor and with professional discipline – the proper domain of the Ordre. When, in mid-1956, the CSMF had agreed to negotiate with Gazier, it had been embarrassed almost immediately by the intervention of the Ordre, another case where competition between representative associations created difficulties in reaching compromises, Hatzfeld, p. 141–2. At the same time, the Rhône branch had threatened scission from the CSMF, Hatzfeld, p. 147.

79 *Le Monde*, 6 Feb 1957. Alternate projects were deposited by the MRP's Bacon (*Le Monde*, 13 April 1957) and Bernard Lafay (RGR) (*Le Monde*, 31 Jan 1957), and were more flexible on the question of exemptions.

80 *Le Monde*, 12/13/May 1957.

81 Philip M. Williams, *Crisis and Compromise: Politics in the Fourth Republic 3rd Ed* (Hamden, CT: Archon Books, 1964); Stanley Hoffmann "Paradoxes of the French Political Community," in Hoffmann, ed., *In Search of France* (Cambridge, MA: Harvard University Press, 1976), pp. 1–117.

82 Rapporteur of the Commission de la Santé cited and elaborated on in *La réforme hospitalière*, Notes et Etudes Documentaires, no. 2555, Série Français CDXII, Série Sociale CV, 9 Juillet 1959 (Paris: La Documentation Française, 1959); Jean Imbert, "La réforme hospitalière," *Droit Social*, *21*, no. 9–10 (Sept–Oct 1958), pp. 496–505.

83 Duverger, *Le système politique français*, p. 123; MacRae, *Parliament, Parties and Society in France*, pp. 4–10; Didier Maus, "Parliament in the Fifth Republic 1958–1988," in Godt, ed., *Policymaking in France* (London and NY: Pinter, 1989): p. 13; Vincent Wright, *The Government and Politics of France. 2nd Ed.* (London: Hutchinson, 1983), pp. 129–136.

83a MacRae, *Parliament, Parties and Society in France*.

84 On decree laws, Duverger, *Le système politique français*, pp. 79, 112–3. The institutional changes stressed by various writers depends on their analysis of the problems of the Fourth Republic. Duverger stresses the electoral laws and the weak political parties, as well as the failure of the parties to incorporate new social groupings and party militants, as does MacRae. Debré and de Gaulle also located the problem with the parties, but focused on the *ministrables* (those MPs who were eligible for ministerial posts) and on the weak executive. Writers interested in the power of the local notables – for example, Wright – underscore the end of the *cumul des mandats*, and the fact that this separation is not fully enforced in practice. See note 83 for references.

85 *Avant-Projet de loi, July 1957, Relatif à la réforme de l'enseignement médicale*, Comité Interministériel d'Etude des problèmes de l'Enseignement médical, de la structure hospitalière et de l'action sanitaire et sociale, pp. 2, 7, DGS 498 in "Comité Interministériel d'étude des problèmes de l'enseignement médical, de la structure hospitalière et de l'action sanitaire et sociale, 1956–1962," F 17 511, "Réforme Hospitalo-Universitaire," SAN 1781, "Conseil Supérieur des Hôpitaux," DGS 497–498, SAN 1601, Direction des Hôpitaux, Ministère des Affairs Sociales et de la Santé, Archives Nationales, hereafter referred to as "Archives, 1958."

86 In the CHU's, private consultations were limited to two afternoons a week, private beds to 8 percent of beds, no more than 5 percent going to the *chef de service*, Albert Salon, *Les Centres Hospitaliers et Universitaires*, Notes et

Etudes Documentaires, No. 3373, 15 Mars 1967 (Paris: La Documentation Français, 1967). The salaries of part-time hospital physicians would be paid out of the total sum of patient fees (the *masse d'honoraires* that previously had been the privilege of the *chef de service* to distribute), but could not constitute more than 60 percent of full-time salaries, Stephan, *Economie et Pouvoir Médical*; Jean Imbert, *L'Hôpital Français* (Paris: Presses Universitaires de France, 1972). Regional hospital centers (CHR) and certain hospital centers, the two highest categories of hospitals, would be required to appoint radiologists, pathologists, and anesthetists on a full-time basis. The remaining hospital doctors would be encouraged to "integrate" themselves voluntarily into the full-time system through salary benefits. On the reform see, Imbert "Les ordonnances de décembre 1958 sur les établissements de soins," *Droit Social*, 22, no. 6 (June 1959), pp. 356–364; Blanpain, *National Health Insurance and Health Resources*, pp. 103–106; Jamous, *Sociologie de la Décision*; *La réforme hospitalière*, Notes et Etudes Documentaires, no. 2555.

87 Galant, *Histoire Politique de la Sécurité Sociale*, pp. 36–7; see also, Antoinette Catrice-Lorey, *Dynamique Interne de la Sécurité Sociale* (Paris: Centre des Recherches en Sciences Sociales, 1980), pp. 44–5 ff.; Jacques Doublet, "La Sécurité Sociale et son évolution [octobre 1951-juin 1961]," *Revue Française des Affaires Sociales*, 25, no. 2 (April-June 1971), pp. 26–60. Typical conflicts between the regional directors and the local administrative boards are described in a long letter from the regional inspector general, sent under a cover letter from the regional director. The letter complains that there are too many local administrative boards and difficulties in applying legislation, and demands a reduction in the number of elected representatives, parity between employers and employees, an increase in the number of qualified persons named by the Minister of Labor, wants the Director Personnel to have a certain independence from the administrative boards, and that preventative health and social measures (*action sanitaire et sociale*) be controlled at a higher level. The regional director also demands that special regimes be eliminated even if beneficiaries will complain, as they "manifest little good will for administering organizations of such importance," 21 December 1959, SAN 7517, in "Travaux préparatoire à la réforme de la Sécurité Sociale de 1960," SAN 7514–7519, "Sécurité Sociale-Réformes," SS 2711–2, "Honoraires," SS 7082–4, SAN 7557, Direction de la Sécurité Sociale, Ministère des Affaires Sociales et de la Santé, Archives Nationales, hereafter referred to as "Archives, 1960."

88 The threat of local health centers was less direct; exemptions would not be limited to a fixed percentage of the profession; doctors' fees would not be indexed to the minimum wage.

89 Doublet "La Sécurité Sociale et son évolution [octobre 1951-juin 1961]," p. 37; Glaser, *Paying the Doctor*, p. 132–3; Hatzfeld, *Grand Tournant de la Médecine Libérale*, p. 178; Jamous, *Sociologie de la Décision*; François Steudler, "Médecine libérale et Conventionnement," *Sociologie du Travail*, IX, no. 2 (April-June 1977), p. 190; Claudine Herzlich, "The Evolution of Relations between French Physicians and the State from 1880 to 1980," *Sociology of Health and Illness*, 4, no. 3 (1982), p. 248. Although all of these scholars agree that the decrees and the political situation of the Fifth Republic were the immediate cause for the health reforms, most go on to look for underlying causes – modernization, younger doctors, rural doctors.

90 In a letter to the Prime Minister, Bacon explained his reasons for linking the administrative reform with the measures taken to guarantee 80 percent

reimbursement for the insured through controls on doctors' fees. "Certainly, it appeared to me useful, in order to assure a more efficient functioning of the public service of social security, to restore the authority of the state equally in this domain. But the public, which generally has only a limited interest in technical measures concerning the functioning of social security, attaches a greater importance to reforms relating to benefits." Consequently, he suggests, the administrative reforms should not be separated from the reform containing improvements in benefits. Further, Bacon suggests that an information campaign be used to present the reforms to the public. "Public opinion is not sufficiently enlightened on problems of social security: One does not render adequate homage to the study of the services that it renders to the population and one grants too much credit to facile critiques, founded on generalizations of isolated cases. . . . It is advisable to underline to the public the advantages that the ensemble of employees may extract from the initiatives of the government." Bacon concluded by advising that such information be disseminated only once the entire reform had been prepared: "Only when the ensemble of envisioned measures have been finalized definitively, should information be diffused to the public with the aim of making clear the utility and interest of the reform," 16 September 1959, reference number W 2447, SAN 7515, Archives 1960.

91 See the description in Thoenig of de Gaulle's failed attempts to undercut local power with regional reform in 1964, the links between the new elites and the regional level versus the old elites and the local level, and the tension resulting from the fact that "local political power no longer represents relevant political power" but, at the same time, it has proven impossible to replace, "La relation entre le centre et la périphérie," p. 77.

92 Both Debré and Bacon kept their committee deliberations secret. Debré notes in his autobiography that as a condition for presiding over the commission, he had demanded that the commission be composed of "persons chosen for their competence and desire for reform and not the representatives of corporations, unions, diverse groupings, or administrations," *L'honneur de vivre. Témoinage.* (Paris: Hermann et Stock), p. 348. Bacon, too, avoided interest-group consultation and information leaks so successfully that both the FNOSS and the CSMF demanded concrete information on the "rumored" social security reform as late as December 1959 – at a time when Bacon insisted the reform should be introduced in January 1960. Circulaire B76 1959 FNOSS, 18 December 1959, SS 7083, Archives, 1960.

93 Cited in a letter from Minister of Labor to M. le Directeur Régional de la Sécurité Sociale, 14 December 1959, SAN 7515, Archives, 1960; cf. SS 7083.

94 24 February 1960, SAN 7517, Archives, 1960.

95 Florence Lemaire, "La réforme hospitalo-universitaire," Mémoire présenté a l'Institute d'Etudes Politiques de l'Université de Paris, 1964, pp. 115–6.

96 Reported by Dr. Jonchères in *Médecin de France*, cited in Hatzfeld, *Grand Tournant de la Médecine Libérale*, p. 178. Robert Debré also mentions de Gaulle's lack of sympathy for the profession, *L'honneur de vivre*, p. 355.

97 *Le Monde*, 19 May 1960, 20 May 1960. Cf. Doublet "La Sécurité Sociale et son évolution [octobre 1951-juin 1961]," p. 41. Concerning the suggestion that the medical profesion could sign a convention with the government, Minister Bacon replied rather sarcastically, "It does not come within the scope of a professional category, however responsible or important as it may be, to set its own legislative or regulatory status through a direct convention with the public authorities," cited in Hatzfeld, *Grand Tournant de la Médecine Libérale*, p. 183.

98 *Le Monde* 19/20 May 1960, cf 15/16 May, 17 May, 20 May and 21 Sept 1960.
99 Dr. Jonchères, president of the CSMF, stated on July 2, "The majority of the unions in the provinces have the impression that the decree is directed especially against the large departments like the Seine and the Rhône and against certain others hostile to all conventions. And many are the fellow members of the profession that tell us that they have had enough of fighting for the Seine and for the Rhône," cited in Hatzfeld, *Grand Tournant de la Médecine Libérale*, p. 188.
100 Hatzfeld, *Grand Tournant de la Médecine Libérale*, p. 178.
101 The funds agreed not to start local health centers without the prior approval of the local medical union, and not to sign individual conventions unless all avenues of collective bargaining had been exhausted. As a concession to the funds, the CSMF agreed to allow direct third-party payment in certain cases and the extension of all conventions for three months after expiration to prevent interruptions in reimbursements at 80 percent if negotiations were slowed. XXX (anonymous author), "Les rapports entre le corps médical et la sécurité sociale depuis le décret du 12 mai 1960," *Droit Social*, 25, no. 3 (Mar 1962), p. 175.
102 The FMF acquired its definite status in 1968, and now claims to represent 13,000 doctors, compared with the 20–25,000 enrolled in the CSMF, Stephan, *Economie et Pouvoir Médical*, pp. 38–9. Figures on French unions vary wildly, however. See Roland Mane, "Où va le syndicalisme médical?" *Droit Social*, 25, no. 9–10 (Sept–Oct 1962), pp. 516–529; Jean Savatier, "Une Profession libérale face au mouvement contemporain de socialisation," *Droit Sociale*, 25, no. 9–10 (Sept–Oct 1962), pp. 477–9. Not only did new unions emerge, but political "groupings," such as the Groupement d'Etudes et de Recherches pour une Médecine Moderne (GERMM, for negotiation), or Groupement International de défense et d'organisation de la Médecine (GIDOM, against negotiation), C.E.R.S., *Sécurité sociale et conflits de classes*; *France Observateur*, 9 June 1960.
103 On the position of CGT, SAN 7517, Archives, 1960; see *Droit Social*, 1960, no. 3, March, p. 179, and no. 4 April, p. 242 for other union opinions. The CGC, in an interesting parallel to the Swedish white-collar union TCO (see Chapter 5 and the Seven Crowns reform), was concerned about the individual convention as an infringement on the "free choice of doctor," and preferred a reasonable reimbursement fee schedule: "The CGC is absolutely opposed to anything that could lead to the introduction of two or more categories of doctors, to be distinguished according to whether their fees would or would not be reimbursed by social security. This would inevitably interfere with the free choice of doctor, to which we are particularly attached," 25 February 1960, SAN 7517.

There was a general feeling among the funds that the controls on doctors were insufficient and would not guarantee 80 percent reimbursement, and at the same time that the funds were being pressured to go along with the administrative reforms. They noted further that it was useless to hope to rally the insured to oppose the government reorganization, because the insured "are not really interested in the administrative organization of Social Security." M. Texier cited in the minutes of the meeting of the administrative board of the local social security fund of Cher, March 1960. See also minutes from the FNOSS meeting of 4 March 1960, SAN 7516.
104 File on "AVIS," artisans and merchants contains statements from local chambers of commerce and small unions – for example, Syndicat National

des Selliers, Bourreliers, Garnisseurs, Litiers, Tapissiers de France et Professions, SAN 7517, Archives 1960. Refer to Doublet, "La Sécurité Sociale et son Évolution [octobre 1951-juin 1961]," pp. 41–2 for details on the special service.

105 *Volonté*, June 1960, no. 143, p. 1. But the editorial also makes clear that there could be more cooperation between these groups, to fight the "common dangers that menace the structures of the private economy," which is hampered by indifference, "as they imagine that their problems are particular, although they flow from the application of the same principles of thought . . . Throughout France, the CGPME is fighting a tough battle against the technocrats and their good apostles . . . and the return to a spirit of 'Dirigisme exterminateur,'" pp. 1–2.

106 As early as 1953, in fact, the employer representatives in the funds and in the FNOSS had disagreed with the accords reached by the CSMF and the FNOSS, arguing that they entailed large increases in the tariffs without sufficient guarantees that doctors would limit themselves to these fees. *Conseil National du Patronat*, no. 159, April 1957, pp. 7–9. At that time, George Villiers, the president of the CNPF, stated that "the CNPF would support the Gazier proposal only if the clause pertaining to financial restraints were retained. This is not to say, however, that the CNPF fully supported the reform. He disputed the tendentious and political interpretation that has been made by certain communiqués and certain journals that presents a position on strictly technical points . . . as approval of the whole project and its fundamental principles. This utilization shows that, in certain quarters, one is less interested in the regulation of a difficult technical problem than in the realization of a new stage in the path of state intervention. The CNPF intends to keep itself outside of a debate on the regulatory modalities of application and sanctions, for conventions that affect a liberal profession that it does not represent. It remains attentive only to the defense of our economy against a particularly inopportune augmentation of charges. But it does not wish that its abstention, in a debate that is in large part exterior to it, may place in doubt the respect and sympathy that it carries for the memory of those that have created the grandeur of French medicine and to their successors that continue to assure it an uncontested influence," *Conseil National du Patronat Français*, no. 157, April 1957, p. 7. So the CNPF in March 1957 did not wish to allow its support for cost control in the social security funds to be mistaken for full support for socialist measures to control the medical profession. The CNPF was not willing, however, to go beyond a restrained expression of its "respect and sympathy" for the profession. Its views are not recorded in the Archives relating to the 1960 decrees, but its former position was certainly known to the administration. There is no reference in its journal, the *Conseil National du Patronat Français*, in 1960, pertaining to the reforms. In 1961, however, the CNPF began publishing critiques of social security that became increasingly critical of the role of doctors' fees in inflating medical costs. See *Patronat Français*, June 1965 and December 1968; Steffen, *Régulation Politique et Stratégies Professionnelles*; B. Jobert and J.F. Paoli, "Les syndicats médicaux et la Sécurité sociale," *Prévenir*, No. 5, special issue, "Sécurité sociale et Santé," Marseille (March 1982), pp. 109–115.

107 In the Seine, 2,200 doctors had signed individual conventions, out of a total of 4,500 doctors enrolled in medical unions and 8,000 practicing physicians. By 1962, 86 conventions were in place for 77 departments, covering 8.6 out

of 13 million insured. Of the 12,874 doctors in departments without conventions, 5,330, or 41.4 percent, had signed individual conventions, although the percentage varied widely by region (for the Seine, the figure was 43 percent). For physicians in "liberal" practice, 29,350 out of 36,900 doctors, or 79.5 percent, were covered by conventions. *Droit Social*, March 1962, No. 3, pp. 176–8; figures are the same as in the report of the Commission prévue par l'article 24 du Décret du 12 Mai 1960, SS 2712, Archives, 1960. Christian Prieur, "L'évolution historique de l'organisation des relations entre la médecine libérale et les régimes d'assurance maladie: 1930–1976," *Revue Trimestrielle de Droit Sanitaire et Sociale*, *12*, no. 46 (April–June 1976), p. 313, gives figures of 70 percent and 80 percent of doctors under conventions for 1963 and 1970, respectively, but does not specify whether he refers only to doctors in liberal practice or to all doctors.

108 For the general regime, the cost of reimbursing doctors' fees increased from 578.8 million new francs in 1960 to 889.7 in 1961, or by 53.7 percent. The total increase for medical fees between 1959 and 1961 was 80.9 percent. For surgical fees, the figures were 30.8 percent and 75.6 percent for the 1960–1961 and the 1959–1961 increases, respectively. SS 2712, Archives, 1960.

109 In 1962, exemptions averaged less than 10 percent of cases, *Droit Social*, March 1962, No. 3, pp. 176–8; figures are the same as in the report of the Commission prévue par l'article 24 du Décret du 12 Mai 1960, SS 2712, Archives, 1960.

110 SS 2712, Archives, 1960; Glaser, *Paying the Doctor*, p. 134.

111 Prieur, "L'évolution historique de l'organisation des relations entre la médecine libérale et les régimes d'assurance maladie: 1930–1976," pp. 317–8.

112 See Godt, "Social Policy in France."

113 The CNPF would hold the nine employer seats. The unions would split the nine employee seats between them, with three seats going to the CGT, two to the CFDT, two to the FO, one to the CFTC, and one to the CGC, Steffen, *Régulation Politique et Stratégies Professionnelles*.

114 The Debré reform was slow to take effect. There were problems with the interministerial coordination required by the reform, and with local level implementation. Nevertheless, the reform was an important first attempt to modernize the hospital system and to introduce elements of coordinated planning aside from the inclusion of hospitals in the more general five-year plans. See Salon, *Les Centres Hospitaliers et Universitaires*. The reform was responsible for the creation of 15,000 full-time hospital posts between 1965 and 1980, J.F. Lacronique, "The French Health Care System," in Maynard and McLachlan, *The Public/Private Mix for Health*, pp. 265–288. This growth in the number of salaried physicians changed the composition of the profession. From 11 percent of physicians in full-time salaried practice in 1956, the percentage increased to 35 percent in 1975, whereas out of the remaining 65 percent, nearly half had some form of salaried activity. In the CHUs, 39.2 percent of the medical personnel held full-time posts in 1965; 81.34 percent by 1972. For public hospitals, the figures were 10 percent and 23.5 percent for 1965 and 1972, respectively, Steudler, "Médecine libérale et Conventionnement." Stephan describes the changes in terms of the reduction of the proportion of physicians in "liberal" practice: 92 percent in 1954, 75 percent in 1971, less than 66 percent in 1975, *Economie et Pouvoir Médical*.

115 A continuing issue since the passage of the Debré reform was the relationship of private clinics to public hospitals. It was claimed that the greater control on hospital expansion introduced by the Ordinances of 11 December 1958

had a greater impact on the expansion of public hospitals. This, along with the more advantageous social security reimbursement for care in private clinics (where doctors' fees are billed separately, rather than at a flat rate as in the public sector, in which public fees are supposed to be based on conventions, but are much lower), resulted in a greater growth of private clinics during the 1960s, despite the measures taken to control and coordinate this growth. Between 1970 and 1980, the private sector grew by 15,000 beds, whereas the public sector increased by only 51,000. Some of the difference is accounted for by the fact that efforts to eliminate beds have been more successful in the public sector. Lacronique, "The French Health Care System." Between 1963 and 1978, the private sector grew from 26.4 percent of total bed capacity to 34.3 percent, Jean de Kervasdoué, "La Politique de l'Etat en Matière d'Hospitalisation Privée, 1962–1978," *Annales Economiques 16* (1980): 23–57; see Emile Lévy, *Hospitalisation Publique, Hospitalisation Privée*, Laboratoire d'économie et de gestion des organisations de Santé (LEGOS), Actions Thématiques Programmées A.T.P. No. 22, Paris: Editions du Centre National de la Recherche Scientifique 1979, for comparisons of public and private sectors. The 1970 Hospital Law was intended to encourage better cooperation between the public and the private sectors, new interhospital structures, and more flexible management. It introduced authorization procedures for hospital construction and expansion that were to be based on a national plan, or *Carte Sanitaire*. The prerogatives of hospital directors were made stronger at the expense of those of the administrative boards. See Blanpain, *National Health Insurance and Health Resources*; Ministère de la Santé publique et de la Sécurité sociale, *Pour une politique de la Santé. Rapports présentées à Robert Boulin. Tome III. L'hôpital*, Présenté par M. Roger Grégoire, Conseilleur d'Etat (Paris: Documentation Française, 1971); Imbert, *L'Hôpital Français*.

116 Under the Socialist government of François Mitterrand, it was decided to eliminate the right of hospital physicians to treat private patients. Private beds were to be phased out by 31 December 1983, private consultations by January 1986. These deadlines were later extended to 31 March 1984 and January 1987. These reforms were later reversed. Demichel, 1983; Loi 28 October 1982, décret 29 December 1982, JO 29 October 1982, p. 3268; JO 30 December 1982; *Le Monde* 15 January 1983; *Le Monde* 14 December 1983; Paul Godt, "Health Care: The Political Economy of Social Policy," in Godt, ed., *Policy-Making in France* (London and NY: Pinter Publishers, 1989), pp. 191–207.

117 Imbert, *L'Hôpital Français*, pp. 12–3, points to the role of parliamentary doctors in weakening the 1970 law, noting that three-quarters of the deputies present after the second parliamentary session on the law were doctors, out of a total of 30–35 deputies present. They managed to preserve the *"honoraires forfaitaires"* (special fees charged at hospitals to ensure that hospital fees were commensurate with fees in liberal practice, which were paid to the hospital whether or not these services were actually performed) and to make the definitions of the function of the public hospital more narrow, specifying that the public hospital would not exercise a monopoly on institutional care.

118 For a discussion of the effects of this regime shift on the relative power of several French interest groups, including farmers, artisans, and shopkeepers, see Suzanne Berger, "Regime and Interest Representation: The French Traditional Middle Classes," in Berger, ed., *Organizing Interests in Western Europe* (Cambridge: Cambridge University Press, 1981), pp. 88–9.

Chapter 4

1 The term "gatekeeper" is taken from Deborah Stone's article, "Physicians as Gatekeepers," *Public Policy 27* (1979), pp. 227–254.

2 The earlier Swiss confederation had its roots in an alliance of cantons from the thirteenth and fourteenth centuries. Although these cantons formed a representative body, the Federal Diet, there was no federal government, as such. Nor were national military or administrative institutions created or customs barriers lifted. After the French invasion, national unification was imposed in 1803. With the collapse of the Napoleonic Empire in 1815, however, the cantons returned to a confederational form of government, banding together in a confederal pact, and reconstituting the Diet. For a summary of this constitutional history, see Jean-François Aubert, "Switzerland," in David Butler and Austin Ranney, eds., *Referendums. A Comparative Study of Practice and Theory* (Washington, DC: American Enterprise Institute, 1978), pp. 39–66; Erich Gruner, "Le fonctionnement du système représentatif dans la Conféderation Suisse," paper presented at the 7th World Congress, International Political Science Association, 18–23 September 1967; Alfred Maurer, "Switzerland," in Peter A, Köhler, Hans F. Zacher (eds), *The Evolution of Social Insurance. 1881–1981. Studies of Germany, France, Great Britain, Austria and Switzerland* (London & NY: Frances Pinter and St. Martin's Press, 1982), pp. 384–453; Christopher Hughes, *The Parliament of Switzerland* (London: Cassell, 1962).

3 On referendum and initiative, see Aubert, "Switzerland," pp. 39–40; Erich Gruner, *Die Parteien in der Schweiz* (Bern: Francke Verlag, 1969), pp. 49–55. The term "direct democracy" refers to two institutions: cantonal councils based on direct representation – all citizens with voting rights directly participate; and the referendum, which is actually semidirect, as citizens respond to legislation with yes or no votes. The referendum has its origins in the Middle Ages, was suppressed in the seventeenth and eighteenth centuries, and reemerged in the 1830s. A referendum was used to establish the Helvetic Republic in 1803 – and passed because there were more abstentions than yes or no votes.

4 On integration, see Karl W. Deutsch, *Die Schweiz als ein paradigmatischer Fall politischer Integration*, Staat und Politik no. 16 (Bern: Verlag Paul Haupt, 1976). On institutions and concordance, see Gerhard Lehmbruch, *Proporzdemokratie. Politisches System und politische Kultur in der Schweiz und in Österreich*, Recht und Staat Heft 335/336 (Tübingen: J.C.B. Mohr/ Paul Siebeck, 1967). On the referendum, see Aubert, "Switzerland," and *Exposé des institutions politiques de la Suisse à partir de quelques affaires controverseés, 2nd Ed.* (Lausanne: Edition Payot, 1983); Maurer, "Switzerland;" Leonhard Neidhart, *Plebiszit und pluralitäre Demokratie. Eine Analyse der Funktion des Schweizerischen Gesetzreferendums* (Bern: Francke Verlag, 1970). On changes in the parties and electoral laws, see Gruner, *Die Parteien in der Schweiz*, pp. 180–192.

5 Aubert, "Switzerland," p. 46. In other European nations, referenda are often called by executive governments and legislatures, and are often consultative, not mandatory as in Switzerland. Italy provides for popular referendum challenges, but a petition of 500,000 rather than 50,000 signatures is necessary. Butler and Ranney specifically mention that "Switzerland and Australia offer evidence for the proposition that referendums are essentially conservative in nature, though the lesson from the American States is less clear," *Referendums*, p. 16, more generally, 16–21.

6 On a 1987 referendum on health insurance, see Schweizerische Gesellschaft
   für praktische Sozialforschung (GFS), *Analyse der eidgenössischen Abstim-
   mung vom 6. Dezember 1987*, GFS Publication No. 34 (Bern, 1988); on Swiss
   voting, see GFS, *Analyse der Nationalratswahlen 1987*, Publication No. 33
   (Bern, 1987); on hypersensitivity to potential losses, see Daniel Kahneman,
   Paul Slovic, and Amos Tversky, eds., *Judgment under Uncertainty: Heuristics
   and Biases* (Cambridge: Cambridge University Press, 1982); Mancur Olson,
   The Logic of Collective Action (Cambridge, MA: Harvard University Press,
   1965); James Q. Wilson, *The Politics of Regulation* (NY: Basic Books, 1980),
   pp. 367–370.
7 Butler and Ranney, *Referendums*, p. 19.
8 Aubert, "Switzerland," p. 46.
9 Aubert, "Switzerland," p. 48–9.
10 On mechanisms for limiting the number of doctors see Gebert, "Cooperative
   Federalism or Muddling-Through." On the history of the Swiss Medical Association and the professionalization process, see Rudolf Braun, "Zur Professionalisierung des Ärztestandes in der Schweiz" in Jürgen Kocka, ed.,
   Bildungsbürgertum im 19. Jahrhundert (Stuttgart: Klett-Cotta, 1985), pp.
   332–357; Ramsey, "The Politics of Professional Monopoly in Nineteenth-
   Century Medicine;" Gerhard Kocher, *Verbandseinfluss auf die Gesetzgebung.
   Ärzteverbindung, Krankenkassenverbände und die Teilrevision 1964 des
   Kranken- und Unfallversicherungsgesetzes*, 2nd ed (Bern: Francke Verlag,
   1972), p. 25. Numbers of doctors and membership figures from Table 6.
11 This section draws heavily on the account found in Neidhart, *Plebiszit und
   pluralitäre Demokratie*, as well as "Zweite KUV-Vorlage vom 13. Juni 1911
   (am 4. Feb. 1912 vom Schweizervolk angenommen)," EDI 27, Bd 5 & 6,
   and "Assurances maladies et accidents: imprimés," 3340 (A) 1, Bd 91–
   97, Bundesarchiv, Bern, hereafter referred to as "Archives, 1911." See
   also Maurer, "Switzerland," and Jürg H. Sommer, *Das Ringen um soziale
   Sicherheit in der Schweiz*, Hochschule St. Gallen für Wirtschafts- und Sozialwissenschaften, Dissertation Nr. 703 (Diessenhofen: Verlag Rüegger, 1978).
12 "Botschaft des Bundestrates an die Bundesversammlung zu dem Entwurf
   eines Bundesgesetzes betreffend die Kranken- und Unfallversicherung (vom
   10. Dezember 1906)," 3340 (A) 1, Bd. 91, in Archives, 1911.
13 On Industrial accident laws, see Maurer, "Switzerland," p. 409; Paul
   Biedermann, *Die Entwicklung der Krankenversicherung in der Schweiz*,
   Diss., medizinische Fakultät der Universität Zürich, 1955, pp. 25–7. On parliamentary seats, see Gruner, *Die Parteien in der Schweiz*, pp. 184–5. On
   referendum results, Maurer, pp. 410–411.
14 Maurer, "Switzerland," pp. 410–411.
15 Neidhart, *Plebiszit und pluralitäre Demokratie*, pp. 150–151.
16 Gruner, *Die Parteien in der Schweiz*, p. 181.
17 *Amtliches Stenographisches Bulletin der schweizerischen Bundesversammlung.
   Nationalrat*, (Parliamentary debates of the National Council, *Stenbull NR*)
   1904, p. 199.
18 H. Stüssi, 1 June 1900, "Einige Gedanken zur Gestaltung der schweizerischen
   Kranken- und Unfallversicherung," EDI 27, Bd 5, Archives, 1911; Biedermann, *Entwicklung der Krankenversicherung in der Schweiz*, p. 28; Maurer,
   "Switzerland," p. 411; Glaser, *Paying the Doctor*, p. 35; Neidhart, *Plebiszit
   und pluralitäre Demokratie*, p. 150–1.
19 Under the *Lex Forrer*, sickness funds would cover the costs of medical
   treatment and would provide cash benefits equivalent to 60 percent of daily
   wages. The system would be financed by a combination of federal, employer

and employee contributions, totalling 0.6 percent, 1.4 percent, and 1.4 percent of wages, respectively. Employers would pay for a greater proportion of the associated system of industrial accident insurance, which brought the total employer contribution up to 2.5 percent of wages or 46 percent of total costs for the compulsorily insured, whereas the federal government would support 22 percent of total costs and the insured 32 percent. In addition to the sickness and accident insurance, the law provided for military insurance that would cover illness and disability for those in active military service. For all three programs, the federal government would spend 7.5 million Swiss francs, to cover approzimately 600,000 compulsorily insured members and about 300,000 voluntary members. "Botschaft des Bundesrates an die Bundesversammlung zu dem Entwurf eines Bundesgesetzes betreffend die Kranken- und Unfallversicherung."

20 EDI 27, Bd 5, Archives, 1911. Sickness insurance would be administered by the preexisting factory funds and voluntary private funds, and, in addition, a network of public funds (*Kreiskrankenkassen*) that were to be subsidized by the cantons would be created. Sickness fund officials feared that the public funds with their cantonal subsidies would be able to offer memberships at lower rates and would gradually replace the private funds.

21 BR-Delegation, Protokoll 4 March 1905, EDI 27, Bd 5, Archives, 1911; Maurer, "Switzerland," p. 410; Biedermann, *Entwicklung der Krankenversicherung in der Schweiz*, pp. 28–9.

22 Erich Wyss, Heilen und Herrschen, Medikalisierung, Krankenversicherung und ärztliche Professionalisierung, 1870–1911, Lizentiatsarbeit, Universität Zürich, 1982, p. 90.

23 For polls, see Richard M. Coughlin, *Ideology, Public Opinion & Welfare Policy*, Institute of International Studies Research Series No. 42 (Berkeley: University of California, 1980), pp. 156, 160–161; Theodore Marmor, *The Politics of Medicare* (Chicago: Aldine, 1973).

24 "Botschaft des Bundesrates an die Bundesversammlung zu dem Entwurf eines Bundesgesetzes betreffend die Kranken- und Unfallversicherung (vom 10. Dezember 1906)," p. 246, cited in Sommer, *Ringen um soziale Sicherheit*, p. 99, and Alfred Maurer, "Landesbericht Schweiz," in Peter A. Köhler and Hans F. Zacher, *Ein Jahrhundert Sozialversicherung*, Schriftenreihe für Internationales und Vergleichendes Sozialrecht Band 6 (Berlin: Duncker & Humbolt, 1981), p. 785. (This is the German edition of *The Evolution of Social Insurance*.)

25 Although compulsory health insurance was ruled out at the national level, individual cantons could declare health insurance obligatory for all or parts of the cantonal population. The cantons could also require employers to pay contributions for the compulsorily insured (article 2 of the law), but this provision has never been used. According to W. Siegrist (administrator of a public sickness fund in Basel), the Swiss parliament forbade the cantons from implementing this portion of the law, *Revue Syndicale Suisse*, *53*, no. 5 (May 1961), p. 151. Under the 1906 proposal, Federal subsidies would total 3.25 million francs for health insurance and 3.65 million for accident insurance, a total of 6.9 million. Funds were to be liable for medical care, at rates to be negotiated between medical accociations and funds, subject to the approval of the cantons. The only exclusive insurance practice would occur in regions where supplementary subsidies for under-doctored regions were provided. The accident insurance would be administered by a national fund, to be administered by representatives of employers and employees. The accident insurance would cover 80 percent of salary. See "Botschaft des Bundesrates

an die Bundesversammlong zu dem Entwurf eines Bundesgesetzes betreffend die Kranken- und Unfallversicherung (vom 10. Dezember 1906)."

26 Erich Gruner, *Arbeiterschaft und Wirtschaft in der Schweiz. 1880–1914. Vol. 2/1* (Zürich: Chronos, 1988), p. 175.

27 On the compromise worked out at a delegates' meeting in Olten, "Botschaft des Bundesrates an die Bundesversammlung zu dem Entwurf eines Bundesgesetzes betreffend die Kranken- und Unfallversicherung (vom 10. Dezember 1906)"; on the development of the funds, Biedermann, *Entwicklung der Krankenversicherung in der Schweiz*.

28 Statements from *Schw. Katholischer Volksverein*, 7 Okt. 1907, *Schw. Arbeiterbund*, 3 March 1907, *Schw. Landwirtschaftsverein*, 30 Juli 1907, *Schw. Metallarbeiterverband*, n.d., *Textilarbeiter und Arbeiterinnen*, *Schw. Holzarbeiterverband*, and *Bundesrat* committee Protokoll 4 March, 1905, EDI 27, Bd 5, Archives, 1911.

29 Stenbull NR, 13 April 1904, p. 213.

30 *Bundesrat*, Komitee Protokoll 4 March 1905, p. 9, EDI 27 Bd 5, Archives, 1911. Instead, extra federal subsidies for cantonal support for hospitals and for supplementary payments to sickness funds in areas lacking sufficient physicians (*Wartegeld*, or "waiting payments") were added as a minor concession to the proponents of state aid for free medical care.

31 *Schw. Bürgerzeitung*, 9 June 1908, p. 1.

32 Schweizerische Ärztekommission, 29 April 1905, and Dr. A. Kraft, "Krankenkassen und Ärzte," Verlag des Schweitzerischen Grütlivereins, 1910, 3340 (A) 1, Bd 97, Archives, 1911.

33 Neidhart, *Plebiszit und pluralitäre Demokratie*, p. 163–170.

34 On the railway compromise (*"Promesse Comtesse"*), see Neidhart, *Plebiszit und pluralitäre Demokratie*, p. 170; on regional votes, see Albert Gyger, *50 Jahre Konkordat der Schweizerischen Krankenkassen, 1891–1941* (Solothurn: Konkordat/Buchdruckerei Vogt-Schild, 1942), p. 26; on the Factory Act of 1877, Maurer, "Switzerland," p. 400.

35 Neidhart, *Plebiszit und pluralitäre Demokratie*, pp. 139–181.

36 Gruner, *Die Parteien in der Schweiz*, pp. 126, 129–131, 135–142.

37 On proportional representation, see Gruner, *Die Parteien in der Schweiz*, pp. 187–189; unionization figures from Peter J. Katzenstein, *Corporatism and Change: Austria, Switzerland, and the Politics of Industry* (Ithaca & London: Cornell University Press, 1984), p. 101; Stephens, *Transition from Capitalism to Socialism*, pp. 115–116.

38 Many of these reforms stemmed from the Emergency Act of 30 August 1939, which authorized the Federal Council to enact legislation directly in order to protect Swiss security. (A similar decision had been made during the First World War.) These powers were used to set up income-substitution funds for soldiers, who did not receive wages. Employers were required to deduct 2 percent of wages and to contribute an equal amount to an equalization fund. These funds were run by employer branch organizations, with cantonal funds and a federal fund for equalization purposes. This administrative structure, considered a breakthrough for Swiss social policy, was used for the implementation of old-age, survivors', and disability insurance. Maurer, "Switzerland," pp. 418–420. The similarity of this type of employer-run scheme to the kinds of social insurance schemes preferred by many American employers in the 1920s and 1930s – for example, the Ohio plan for unemployment insurance – is rather striking.

38a The return to democracy (popular initiative) affected the emergency legislation only; other laws had continuously been subject to the referendum.

39 *Konkordat der Schweizerischen Krankenkassenverbände,* (KSK), "Bericht über die Tätigkeit des Leitenden Ausschusses, 1920–1924," p. 41; Biedermann, *Entwicklung der Krankenversicherung in der Schweiz,* tables.

40 *KSK, Tätigkeitsbericht 1948–50,* p. 22, cf. 23–5, *KSK, Tätigkeitsbericht 1945–48,* pp. 48–50.

41 Biedermann, *Entwicklung der Krankenversicherung in der Schweiz,* pp. 49–50.

42 A. Saxer, *Die soziale Sicherheit in der Schweiz,* 4th ed (Bern: Verlag Paul Haupt, 1977); Sommer, *Ringen um soziale Sicherheit in der Schweiz,* pp. 178–286. The issue of family allowances was separated from maternity insurance, and debated in different conflicts than those discussed here. No satisfactory solution was found for either issue.

43 The Federal Office of Social Insurance presented a plan for compulsory health insurance for low-income earners to an expert commission of fifty interest-group and government representatives, in December 1948. The most important conflict in these deliberations concerned the issue of compulsory health insurance coverage. The sickness funds argued that the cantons should set the income limits for compulsory coverage, but insisted that at least 50 percent of the population in each canton should be compulsorily insured. The medical profession, on the other hand, wanted guarantees that no more than 30 percent of the population could be compulsorily insured. The sickness funds thus, sought to expand compulsory coverage, whereas the medical profession sought to keep middle- and higher-income patients out of compulsory coverage. *KSK Tätigkeitsbericht 1945–48.*

44 Neidhart, *Plebiszit und pluralitäre Demokratie,* pp. 270–271.

45 *Schw. Ärztezeitung* (Journal of the Swiss Medical Association), 1949, Nr. 8 and Nr. 11, pp. 185–190.

46 *J. des Associations Patronales* (Journal of the Swiss Employers' Associations), 13 May 1949, *44,* Nr. 19, p. 409.

47 *Schw. Gewerbeverband Tätigkeitsbericht* (Annual Report of the Swiss Small Business Association) 1949, pp. 100–1.

48 Stephens, *Transition from Capitalism to Socialism,* pp. 115–6.

49 Biedermann, *Entwicklung der Krankenversicherung in der Schweiz,* p. 68. Biedermann reports 1.27 million male members for 1950, but notes that this figure is substantially inflated as persons belonging to more than one fund, a common occurrence, are counted twice.

50 The Konkordat was founded in 1891 to represent the interests of sickness funds in the German-speaking regions of Switzerland. A second regional association was formed for the French funds in 1893. In 1916, however, this organization agreed to cooperate with the Konkordat, taking responsibility for all matters pertaining to the federal government. Though there are still three separate sickness fund associations, the Konkordat speaks for all on official matters. Thus, even though one might have expected regional and linguistic differences to have split the sickness funds movement, this has not been the case in practice.

51 Gruner, *Die Parteien in der Schweiz,* pp. 186–7.

52 *Schw. Krankenkassenzeitung,* 1 June 1949, pp. 137–8.

53 *KSK, Tätigkeitsbericht 1958–1950,* p. 47; Gruner, *Regierung und Opposition im schweizerischen Bundesstaat,* Series Staat und Politik no. 7 (Bern: Verlag Paul Haupt, 1969), pp. 17–8.

54 *Schw. Arbeitgeberzeitung,* 3 June 1949, p. 441.

55 "Bericht und Vorentwurf der Expertenkommission 1954," Archive/E 1954/5 Bd. 73–74, Files 214210-2142115, Bundesamt für Sozialversicherung, referred to as "Archives, 1954." Federal subsidies for health insurance were to

be increased from 23.1 million Swiss francs annually to 43.6 million; for maternity insurance they would be raised from 1.8 to 12.5 million. The federal subsidies would total 71 million for the first year (an increase of 36 million); 79.5 million after ten years. See "Bericht und Vorentwurf zu einem Bundesgesetz über die Kranken- und die Mutterschaftsversicherung (vom 3. Februar 1954)," offprint, pp. 138–9. The reform also had some implications for the development of private health insurance: Group policies and family policies, which existed in practice but which lacked a clear legal status, were explicitly incorporated into the system and would be eligible for subsidies. It was decided within the executive that employer contributions would best be left to collective bargaining. See A. Saxer, Press Conference, 30 August 1954, and Memorandum from the *Bundesamt für Industrie, Gewerbe und Arbeit* to the *Bundesamt für Sozialversicherung*, 23 October 1954, Bd 73, Archives, 1954.

56 "Botschaft des Bundesrates an die Bundesversammlung zum Entwurf eines Bundesgesetzes betreffend die Änderung des Ersten Titels des Bundesgesetzes über die Kranken- und Unfallversicherung (vom 5. Juni 1961)," *Bundesblatt*, 113, no. 25, I, p. 1418.

57 Zentralverband/Vorort, *Vernehmlassung*, pp. 19–20, Bd 74, Archives, 1954.

58 Verbindung Schweizerärzte, *Vernehmlassung*, p. 2, Bd 74, Archives, 1954.

59 Konkordat, *Vernehmlassung*, p. 2, Bd 74, Archives, 1954.

60 The most important groups were the Association Populaire d'entr'aide Familiale, the Schweizerische Frauenverein, the Katholische Frauenverband and the Schweizerische Vereinigung für Sozialpolitik, Bd 73, Archives, 1954.

61 Bd 74, Archives, 1954.

62 Aside from the interest associations, most political parties, other than the Social Democrats, opposed the reform. Many, such as the Catholic Conservatives, the Farmers', Citizens' and Artisans' Party, and the Democratic Party, objected not only to the increased subsidies and maternity insurance but also to the income classes. The cantons were divided on the increased federal subsidies, but some supported the maternity insurance and most objected to the income classes. Bd 74, Archives, 1954.

63 BSV in Neidhart, *Plebiszit und pluralitäre Demokratie*, p. 337.

64 The Federal Council is composed of two members from each of the three leading parties – the Radical-Democrats, the Christian-Socialists (formerly the Conservative-Catholics, then renamed Conservative-Christian-Socialists), and the Social-Democrats – as well as one member from the Swiss People's Party (formerly the Farmers', Artisans' and Citizens' Party).

65 "Die Revision der Krankenversicherung. Grundsätze, Erläuterungen, Finanzielle Auswirkungen," *Report Eidgenössisches Department des Innern*, 25 May 1960.

66 The Konkordat had already agreed in 1958 to support the government in its decision to refrain from demanding national health insurance, and in fact it was a representative of the Farmers', Artisans' and Citizens' Party with very close ties to the sickness fund movement's National Councilor Gnägi, who sponsored the parliamentary motion that invited the Federal Council to draft a proposal for a limited, partial revision of the sickness and accident insurance law.

67 Gerhard Kocher, *Verbandseinfluss auf die Gesetzgebung. Ärzteverbindung, Krankenkassenverbände und die Teilrevision 1964 des Kranken- und Unfallversicherungsgesetzes*, 2nd ed (Bern: Francke Verlag, 1972); *Domaine Public* (*DP*, Public Domain, critical journal), 22 Nov. 1973.

68 "Grundsätz und Erläuterungen f.d. Revision d. Krankenversicherung,"

Archiv/E, Bd. 61–2, Files 21404110-21404114, Bundesamt für Sozialversicherung, referred to as Archives, 1960. Business Vernehmlassungs statement is in Bd 62.

69 Bd 62, Archives, 1960.

70 Bd 73, Archives, 1954.

71 Bd 62, Archives, 1960. The law actually stated the members paying equal contributions should be eligible for equal benefits, a provision that had been interpreted by the federal courts to mean that physicians could not charge members of the same sickness funds at different rates and that the sickness funds could not sign contracts with local medical associations that provided for sliding fees. The Association of Public Employees had argued as early as 1959 that the funds were making a mistake by agreeing to a partial reform, for political opposition to a partial reform would be as great as to a total reform, and that therefore the funds should go ahead and fight for their real demands. Kocher, *Verbandseinfluss auf die Gesetzgebung*, p. 33.

72 "Botschaft des Bundesrates an die Bundesversammlung zum Entwurf eines Bundesgesetzes betreffend die Änderung des Ersten Titels des Bundesgesetzes über die Kranken- und Unfallversicherung (vom 5. Juni 1961)," *Bundesblatt*, 113, no. 25, I: 1417–1528.

73 Legislative proposals are arbitrarily sent to either one of the two houses of parliament for preliminary consideration. The *Ständerat* committee was composed of five members of the Conservative-Christian-Socialist fraction, four Radical-Democrats, one Social-Democrat, one member of the Democratic and Evangelical faction, and one member of the Farmers', Artisans' and Citizens' Party.

74 The offending provision clarified the competence of the Federal Insurance Court to rule in conflicts between physicians and sickness funds, and allowed not only these parties but also the Federal Council to appeal decisions of lower courts at the federal level. Kocher, *Verbandseinfluss auf die Gesetzgebung*, p. 41.

75 17 August 1961, "Verhandlungen der eidg. Räte 1961/2, Kommission des Ständerates für die Vorberatung des Entwurfes eines Bundesgesetzes betreffend die Änderung des Ersten Titels des Bundesgesetzes über die Kranken- und Unfallversicherung vom 13. Juni 1911," 1961, Bd. 67, File 2140413, Bundesamt für Sozialversicherung.

76 Many of the funds' problems stemmed from the controversial provision of the 1911 law that had allowed any Swiss doctor to treat insurance patients ("free choice of doctor"). The funds had no legal means to exclude doctors who overcharged patients or treated too many patients from insurance practice; they could merely refuse to reimburse patients for fees above a certain level, or they could bring charges of malpractice to the local cantonal medical society. As in France, when negotiations between doctors and sickness funds took place at the *local* rather than the *national* level and when any doctor could treat the insured, the funds had little leverage over the medical profession; medical societies had no real incentive to sign collective agreements with the sickness funds. In order to induce the local medical societies to negotiate, the funds insisted that doctors should be penalized for failing to reach agreements with the funds. Income classes should be legal only within the framework of contracts negotiated with the funds. Should these contracts lapse, this privilege should be revoked, and doctors' fees should be strictly regulated by the cantonal authorities. Because cantonal fee schedules had been ignored in the past, the funds wanted it made absolutely clear that these limitations on fees were legally binding. Finally, the cantons should be

empowered to force doctors to treat fund patients in areas where there was a shortage of fund doctors.

77 "Ergänzungsbotschaft des Bundesrates an die Bundesversammlung zum Entwurf eines Bundesgesetzes betreffend die Änderung des Ersten Titels des Bundesgesetzes über die Kranken- und Unfallversicherung (vom 16. Nov. 1962)," *Bundesblatt*, II: 1265–1292. The cantonal schedules would include minimum and maximum rates, with doctors free to set the exact fee according to the difficulty of the case. The profession's demand to be able to take the economic circumstances of the patient into account, however, was rejected. Income would be relevant only if separate cantonal tariffs for different income classes were drawn up. See the French case, where the issue of whether the patient's income (*fortune du malade*) could be taken into account by doctors when determining their fees was a critical issue in the 1950s debates.

78 *Schw. Ärztezeitung*, cited in *Stenbull SR* 1962, p. 119; see also Kocher, *Verbandseinfluss auf die Gesetzgebung*, p. 66.

79 Cited in Fritz Schären, *Die Stellung des Arztes in der sozialen Krankenversicherung* (Zürich: Schulthess Polygraphischer Verlag, 1973), p. 72.

80 Kocher, *Verbandseinfluss auf die Gesetzgebung*, p. 147.

81 Kocher, *Verbandseinfluss auf die Gesetzgebung*, p. 73.

82 Obrecht, *Stenbull SR* 1963, p. 104.

83 Kocher, *Verbandseinfluss auf die Gesetzgebung*, p. 93.

84 Obrecht, *Stenbull SR* 1963, p. 105.

85 Stüssi, *Stenbull SR* 1962, p. 128.

86 Kocher, *Verbandseinfluss auf die Gesetzgebung*, p. 87.

87 Kocher, *Verbandseinfluss auf die Gesetzgebung*, p. 93.

88 With 26.5 percent of the popular vote in 1963, the Social Democrats controlled 25.5 percent of the seats in the Nationalrat but only 7 percent of the seats in the Ständerat. Gruner, *Die Parteien in der Schweiz* 1977: 184–6; Jean-François Aubert, *Exposé des institutions politiques de la Suisse à partir de quelques affaires controverseés, 2nd Ed* (Lausanne: Editions Payot, 1983), pp. 280–1. Measured by profession, the Ständerat has a greater proportion of self-employed persons, who in the French case constituted an ally for doctors – 52 percent compared with 37.5 percent in the Nationalrat – whereas the Nationalrat has more professional politicians (full-time MPs, local government representatives, interest-group and political party employees) – 43 percent compared with 29.5 percent in the *Ständerat*. Gruner, *Politische Führungsgruppen im Bundestaat* (Bern: Francke Verlag, 1973), p. 58–9. The Nationalrat committee was composed of seven representatives each from the Conservative-Christian Socialist, Radical-Democratic and Social Democratic fractions, and three members from the Farmers' Artisans' and Citizens' Party, one Democrat, one Liberal and one Independent.

89 The cantons were to "assure" medical treatment for low-income earners by setting legally binding fee schedules and requiring doctors to treat fund patients if necessary. Though the explicit sanctions proposed by the Federal Council had been removed, these provisions constituted a weakened form of these controls on the medical profession.

90 This change came about almost by chance: Because the vote on liability was tied, the president of the Nationalrat settled this question.

91 NR chairman Wyss, cited in Sommer, *Ringen um soziale Sicherheit in der Schweiz*, p. 472. On the number of female petitioners, see Kocher, *Verbandseinfluss auf die Gesetzgebung*, p. 114.

92 NR Forel, cited in Sommer, *Ringen um soziale Sicherheit in der Schweiz*, p. 473; See also Gnägi, *Stenbull NR* 1963, p. 432.

93 The NR had inserted a clause stating that "the cantons will assure the medical treatment of low-income earners," but this was too vague to be effective, especially without sanctions. One year later, the Konkordat noted in its annual report that the system was not working. The 1964 revision was based on the assumption that negotiated contracts would regulate relations between doctors and funds, the Konkordat wrote, but the more prevalent situation was one where such agreements had lapsed and there was no incentive for cantonal medical societies to sign new contracts. Furthermore, the cantonal fee schedules that were to come into force precisely under this situation did not regulate fees in a satisfactory manner. *KSK, Tätigkeitsbericht 1964–5*, pp. 11–14.

94 Hänggi, 24 March 1964, cited in Kocher, *Verbandseinfluss auf die Gesetzgebung*, p. 131.

95 *DP*, 250, 22 Nov. 1973.

96 *Statistik über die vom Bunde anerkannten Krankenkassen und Tuberkulose-Versicherungsträger*, Bern: Bundesamt für Sozialversicherung, 1963), p. 20; 1964 edition, p. 19.

97 The original report of June 1960 had proposed that the federal government reimburse the funds for 10 percent, 15 percent, and 25 percent of the costs of medical care for men, women, and children, respectively; successive increases during the parliamentary consideration of the law raised these percentages to 10 percent, 35 percent, and 30 percent in the final law. Hospital coverage was increased to 720 days within a 900-day period; coverage for ambulatory care became unlimited; sickness cash benefits were raised from 1 to 2 Swiss francs per day, for 720 days within the 900-day period. Previous limits for ambulatory, hospital, and sickness cash benefits had been 180 days for each 360 day period, raised to 270 out of 360 for health care if cost-sharing were required. Most funds, however, provided considerably higher benefits. Thus, although the law certainly increased the average benefits to the insured, one of its main effects was to bring the benefits of the smaller and medium-sized funds up to the standards of the larger funds.

98 Maurer, "Switzerland," p. 433.

99 The main difference between the Social Democratic initiative and the government's counterproposal was that the government's plan was largely voluntary. Both plans, however, called for financing through a payroll tax, with significant contributions by employers. The Social Democratic initiative was financed by federal and cantonal contributions (18.8 percent), employer contributions (34 percent), and contributions by the insured (47.2 percent, 7.4 percent as cost-sharing, and 39.8 percent as payroll tax). Under the government's counterproposal, public subsidies would pay for 19.3 percent, employers for 20.9 percent, and the insured for 59.8 percent (14.3 percent as cost-sharing, 17.4 percent as premiums, 28.1 percent as payroll tax). Sommer, *Ringen um soziale Sicherheit in der Schweiz*, pp. 477–532; Gebert, "Cooperative Federalism or Muddling-Through;" Felix Gutzwiller, "Cost and Cost-Sharing in the Health Services of Switzerland," Paper presented at the International Conference on "Policies for the Containment of Health Care Costs and Expenditures," Fogarty International Center, National Institutes of Health, Bethesda, MD, 1976, pp. 11–12.

100 Interview, Department of Social Insurance, 19 December 1989.

100a Maurer, "Switzerland," pp. 436–7.

101 Harold Wilensky, *The Welfare State and Equality* (Berkeley, CA: University of California Press, 1975). Coughlin, *Ideology, Public Opinion & Welfare Policy*; Robert Y. Shapiro and John T. Young, "Public Opinion and the Welfare State"; *Political Science Quarterly 104* 1 (Spring 1989): 58–89.

102 Gruner, *Die Parteien in der Schweiz*; Jean Meynaud, *Les organisations professionnelles en Suisse* (Lausanne: Editions Librairie Payot, 1963). The weak party structure provides a further route of interest group influence as the interest groups maintain parliamentary groups that cut across the parties as well as directly employing members of parliament.

103 Lehmann, Gutzwiller, and Martin, "The Swiss Health System: The Paradox of Ungovernability and Efficacy."

104 See Table 5, Chapter 2.

105 Gruner, *Die Parteien in der Schweiz*; Henry H. Kerr, *Parlement et Société en Suisse* (St. Saphorin: Editions Georgi, 1981); Katzenstein, *Corporatism and Change*; Neidhart, *Plebiszit und pluralitäre Demokratie*.

Chapter 5

1 Douglas V. Verney, *Parliamentary Reform in Sweden, 1866–1921* (Oxford: Clarendon Press, 1957).

2 Royal Committees are appointed by the government to investigate specific policy problems and to draft legislative proposals. Originally divided into "expert" committees and "political" committees (*sakkunniga* and *politiska kommittéer*), the two functions are now virtually merged, with both technical and political experts appointed to the same committees. Proposals formulated by government departments and/or the Royal Committees are sent to interest-group and government representatives for comment. Their written responses are called "*remiss*" statements. Gunnar Hesslén, *Det Svenska Kommittéväsendet intill år 1905. Dess uppkomst, ställning och betydelse*, diss., filosofiska fakultet i Uppsala humanistiska sektion, Uppsala, 1927. See also Steven Kelman, *Regulating America, Regulating Sweden: A Comparative Study of Occupational Safety and Health Policy* (Cambridge, MA: MIT Press, 1981), 131–2.

3 Hesslén, *Svenska Kommittéväsendet*, pp. 357, 360, 377. In his study of late nineteenth-century social legislation, Englund also stresses the importance of this political form. Karl Englund, *Arbetarförsäkringsfrågan i svensk politik 1884–1901*, Acta Universitatis Uppsaliensis, Studia Historia Uppsaliensia (Stockholm: Almqvist & Wicksell International, 1976), pp. 96, 186.

4 Thomas J. Anton, "Policy-Making and Political Culture in Sweden," *Scandinavian Political Studies 4* (1969), pp. 88–102; Hans Meijer, "Bureuacracy and Policy Formulation in Sweden," *Scandinavian Political Studies 4* (1969), pp. 103–116; Hugh Heclo, *Modern Social Politics in Britain and Sweden* (New Haven: Yale University Press, 1974); Hugh Heclo and Henrik Madsen, *Policy and Politics in Sweden: Principled Pragmatism* (Philadelphia: Temple University Press, 1987).

5 SOU 1968: 47, pp. 111–112, cited in Odin Anderson, *Health Care: Can There be Equity? The United States, Sweden and England* (NY: John Wiley, 1972), p. 42, fn 10.

6 See discussion of proportional representation and the Rokkan model in Esping-Andersen, *Politics Against Markets*, p. 72.

7 Verney, *Parliamentary Reform in Sweden*, pp. 206–7, 216–7, 226–7.

8 O. Nyman, *Svensk Parlamentarism 1932–1936. Från Minoritetsparlamentarism till majoritetskoalition*. No. 27, *Skrifter Utgivna av Statsvetenskapliga*

Föreningen i Uppsala genom Axel Brusewitz. (Uppsala: Almqvist & Wicksell, 1947); On the role of the First Chamber, see Verney, *Parliamentary Reform in Sweden*, p. 217.

9 MacRae, *Parliament, Parties and Society in France.*

10 Odin W. Anderson, *Health Care: Can There Be Equity?*, pp. 7, 38, 43. Cf. Karl J. Höjer, *Svensk Socialpolitisk Historia* (Stockholm: P.A. Norstedt & Söners Förlag, 1952).

11 Bo Hjern, "The Swedish Health Services from the Standpoint of the Profession – Negotiating and Bargaining," unpublished presentation, Chicago, 12 April 1976, 10.

12 Gunnar Biörck "How to be a Clinician in a Socialist Country," *Annals of Internal Medicine* 86 (1977): 815–6.

13 This is the view of Theodore R. Marmor and David Thomas, "Doctors, Politics and Pay Disputes: 'Pressure Group Politics' Revisited," *British Journal of Political Science* 2 (1972): 436–437.

14 Peter Garpenby, *The State and the Medical Profession. A Cross-National Comparison of the Health Policy Arena in the United Kingdom and Sweden 1945–1985* (Linköping: Linköping Studies in Arts and Sciences, 1989); Hans Berglind and Ulla Petersson, *Omsorg som yrke eller omsorg on yrket* (Stockholm: Trosa Tryckeri/Sekretariatet for framtidsstudier, 1980).

15 Anderson, *Health Care: Can There Be Equity?*, p. 43.

16 In 1915, a law was passed at Liberal insistence that allowed the monarch to recognize unlicensed practitioners, but this had no practical effect. Ramsey, "The Politics of Professional Monopoly in Nineteenth-Century Medicine."

17 Bjurulf, Bo and Swahn, Urban, "Health Policy Recommendations and What Happened to them: Sampling the Twentieth Century Record," pp. 75–98 in Heidenheimer & Elvander, eds., *The Shaping of the Swedish Health System* (London: Croom Helm, 1980); Andrew Twaddle and Richard Hessler, "Power and Change: The Case of the Swedish Commission of Inquiry on Health and Sickness Care," *Journal of Health Politics, Policy and Law 11*, no. 1, 1986, pp. 14–40.

18 *Läkartidningen* (Journal of the Swedish Medical Association), 75, no. 2 (1986), pp. 1986–2000.

19 See Gösta Esping-Andersen and Walter Korpi, "Social Policy as Class Politics in Post-War Capitalism," *Crisis and Order in Contemporary Capitalism*, ed. J. Goldthorpe (Oxford: Clarendon Press, Oxford University Press, 1984), 179–208, and Gösta Esping-Andersen, *Politics Against Markets: The Social Democratic Road to Power* (Princeton: Princeton University Press, 1985).

20 Bo Särlvik, "Party Politics and Electoral Opinion Formation," *Scandinavian Political Studies 2* (1967): 167–202; Nils Elvander, *Intresseorganisationerna i dagens Sverige* (Lund: CWK Gleerup Bokförlag, 1966).

21 After the passage of the 1911 Sickness and Accident Insurance Law, Swiss federal subsidies grew from covering 6.3 percent of sickness fund expenditures in 1892–5 to 20.5 percent in 1915. In Sweden, government subsidies covered only 12.8 percent of fund expenditures in 1915. By 1935, however, after the 1931 Sickness Fund Law was passed, the Swedish state subsidies covered a larger portion of costs (26 percent) than the Swiss subsidies, 18.6 percent in 1935. In France, state subsidies covered 6.7 percent of fund expenditures in 1919; no figures were found for 1935, after the 1930 Social Insurance Law was passed. "Bericht und Vorentwurf zu einem Bundesgesetz über die Kranken- und die Mutterschaftsversicherung (vom 3. Februar 1954)," offprint, pp. 208–209, listed in Swiss references; Statistiska Centralbyrån, *Historisk Statistik för Sverige. Statistiska Översiktstabeller* (Stockholm: Statistiska Centralbyrån,

1960) p. 143; Ass. S. Carton 5, "Rapport Grinda," Archives, 1930, listed in French references.

22 On 1899, see Englund, *Arbetarförsäkringsfrågan*, p. 99. On 1910, see Höjer, *Svensk Socialpolitisk Historia*; It is literally the case that the newspaper coverage of the Sickness Fund Law was completely overshadowed by the Ådalen story, which filled the papers exactly when the law was debated in the Riksdag. See, for example, *Socialdemokraten* and *Dagens Nyheter* from May 15, 1931 to the end of the month.

23 Arnold J. Heidenheimer "Unions and Welfare State Development in Britian and Germany: An Interpretation of Metamorphoses in the Period 1910–1950," International Institute for Comparative Social Research SP-II Discussion Paper, IIVG/dp/80–209 (Berlin: Wissenschaftszentrum Berlin, 1980) points out the significance of union-sickness fund linkages for the formation of government programs in health. When unions used the sickness funds as an organizational tool, as in Germany, government-administered health programs were impeded.

24 In 1909, for example, among local sickness funds, 116 were officially linked to the Temperance movement, 40 to unions, and 27 to the Free Religious movement. Among the national funds, the largest was a Temperance fund, *Nykterhetsvännernas allmänna sjukkassa*, headed by C.G. Ekman, the Liberal leader who became prime minister from 1926 to 1928 and from June 1930 to August 1932. The Temperance movement was most closely tied to the Liberal Party, although there were many Social Democrats who also participated in the movement. The movement was extremely well-connected in the Second Chamber of the Swedish Riksdag, with 82 out of 230 MPs in the Second Chamber – mostly Liberals and Social Democrats – belonging to the movement in 1903, compared with 4 in the Social Democratic Party, 3 in LO, and 32 in the Free Religous movement. In 1912, the figures were 122 MPs affiliated with the Temperance movement, 64 belonging to SAP, 33 to LO, 41 to the Free Religious movement. Lindeberg, *Svensk Sjukkasserörelsens Historia*; Bengt Lindroth, *Bingo! En kritisk granskning av folkrörelserna i Sverige. 1850–1975*, Verdandi-Debatt Nr. 76, (Stockholm: Prisma, 1975), p. 34.

25 Gösta Lindeberg, *Den Svenska Sjukkasserörelsens Historia* (Lund: Svenska Sjukkasseförbundet/Carl Bloms Boktryckeri, 1949), p. 121.

26 Lindeberg, *Svenska Sjukkasserörelsens Historia*, p. 288; on industrial accident insurance, see Englund, *Arbetarförsäkringsfrågan*, pp. 99, 181, 186; cf. Anita Dahlberg, "Socialförsäkringens utveckling. Ersättningar vid sjukdom, arbetsskada och ålderdom – utvecklingen i tre faser," unpublished mimeo, Institutionen för Socionomutbildningen (Socialhögskolan), Stockholm, 1978.

27 K.J. Höjer, *Svensk Socialpolitisk Historia*, p. 71.

28 Lindeberg, *Svenska Sjukkasserörelsens Historia*, p. 355; SOU (Statens Offentliga Utredingar, Royal Committee Reports) 1925: 8, *Statens Besparingskommitté. Betänkande om Socialförsäkringarnas Organisation.* Hirobumi Ito lists the 1925 figures as 13.3 percent for Sweden, 42.5 percent for Denmark, and 32 percent for Germany, "Health Insurance and Medical Services in Sweden and Denmark. 1850–1950," in Heidenheimer and Elvander, *The Shaping of the Swedish Health System*, pp. 44–67. Flora and Alber lists the 1925 figures in terms of members as a percentage of the active labor force: Sweden, 29 percent; France, 21 percent; Switzerland, 50 percent; Germany, 57 percent; Denmark: 99 percent. There are of course problems with this type of comparison. Swedish children, for example, are not counted as members, even though they are insured by their parents. The Swiss figures are inflated

because so much double-counting occurs. See Flora and Alber's "Modernization, Democratization, and the Development of Welfare States," p. 75.

29 Lindeberg, *Svenska Sjukkasserörelsens Historia*, p. 318, 321; Höjer, *Svensk Socialpolitisk Historia*, p. 114; States Offentliga Utredningar 1944: 15, *Socialvårdskommittéens betänkande VII: Utredning och förslag angående Lag om Allmän Sjukförsäkring* (STH: Socialdepartementet).

30 SOU 1944: 15, p. 57; Lindeberg *Svensk Socialpolitisk Historia*, p. 328. Bo Rothstein describes Möller's clever use of institutional reforms, in *The Social Democratic State*.

31 Lindeberg, *Svenska Sjukkasserörelsens Historia*, p. 277; Thomas Fürth, *Folkrörelse eller Myndighetstradition. Organisationssyn och teknikval i Socialförsäkringshistoria* (Stockholm: Arbetslivscentrum, 1980), p. 13.

32 SOU 1929: 24, in Socialdepartementets Konseljakt 28 February 1930, Nr. 47 (Prop. Nr. 154 med förslag till lag om ändring till lag om ändring i vissa delar av lagen om understödsföreningar), Riksarkivet, herafter referred to as "Archives, 1930"; Lindeberg, *Svenska Sjukkasserörelsens Historia*, pp. 442–3. In 1934, the two organizations merged to become The Swedish Sickness Fund Association (*Svenska Sjukkasseförbundet*).

33 Lindeberg, *Svenska Sjukkasserörelsens Historia*; Sveriges Läkarförbund (The Swedish Medical Association), *Sveriges Läkarförbunds Historia* (The Swedish Medical Association's History), unpublished manuscript, approximate date 1953; *Läkartidningen*, 25, no. 20 (1978), pp. 1986–2000.

34 Letter from *Värmlandsföreningen*, a local medical association, to *Sveriges Läkarförbunds fullmäktige*, the central steering committee of the Swedish Medical Association, reprinted in *Läkartidningen* (*LT*), October 1930, p. 1266.

35 *Läkartidngningen* (*LT*), 10 October 1930, pp. 1285–1303.

36 Sveriges Läkerförbund, *Sveriges Läkarförbunds Historia*, p. 218.

37 Petrén, *LT*, 17 April 1931, p. 585.

38 *LT*, 6 March 1931, p. 528; cf. 6 March 1930, p. 370; 24 April 1931, p. 633; 8 May 1931; 22 May 1931.

39 "*Läkaruttalanden i sjukförsäkringsfrågan, ur officiella handlingar utgivna av skattebetalarnas förening*" (Doctors' Opinions on the National Health Insurance Issue, from Official Documents Published by the Taxpayers' Association) 31 December 1930; for discussions of the role of the Taxpayers' Association, see SvD May 22 1931, p. 6; *Socialdemokraten*, 15 May 1931, p. 4; DN 27 May 1931, p. 4. SAF's journal, *Industria*, was scanned for articles pertaining to the sickness fund law. One article described the Taxpayers' Association's opposition to the law on cost grounds (1926, no. 10, p. 261), but without adding SAF's position or relationship to the organization; all others were limited to brief descriptions of the legislative process.

40 *Svenska Sjukkassetidningen*, Vol. 23, No. 6, June 1930, p. 111 in Socialdepartementets Konseljakt 6 February 1931, Nr. 63 (Kungl. Maj:t Prop. Nr. 75 till Riksdagen med förslag till lag om ändring i vissa delar an lagen den 29 juni 1912 (nr. 184) om understödsföreningar mm.), Riksarkivet, referred to as "Archives, 1931"; *Läkartidningen*, 6 March 1931, p. 370; *Sveriges Läkarförbunds Historia*, nd, pp, 217, 219, 265.

41 *Riksdagen Protokoll*, Andra Kammaren (Parliamentary Debates of the Second Chamber) Samling 6, 35 (1931) p. 45.

42 Kungl. Majet Proposition 1926: 117 (I Saml., Band II, Prop. 110–131, 1926); Riksarkivet, Socialdepartementets Konseljakt 28 February 1930, Nr. 47 (Prop. Nr. 154 med förslag till lag om ändring i vissa delar av lagen om understöds-

föreningarj; RA, Socialdepartementets Konseljakt 6 February 1931, Nr. 63 (Kungl. Maj:t Prop. Nr. 75 till Riksdagen med förslag till lag om ändring i vissa delar av lagen den 29 Juni 1912 nr. 184 om understödsföreningar mm).

43 Nils Elvander, "Interest Groups in Sweden," *Annals of the American Academy of Political and Social Science*, 413 (1974), p. 27.

44 The 1931 law increased state subsidies for sickness funds, from about 3.6 million Swedish crowns annually in 1930 to 10.7 million by 1935, or, in terms of sickness fund expenditures, from covering 13.9 percent of expenditures to covering 27 percent, Statistiska Centralbyrån, *Historisk Statistik för Sverige. Statistiska Översiktstabeller* (Stockholm: SCB, 1960), p. 143; Rolf Broberg *Så formades tryggheten: Socialförsäkringens historia, 1946–1972* (Stockholm: Försäkringskasseförbundet, 1973), p. 194.

44a Between 1930 and 1945, LO's membership increased from 553,456 to 1,106,917, SAF's from 2,969 to 8,645 (covering 306,520 and 530,161 employees, respectively), TCO's from 20,000 in 1931 (DACO) to 204,653 in 1945. SACO was founded in 1947 with about 15,000 members, SR (government employees) was founded in 1946 with about 18,100 members, RLF (an agricultural organization) increased from 19,237 members in 1930 to 154,339 in 1945, Stig Hadenius, Björn Molin, and Hans Wieslander, *Sverige Efter 1900. En Modern Politisk Historia. 8th Ed.* (Stockholm: Aldus/Bonniers, 1978), p. 336. On the shift in parties, see Nyman, *Svensk Parlamentarism 1932–1936.* On the labor movement, see Esping-Andersen, *Social Democratic Road to Power*; Walter Korpi, *The Democratic Class Struggle.*

45 Verney, *Parliamentary Reform in Sweden*, p. 229.

46 Unemployment insurance was, on the other hand, not considered a "pillar" of social policy, for full employment was to be a priority. In addition, unions did not wish to give up their independent unemployment insurance funds, and the system is still based on this so-called "Ghent" system. See Bo Rothstein, in Steinmo Thelan and Longstreth, *Structuring Politics.*

47 *TCO-remiss*, p. 3, in Socialdepartementet Konseljakt 27 September 1946, nr. 123, prop. 312 del I. Remiss betr. SOU 1944: 15, 16 (ang. lag om allmänn sjukförsäkring) Dnr 2038/44, Stockholm 19 Maj 1944. Riksarkivet, hereafter referred to as "Archives, 1946." Many of the *remiss* answers refer to the increasing use of collective bargaining agreements to regulate labor relations. The Employers' Association pointed out that employers were increasingly paying for their employees' sickness fund contributions through negotiated agreements, thereby replacing the direct provision of benefits typical of more "patriarchal circumstances," *SAF-remiss.* Similarly, the Rural Employers' Federation (Svenska Lantarbetsgivarföreningen) noted that according to the collective agreement signed with the Association of Rural Laborers, each laborer was obligated to insure himself. Furthermore, this organization supported the idea that all self-employed persons should be included in the national health insurance system.

47a The specific demands of the profession followed the "market-protection" logic mentioned in conjunction with earlier reforms: Patients should be reimbursed for only two-thirds rather than three-quarters of medical expenses, and the waiting period for benefits should be increased.

48 *Hantverk och Industri*, 1948, nr. 1, p. 8, and 1948, nr. 9, p. 6.

49 The commune reform was to reduce the number of primary communes, the most local unit of government, from 2,400 to 800. This consolidation was intended to produce local government bodies more able to provide the necessary administrative and financial base for many of the postwar social reforms.

50 Disputes arose over the cash benefits portion of the law, with factions within

the Social Democratic Party split between flat-rate benefits, as under the Beveridge plan, versus a system of benefits graduated according to income. Social Minister Gustav Möller, a staunch supporter of the Beveridge Plan, insisted on the flat-rate benefits. This was not the only time that Möller took a straight "Beveridge" position on social reforms. He won out over Wigforss and Hansson on a relatively high basic pension that was to be equal for all citizens, rather than a lower basic pension with income-tested supplements. The Social Services Committee, Prime Minister Erlander, Finance Minister Sträng, and Axel Strand, head of LO, on the other hand, supported the income-related benefits on the grounds that this was politically more attractive and financially more feasible. With income-related benefits, contributions could be set at higher rates for high-income earners. Such a system, it was thought, would appeal to these groups and broaden political support for national health insurance. Further, it would bring more money into the system. In fact, even Axel Strand criticized Möller's proposal for entailing a basic shift in financing from contributions to taxes. The issue was complicated by the independent development of industrial accident insurance. Since 1918, employers had been required to insure their employees for industrial accidents. Many had supplemented these schemes with additional voluntary coverage. Consequently, most skilled workers were covered for income loss during illness at generous rates, as well as for medical treatment even for illnesses unrelated to work accidents. Income-related benefits under national health insurance would allow coordination with the accident insurance in such a way that more equal health insurance coverage for all wage earners could be introduced without reducing the benefits of the previously covered skilled workers. Hadenius et al., *Sverige Efter 1900*, p. 182–3; Höjer, *Svensk Socialpolitisk Historia*, p. 258–9, Åke Elmér, *Från Fattigsverige till valfärdstaten. Sociala förhållanden och Social politik i Sverige under 1900-talet* (Stockholm: Bokförlaget Aldus/Bonniers, 1963); Rolf Broberg, *Så Formades Tryggheten: Socialförsäkringens historia 1946–1972* (Stockholm: Försäkringskasseförbundet, 1973), p. 243; Fürth, *Folkrörelse eller Myndighetstradition.*
51 Statens Offentliga Utredningar (SOU) 1948: 14, *Den öppna läkarvården i riket. Utredning och förslag av medicinalstyrelsen* (STH: Inrikesdepartementet) 241; SOU 1948: 24, *Bilagor till medicinalstyrelsens utredning om den öppna läkarvården i riket (SOU 1948: 14)* (STH: Inrikesdepartementet); Anita Jarild Ög, "Diskussion kring Medicinalstyrelsens betänkande, 'Den öppna läkarvården i riket,'" unpublished paper from the pro-seminar in Political Science, Uppsala University, 1962; Arnold J. Heidenheimer, "Conflict and Compromise Between Professional and Bureaucratic Health Interests. 1947–1972," *The Shaping of the Swedish Health System*, eds. Heidenheimer & Elvander (London: Croom Helm, 1980), 119–142; Anderson, *Health Care: Can There be Equity?*
52 Anderson, *Health Care: Can There Be Equity?*, pp. 78–9.
53 *SvD*, March 10, 1948, p. 3–4. *DN*, 10 March 1948, p. 4. *MT*, 10 March 1948, p. 4.
54 *SvD*, 12 March 1948, p. 2.
55 SAF-*remiss*, in Inrikeskonseljakt 30 April 1954 Nr. 82, betänkande angående den öppna sjukvården i riket (1948: 14) och bilagor (SOU 1948: 24), hereafter referred to as "Archives, 1954."
56 The Swedish Medical Association objected to the pressing work tempo and low fees of the *polikliniks*, as well as to the long lines of patients. The Association had recommended that hospitals instead subcontract this outpatient work to private practitioners. Hospitals, on the other hand, wished to

continue with the *polikliniks*, but had trouble staffing them and often required *poliklinik* service as part of the contracts of junior hospital doctors. Sveriges Läkarförbund *Utredning angående Poliklinikväsendet i Sverige, angiven av Sveriges Läkarförbundspolikliniksakkunige* (STH: 1944). SOU 1978: 74, *Husläkare – en enklare och tryggare sjukvård. Betänkande av Kontinuitetsutredningen* (STH: Socialdepartementet).

57 Heidenheimer, "Conflict and Compromise," p. 122; Ög, "Diskussion kring Medicinalstyrelsens betänkande, 'Den öppna läkarvården i riket,'" p. 10; J Axel Höjer, *Hälsovård i går- i dag- i morgon* (STH: Kooperativa Förbundets Förlag, 1949); Höjer *En Läkares Väg. Från Visby till Vietnam* (STH: Bonniers, 1975); *Motpol*, 60.2 (1982): 7–18. Representative articles in *Läkartidningen* can be found in *LT* 9 April 1948: 711; 16 April 1948: 966–9; 13 August 1948; 1576; 20 August 1948: 1623–5. Höjer stated in *Morgon Tidningen* that the Medical Association leadership had organized an opinion in advance among the doctors and the press (*MT* 5 April 1948 cited in Ög, p. 11). Later he called the Medical Association "a collection of private doctors" (*SvD* 13 November 1948, in Ög, p. 12).

58 Nils Elvander, *Svensk Skattepolitik 1945–1970. En Studie i partiers och organisationers funktioner* (Stockholm: Rabén och Sjögren, 1972), Chapter II.

59 Although sickness fund membership had continued to grow after the war, the national health insurance law expanded coverage considerably, from 3.17 million in 1954 to 5.4 million in 1955, or from 48 percent of the adult population in 1945 and 60 percent in 1954, to 78 percent of the population in 1955. With family members, 100 percent of the population was insured. With the introduction of national health insurance, the voluntary contributions were eliminated and contributions were shared between the national government (29 percent, employers 27 percent), and the insured (44 percent). Broberg, *Så Formades Tryggheten*, pp. 45, 194, 206. Carl G. Uhr quotes financing as 19 percent by the insured, 11 percent from employer contributions, and 70.4 percent from national and local government revenues for 1962; his figures for 1955 are about the same, *Sweden's Social Security System. An Appraisal of its Economic Impact in the Postwar Period*, Social Security Administration, Research Report No. 14. (Washington, DC: U.S. Dept. of Health Education and Welfare, 1966), p. 85.

60 Leif Lewin, *Planhushållningsdebatten. 3rd Ed* (STH: Almqvist & Wicksell, 1970); Nils Elvander *Svensk Skattepolitik 1945–1970. En Studie i partiers och organisationers funktioner.* (Stockholm: Rabén och Sjögren, 1972).

61 Hadenius et al., *Sverige Efter 1990*, pp. 306–7; Verney, *Parliamentary Reform in Sweden*, p. 217.

62 Glaser, *Paying the Doctor*, 110; Andrew Martin, "The Dynamics of Change in a Keynesian Political Economy: The Swedish Case and its Implications," *State and Economy in Contemporary Capitalism*, ed. C. Crouch (London: Croom Helm, 1979), 89–121.

63 Referenda were used in 1922 for prohibition, in 1955 for driving on the right side of the road, and in 1958 for a pension reform. Prohibition was narrowly rejected, as was right-hand traffic. Nevertheless, the right-hand traffic proposal was subsequently introduced by parliament in 1967, an example that is often cited to show that Swedish democracy is truly representative rather than direct. Butler and Raney, *Referendums*, p. 16; Joseph P. Board, *The Government and Politics of Sweden* (Boston: Houghton and Mifflin, 1970), p. 116. The 1958 superannuated pensions election, on the other hand, provided for an electoral realignment, in which the Liberal Party lost one-half of its support. The referendum did not bind the executive, however, as the

majority of voters voted for plans other than the Social Democratic proposal. In contrast to the Swiss referenda, only the political parties can call the referenda, and the proposals are not limited to ratifying or supported an already enacted law or a constitutional initiative. On this period, see Nils Elvander, "The Politics of Taxation in Sweden 1945–1970: A Study of the Functions of Parties and Organizations," *Scandinavian Political Studies 7* (1972), pp. 63–82, and Sven Steinmo, "Political Institutions and Tax Policy in the United States, Sweden, and Britain," *World Politics 41* No. 4 (July 1989), pp. 500–535.

64 In 1960, 50 doctors were attached to the private clinics known as "*Läkarhus.*" By 1978, the number had grown to 390, compared with over 10,000 active physicians. These private clinics have been much more successful for dentists, whose number grew from 30 affiliated dentists in 1966 to 1,720 in 1978. (Figures from *Praktikertjänst AB*, the company that organizes the clinics.) Recently, there have been new (and controversial) attempts to start private clinics, and they have had more success, notably *Stockholm Akuten*, an emergency care service.

65 Socialdepartementet Stencil 1969: 2, "Promemoria med förslag till ändringar av sjukförmånerna inom sjukförsäkringen mm."

66 Heidenheimer, "Conflict and Compromise," pp. 121, 127–8; Biörck, "How to be a Clinician in a Socialist Country," p. 814; Carin Oldfelt, "Läkarförbundets inflytande på intagningen av medicine studerande och frågan om landets läkarbehov 1946–1959," unpublished paper from the pro-seminar in Political Science, Uppsala University, 1962.

67 Younger doctors, interested in better relations with the government, were important for the passage of the 1959 Hospital Law. This does not mean that enactment of the law came free of disputes. The Medical Association insisted that the hospital outpatient clinics be limited to specialist care. Later, these restrictions were lifted by the 1963 and 1972 Hospital Laws. SOU 1978: 74, p. 27; Heidenheimer, "Conflict and Compromise"; Uncas Serner, "Swedish Health Legislation: Milestones in Re-Organization Since 1945," *The Shaping of the Swedish Health System*, eds. Heidenheimer and Elvander (London: Croom Helm, 1980), pp. 99–116. Mack Carder and Bendix Klingeberg, "Towards a Salaried Medical Profession: How 'Swedish' was the Seven Crowns Reform?", *The Shaping of the Swedish Health System*, eds. Heidenheimer and Elvander, pp. 146, 143–172.

68 Interviews, 30 January 1980, 18 April 1980, Dr. Karl-Evert Mosten, negotiator for *Sveriges Practiserande Läkares Förening* and *Praktiker Bolaget AB*; 1 April 1980, S.-Åke Lindgren, Surgeon General of Sweden.

69 Carder and Klingeberg, "How 'Swedish' was the Seven Crowns Reform?", p. 150.

70 Sven Aspling, former Social Minister, interview, June 1980.

71 Carder and Klingeberg, "How 'Swedish' was the Seven Crowns Reform?", p. 150.

72 Patients at the hospital *polikliniks* and at district doctors would pay 7 crowns, whereas at private practitioners' offices they would pay the full fee, with reimbursement for 75 percent of the official fee as under the fee schedule. Because private doctors – or public doctors in their private hours – charged above officially recognized rates, the actual rates of reimbursement to patients were significantly lower than those guaranteed by law. This overcharging, as well as the theory that these increases in fees created a market pressure to increase the fee schedule for all doctors, was part of the motivation for the Seven Crowns reform.

73 In addition, the reform was triggered by the County Councils' plan to raise the
    cost of inpatient care from 5 to 10 crowns per day; the introduction of the
    7 crowns flat fee for outpatient care would compensate patients for this
    increase. Pensioners, the group most likely to be hurt by the increased in-
    patients fees, were placated by doubling the number of free hospital days
    available to them, from 180 days to a full year. The shift in outpatient care
    financing from reimbursement to flat fee was estimated to cost 250 million
    crowns annually, 200 million of which would be financed through an increase
    in the employer contribution to health insurance from 2.5 percent to 2.9
    percent of the wage bill.
74 An alternate solution would have been to make the reimbursement fee schedule
    binding on all doctors, not just junior hospital physicians, which was the route
    taken in France. The elimination of fees and the substitution of salary for
    hospital outpatient care was a more reliable route, however. For the re-
    imbursement schedule – binding for junior hospital physicians – was con-
    tinually driven upward by the fees of private practitioners and senior doctors
    who were not bound by it. The reimbursement schedule had not been nego-
    tiated on a regular basis until 1965. Although the Swedish Medical Association
    was consulted about the schedule, it took care not to participate as a nego-
    tiating body, for fear that the schedule would become binding on all physicians.
    In 1965, junior hospital doctors threatened to go on strike unless the schedule,
    which had remained more or less the same since 1955, was revised, Glaser,
    Paying the Doctor, p. 49. Nevertheless, despite regular negotiations, the
    reimbursement schedule failed to keep up with the fees of the private scetor.
    On the recommendation of the Hultström report of 1967, the reimbursement
    schedule was raised an average of 35 percent in 1968, yet already in September
    1968 the average fee in Stockholm surpassed the schedule by 31.4 percent.
    Stockholm private practitioners charged 42.5 percent above the schedule,
    hospital chiefs-of-staff 33.4 percent. Outside Stockholm, private practitioners
    overcharged by 32 percent, but because hospital doctors charged less, the
    average fee was only 9.6 percent above the schedule. Consequently, average
    reimbursement rates to patients were 55.8 percent in Stockholm and 68.6
    percent elsewhere, compared with the legislated 75 percent. In 1966, they had
    been 52 percent and 64.2 percent, respectively, a situation that the 1968
    increases had intended to remedy. Socialdepartementet Stencil 1969: 2.

75 Carder and Klingeberg, "How 'Swedish' Was the Seven Crowns Reform?",
    p. 163.
76 Heidenheimer, "Conflict and Compromise."
77 Gunnar Biörck, *SvD*, 17 Nov 1969, p. 4.
78 LF-*remiss*, 29 April, 1969, in Socialdepartementet Konseljakt 17 October
    1969, Nr. 60 (Prop. 125), Prop. med förslag till ändring i lagen den 25 maj
    1962 (Nr. 381) om allmänn försäkring mm. Socialdepartementet, hereafter
    referred to as "Archives, 1969."
79 Even after the large increase in the number of doctors in Sweden, there were
    only 13.9 physicians per 10,000 persons, compared with 15.4 in the United
    States, 17.8 in West Germany, and 13.9 in France. Table adapted from
    Maxwell in Christa Altenstetter, "The Impact of Organizational Arrange-
    ments," *Changing National-Subnational Relations in Health*, ed. C. Altenstetter
    (Washington, DC: Fogerty International Center and Department of Health,
    Education and Welfare, 1976), pp. 22, 3–33. See Table 6, Chapter 3.
80 Socialdepartementet Konseljakt 17 October 1969, nr. 60 (Prop. 125) prop.
    med förslag till ändring i lagen den 25 maj 1962 om allmänn försäkring mm.

81 Carder and Klingeberg, "How 'Swedish' Was the Seven Crowns Reform?", p. 143.
82 Elvander, *Svensk Skattepolitik 1945–1970*, chapter VIII.
83 Rolf Evjegård, *Landstingsförbundet. Organisation. Beslutsfattande. Förhållande till Staten* (Stockholm: Landstingsförbundet, 1973), pp. 335, 337.
84 *SvD*, 17 November 1969, cited in Evjegård, *Landstingsförbundet*, p. 394.
85 *Riksdagens protokoll FK* 1969, 39:72.
86 *Handelstidningen*, reprinted in *Dagen's Nyheter* 25 November 1969.
87 *Göteborgs Handels & Sjöfartstidning*, 10 December 1969, 31 December 1969.
88 *LT*, 5 November 1969, p. 4625–8; 19 November 1969, p. 4826; *LT*, December 1969, p. 4964. See also Carder and Klingeberg, "How 'Swedish' was the Seven Crowns Reform?"
89 Letter from Medical Association to Social Department, 1979–02–06, Brev till Socialdepartementet från Sveriges Läkarförbund, 1979–02–06, Olle Westerborn/Bo Hjern.
90 Björn Smedby, "Primary Care Financing in Sweden," pp. 247–251 in C.D. Burrell and C.G. Sheps, eds., *Primary Health Care in Industrialized Nations. Annals of the New York Academy of Sciences, 310* (NY: NY Academy of Sciences, 1978), p. 250.
91 The hospital positions were full-time positions – these spare-time practices were all carried out in overtime hours. In Britain in the late 1960s, 70 percent of hospital consultants had part-time private practices and worked in the hospitals on a part-time basis. Anderson, *Health Care: Can there be Equity?"*, p. 196.
92 *Socialdepartementet*, Ds S 1982:9; Serner "Swedish Health Legislation: Milestones in Reorganization Since 1945," p. 112.
93 Proposition 1983/84: 190, "Regeringens Proposition om vissa ersättningar till sjukvårdshuvudmänen mm." 5 April 1984. On growth of private practice, see also Marilynn M. Rosenthal, "Beyond Equity: Swedish Health Policy and the Private Sector," *The Milbank Quarterly 64*, Vol. 1, No. 4, (1986), pp. 592–621.

Chapter 6

1 See Shepsle, "Institutional Equilibrium and Equilibrium Institutions," on structure-induced equilibrium and partitioning into jurisdictions, and Hammond and Miller, "The Core of the Consitution," on cores.
2 Stephens, *Transition from Capitalism to Socialism*, p. 216, fn 9, gives Switzerland a score of zero on his "socialist rule index," arguing that "since the Swiss Social Democrats have always had two members in the Bundesrat, the seven-member executive, [it might be argued] that Switzerland should be coded as 7 not as 0. However, membership in the Bundesrat does not give one effective power over policy making. It is not a coalition government, operating on the basis of parliamentary support, making policy, [and so on]. The effective policymaking mechanism is the referendum, which impedes coalition formation and isolates the Social Democrats from any effective influence over policy making. Thus, since the party has no direct power over state policy, Switzerland should be coded 0 on the "socialist rule index". I argue, by contrast, that because political institutions have such strong effects on policy making, they should be at the center of models that analyze the effects of politics on policy making.
3 Jean Meynaud, *Les organisations professionnelles en Suisse* (Lausanne: Editions Librairie Payot, 1963), p. 181.

4 Meynaud, *Organisations Professionnelles*. In a careful study of union and employee association membership figures, Jelle Visser estimates the total union-employee association density (members divided by potential members) at 73 percent, 19.8 percent, and 30.3 percent for Sweden, France, and Switzerland, respectively. Swedish and Swiss figures are for 1960, French for 1962. *Dimensions of Union Growth in Postwar Western Europe*. European University Institute Working Paper No. 89. (Badia Fiesolana, San Domenico, FI: European University Institute, 1984, pp. 29, 65, 77. See Table 7.

5 Abram de Swaan, *In Care of the State. Health Care, Education and Welfare in Europe and the USA in the Modern Era* (Oxford: Polity Press/Basil Blackwell, 1988), p. 148.

6 Ashford, *Emergence of the Welfare States*; Heidenheimer, "Conflict and Compromise."

7 Gary P. Freeman, "National Styles and Policy Sectors: Explaining Structured Variation," *Journal of Public Policy*, 5, part 4 (October 1985); 467–496; Jeremy Richardson, *Policy Styles in Western Europe* (London: George Allen & Unwin, 1982).

8 On Britain, see Klein, *Politics of the National Health Service*; Eckstein, *Pressure Group Politics*. On Italy, see Lange and Regini, *State, Market, and Social Regulation*, pp. 257–261.

8a Altmeyer, *The Formative Years of Social Security*.

9 Rosewitz and Webber, *Reformversuche und Reformblockaden im deutschen Gesundheitswesen*.

10 Arthur Altmeyer, *The Formative Years of Social Security* (Madison: University of Wisconsin Press).

11 As Giovanni Sartori argued, "We are the victims of an *objectivist bias*. The underlying argument goes something like this: The polity (and politics) is an 'artifact,' whereas in the society we find the 'facts'," "From the Sociology of Politics to Political Sociology," in S.M. Lipset, ed, *Politics and Social Sciences*, (London, New York, Toronto: Oxford University Press, 1969), p. 85.

Bibliography and sources cited

French, Swiss, and Swedish sources are cited separately at the end of the general bibliography

Abbott, Andrew (1988). *The System of the Professions. An Essay on the Division of Expert Labor.* Chicago: University of Chicago Press.

Abel-Smith, Brian (1965). "The Major Pattern of Medical Financing and the Organization of Medical Services that Have Emerged in Other Countries," *Medical Care*, Vol. 3, No. 1 (January–March), pp. 33–40.

Alber, Jens (1982). *Vom Armenhaus zum Wohlfahrtsstaat. Analysen zur Entwicklung der Sozialversicherung in Westeuropa.* Frankfurt: Campus Verlag.

Alford, Robert R. (1975). *Health Care Politics: Ideological and Interest Group Barriers to Reform.* Chicago: University of Chicago Press.

Altenstetter, Christa (1976). "The Impact of Organizational Arrangements," pp. 3–33 in C. Altenstetter (ed.), *Changing National-Subnational Relations in Health.* Washington, DC: Fogerty International Center and Department of Health, Education and Welfare.

Altmeyer, Arthur (1966). *The Formative Years of Social Security.* Madison: University of Wisconsin Press.

Anderson, Odin W. (1972). *Health Care: Can There Be Equity? The United States, Sweden and England.* New York: John Wiley.

(1989). "Issues in the Health Services of the United States," pp. 49–71 in Mark G. Field (ed.), *Success and Crisis in National Health Systems: A Comparative Approach.* New York: Routledge.

Ashford, Douglas E. (1978). *Comparing Public Policies: New Concepts and Methods.* Beverly Hills, CA: Sage Publications.

(1986). "The British and French Social Security Systems: Welfare State by Intent and by Default," pp. 96–122 in Douglas E. Ashford and E.W. Kelley, (eds.), *Nationalizing Social Security.* Greenwich, CT: JAI Press.

(1986). *The Emergence of the Welfare States.* Oxford and New York: Blackwells.

Baernreither, J.M. (1889). *English Associations of Working Men.* London: Swann Sonnenschein & Co., republished by Gale Research Co., Detroit, 1966.

Baldwin, Peter (1988). *The Politics of Social Solidarity and the Bourgeois Origins of the European Welfare State, 1875–1975.* Cambridge: Cambridge University Press.

Bates, Robert H. (1988). "Contra Contractarianism: Some Reflections on the New Institutionalism," *Politics & Society*, Vol. 16, No. 2–3 (June-Sept.), pp. 387–401.

Baumol, William J. (1988), "Containing Medical Costs: Why Price Controls Won't Work," *The Public Interest* No. 93, (Fall), pp. 37–53.

Begin, Monique (1988). *Medicare Canada's Right to Health*. Montreal: Optimum Publishing International.

Berlant, Jeffrey (1975). *Profession and Monopoly*. Berkeley: University of California Press.

Björkman, James Warner (1985). "Who Governs the Health Sector?" *Comparative Politics 17*. 4 (July), pp. 399–420.

Block, Fred (1977). "The Ruling Class Does Not Rule." *Socialist Revolution*, Vol. 7 No. 33, pp. 6–28

Brown, Lawrence D. (1986). "Introduction to a Decade of Transition," *Journal of Health Politics, Policy and Law*, Vol. 11, No. 4 (Winter), pp. 569–583.

Cameron, David (1978). "The Expansion of the Public Economy: A Comparative Analysis," *American Political Science Review 72*, No. 4, (December), pp. 1243–61.

Carr-Saunders, Alexander Morris, and Paul Alexander Wilson (1962). *The Professions*. London: Frank Case.

Castles, Francis G. (1982). "The Impact of Parties on Public Expenditures," pp. 21–96 in Castles (ed.), *The Impact of Parties*. Beverly Hills: Sage.

Chubb, John E. (1983). *Interest Groups and the Bureaucracy. The Politics of Energy*. Stanford: Stanford University Press.

Cobb, Roger and Charles Elder (1972). *Participation in American Politics: The Dynamics of Agenda Building*. Boston: Allyn and Bacon.

Cutright, Phillips (1965). "Political Structure, Economic Development and National Social Security Programs," *American Journal of Sociology 70*, No. 3 (March), pp. 537–50.

Cyert, Richard M. and James March (1963). *A Behavioral Theory of the Firm*. Englewood Cliffs, NJ: Prentice Hall.

Derthick, Martha (1979). *Policy-Making for Social Security*. Washington, DC: The Brookings Institution.

Domhoff, William (1987). *Power Elites and Organizations*. Newbury Park, CA: Sage Publications.

Eckstein, Harry (1960). *Pressure Group Politics: The Case of the British Medical Association*. London: Allen & Unwin.

Edelman, Murray (1964). *The Symbolic Uses of Politics*. Urbana: University of Illinois Press.

Esping-Andersen, Gösta and Walter Korpi (1984). "Social Policy as Class Politics in Post-War Capitalism," in Goldthorpe (ed.), *Crisis and Order in Contemporary Capitalism*. Oxford: Clarendon Press, Oxford University Press.

Esping-Andersen, Gösta (1990). *The Three Worlds of Welfare Capitalism*. Princeton: Princeton University Press.

Evans, Robert G. (1984). *Strained Mercy. The Economics of Canadian Health Care*. Toronto: Butterworths.

(1986). "Finding the Levers, Finding the Courage: Lessons from Cost Containment in North America," *Journal of Health Politics, Policy and Law*, Vol. 11, No. 4, (Winter), pp. 585–615.

Fein, Rashi (1989). *Medical Care, Medical Costs. The Search for a Health Insurance Policy*. Cambridge, MA: Harvard University Press.

Ferejohn, John A. (1988). "The Structure of Agency Decision Processes," pp. 441–461 in Mathew D. McCubbins and Terry Sullivan eds., *Congress: Structure and Policy*. Cambridge: Cambridge University Press.

Field, Mark G. (1980). "The Health System and the Polity: A Contemporary American Dialectic," Vol. 14A, pp. 397–413.

ed. (1989). *Success and Crisis in National Health Systems: A Comparative Approach.* New York: Routledge.

Flora, Peter and Alber, Jens (1981). "Modernization, Democratization, and the Development of Welfare States in Western Europe," pp. 37–80 in Flora and Heidenheimer (eds.), *The Development of Welfare States in Europe and America.* New Brunswick, NJ: Transaction Books.

Flora, Peter, ed., (1986). *Growth to Limits. The Western European Welfare States Since World War II.* Vol. 1. *Sweden, Norway, Finland, Denmark.* European University Institute, Series C. Political and Social Science, 6.1 Berlin, New York: Walter de Gruyter.

(1986). *Growth to Limits. The Western European Welfare States Since World War II.* Vol. 2. *Germany, United Kingdom, Ireland, Italy.* European University Institute. Series C. Political and Social Science. 6.2 Berlin, New York: Walter de Gruyter.

(1987). *Growth to Limits. The Western European Welfare States Since World War II.* Vol. 4. *Appendix (Synopses, Bibliographies, Tables)* European University Institute. Series C. Political and Social Science. 6.4 Berlin, New York: Walter de Gruyter.

Fox, Daniel M. (1986). *Health Policies. Health Politics. The British and American Experience, 1911–1965.* Princeton: Princeton University Press.

Fraser, Derek (1973). *The Evolution of the British Welfare State. A History of Social Policy Since the Industrial Revolution.* NY: Harper & Row.

Freddi, Giorgio and James Warner Björkman (1989). *Controlling Medical Professionals. The Comparative Politics of Health Governance.* London: Sage Publications.

Freeman, Gary P. (1985). "National Styles and Policy Sectors: Explaining Structured Variation." *Journal of Public Policy,* Vol. 5, Part 4 (October), pp. 467–496.

Freidson, Eliot (1970). *Profession of Medicine: A Study of the Sociology of Applied Knowledge.* New York: Dodd, Mead & Company.

Friedman, Milton (1962). *Capitalism and Freedom.* Chicago: Chicago University Press.

Gilbert, Bentley B. (1966). *The Evolution of National Insurance in Great Britain. The Origins of the Welfare State.* London: Michael Joseph.

Glaser, William A. (1970). *Paying the Doctor: Systems of Remuneration and their Effects.* Baltimore: Johns Hopkins University Press.

(1976). *Paying the Doctor Under National Health Insurance: Foreign Lessons for the United States,* 2nd ed. Springfield, VA: National Technical Informations Service, US Dept. of Commerce.

(1978). *Health Insurance Bargaining: Foreign Lessons for Americans.* NY: Gardener Press.

(1984). "Health Politics: Lessons From Abroad," pp. 305–338 in Theodor J. Litman ed., *Health Politics and Policy.* New York: John Wiley.

(1989). "The Politics of Paying American Physicians," *Health Affairs.* Vol. 8, No. 3 (Fall), pp. 129–146.

Godt, Paul J. (1987). "Confrontation, Consent, and Corporatism: State Strategies and the Medical Profession in France, Great Britain, and West Germany," *Journal of Health Politics, Policy and Law,* Vol. 12, No. 3 (Fall), pp. 459–481.

Goldthorpe, John (1984). *Order and Conflict in Contemporary Capitalism.* Oxford: Clarendon Press, New York: Oxford University Press.

Gosden, P.H.J.H. (1961). *The Friendly Societies in England 1815–1875.* Manchester: Manchester University Press, 1961.

Gough, Ian (1979). *The Political Economy of the Welfare State.* London: Macmillan.

Gusfield, Joseph (1981). *The Culture of Public Problems.* Chicago: Chicago University Press.

Gutman, Amy, ed., (1988). *Democracy and the Welfare State.* Princeton: Princeton University Press.

Habermas, Jürgen (1983 [1962]). *Strukturwandel der Öffentlichkeit.* Darmstadt und Neuwied: Hermann Luchterhand Verlag.

Hall, Peter A. (1986). *Governing the Economy: the Politics of State Intervention in Britain and France.* Cambridge: Polity Press.

Ham, Christopher (1988). "Governing the Health Sector: Power and Policy Making in the English and Swedish Health Services," *The Milbank Quarterly.* Vol. 66, No. 2, pp. 389–414.

Hammond, Thomas H. and Gary J. Miller (1987). "The Core of the Constitution," *American Political Science Review,* Vol. 81, No. 4, (December), pp. 1155–1173.

Hattam, Victoria C. (1992). *Changing Conceptions of Class and American Political Development, 1806–1896.* Princeton, NJ: Princeton University Press.

Havighurst, Clark C. (1986). "The Changing Locus of Decision Making in the Health Care Sector," *Journal of Health Politics, Policy and Law,* Vol. 11, No. 4, (Winter), pp. 697–735.

Heclo, Hugh (1974). *Modern Social Politics in Britian and Sweden.* New Haven and London: Yale University Press.

Heidenheimer, Arnold J. (1985). "Comparative Public Policy at the Crossroads," *Journal of Public Policy,* Vol. 5, No. 4 (October), pp. 441–465.

Hewitt, Christopher (1977). "The Effect of Political Democracy and Social Democracy on Equality in Industrialized Societies: A Cross-National Comparison," *American Sociological Review 42,* (June), 450–464.

Hibbs, Douglas A. (1977). *Trade Union Power, Labor Militancy, and Wage Inflation: A Comparative Analysis.* Cambridge, MA: Center for International Studies, Massachusetts Institute of Technology.

(1977). "Political Parties and Macroeconomic Policy." *American Sociological Review 71.*

Hogarth, James (1963). *The Payment of the Physician. Some European Comparisons.* NY: Macmillan Co. (Pergamon Press).

Hollingsworth, J. Rogers (1986). *A Political Economy of Medicine: Great Britain and the United States.* Baltimore: Johns Hopkins University Press.

Honigsbaum, Frank (1979). *The Division in British Medicine. A History of the Separation of General Practice from Hospital Care, 1911–1968.* London: Kogan Page.

Ikenberry, G. John (1988). "Conclusion: An Institutional Approach to American Foreign Economic Policy," *International Organization,* Vol. 42, No. 1 (Winter), pp. 219–243.

Janowitz, Morris (1976). *The Social Control of the Welfare State.* NY: Elsevier.

Jenson, Jane (1986). "Gender and Reproduction: Or, Babies and the State." *Studies in Political Economy 20* (Summer): 9–43.

Johnston, J. Bruce and Uwe E. Reinhardt (1989). "Addressing the Health of a Nation: Two Views." *Health Affairs,* Vol. 8, No. 2 (Summer), pp. 5–23.

Jost, Timothy S. (1990). *Assuring the Quality of Medical Practice.* London: King Edward's Hospital Fund for London.

Kaufmann, Franz-Xavier, Giandomenico Majone, Vincent Ostrom and Wolfgang Wirth eds. (1986). *Guidance, Control and Evaluation in the Public Sector*. Berlin, New York: Walter de Gruyter.

Klass, Gary M. (1985). "Explaining America and the Welfare State: An Alternative Theory," *British Journal of Political Science*, Vol. 15, Part 4, (October), pp. 427–450.

Katznelson, Ira (1981). *City Trenches: Urban Politics and the Patterning of Class in the United States*. NY: Pantheon, 1981.

Klein, Rudolf (1983). *The Politics of the National Health Service*. London: Longman.

Korpi, Walter (1983). *The Democratic Class Struggle*, London: Routledge and Kegan Paul.

Krasner, Stephen D. (1984). "Approaches to the State: Alternative Conceptions and Historical Dynamics," *Comparative Politics*, Vol. 16, No. 2, (January), pp. 223–246.

Kuhnle, Stein (1975). *Patterns of Social and Political Mobilization: A Historical Analysis*. London, Beverly Hills: Sage Publications.

Lange, Peter, and Marino Regini, eds. (1989). *State, Market, and Social Regulation. New Perspectives on Italy*. Cambridge: Cambridge University Press.

Larson, Magali Sarfatti (1977). *The Rise of Professionalism. A Sociological Analysis*. Berkeley: University of California Press.

Leichter, Howard M. (1979). *A Comparative Approach to Policy Analysis: Health Care Policy in Four Nations*. Cambridge: Cambridge University Press.

Light, Donald, and Sol Levine (1988). "The Changing Character of the Medical Profession: A Theoretical Overview," *The Milbank Quarterly*, Vol. 66, Suppl. 2, pp. 10–32.

Lijphart, Arend (1968). *The Politics of Accommodation. Pluralism and Democracy in the Netherlands*. Berkeley: University of California Press.

Lipsky, Michael (1968). "Protest as a Political Resource." *American Political Science Review 62*, No. 4, (December), pp. 1144–1158.

Lowi, Theodore J. (1979). *The End of Liberalism*. 2nd ed. New York: W.W. Norton.

Lubove, Roy (1968). *The Struggle for Social Security*. Cambridge, MA: Harvard University.

Maier, Charles S. (1975). *Recasting Bourgeois Europe*. Princeton: Princeton University Press.

March, James and Herbert Simon (1958). *Organizations*. New York: John Wiley and Sons.

March, James and Johan Olsen (1984). "The New Institutionalism: Organization Factors in Political Life," *American Political Science Review*, 78, no. 3, (Sept): 734–749.

(1983). "Organizing Political Life: What Administrative Reorganization Tells Us About Government," *The American Political Science Review*, Vol. 77, No. 2, pp. 281–296.

(1986). "Popular Sovereignty and the Search for Appropriate Institutions," *Journal of Public Policy*, Vol. 6, No. 4, (Oct–Dec), pp. 341–370.

(1989). *Rediscovering Institutions. The Organizational Basis of Politics*. New York: Free Press.

Marmor, Theodore with assistance of Jan S. Marmor (1973). *The Politics of Medicare*. Chicago: Aldine.

Marmor, Theodore R. (1983). *Political Analysis and American Medical Care*. Cambridge: Cambridge University Press.

(1986). "American Medical Policy and the 'Crisis' of the Welfare State: A Comparative Perspective," *Journal of Health Politics, Policy and Law*, Vol. 11, No. 4, Tenth Anniversary Issue, (Winter), pp. 617–631.

Marshall, T.H. (1964). "Citizenship and Social Class," pp. 71–134 in T.H. Marshall, *Class, Citizenship and Social Development*. Chicago: University of Chicago Press.

Maxwell, Robert J. (1981). *Health and Wealth. An International Study of Health Care Spending*. Lexington, MA: Lexington Books, D.C. Heath for Sandoz Institute for Health and Socio-Economic Studies.

McFarland, Andrew S. (1987). "Interest Groups and Theories of Power in America," *British Journal of Political Science*, Vol. 17, Part 2, (April), pp. 129–147.

Moe, Terry M. (1989). "The Politics of Bureaucratic Structure," pp. 267–329 in John E. Chubb and Paul E. Peterson (eds.), *Can the Government Govern?* Washington, DC: The Brookings Institution.

Myles, John (1984). *Old Age in the Welfare State*. Boston: Little Brown.

Naschold, Frieder (1967). *Kassenärzte und Krankenversicherungs-reform. Zu einer Theorie der Statuspolitik*. Freiburg im Breisgau: Verlag Rombach & Co.

Naylor, C. David (1986). *Private Practice, Public Payment. Canadian Medicine and the Politics of Health Insurance, 1911–1966*. Kingston: McGill-Queen's University Press.

Nelson, Barbara J. (1984). *Making An Issue of Child Abuse: Political Agenda-Setting for Social Problems*. Chicago: University of Chicago Press.

O'Connor, James (1973). *The Fiscal Crisis of the State*. NY: St. Martin's Press.

Offe, Claus (1984). *Contradictions of the Welfare State*. Cambridge: MIT Press.

(1987). "II. Democracy Against the Welfare State? Structural Foundations of Neoconservative Political Opportunities," *Political Theory*. Vol. 15, No. 4 (November), pp. 501–537.

Orloff, Ann Shola and Skocpol, Theda (1984). "Why Not Equal Protection? Explaining the Politics of Public Social Spending in Britain, 1900–1911, and the United States, 1880s–1920," *American Sociological Review*, 49, No. 6 (Dec): 726–750.

Ostrom, Elinor (1986). "A Method of Institutional Analysis," in Franz-Xavier Kaufmann, Giandomenico Majone, Vincent Ostrom, and Wolfgang Wirth (eds.), *Guidance, Control, and Evaluation in the Public Sector*, Berlin, New York: Walter de Gruyter.

Parsons, Talcott (1951). *The Social System*. Glencoe, IL: Free Press.

Pelling, Henry (1987). *A History of British Trade Unionism*. Fourth Ed. London: Macmillan.

Polanyi, Karl (1944). *The Great Transformation*. Boston: Beacon Press.

Pryor, F. (1968). *Public Expenditure in Communist and Capitalist Nations*. Homewood, IL: Irwin.

Quadagno, Jill (1984). "Welfare Capitalism and the Social Security Act of 1935." *American Sociological Review* 49: 632–47.

(1985). "Two Models of Welfare State Development: Reply to Skocpol and Amenta." *American Sociological Review* 50: 575–577.

Reulecke, J. (1981). "English Social Policy Around the Middle of the Nineteenth Century As Seen by German Social Reformers," pp. 32–49 in W.J. Mommsen (ed.), *The Emergence of the Welfare State in Britain and Germany 1850–1950*. London: Croom Helm.

Richardson, Jeremy (1982). *Policy Styles in Western Europe*. London: George Allen & Unwin.

Rimlinger, Gaston V. (1971). *Welfare Policy and Industrialization in Europe, America and Russia.* NY: John Wiley.

Riska, Elianne (1988). "The Professional Status of Physicians in the Nordic Countries," *The Milbank Quarterly, 66,* Suppl. 2: 133–147.

Roemer, Milton (1977). *Comparative National Policies on Health Care.* New York: Marcel Dekker.

Rosewitz, Bernd and Douglas Webber (1990). *Reformversuche und Reformblockaden im deutschen Gesundheitswesen.* Frankfurt: Campus.

Ruggie, Mary (1984). *The State and Working Women: A Comparative Study of Britain and Sweden.* Princeton: Princeton University Press.

Rothstein, Bo (forthcoming). *The Social Democratic State.* Cambridge and New York: Cambridge University Press.

Safran, William (1967). *Veto Group Politics: The Case of Health Insurance Reform in West Germany.* San Francisco: Chandler.

Sarfatti Larson, Magali (1977). *The Rise of Professionalism. A Sociological Analysis.* Berkeley: University of California Press.

Scharpf, Fritz W. (1986). "Policy Failure and Institutional Reform: Why Should Form Follow Function?" *International Social Science Journal, 38,* Special Issue, "The Study of Public Policy 108," No. 2: 179–189.

(1989). "Decision Rules, Decision Styles, and Policy Choices," *Journal of Theoretical Politics, 1*: 149–76.

Schattschneider, E.E. (1960). *The Semi-Sovereign People.* New York: Holt, Rinehart & Winston.

Schieber, George J. and Jean-Pierre Poullier (1989). "International Health Care Expenditure Trends: 1987," *Health Affairs,* Vol. 8, No. 3 (Fall), pp. 169–151.

Schmitter, Philippe C. and Gerhard Lembruch (eds.) (1979). *Trends Towards Corporatist Intermediation.* London and Beverly Hills: Sage Publications.

(1981). "Interest-Intermediation and Regime Governability in Contemporary Western Europe and North America," pp. 287–327 in S. Berger (ed.), *Organizing Interests in Western Europe.* Cambridge: Cambridge University Press.

Schmitter, Philippe C. and Wolfgang Streeck (1985). *Private Interest Government: Beyond Market and State.* London, Beverly Hills: Sage Publications.

Schneider, Markus, Jürg H. Sommer, Aynur Keçeci, Léa Scholtes, Arno Welzel (1989). *Gesundheitsysteme im internationalen Vergleich* 2d Ed. Bundesministerium für Arbeit und Sozialordnung Forschungsbericht No. 160. Bonn: Bundesministerium für Arbeit und Sozialordnung.

Scott, W. Richard (1987). "The Adolescence of Institutional Theory," *Administrative Science Quarterly,* Vol. 32, (December), pp. 493–511.

Selznick, Philip (1949). *TVA and the Grass Roots: A Study of Politics and Organization.* Berkeley, Los Angeles, London: University of California Press.

Shapiro, Robert Y. and John T. Young (1989). "Public Opinion and the Welfare State: The United States in Comparative Perspective," *Political Science Quarterly,* Vol. 104, No. 7, (Spring), pp. 59–89.

Shepsle, Kenneth (1986). "Institutional Equilibrium and Equilibrium Institutions," in Herbert F. Weisberg (ed.), *Political Science: The Science of Politics.* New York: Agathon Press.

Shepsle, Kenneth A, and Barry R. Weingast (1987). "The Institutional Foundations of Committee Power," *American Political Science Review,* Vol. 81, No. 1 (March), pp. 85–103.

Simon, Herbert (1976). *Administrative Behavior.* New York: Free Press.

Skocpol, Theda (1980). "Political Response to Capitalist Crisis: Neo-Marxist Theories of the State and the Case of the New Deal," *Politics and Society* 10, pp. 155–201.

(1985). "Bringing the State Back In: Strategies of Analysis in 'Current Research," pp. 3–37 in P.B. Evans, D. Rueschemeyer, and T. Skocpol (eds.), *Bringing the State Back In.* Cambridge: Cambridge University Press.

Smith, Tom W. (1987). "The Polls – A Report. The Welfare State in Cross-National Perspective," *Public Opinion Quarterly*, Vol. 51, (Fall), pp. 404–421.

Starr, Paul (1982). *The Social Transformation of American Medicine.* NY: Basic Books.

Steinmo, Sven, Kathleen Thelen, and Frank Longstreth, eds., (1992). *Structuring Politics: Historical Institutionalism in Comparative Politics*, Cambridge and New York: Cambridge University Press.

Stephens, John (1979). *The Transition from Capitalism to Socialism.* London: Macmillan.

Stevens, Rosemary (1966). *Medical Practice in Modern England: The Impact of Specialization and State Medicine.* New Haven, CT: Yale University Press.

Stigler, George (1971). *Can Regulatory Agencies Protect Consumers?* Washington, DC: American Enterprise Institute for Public Policy Research.

Stone, Deborah A. (1980). *The Limits of Professional Power.* Chicago: University of Chicago Press.

Swaan, Abram de (1986). "Workers' and Clients' Mutualism Compared: Perspectives from the Past in the Development of the Welfare State," *Government and Opposition*, 21, pp. 36–55.

(1988). *In Care of the State. Health Care, Education and Welfare in Europe and the USA in the Modern Era.* Oxford: Polity Press/Basil Blackwell.

Taylor, Rosemary C.R. (1984). "State Intervention in Postwar Western European Health Care: The Case of Prevention in Britain and Italy," pp. 91–111 in S. Bornstein, D. Held and J. Krieger (eds.), *The State in Capitalist Europe.* London: George, Allen & Unwin.

Therborn, Göran (1987). "Welfare States and Capitalist Markets," *Acta Sociologica 30*, 3/4, pp. 237–254.

Thurow, Lester C. (1985). "Medicine Versus Economics," *The New England Journal of Medicine*, Vol. 313, No. 10, pp. 611–614.

Tilly, Charles (1978). *From Mobilization to Revolution.* Reading, MA: Addison-Wesley.

Titmuss, Richard M. (1976). *Commitment to Welfare.* London: George Allen and Unwin.

Tsebelis, George (1990). "Elite Interaction and Constitution Building in Consociational Democracies," *Journal of Theoretical Politics*, Vol. 2, No. 1, (January), pp. 5–29.

Visser, Jelle (1984). *Dimensions of Union Growth in Postwar Western Europe.* European University Institute Working Paper No. 89. Badia Fiesolana, San Domenico (FI): European University Institute.

Webb, Sidney and Beatrice (1965). *The History of Trade Unionism.* New York: Augustus M. Kelley.

Weir, Margaret (1992). *Politics and Jobs: The Boundaries of Employment Policy in the United States.* Princeton, NJ: Princeton University Press.

Weir, Margaret and Skocpol, Theda (1985). "State Structures and the Possibilities for 'Keynesian' Responses to the Great Depression in Sweden, Britain and the United States," pp. 107–163 in P.B. Evans, D. Rueschemeyer, and

T. Skocpol (eds.), *Bringing the State Back In*. Cambridge: Cambridge University Press.

Weller, G.R. (1977). "From 'Pressure Group Politics' to 'Medical-Industrial Complex': The Development of Approaches to the Politics of Health," *Journal of Health Politics, Policy and Law*, Vol. 7, No. 4 (Winter), pp. 444–470.

Wilensky, Harold and Charles Lebeaux (1958). *Industrial Society and Social Welfare: The Impact of Industrialization on the Supply and Organization of Social Welfare Services in the U.S.* New York: Russell Sage Foundation (2nd edition 1965, New York: Free Press).

Wilensky, Harold (1964). "The Professionalization of Everyone?" *American Journal of Sociology* Vol. 70, No. 2 (September), pp. 137–158.

(1975). *The Welfare State and Equality*. Berkeley, CA: University of California Press.

(1976). *The "New Corporatism," Centralization and the Welfare State*. Beverley Hills, CA: Sage.

(1981). "Leftism, Catholicism, and Democratic Corporatism: The Role of Political Parties in Recent Welfare State Development." pp. 345–382 in Peter Flora and Arnold Heidenheimer, *The Development of Welfare States in Europe and America*. New Brunswick, NJ: Transaction Press.

Wilsford, David (1987). "The Cohesion and Fragmentation of Organized Medicine in France and the United States," *Journal of Health Politics, Policy and Law*, Vol. 12, No. 3 (Fall), pp. 481–503.

Wolin, Sheldon S. (1987). "Theorizing the Welfare State. I. Democracy and the Welfare State. The Political and Theoretical Connections Between Staatsräson and Wohlfahrtsstaatsräson," *Political Theory*, Vol. 15, No. 4 (Nov), pp. 467–500.

Wolinsky, Fredric D. (1988). "The Professional Dominance Perspective, Revisited," *The Milbank Quarterly*, Vol. 66, Suppl. 2, pp. 33–47.

FRENCH SOURCES

Primary sources

Archives

Archives (1930). Archives Nationales. Ministère du Travail. "Assurances sociales," Ass. S., cartons 1–7.

Archives (1958). Archives Nationales. Direction des Hôpitaux. Ministère des Affaires Sociales et de la Santé. "Comité Interministèriel d'étude des problèmes de l'enseignement médical, de la structure hospitalière et de l'action sanitaire et sociale, 1956–1962," F 17 511. "Réforme Hospitalo-Universitaire," SAN 1781. "Conseil Supérieur des Hôpitaux," DGS 497–498. SAN 1601.

Archives (1960). Archives Nationales. Direction de la Sécurité Sociale. Ministère des Affaires Sociales et de la Santé. "Travaux préparatoire à la réforme de la Sécurité Sociale de 1960," SAN 7514–7519. "Sécurité Sociale- Réformes," SS 2711–2. "Honoraires," SS 7082–4. SAN 7557.

Government documents

Centre de Recherche pour l'Etude et l'Observation des Conditions de Vie (CREDOC). Institut Nationale de la Statistique et des Etudes Economiques

(INSEE). Ministère de la Santé. *Comptes Nationaux de Santé. Résultats 1950–1977.* 1979.

Cour de Comptes. *Rapport au Président de la République, suivi des réponses des Administrations.* Paris: Journal Officiel (JO).

Inspection Générale des Affaires Sociales. *Rapport Annuel 1977–1978. Les Etablissements Sanitaires et Sociaux.* Paris: Documentation Française, 1979.

Journal Officiel. Lois et Décrets (laws and decrees).

Journal Officiel. Débats parlementaires, Assemblée Nationale (parliamentary debates, national assembly).

Journal Officiel. Débats parlementaires, Sénat (parliamentary debates, senate).

Ministère de la Santé publique et de la Sécurité sociale. *Pour une politique de la Santé. Rapports présentées à Robert Boulin. Tome III. L'hôpital.* Présenté par M. Roger Grégoire, Conseilleur d'Etat. Paris: Documentation Française, 1971.

Newspaper archives

Press Archives of *Le Monde.* "Sécurité sociale," (1956–1960); "Médecins," (1981–1983); "Hôpitaux," (1965–1970).

Dossiers de Presse (DdP). Press archives of the Fondation Nationale des Sciences Politiques. Dossiers 421/01 (1945–7); 421/04 (1949–1965); 474 (1955–9); 474/2 (1979–1981).

Journals and annuals

L'Année Politique (AP). Selected years. Paris: Presses Universitaires de France.

Bulletin du Conseil National du Patronat Français. Le Patronat (journal of the CNPF, the organization of employers), April 1957, June 1965, December 1968.

Le Concours Médicale, 1926, 1945, and selected years.

Esprit. "Les Médecins parlent de la médecine," 25, special issue No. 247 (February 1957): 161–387.

Le Médecin de France. Journal officiel de la confédération des syndicats médicaux français (journal of the CSMF, the main French medical association), 1929–1930.

Le Médecin Syndicaliste (journal of the USMF, an early medical association), 1925–7.

Revue "Paysans" (journal of the Peasants' Association), June–July 1957, 1959.

Revue de la Sécurité sociale (journal of the FNOSS, the organization of social security funds), April 1951, April 1957, March 1957, May 1957, March 1960, 1956–1960.

Sondages. Bulletin d'Information de l'Institut Français d'Opinion Publique. Revue Françise de l'Opinion Publique. 1945–1976. "Les Français et leur Médecin," 22, special issue No. 1 & 2 (1960).

La Volonté de Commerce et l'Industrie. Organe Mensuel de la Confédération générale des petits et moyennes entreprises (journal of the CGPME, the assocation of small and medium-sized firms), 1957, June 1960.

Secondary sources

Adam, Gérard (1964). *Atlas des élections sociales en France.* Cahiers de la Fondation Nationale des Sciences Politiques, Partis et Elections. Paris: Librairie Armand Colin.

Ashford, Douglas E. (1981). *British Dogmatism and French Pragmatism: Central-Local Policy-making in the Welfare State.* London: Allen & Unwin.

(1982). *Policy and Politics in France: Living with Uncertainty.* Philadelphia: Temple University Press.

Association Française de Science Politique (AFSP) (1957), "Les Intellectuels Dans la Société Française Contemporaine," Table Ronde de Juin 1957. Paris: AFSP.

Baszanger, Isabelle (1981). "La socialisation professionnelle des étudiants en médecine," *Revue Française de Sociologie*, XXII-2 (April–June): 223–245.

Baumgartner, Frank R. and Jack L. Walker, "Educational Policymaking and the Interest Group Structure in France and the United States," *Comparative Politics, 21,* 3 (Apr): 273–288.

Benar, Georges (1957). "Le contrôle de l'état sur les organismes de sécurité sociale," *Droit Social, 20* (Nov–Dec): 565–582; 644–647.

Berger, Suzanne (1974). "The French Political System," pp. 333–470 in S. Beer and A. Ulam (eds), *Patterns of Government*, 2nd ed. NY: Random House.

(1981). "Regime and Interest-Representation: The French traditional middle classes," pp. 83–101 in S. Berger (ed), *Organizing Interests in Western Europe.* Cambridge: Cambridge University Press.

Birnbaum, Pierre (1977). *Les Sommets de l'Etat.* Paris: Editions du Seuil.

Blanpain, Jan, with Luc Delesie and Herman Nys (1978). *National Health Insurance and Health Resources: The European Experience.* Cambridge: Harvard University Press.

Boltanski, Luc (1970). "Consommation médicale et rapport au corps," unpublished paper, Centre de Sociologie Européene, Maison de Sciences de l'Homme, Paris.

Brugeneur, Michel (1977). "La France malade de sa médecine?" *Revue Politique et Parlementaire*, (Sept–Oct): 63–74.

Brunet-Jailly, Joseph (1971). *Essai sur l'économie générale de la Santé.* Paris: Editions Cujas.

Bungener Lapadu-Hargues, Martine (1980). "Besoins en médecins et fonctions sociales de la médecine." Thesis, U.E.R. Sciences des Organisations, Université Paris IX Dauphine, Paris.

Antoinette Catrice-Lorey (1982). *Dynamique Interne de la Sécurité Sociale. 2nd ed.* Paris: Centre des Recherches en Sciences Sociales.

Antoinette Catrice-Lorey (1980). *Dynamique Interne de la Sécurité Sociale.* Paris: Centre des Recherches en Sciences Sociales.

Cayla, J.-S. (1976). "Le Conventionnement des honoraires médicaux," *Revue Trimestrielle de Droit Saniatire et Sociale, 12,* No. 46 (April–June): 327–343.

(C.E.R.S.) Centre d'étude des Relations sociales (1962). *Sécurité sociale et conflits de classes.* Economie et Humanisme. Paris: Les Editions Ouvrières.

Chapsal, Jacques (1981). *La Vie Politique sous la Ve République.* Paris: Presses Universitaires de France.

Chenot, Bernard (1960). "Les problèmes de la Santé Publique," *La Revue des Deux Mondes*, (1 May): 19–28.

Cibrie, Paul (President of the CSMF) (1954). *Syndicalisme Médical.* Paris: Confédération des Syndicats Médicaux Français (CSMF).

Clément, J.-M. (1982). "Le préfet et l'hôpital," *Revue de Droit Sanitaire et Sociale, 18,* no. 69 (Jan–Mar): 18–31.

Comité de Liaison, d'Etude et d'Action Républicains (CLEAR) (1970). *L'Hôpital en Question. Dossier Pour la Réforme Hospitalière.* Paris: Editions Emile-Paul.

Comet, P. (1959). "La Réforme Hospitalière," *La Revue Administrative, 12,* 67 (Jan–Feb): 12–18.

Debré, Robert (1974). *L'honneur de vivre. Témoinage.* Paris: Hermann et Stock.

G. Dorion and A. Guionnet (1983). *La Sécurité Sociale*, Que Sais-Je? No. 294. Paris: Presses Universitaires de France.

Doublet, Jacques (1971). "La Sécurité Sociale et son évolution [octobre 1951–juin 1961]," *Revue Française des Affaires Sociales*, 25, No. 2 (April–June): 26–60.

(1972). *Sécurité Sociale, 5e Edition*. Paris: Presses Universitaires de France.

Dupeyroux, Jean-Jacques (1960). "Nouvelles remarques sur la réforme du 12 mai 1960," *Droit Social*, 23, No. 11 (Nov): 567–572.

(1984). *Droit de la Sécurité Sociale*. Paris: Dalloz.

(1988). *Droit de la Sécurité Sociale. 11th Ed*. Paris: Dalloz.

Duverger, Maurice (1976). *Institutions politiques et droit constitutionnel. Vol. 2 Le système politique français*. Paris: Presses Universitaires de France.

Ehrmann, Henry W. (1957). *Organized Business in France*. Princeton: Princeton University Press.

(1976). *Politics in France, Third Ed*. Boston: Little Brown & Co.

Galant, Henry C. (1955). *Histoire Politique de la Sécurité Sociale Française. 1945–1952*. Cahiers de la Fondation Nationale des Sciences Politiques No. 76. Paris: Librairie Armand Colin.

Glaser, William A. (1970). *Paying the Doctor: Systems of Remuneration and their Effects*. Baltimore & London: Johns Hopkins University Press.

Paul Godt, "Health Care: the Political Economy of Social Policy," in Godt, ed., *Policy-Making in France* (London and NY: Pinter Publishers, 1989), pp. 191–207.

Goguel, François (1958). *La Politique des Partis sous la IIIe République, 3e Edition*. Paris: Editions du Seuil.

Goguel, François and Alfred Grosser (1967). *La Politique en France, 3e Edition*. Paris: Librairie Armand Colin.

Grémion, Pierre (1976). *Le pouvoir périphérique*. Paris: Le Seuil.

Guillemard, Anne-Marie (1980). *La Vieillesse et l'Etat*. Paris: Presses Universitaires de France.

Hall, Peter A. (1986). *Governing the Economy*. Oxford: Oxford University Press.

Hatzfeld, Henri (1963). *Le Grand Tournant de la Médecine Libérale*. Paris: Les Editions Ouvrières.

(1971). *Du Paupérisme à la Sécurité Sociale. Essai sur les Origines de la Sécurité Sociale en France. 1850–1940*. Paris: Librairie Armand Colin.

Herzlich, Claudine (1973). "Types de clientèle et fonctionnement de l'institution hospitalière," *Revue Française de Sociologie*, XIV, special issue: 41–59.

(1982). "The Evolution of Relations Between French Physicians and the State from 1880 to 1980," *Sociology of Health and Illness*, 4, No. 3: 241–252.

Hilaire, Dr., Chargé de Mission à la Direction Générale de la Sécurité Sociale au Ministère du Travail, (1946). "Les médecins devant la sécurité sociale," *Revue Française de Travail*, I, No. 7 (Oct): 566–574.

Hoffmann, Stanley (1956). *Le Mouvement Poujade*. Cahiers de la Fondation Nationale des Sciences Politiques No. 81. Paris: Presses de la Fondation Nationale des Sciences Politiques.

(1976). "Paradoxes of the French Political Community," pp. 1–117 in Hoffmann (ed), *In Search of France*. Cambridge: Harvard University Press.

Imbert, Jean (1958). "La réforme hospitalière," *Droit Social*, 21, no. 9–10 (Sept–Oct): 496–505.

(1959). "Les ordonnances de décembre 1958 sur les établissements de soins," *Droit Social*, 22, No. 6 (June): 356–364.

(1972). *L'Hôpital Français*. Paris: Presses Universitaires de France.

Jambu-Merlin, Roger (1970). *La Sécurité Sociale*. Paris: Librairie Armand Colin.

Jamous, Haroun (1969). *Sociologie de la décision: la réforme des études médicales et des structures hospitalières.* Paris: Editions du Centre Nationale de la Recherche Scientifique.

Jobert, B. and Paoli, J.F. (1982). "Les syndicats médicaux et la sécurité sociale," *Prévenir*, No. 5, special issue, "Sécurité sociale et Santé," Marseille, (March): 109–115.

Jean de Kervasdoué, "La Politique de l'Etat en Matière d'Hospitalisation Privée, 1962–1978," *Annales Economiques 16* (1980): 23–57.

Lacronique, J.F. (1982). "The French Health Care System," pp. 265–288 in A. Maynard & G. McLachlan (eds), *The Public/Private Mix for Health.* London: The Nuffield Provincial Hospitals Trust.

Laroque, Pierre (1948). "De l'assurance sociale a la sécurité sociale. L'experience française," *Revue Internationale de Travail, LVLL,* No. 6 (June): 621–649.

(1971). "La Sécurité Sociale de 1944 à 1951," *Revue Française des Affaires Sociales,* 25, No. 2 (April–June): 11–25.

Lavielle, Roman (1964). *Histoire de la mutualité. Sa place dans le régime français de la Sécurité Sociale.* Paris: Librairie Hachette.

Lefranc, Georges (1950). *Les Expériences Syndicales en France de 1939 à 1950.* Paris: Aubier, Editions Montaigne.

Lemaire, Florence (1964). "La réforme hospitalo-universitaire." Mémoire présenté a l'Institute d'Etudes Politiques de l''Université de Paris.

Lévy, Emile (1977). *Hospitalisation Publique, Hospitalisation Privée.* Laboratoire d'économie et de gestion des organisations de Santé (LEGOS), Actions Thématiques Programmées A.T.P. No. 22. Paris: Editions du Centre Nationale de la Recherche Scientifique.

Loux, Françoise (1973). "Les représentations de l'hopital à travers la presse populaire," *Cahiers de Sociologie et de Démographie Médicales, XIII,* No. 2 (April–June): 55–60.

Machin, A. (1979). "Traditional Patterns of French Local Government," pp. 28–41 in Jacques Lagroye & Vincent Wright (eds), *Local Government in Britain and France. Problems & Aspects.* London: George Allen & Unwin.

MacRae, Duncan (1967). *Parliament, Parties and Society in France, 1946–1958.* NY: St. Martin's Press.

Malissol, J. (1959). "Quelques pas à travers l'histoire de la protection sociale des agriculteurs" (and editors' introduction), *Revue Paysans,* 4, no. 2 (Aug–Sept): 1–2 & 4–11.

Mane, Roland (1962). "Où va le syndicalisme médical?" *Droit Social,* 25, no. 9–10 (Sept–Oct): 516–529.

Maus, Didier (1989). "Parliament in the Fifth Republic 1958–1988," pp. 12–27 in Paul Godt, ed., *Policymaking in France.* London and NY: Pinter.

Meynaud, Jean (1958). *Les Groupes de Pression en France.* Cahiers de la Fondation Nationale des Sciences Politiques No. 95. Paris: Librairie Armand Colin.

Massin, Gérard (1978). "Le Patronat Français et le système de Santé." Mémoire de fin d'assistant, Ecole Nationale de la Santé Publique, Rennes.

Michel, Clément (1960). "La réforme de l'assurance-maladie; éléments d'un dossier: A propos du décret du 12 mai sur les honoraires médicaux," *Droit Social,* 23, no. 11 (Nov): 556–567.

(1980). *La Consommation médicale des français.* Notes et Etudes Documentaires, 4555–6. Paris: La Documentation Française.

Notes et Etudes Documentaires (1957). *L'Organisation hospitalière en France,* Notes et Etudes Documentaires, no. 2330, Série Français CCCLXXXII, Série Sociale LXXXV, 26 Sept 1957. Paris: La Documentation Française.

(1959). *La réforme hospitalière*. Notes et Etudes Documentaires, no. 2555, Série Français CDXII, Série Sociale CV, 9 Juillet 1959. Paris: La Documentation Française.

Prieur, Christian (1976). "L'évolution historique de l'organisation des relations entre la médecine libérale et les régimes d'assurance maladie: 1930–1976," *Revue Trimestrielle de Droit Sanitaire et Sociale, 12*, no. 46 (April–June): 305–325.

Ramsey, Matthew (1984). "The Politics of Professional Monopoly in Nineteenth-Century Medicine: the French Model and its Rivals," pp. 225–305 in Gerald Geison (ed), *Professions and the French State, 1700–1900*. Philadelphia: University of Pennsylvania Press.

Rodwin, Victor G. (1982). "Management without objectives: the French health policy gamble," pp. 289–325 in A. Maynard and G. McLachlan (eds.), *The Public/Private Mix for Health*. London: The Nuffield Provincial Hospitals Trust.

(1984). *The Health Planning Predicament: France, Québec, England and the United States*. Berkeley: University of California Press.

(1989). "New ideas for health policy in France, Canada, and Britain," pp. 265–285 in Mark G. Field (ed.). *Success and Crisis in National Health Systems*. New York: Routledge.

Saint-Jours, Yves (1982). "France," pp. 93–149 in Peter A. Köhler and Hans F. Zacher (eds.), *The Evolution of Social Insurance. 1881–1981. Studies of Germany, France, Great Britain, Austria and Switzerland*. London: Frances Pinter, NY: St. Martin's Press.

Salon, Albert (1967). *Les Centres Hospitaliers et Universitaires*. Notes et Etudes Documentaires, No. 3373, 15 Mars 1967. Paris: La Documentation Française.

Sandier, Simone (1983). "Les dépenses de soins médicaux en France depuis 1950," *Revue Français de finances publiques*, no. 2: 5–30.

Savatier, Jean (1962). "Une profession libérale face au mouvement contemporain de socialisation," *Droit Sociale, 25*, no. 9–10 (Sept–Oct): 477–9.

Sellier, François (1961). *Stratégie de la Lutte Sociale*. Collection "Relations Sociales." Paris: Les Editions Ouvrières, Editions Economie et Humanisme.

(1970a). "Le rôle des organisations et des institutions dans le développement des besoins sociaux. Le cas du besoin de santé et de l'assurance maladie," *Sociologie du Travail, 2*: 1–14.

(1970b). *Dynamique des Besoins Sociaux*. Collection "Relations Sociales." Paris: Editions Ouvrières, Editions Economie et Humanisme.

Steffen, Monika (1983). *Régulation Politique et Stratégies Professionnelles: Médecine Libérale et Emergence des Centres de Santé*. Thèse d'Etat. Institute d'Etudes Politiques. Université des Sciences Sociales de Grenoble II, Grenoble.

(1987). "The Medical Profession and the State in France," *Journal of Public Policy, 7*, 2, 189–208.

Stephan, Jean-Claude (1978). *Economie et Pouvoir Médical*. Paris: Economica.

Steudler, François (1977). "Médecine libérale et Conventionnement," *Sociologie du Travail, IX*, no. 2 (April–June): 176–198.

Tarrow, Sidney (1977). *Between-Center and Periphery: Grassroots Politicians in Italy and France*. New Haven & London: Yale University Press.

Thoenig, Jean-Claude (1975). "La relation entre le centre et la périphérie," *Bulletin de l'Institut International d'Administration Publique*, no. 36 (Oct–Dec): 77–123.

(1979). "Local Government Institutions and the Contemporary Evolution of French Society," pp. 74–104 in Jacques Lagroye & Vincent Wright (eds), *Local Government in Britain and France. Problems & Aspects*. London: George, Allen & Unwin.

Tocqueville, Alexis de (1958 [1856]). *The Ancien Régime and the French Revolution*. NY: Doubleday, Anchor Books.

Williams, Philip M. (1964). *Crisis and Compromise: Politics in the Fourth Republic, 3rd ed*. Hamden, CT: Archon Books.

Wilson, Frank L. (1983). "French Interest Group Politics: Pluralist or Neo-Corporatist?" *American Political Science Review*, 77, 4 (Dec): 895–910.

Worms, Jean-Pierre (1966). "Le Préfet et ses notables," *Sociologie du Travail*, 8, no. 3 (July–Sept): 249–275.

Vincent Wright (1983). *The Government and Politics of France. 2nd Ed*. (London: Hutchinson).

XXX (1962). "Les rapports entre le corps médical et la sécurité sociale depuis le décret du 12 mai 1960," *Droit Social*, 25, no. 3 (Mar): 174–180.

Zeldin, Theodore (1973). *France. 1848–1945. Vol. 1, Ambition, Love, and Politics*. Oxford: Clarendon Press, Oxford University Press.

SWISS SOURCES

Primary sources

Archives

Archives (1911). Bundesarchiv. "Zweite KUV-Vorlage vom 13. Juni 1911 (am 4. Feb. 1912 vom Schweizervolk angenommen)," EDI 27, Bd 5 & 6. "Assurances maladies et accidents: imprimés", 3340 (A) 1, Bd 91–97.

Archives (1954). Bundesamt für Sozialversicherung. "Bericht und Vorentwurf d. Expertenkommission 1954," Archive/E 1954/5 Bd. 73–74, Files 214210–2142115.

Archives (1960). Bundesamt für Sozialversicherung. "Grundsätze und Erläuterungen f.d. Revision d. Krankenversicherung," Archiv/E, Bd. 61–2, Files 21404110–21404114.

"Verhandlungen der eidg. Räte 1961/2, Kommission des Ständerates für die Vorberatung des Entwurfes eines Bundesgesetzes betreffend die Änderung des Ersten Titels des Bundesgesetzes über die Kranken- und Unfallversicherung vom 13. Juni 1911," 1961, Bd. 67, File 2140413.

Archives (1967). Bundesamt für Sozialversicherung. "Totalrevision KUVG-Flimsermodell" 1967–1973, Bd 90–91, Files 214811–214811211.

Government documents

Botschaft (1906). "Botschaft des Bundesrates an die Bundesversammlung zu dem Entwurf eines Bundesgesetzes betreffend die Kranken- und Unfallversicherung (vom 10. Dezember 1906)," in Archives (1911): 3340 (A) 1, Bd. 91.

Bericht (1954). "Bericht und Vorentwurf zu einem Bundesgesetz über die Kranken- und die Mutterschaftsversicherung (vom 3. Februar 1954)," offprint.

Botschaft (1961). "Botschaft des Bundesrates an die Bundesversammlung zun Entwurf eines Bundesgesetzes betreffend die Änderung des Ersten Titels des Bundesgesetzes über die Kranken- und Unfallversicherung (vom 5. Jun 1961)," *Bundesblatt*, 113, no. 25, I: 1417–1528.

Botschaft (1962). "Ergänzungsbotschaft des Bundesrates an die Bundesversammlung zum Entwurf eines Bundesgesetzes betreffend die Änderung des Ersten Titels des Bundesgesetzes über die Kranken- und Unfallversicherung (vom 16. Nov. 1962)," *Bundesblatt*, II: 1265–1292.

Rapport (1972). "Rapport de la commission féderale d'experts chargeé d'examiner un nouveau régime d'assurance maladie (du 11 février 1972)," offprint.

Bericht (1977). "Bericht der Expertenkommission für die Teilrevision der Krankenversicherung (vom 5. Juli 1977)," offprint.

Bericht (1978). "Teilrevision der Krankenversicherung. Bericht und Vorentwurf. November 1978," offprint.

Rapport (1979). *Rapport sur l'évolution des revenues des personnes exerçant une activité dans le domaine médical et sur celle des prix des médicaments*. Bern: Office fédéral des assurances sociales.

Botschaft (1981). "Botschaft über die Teilrevision der Krankenversicherung (vom 19. August 1981)," offprint.

Botschaft (1982). "Botschaft über die Volksinitiative für einen wirksamen Schutz der Mutterschaft," offprint.

Bundesamt für Sozialversicherung. *Statistik über die vom Bunde Anerkannten Versicherungsträger der Krankenversicherung*. Bern: BSV.

Stenbull NR. *Amtliches Stenographisches Bulletin der schweizerischen Bundesversammlung. Nationalrat* (parliamentary debates of the National Council).

Stenbull SR. ——*Ständerat* (parliamentary debates of States' Council.)

Newspapers, annual reports, journals

(DP) *Domaine Public* (Public Domain, critical journal).

(KSK) *Konkordat der schweizerischen Krankenkassen, Tätigkeitsberichte* (Konkordat of Sickness Funds, annual reports): 1920/1924, 1924/1926, 1926/1928, 1945/48, 1948/50, 1954/55, 1960/1961, 1962/63, 1964/65, 1972/73, 1974/75, 1982/83.

Schweizerische Ärztezeitung (Swiss Medical Journal).

(SAZ) *Schweizerische Arbeitgeberzeitung/Journal des Associations patronales* (Swiss Employers' Journal), 13 May 1949, 30 Jan 1964.

Schweizerische Bauernzeitung (Swiss Farmers' Journal), May 1949, March & April 1964.

Schweizerischer Gewerbeverband, Bericht über die Tätigkeit des Verbands (Swiss Artisans' Association, Report on the Activities of the Association), 1949, 1963, 1964.

(SGB) *Schweizerischer Gewerkschaftsbund, Tätigkeitsberichte* (Swiss Trade Union Confederation, annual reports): 1947/49, 1953/56, 1963/5.

(SKZ) *Schweizerische Krankenkassenzeitung* (Swiss Sickness Funds' Journal).

Zentralverband schweizerischer Arbeitgeber-Organisationen, Bericht des Vorstandes an die Mitglieder (Federation of Swiss Employer Associations, Report of the Governing Board to the Members), 1910–12, 1947–9, 1953–5, 1960–4, 1971–4.

Secondary sources

Aubert, Jean-François (1978). "Switzerland," pp. 39–66 in David Butler and

Austin Ranney (eds.), *Referendums. A Comparative Study of Practice and Theory.* Washington, DC: American Enterprise Institute.

(1983). *Exposé des institutions politiques de la Suisse à partir de quelques affaires controveseés, 2nd Ed.* Lausanne: Editions Payot.

Biedermann, Paul (1955). *Die Entwicklung der Krankenversicherung in der Schweiz.* Diss., medizinische Fakultät der Universität Zürich.

Braun, Rudolf (1985). "Zur Professionalisierung des Ärztestandes in der Schweiz," pp. 332–357 in Jürgen Kocka (ed), *Bildungsbürgertum im 19. Jahrhundert.* Stuttgart: Klett-Cotta.

Butler David and Austin Ranney (1978). *Referendums. A Comparative Study of Practice and Theory.* Washington, DC: American Enterprise Institute.

Deutsch, Karl W. (1976). *Die Schweiz als ein paradigmatischer Fall politischer Integration.* Staat und Politik no. 16. Bern: Verlag Paul Haupt.

Frey, U., G. Kocher and M. Steinmann (1980). *Des schweizerische Gesundheitswesen im Spiegel der Öffentlichkeit.* Bern: SRG-Forschungsdienst.

Furrer, Alfons (1952). *Entstehung und Entwicklung der schweizerischen Sozialversicherung.* Diss., Juristische Fakultät der Universität Freiburg.

Gebert, Albert J. (1976). "Cooperative Federalism or Muddling-Through: The Swiss Case," pp. 95–139 in Altenstetter (ed.), *Changing National-Subnational Relations in Health.* Washington, DC: Fogerty International Center and Department of Health, Education and Welfare.

Gilliand, Pierre (1976). *Démographie médicale en Suisse, Santé publique et prospective 1900–1974–2000.* OSEV (DEMODED).

(1980). "L'hospitalisation en Suisse. Statistiques 1936–1978. Quel Avenir?" *Cahiers d'études de l'Institut Suisse des Hôpitaux*, No. 15. Aarau: ISH.

Glaser, William A. (1970). *Paying the Doctor: Systems of Remuneration and their Effects.* Baltimore & London: The Johns Hopkins Press.

(1976). *Paying the Doctor Under National Health Insurance: Foreign Lessons for the United States, 2nd ed.* Springfield, VA: National Technical Informations Service, US Dept. of Commerce.

(1978). *Health Insurance Bargaining: Foreign Lessons for Americans.* NY: Gardener Press.

(1979). "Paying the Hospital in Switzerland." Manuscript, Center for the Social Sciences at Columbia University, NY.

Gruner, Erich (1967). "Le fonctionnement du système représentatif dans la Conféderation Suisse." Paper presented at the 7th World Congress, International Political Science Association, 18–23 September.

(1968). *Die Arbeiter in der Schweiz im 19. Jahrhundert. Soziale Lage, Organisation, Verhältnis zu Arbeitgeber und Staat. Helvetia Politica* Series A, Vol. III. Bern: Francke Verlag.

(1969). *Die Parteien in der Schweiz.* Bern: Francke Verlag.

(1969). *Regierung und Opposition im schweizerischen Bundesstaat.* Series Staat und Politik, No. 7. Bern: Verlag Paul Haupt.

ed. (1971). *Die Schweiz seit 1945. Beiträge zur Zeitgeschichte.* Bern: Francke Verlag.

(1973). *Politische Führungsgruppen im Bundestaat.* Bern: Francke Verlag.

Gyger, Albert (1942). *50 Jahre Konkordat der Schweizerischen Krankenkassen, 1891–1941.* Solothurn: Konkordat/Buchdruckerei Vogt-Schild.

Gygi, Pierre and Peter Tschopp (1968). *Sozial-medizinische Sicherung.* Bern & Stuttgart: Verlag Hans Huber.

Gygi, Pierre and Heiner Henny (1977). *Das schweizerische Gesundheitswesen. Aufwand, Struktur und Preisbildung im Pflegebereich, 2nd revised ed.* Bern: Verlag Hans Huber.

Gygi, Pierre and Andreas Frei (1980). *Das schweizerische Gesundheitswesen 1980. 2. Ergänzungsband.* Basel: G. Krebs AG.

Gutzwiller, Felix (1976). "Cost and Cost-Sharing in the Health Services of Switzerland." Paper presented at the International Conference on 'Policies for the Containment of Health Care Costs and Expenditures,' Fogerty International Center, National Institutes of Health, Bethesda, MD.

Hogarth, James (1963). *The Payment of the Physician. Some European Comparisons.* NY: Macmillan Co. (Pergamon Press).

Holtz, Beat (1979). "Die Nachkriegsentwicklung von Wirtschaft und Gesellschaft als Zwang zur Planung staatlicher Problemlösung," pp. 53–79 in Wolf Linder, Beat Holtz, Hans Werder (eds), *Planung in der schweizerischen Demokratie.* Bern & Stuttgart: Verlag Paul Haupt.

Katzenstein, Peter J. (1984). *Corporatism and Change: Austria, Switzerland, and the Politics of Industry.* Ithaca & London: Cornell University Press.

(1985). *Small States in World Markets: Industrial Policy in Europe.* Ithaca & London: Cornell University Press.

Kerr, Henry H. (1974). *Switzerland: Social Cleavages and Partisan Conflict.* London & Beverly Hills: Sage Publications.

(1981). *Parlement et Société en Suisse.* St Saphorin: Editions Georgi.

Kocher, Gerhard (1972). *Verbandseinfluss auf die Gesetzgebung. Ärzteverbindung, Krankenkassenverbände und die Teilrevision 1964 des Kranken- und Unfaleversicherungsgesetzes, 2nd ed.* Bern: Francke Verlag.

ed. (1979). *Von der Spitalplanung zur Gesundsheitsplanung. Möglichkeiten zur Verbesserung der Planungsqualität.* Schriftenreihe der Schweizerischen Gesellschaft für Gesundsheitpolitik, No. 1.

Linder, Wolf (1983). "Politisch-ökonomischer Kontext. Entwicklung, Strukturen des Wirtschafts- und Sozialstaats in der Schweiz," pp. 255–382 in *Handbuch Politisches System der Schweiz. I. Grundlagen.* Bern & Stuttgart: Verlag Paul Haupt.

Maurer, Alfred (1982). "Switzerland," pp. 384–453 in Peter A. Köhler and Hans F. Zacher (eds), *The Evolution of Social Insurance. 1881–1981. Studies of Germany, France, Great Britain, Austria and Switzerland.* London & NY: Frances Pinter and St. Martin's Press.

Meynaud, Jean (1963). *Les organisations professionnelles en Suisse.* Lausanne: Editions Librairie Payot.

Neidhart, Leonhard (1970). *Plebiszit und pluralitäre Demokratie. Eine Analyse der Funktion des Schweizerischen Gesetzreferendums.* Bern: Francke Verlag.

(1975). *Föderalismus in der Schweiz. Zusammmenfassender Bericht über die Föderalismus-Hearings der Stiftung für eidgenössische Zusammenarbeit in Solothurn.* Zürich & Köln: Benziger Verlag.

November, Andraàs (1981). *Santé 80. Enquête auprès des ménages à Genève.* Cahiers de l'Institut Sandoz d'études en matière de santé et d'économie sociale, No. 3. Geneva: Institut Sandoz.

Saxer, A. (1961). "Social Security in Switzerland," *Bulletin of the International Social Security Association, 14* No. 9 (Sept), 457–520.

(1977). *Die soziale Sicherheit in der Schweiz, 4th ed.* Bern: Verlag Paul Haupt.

Schären, Fritz (1973). *Die Stellung des Arztes in der sozialen Krankenversicherung.* Zürich: Schulthess Polygraphischer Verlag.

Schoch, Hans (1984). "Das Privatspital im sozialpolitischen Umfeld," *Schweizerische Ärztezeitung, 65* No. 32 (August): 1528–1531.

Sidjanski, Dusan (1974). "Interest Groups in Switzerland," *Annals of American Academy of Political and Social Science, 413* (May): 101–123.

Siegrist, W. (administrator of a public sickness fund in Basel) (1961). *Revue Syndicale Suisse*, *53*, No. 5 (May): 141–152.

Sommer, Jürg H. (1978). *Das Ringen um soziale Sicherheit in der Schweiz*. Hochschule St. Gallen für Wirtschafts- und Sozialwissenschaften. Dissertation No. 703. Diessenhofen: Verlag Rüegger.

Steiner, Jürg (1970). *Gewaltlose Politik und kulturelle Vielfalt. Hypothesen entwickelt am Beispiel der Schweiz*. Bern: Verlag Paul Haupt.

Stephens, John D. (1979). *The Transition from Capitalism to Socialism*. Atlantic Highlands, NJ: Humanities Press.

Wyss, Erich (1982). Heilen und Herrschen. Medikalisierung, Krankenversicherung und ärztliche Professionalisierung, 1870–1911. Lizentiatsarbeit, Universität Zürich.

SWEDISH SOURCES

Primary sources

Archives

Archives (1930). Riksarkivet. Socialdepartmentets Konseljakt 28 February 1930, Nr. 47 (Prop. Nr. 154 med förslag till lag om ändring i vissa delar av lagen om understödsföreningar).

Archives (1931). Riksarkivet. Socialdepartementets Konseljakt 6 February 1931, Nr. 63 (Kungl. Majet Prop. Nr. 75 till Riksdagen med förslag till lag om ändring i vissa delar av lagen den 29 juni 1912 (nr. 184) om understödsföreningar mm.)

Archives (1946). Riksarkivet. Socialdepartementet Konseljakt 27 September 1946, nr. 123, prop. 312 del I. Remiss betr. SOU 1944: 15, 16 (ang. lag om allmänn sjukförsäkring) Dnr 2038/44.

Archives (1954). Riksarkivet. Inrikesdepartementet Konseljakt 30 April 1954, Nr. 82, betänkande angående den öppna sjukvården i riket (1948: 14) och bilagor (SOU 1948: 24)

Archives (1969). Socialdepartementet. Socialdepartmentet Konseljakt 17 October 1969, Nr. 60 (Prop 125), Prop. med förslag till ändring i lagen den 25 maj 1962 (Nr. 381) om allmänn försäkring mm.

Government documents

Proposition (legislative proposal) 1926: 117, "Kungl. Maj:ts proposition till riksdagen med förslag till lag angående anslag till sjukkasseväsendets befrämjande mm, given Stockholms slott den 25 februari 1926.

Proposition 1969 Nr. 125, 17 October 1969.

Proposition 1983/84: 190, "Regeringens Proposition om vissa ersättningar till sjukvårdshuvudmänen mm." 5 April 1984.

Riksdagens Protokoll, FK (parliamentary debates of the First Chamber).

Riksdagens Protokoll, AK (parliamentary debates of the Second Chamber).

Riksföräkringsverket. *Allmänn Försäkring*.

Socialdepartementet Stencil 1969: 2, "Promemoria med förslag till ändringar av sjukförmånerna inom sjukförsäkringen mm."

Socialdepartementet Stencil 1973: 5, "Sjukförsäkrings ersättningesregler vid privat läkarvård. Utrdning och förslag," Riksförsäkringsverket och Socialstyrelsen.

Socialdepartementet Ds S 1982: 9, "Promemoria om nyrekrytering av privatpraktiserande läkare."
SOU (Statens Offentliga Utredingar, Royal Commission Reports) 1925: 8, *Statens Besparingskommitté. Betänkande om Socialförsäkringarnas Organisation.*
SOU 114: 15, *Socialvårdskommitténs betänkande VII: Utredning och förslag angående Lag om Allmänn Försäkring.*
SOU 1948: 14, *Den öppna läkarvården i riket. Utredning och förslag av medicinalstyrelsen.* STH: Inrikesdepartementet.
SOU 1948: 24, *Bilagor till medicinalstyrelsens utredning om den öppna läkarvården i riket (SOU 1948: 14).*
SOU 1963: 21, *Sjukhus och öppen vård. Betänkande av ÖHS-kommittén.* STH: Inrikesdepartementet.
SOU 1967: 63, *Förmåner och avgifter i sluten sjukvård mm av 1961 års sjukvårdsförsäkringsutredning. Betänkande III.* STH: Socialdepartementet.
SOU 1978: 74, *Husläkare – en enklare och tryggare sjukvård. Betänkande av Kontinuitetsutredningen.* STH: Socialdepartementet.
Statistiska Centralbyrån. *Historisk Statistik för Sverige. Statistiska Översiktstabeller.* 1960.
Statistiska Centralbyrån. *Appendix 1 till Nationalräkenskaper Årsrapport 1970–1983.* Sveriges Officiella Statistik. SM N 1984: 5.5.

Newspapers

(DN) *Dagens Nyheter,* systematic review of Februrary and May, 1931, January, 1969, and 17 October 1969–4 December 1969.
(GHSJT) *Göteborgs Handels & Sjöfartstidning.*
(GP) *Göteborgs Posten.*
(MT) *Morgontidningen.*
Socialdemokraten. Systematic review February and May 1931.
(SDS) *Sydsvenska Dagbladet Snällposten.*
(SvD) *Svenska Dagbladet.* Systematic review February and May 1931, January 1969 and 17 October–4 December 1969.

Journals and annual reports

(LO) Landsorganisationen i Sverige (The Swedish Trade Union Federation). *LO-Tidningen (Fackföreningsrörelsen)* 1949, 1969.
(LF) Sveriges Läkarförbund (The Swedish Medical Association). *Sveriges Läkarförbunds Historia* (The Swedish Medical Association's History). Unpublished manuscript, approximate date 1953.
Utredning angående Poliklinikväsendet i Sverige, angiven av Sveriges Läkarförbundspolikliniksakkunige. STH: 1944.
Sveriges Läkarförbunds Årsbok, 1949.
Brev till Socialdepartementet från Sveriges Läkarförbund. 1979-02-06. Olle Westerborn, Bo Hjern.
"The Swedish Health Service from the Standpoint of the Profession – Negotiating and Bargaining." Unpublished mimeo by Bo Hjern, 1976-04-12.
(LT) *Läkartidningen.* (Journal of the Swedish Medical Association). 1926, 1927, 1930, 1931, 1946, 1948, 1969.
(SAF) Svenska Arbetsgivareförening (The Swedish Employers Federation). *Svenska Arbetsgivareföreningens styrelse och revisionsberättelser för år 1930, 1926, 1931, 1946, 1948, 1949, 1955.*
Industria, 1925, 1926, 1931, 1948, 1949.
SAF-Tidningen (Arbetsgivaren), 1969.

SF) Skattebetalarnas Förening (The Taxpayers' Association). *Läkaruttalanden i Sjukförsäkringsfrågan, ur officiella handlingar utgivna av skattebetalarnas Förening, 31 December 1930.*
Svensk Hantverkstidning (Swedish Craftsman's Journal), 1925, 1926.
Hantverk & Industri (Craft and Industry), 1948.

Secondary sources

Anderson, Odin W. (1972). *Health Care: Can There Be Equity? The United States, Sweden and England.* NY: John Wiley.
Anton, Thomas J. (1969). "Policy-Making and Political Culture in Sweden," *Scandinavian Political Studies 4*, pp. 88–102.
Berglind Hans, and Ulla Petersson (1980). *Omsorg som yrke eller omsorg on yrket.* Sekretariatet for framtidsstudier. Stockholm: Trosa Tryckeri.
Biörck, Gunnar (1977). "How to be a Clinician in a Socialist Country," *Annals of Internal Medicine, 86*, No. 6, (June): 813–817.
Bjurulf, Bo and Swahn, Urban (1980). "Health Policy Recommendations and What Happened to Them: Sampling the Twentieth Century Record," pp. 75–98 in Heidenheimer & Elvander, eds., *The Shaping of the Swedish Health System.* London: Croom Helm, 1980.
Broberg, Rolf (1973). *Så Formades Tryggheten: Socialförsäkringens historia 1946–1972.* Stockholm: Försäkringskasseförbundet.
Carder, Mack and Klingeberg, Bendix (1980). "Towards a Salaried Medical Profession: How Swedish was the Seven Crowns Reform?" pp. 143–172 in Heidenheimer and Elvander (eds), *The Shaping of the Swedish Health System.* London: Croom Helm.
Dahlberg, Anita (1978). "Socialförsäkringens utveckling. Ersättningar vid sjukdom, arbetsskada och ålderdom – utvecklingen i tre faser." Unpublished mimeo, Institutionen för Socionomutbildningen (Socialhögskolan), Stockholm.
Elmér, Åke (1963). *Från Fattigsverige till valfärdstaten. Sociala förhållanden och Social politik i Sverige under 1900-talet.* Stockholm: Bokförlaget Aldus/ Bonniers.
——— (1983). *Svensk Social Politik. 15th Ed.* Malmö: Liber Förlag.
Elvander, Nils (1966). *Intresseorganisationerna i dagens Sverige.* Lund: CWK Gleerup Bokförlag.
——— (1972). *Svensk Skattepolitik 1945–1970. En Studie i partiers och organisationers funktioner.* Stockholm: Rabén och Sjögren.
——— (1974). "Interest Groups in Sweden," *Annals of the American Academy of Political and Social Science. 413,* (May): 27–43.
Esping-Andersen, Gösta (1985). *Politics Against Markets: The Social Democratic Road to Power.* Princeton: Princeton University Press.
Englund, Karl (1976). *Arbetarförsäkringsfrågan i svensk politik 1884–1901.* Acta Universitatis Uppsaliensis. Studia Historia Upsaliensia. Stockholm: Almqvist & Wicksell International (Historiska Institutionen vid Uppsala Universitet).
Evjegård, Rolf (1973). *Landstingsförbundet. Organisation. Beslutsfattande. Förhållande till Staten.* Stockholm: Landstingsförbundet.
Fürth, Thomas (1980). *Folkrörelse eller Myndighetstradition. Organisationssyn och teknikval i Socialförsäkringshistoria.* Stockholm: Arbetslivscentrum.
Garpenby, Peter (1989). *The State and the Medical Profession. A Cross-National Comparison of the Health Policy Arena in the United Kingdom and Sweden 1945–1985.* Linköping: Linköping Stduies in Arts and Sciences.

Glaser, William A. (1970). *Paying the Doctor: Systems of Remuneration and the Effects.* Baltimore & London: Johns Hopkins University Press.

Hadenius, Stig, Molin, Björn and Wieslander, Hans (1978). *Sverige Efter 1990. En Modern Politisk Historia. 8th Ed.* Stockholm: Aldus/Bonniers.

Heclo, Hugh (1974). *Modern Social Politics in Britain and Sweden.* New Haven: Yale University Press.

and Henrik Madsen, (1987). *Policy and Politics in Sweden: Principled Pragmatism.* Philadelphia: Temple University Press.

Heidenheimer, Arnold J. (1980) "Conflict and Compromise Between Professional and Bureaucratic Health Interests. 1947–1972," pp. 119–142 in Heidenheimer & Elvander (eds.), *The Shaping of the Swedish Health System.* London: Croom Helm.

(1980b). "Unions and Welfare State Development in Britain and Germany: An Interpretation of Metamorphoses in the Period 1910–1950." Discussion paper, International Institute for Comparative Social Research, SP-II, IIVG/dp/80-209, Berlin.

Herlitz, Nils (1957). *Grunddragen av det Svenska Statsskickets historia. 5e upplagan.* Stockholm: Svenska Bokförlaget/Norstedts. Scandinavian University Books.

Hesslén, Gunnar (1927). *Det Svenska Kommittéväsendet intill år 1905. Dess uppkomst, stållning och betydelse.* Doctoral dissertation, filosofiska fakultetet i Uppsala humanistiska sektion, Uppsala.

Hogarth, James (1963). *The Payment of the Physician. Some European Comparisons.* NY: Macmillan Co. (Pergamon Press).

Höjer, J. Axel (1949). *Hälsovård i går- i dag- i morgon.* STH: Koopreativa Förbundets Förlag.

(1975). *En Läkares Väg. Från Visby till Vietnam.* STH: Bonniers.

and Sjövall, Einar (1945). *Folkhälsan som Samhällsangelägenhet.* STH: Albert Bonniers Förlag.

Höjer, Karl J. (1952). *Svensk Socialpolitisk Historia.* Stockholm: P.A. Norsetdt & Söners Förlag.

Ito, Hirobumi (1980). "Health Insurance and Medical Services in Sweden and Denmark. 1850–1950," pp. 44–67 in Heidenheimer & Elvander (eds), *The Shaping of the Swedish Health System.* London: Croom Helm.

Kelman, Steven (1981). *Regulating America, Regulating Sweden: A Comparative Study of Occupational Safety and Health Policy.* Cambridge, MA: MIT Press, 1981.

Lewin, Leif (1970). *Planhushållningsdebatten. 3rd Ed.* STH: Almqvist & Wicksell.

Lindbeck, Assar (1971). *Svensk Ekonomisk Politik. 5th Ed.* STH: Aldus/Bonniers.

Lindeberg, Gösta (1949). *Den Svenska Sjukkasserörelsens Historia.* Lund: Svenska Sjukkasseförbundet/Carl Bloms Boktrycheri.

Lindroth, Bengt (1975). *Bingo! En kritisk granskning av folkrörelserna i Sverige. 1850–1975.* Verdandi-Debatt Nr. 76. STH: Prisma.

Marklund, Staffan (1982). *Klass, Stat och Socialpolitik. En jämförande studie av socialförsäkringarnas utveckling i några västliga Kapitalistiska länder. 1930–1975.* Lund: Arkiv Förlag.

Martin, Andrew (1979). "The Dynamics of Change in a Keynesian Political Economy: The Swedish Case and its Implications," pp. 89–121 in C. Crouch (ed) *State and Economy in Contemporary Capitalism.* London: Croom Helm.

Meijer, Hans (1969). "Bureaucracy and Policy Formulation in Sweden," *Scandinavian Political Studies 4* pp. 103–116.

Nyman, Olle (1947). *Svensk Parlamentarism 1932–1936. Från Minoritetsparlamentarism till majoritetskoalition.* No. 27, *Skrifter Utgivna av Statsvetenskapliga Föreningen i Uppsala genom Axel Brusewitz.* Uppsala: Almqvist & Wicksell.

Ög, Anita Jarild (1962). "Diskussion kring Medicinalstyrelsens betånkande, 'Den öppna läkarvården i riket.'" Unpublished paper from the pro-seminar in Political Science, Uppsala University.

Oldfelt, Carin (1962). "Läkarförbundets inflytande på intagningen av medicine studerande och frågan om landets läkarbehov 1946–1959," Unpublished paper from the pro-seminar in Political Science, Uppsala University.

Rosenthal, Marilynn M. (1986). "Beyond Equity: Swedish Health Policy and the Private Sector," The Milbank Quarterly, *64*, 4: 592–621.

Samhälle och Riksdag. Historisk och Statsvetenskaplig Framställning utgiven i anledning av Tvåkammarriksdagens 100-åriga tillvaro. STH: Almqvist och Wicksell, 1966.

Serner, Uncas (1980). "Swedish Health Legislation: Milestones in Re-Organization Since 1945," pp. 99–116, in Heidenheimer & Elvander (eds), *The Shaping of the Swedish Health System.* London: Croom Helm.

Shenkin, Budd (1973). "Politics and Health Care in Sweden: The Seven Crowns Reform," *New England Journal of Medicine, 228*: 555–559.

Sköld, Lars and Halvarson, Arne (1966). "Riksdagens Sociala Sammansättning under Hundra År," pp. 375–493 in *Samhälle och Riksdag. Del I.* STH: Almqvist & Wicksell.

Smedby, Björn (1978). "Primary Care Financing in Sweden," pp. 247–251 in C.D. Burrell & C.G. Sheps (eds), *Primary Health Care in Industrialized Nations. Annals of the New York Academy of Sciences, 310.* NY: NY Academy of Sciences.

Twaddle, Andrew and Richard Hessler. (1986). "Power and Change: the Case of the Swedish Commission of Inquiry on Health and Sickness Care," *Journal of Health Politics, Policy and Law 11*, no. 1, pp. 14–40.

Uhr, Carl G. (1966). *Sweden's Social Security System. An Appraisal of its Economic Impact in the postwar period.* Social Security Administration, Research Report No. 14. Washington, DC: US Dept. of Health, Education and Welfare.

Werkö, Lars (1971). "Swedish Medical Care in Transition," *The New England Journal of Medicine, 284*, no. 7, (18 February): 360–366.

Verney, Douglas V. (1957). *Parliamentary Reform in Sweden, 1866–1921.* Oxford: Clarendon Press.

Index